PRAISE FOR
POLITICS—ACCORDING TO THE BIBLE

"Wayne Grudem is one of the outstanding biblical scholars in America. He's going to handle very well any subject he tackles. I particularly appreciate his work in this area..... There are sections of this book that are uncannily timely.... This can be a wonderful resource as we face growing tensions from an ever more powerful state."
—Chuck Colson, Founder, Prison Fellowship

"If you read this year only one Christian book on politics, read *Politics—According to the Bible*.... Grudem's biblically-based good sense overwhelms the nostrums of Jim Wallis and the evangelical left ... and shows why those seeking a vacation from politics need to rise up and go to work."
—Marvin Olasky, editor-in-chief, *World*, and provost, The King's College, New York City

"Conservative and hard-hitting both biblically and culturally, Grudem's treatise is essentially a giant tract for the times, covering the whole waterfront of America's political debate with shrewd insight and strong argument. This book will be a valued resource for years to come, and right now no Christian can afford to ignore it. An outstanding achievement!"
—James I. Packer, Board of Governors Professor of Theology, Regent College, Vancouver.

"Wayne Grudem's call for men and women of faith to be engaged in the public life of our great country is precisely and exactly the call the rising generation needs to hear."
—Timothy Goeglein, Vice President, External Relations, Focus on the Family

D1013624

Zondervan Books and Products
by Wayne Grudem

Systematic Theology

Bible Doctrine

Christian Beliefs

Systematic Theology Laminated Sheet

The Making Sense Series

Are Miraculous Gifts for Today? 4 Views (General Editor)

Politics — According to the Bible

Voting as a Christian: The Social Issues

VOTING AS A CHRISTIAN

THE ECONOMIC AND FOREIGN POLICY ISSUES

PREVIOUSLY PUBLISHED IN
POLITICS–ACCORDING TO THE BIBLE

WAYNE GRUDEM

ZONDERVAN®

ZONDERVAN.com/
AUTHORTRACKER
follow your favorite authors

We want to hear from you. Please send your comments about this book to us in care of zreview@zondervan.com. Thank you.

ZONDERVAN

Voting as a Christian: The Economic and Foreign Policy Issues
Copyright © 2010, 2012 by Wayne Grudem

Previously published in *Politics – According to the Bible*

This title is also available as a Zondervan ebook. Visit www.zondervan.com/ebooks.

Requests for information should be addressed to:

Zondervan, *Grand Rapids, Michigan* 49530

This edition: ISBN 978-0-310-49599-4 (softcover)

The Library of Congress has cataloged the original edition as:

Grudem, Wayne A.
     Politics – according to the Bible : a comprehensive resource for understanding
  modern political issues in light of scripture / Wayne Grudem.
        p. cm.
     Includes bibliographical references.
     ISBN 978-0-310-33029-5 (hardcover, printed) 1. Politics in the Bible. 2. Bible
  and politics. 3. Christianity and politics. 4. Church and social problems. I. Title.
  BS680.P45G78 2010
  261.7 – dc22   2010022252

Cover design: Rob Monacelli
Cover photography: SuperStock / Masterfile
Interior design: Matthew Van Zomeren

Printed in the United States of America

12 13 14 15 16 17 18 /DCI/ 21 20 19 18 17 16 15 14 13 12 11 10 9 8 7 6 5 4 3 2 1

To Rick and Debbie Nevins
and Steve and Kitty Oman,
special friends,
whose wise counsel and prayers
have helped and encouraged me
on this many other projects

CONTENTS

PUBLISHER'S PREFACE

Wayne Grudem's *Politics — According to the Bible: A Comprehensive Resource for Understanding Modern Political Issues in Light of Scripture* was first published in the fall of 2010. Systematic and wide-ranging, it filled a niche for a thorough resource of conservative biblical thought on politics. Every significant political issue facing the nation was covered — more than 50 areas of public policy — often in great depth. Many thousands of readers purchased the book, and it will rest on their shelves for years to come, ready to be pulled down when considering a variety of topics.

Yet the very strengths of that book also made it unapproachable for some. At 624 pages, it is admittedly a daunting volume to pick up, let alone to crack open and read. Furthermore, we know that many readers who resonate with Prof. Grudem's political vision are more interested in certain issues than others. Many also have limited reading time.

So we've created two abridged volumes of his larger work. The first is this book you're holding, which centers on issues related to national defense, the U.S. economy, and the size of the federal government, topics that dominate political debate during election seasons.

A second book, entitled *Voting as a Christian: The Social Issues*, unpacks from a biblical perspective the moral issues of enduring concern to so many Christian voters. Abortion, homosexual marriage, freedom of speech and religion — all of these and more are tackled in its pages.

We trust that these accessible, affordable books will aid you in biblically assessing the important decisions confronting our nation, and we hope they will be useful as you consider your own decisions the next time you head to your local polling place.

Paul E. Engle
Senior Vice President and Publisher
Church, Curriculum, Academic, and Reference Resources
Zondervan

FOREWORD

"How then should we live?" is a question that Christians have had to struggle with in every age, and the greatest theologians from St. Augustine to Francis Schaeffer have done their best to offer immediate guidance on timeless issues to believers living in the moment. For as long as time continues and the church endures, these offerings of practical guidance will serve Christians, provided the guidance is deeply grounded in true theology and also in the actual complexities of the world in which the Christians live.

It is worse than no good to ground practical advice on politics and flawed understanding of Christ and his teachings, no better than navigating with a broken compass and a centuries-old map.

It is also fruitless—and frustrating—to be offered platitudes by even the best of good-hearted pastors whose grasp of the difficulties of modern politics is limited to an occasional glimpse of a headline or a five-minute report on the latest controversy on Capitol Hill.

American politics is riven with highly contentious, incredibly convoluted issues of enormous moral significance. If, just to consider one, the earth is indeed warming at an alarming rate and that increase in temperature will endanger hundreds of millions with starvation due to crop failures, then the Christian must approach the issue of climate change very differently than if in fact the variation in global temperatures fits a pattern of centuries and is indifferent to human contribution, much less to "eco-engineering." The facts matter, and good theology applied to the present political situation will proceed first from good facts about the disputes at hand.

I am thus slow to take political advice from theologians, even the best of them. My calling is in the intersection where politics, law, and media meet, and I know that amateurs are no more effective in crafting effective resolutions to the most intractable of these disputes than those same amateurs are in the emergency room of a major urban hospital.

But the best theologians have much to offer to the practical resolution of these debates, just as they do to the surgeon, the physicist, and the general. Every aspect of human life that requires moral decision-making ought to use the best in God-driven thinking, the best in applicable Scripture, and the best in prayer-infused thought and analysis.

"Where to begin?" is a very fair question from the legislator, the executive branch appointee, or even just the average voter. "I know these are complicated issues, and I know God has set out rules for living that are timeless, so where do I start, and to whom do I turn?"

I am very happy to suggest that you have a book in your hands that is in fact that starting point, a serious but very readable work by a serious yet very understandable—and understanding—scholar of the first rank, perhaps America's most influential systematic theologian, Dr. Wayne Grudem.

Go ahead, Google him. Don't believe me or the blurbs on the back of the book. Just let fly with Google. It is no small thing to have led the organizations that Dr. Grudem has led, to write the books he has authored, to teach the students he has taught. You should be impressed, indeed very impressed, with Dr. Grudem's record of scholarship.

What you will not know—but which I do from my visits to Phoenix over the years as I have broadcast from there and met Dr. Grudem, interviewed him repeatedly on the air, and met with his students and especially his Sunday school students—is that Wayne Grudem is God's man first and foremost, kind-hearted, wise, and of course smart beyond what any one scholar ought to be allowed to be.

Dr. Grudem undertook this vast and readable project for you—for the mere Christian confronted with a dizzying array of questions, answers, and would-be prophets all eager to tell you how to think and to assure you that God thinks a particular way.

Here at last is a book, comprehensive yet readable, that will help you understand God's plan in this, the early part of the 21st century; remind you of the eternal truths; and prompt you to the reflections that ought to inform your life as a citizen.

Give yourself the gift of understanding, and then pass it or a new copy along to your friends and family struggling to be a good citizen and a good Christian in these tumultuous times. If you are in a small group, adopt this as a text for a season. If you know a pastor or a lay minister, gift them with this comprehensive but accessible source book.

But most of all, dive in and be open to God's call on your life as a citizen—because you can trust Dr. Grudem to have begun each question with God's Word and work, not any agenda or slogan.

Dr. Grudem has been blessed with an incredible intellect and he has used it again to be a blessing to others—in this case every American, young and old, left, right, or center, who must live as a citizen in a free republic—and for that we should all be grateful.

Hugh Hewitt
Professor of law, Chapman University,
and nationally syndicated radio talk show host

INTRODUCTION

This book is a shortened version of my longer book, *Politics — According to the Bible: A Comprehensive Guide for Understanding Modern Political Issues in Light of Scripture* (Zondervan, 2010, 624 pages). In this volume I focus solely on economic and foreign policy issues — such as taxes, government responsibility for the poor, the environment, energy supplies, global warming, war, Islamic jihadism, nuclear weapons, foreign aid, immigration, and Israel.

I have not written this book from the perspective of a lawyer or journalist or professional politician, but from the perspective of a professor with a Ph.D. in New Testament studies and thirty years of experience in teaching the Bible at the M.Div. and (for several years) the Ph.D. level. I wrote this book because I was convinced that God intended the Bible to give guidance to every area of life — including how governments should function!

I support political positions in this book that would be called more "conservative" than "liberal." That is because of my conclusions about the Bible's teaching on the role of government and a biblical worldview. It is important to understand that I see these positions as *flowing out of the Bible's teachings* rather than positions that I hold prior to, or independently of, those biblical teachings. My primary purpose in the book is not to be liberal or conservative, or Democratic or Republican, but to explain a biblical worldview and a biblical perspective on key social issues being debated today.

I hope that Christians who take the Bible as a guide for life will find the political discussions in this book encouraging. I believe the Bible's teachings about politics will bring hope and beneficial change to people in every nation where they are put into practice. When these teachings are put into practice in a nation, it will be good news for those who are oppressed, good news to those who long for justice, good news to those who long for peace, good news for young and old, weak and powerful, rich and poor—good news for everyone who will follow the wonderful paths of freedom and sound government that are taught in the pages of the Bible. The prophet Isaiah extolled the beautiful sound of the feet of a messenger who came running with good news from God himself:

> How beautiful upon the mountains are the feet of him who brings good news, who publishes peace, who brings good news of happiness, who publishes salvation, who says to Zion, "Your God reigns" (Isa. 52:7).

Therefore I hope that as people and nations follow these principles for government, they will begin to see a reversal of the continual decline in peace, civility, liberty, and civic goodness that we have seen in recent decades in our societies, and instead we will begin to see regular progress toward increasingly good, pleasant, productive, low-crime, free, and happy civil societies in which we can live.

I am well aware that the Bible is not an American book, for it was finished nearly 1,700 years before the United States existed! The principles and teachings in the Bible contain wisdom that is helpful for *all* nations and all governments. Therefore I have tried to keep in mind that people in other nations might read this book and find it useful for formulating their own positions on the political issues that they face in their own nations. Yet in my examples and my choice of political issues, I focus primarily on the United States, because that is the country I know best, the country I am proud to be a citizen of, and the country I deeply love.

What about readers who don't believe the Bible to be from God or who may not be sure what they think about the Bible? I hope they will still consider the arguments in this book on their own merits and find them useful—perhaps even persuasive—in formulating their own opinions. If not, their right to disagree with me is still very important to any government that follows the principles in this book. I believe there should be strong protections for freedom of religion in every nation, and I earnestly desire to protect each person's freedom to make decisions about religious belief for himself or herself, totally without any compulsion from government. I want to protect other people's right to disagree with me and to express that disagreement publicly in any nation.

I also want to say at the beginning that I do not hold with equal confidence every position I support in this book. On some issues I think the overall teaching of the Bible is *clear, direct, and decisive*, such as the idea that civil governments are set up by God to punish evil and reward good (Rom. 13:1–7; 1 Pet. 2:13–14).

There is a second set of issues where I depend on *arguments from broader principles*. In these cases I reason not from direct, specific biblical teaching on the topic but from broader biblical principles (such as the equality of all people in the image of God). That kind of argument from broader principles requires wise judgment in applying those principles correctly to a modern situation, and thus there is a greater possibility of making a mistake or failing to balance the principle with other principles that might modify one's conclusions.

Then I have used a third type of argument: *an appeal to facts in the world*. In some sections, much of my argument depends on one's evaluation of the *actual results* of certain policies. Such arguments are different from arguments from *direct biblical statements*, and they are different from arguments from *broader biblical principles*, for they depend not on the Bible but on *an evaluation of the relevant facts* in the world today.

I have not distinguished these three types of argument in the pages that follow. I have not made explicit where I am depending on *direct teachings of the Bible*, where I am depending on *broader biblical principles*, where I am depending on an *evaluation of facts* in the world today, and where I am depending on some combination of these three. But I hope readers will be able to make those distinctions for themselves as they weigh the arguments that I present. And in the end, I hope that most readers will find themselves persuaded by the book.

Many people helped in the writing of the larger book on which this one is based, and I thanked them all in that book. Here I want especially to mention again the irreplaceable research help of Craig Osten, the encouragement of Alan Sears, Ben Bull, and Cathi Herrod, the material support of the partners of Marketplace One, the economic insight of Barry Asmus and David Payne, the wisdom of Calvin Beisner regarding the environment and global warming, the military and just war knowledge of Daniel Heimbach, and the prayer support of many friends who regularly pray for me and my writing projects. Even more, I am continually thankful for the help and daily encouragement of my wonderful wife, Margaret. Above all of these, I am thankful to the Lord who gives me strength to keep writing and, I hope, some measure of good judgment along the way.

Chapter 1

HOW CHRISTIANS SHOULD BE INVOLVED IN GOVERNMENT

Should Christians try to influence laws and politics? Before explaining my own understanding of this question, I need to mention what I think are five wrong views. After that I will propose what I think is a better, more balanced solution.

A. WRONG VIEW #1: GOVERNMENT SHOULD COMPEL RELIGION

The first wrong view (according to my judgment) is the idea that civil government should compel people to support or follow one particular religion.

Tragically, this "compel religion" view was held by many Christians in previous centuries. It played a large role in the Thirty Years' War (1618–48) that began as a conflict between Protestants and Roman Catholics over control of various territories, especially in Germany. There were many other "wars of religion" in Europe, particularly between Catholics and Protestants, in the sixteenth and seventeenth centuries.

Eventually more and more Christians realized that this position is inconsistent with the teachings of Jesus and inconsistent with the nature of faith itself. Today I am not aware of any major Christian group that holds to the view that government should try to compel people to follow the Christian faith.

But other religions still promote government enforcement of their religion. This is seen in countries such as Saudi Arabia, which enforces laws compelling people to follow Islam and where those who fail to comply can face severe penalties from the religious police. The law prohibits public practice of any religion other than Islam and prohibits Saudis from converting to other religions. But it must be noted that other Muslims also favor democracy and allowing for varying degrees of freedom of religion.

In the early years of the United States, support for freedom of religion in the American colonies increased because many of the colonists had fled from religious persecution in their home countries. For example, the New England Pilgrims had fled from England where they had faced fines and imprisonment for failing to attend services in the Church of England and for conducting their own church services.

Several teachings of the Bible show that "government should compel religion" is an incorrect view, one that is contrary to the teachings of the Bible itself.

1. Genuine faith cannot be forced

Government should never try to compel any religion because, according to the Bible, genuine religious belief cannot be compelled by force. Jesus and the New Testament apostles always *taught* people and *reasoned* with them and then *appealed* to them to make a personal decision to follow Jesus as the true Messiah. Jesus invited people, "Come to me, all who labor and are heavy laden, and I will give you rest" (Mat 11:28; compare Acts 28:23; Rom. 10:9–10; Rev. 22:17).

Anyone who has brought up children knows that not even parents can force children to believe in God. You can bring them to church and you can teach them the Bible, but each child must make a personal decision to trust in Jesus as his or her own Lord and Savior. Genuine faith cannot be forced.

Someone might object, "But what about laws in the Old Testament that ordered severe punishments for anyone who tried to teach another religion (see Deut. 13:6–11)? Wasn't that part of the Bible?"

The answer is that those laws *were only for the nation of Israel for that particular time.* They were never imposed on any of the surrounding nations. Such Old Testament laws enforcing religion were never intended for people after Jesus came and established his "new covenant" (Heb. 8:8–9:28).

2. Jesus distinguished the realms of God and of Caesar

Another biblical argument against the "compel religion" view comes from Jesus' teachings bout God and Caesar. Jesus' Jewish opponents were trying to trap him with the question, "Is it lawful to pay taxes to Caesar, or not?" (Matt. 22:18). Taking his opponents by surprise, Jesus said, "Show me the coin for the tax," and "they brought him a denarius" (v. 19). Jesus said to them, "Whose likeness and inscription is this?" They said, "Caesar's." Then he said to them, "Therefore render to Caesar the things that are Caesar's, and to God the things that are God's" (Matt. 22:20–21).

This is a remarkable statement because Jesus shows that there are to be *two different spheres of influence,* one for the government and one for the religious life of the people of God. Some things, such as taxes, belong to the civil government ("the things that are Caesar's"), and this implies that the church should not try to control these things. On the other hand, some things belong to people's religious life ("the things that are God's"), and this implies that the civil government should not try to control those things.

Jesus did not specify any list of things that belong to each category, but the mere distinction of these two categories had monumental significance for the history of the world. It signaled a *different system* from the nation of Israel in the Old Testament, where everybody in the nation was considered a part of the people of God and they all had to obey the religious laws.

3. Freedom of religion is a biblical value

Jesus' new teaching that the realms of "God" and "Caesar" are distinct implies freedom of religion. It implies that all civil governments — even today — should give people freedom regarding the religious faith they follow (or don't follow), and regarding the religious doctrines they hold, and how they worship God. "Caesar" should not control such things, for they are "the things that are God's."

Therefore Christians in every nation should support freedom of religion and oppose any attempt by government to compel any single religion. In fact, *complete freedom of religion* should be the first principle advocated and defended by Christians who seek to influence government.

B. WRONG VIEW #2: GOVERNMENT SHOULD EXCLUDE RELIGION

The opposite error from the "compel religion" view is "exclude religion." This is the view that says we should completely exclude religion from government and politics. According to this view, religious beliefs should never be mentioned in governmental functions or on government property and should never play a role in decision-making processes in politics or government.

This is the view promoted today by the American Civil Liberties Union (ACLU). According to it, religious belief should be kept at home and quiet. There should be no influence from religious groups in the political process.

Examples of this view are seen when people object to prayers being given at the beginning of a city council meeting, or when groups demand that the Ten Commandments be removed from public places. Supporters of this view seek to prohibit religious expression in high schools, student-led Bible studies, prayers before sporting events, or even a valedictorian talking about his or her faith at graduation.

1. It changes freedom of religion into freedom from religion

The "exclude religion" stance is wrong from a Constitutional viewpoint, because it twists the positive ideal of "freedom *of* religion" to mean "freedom *from* all religious influence" — which is entirely different and something the signers of the Declaration of Independence and the framers of the U.S. Constitution never intended.

In fact, the "exclude religion from politics" view would invalidate the very reasoning of the Declaration of Independence, on which the United States of America was first founded. The first two sentences mention God twice in order to say that God's laws authorize independence from Great Britain and that God is the one who gives human beings the rights that governments must protect:

> When in the Course of human events, it becomes necessary for one people to dissolve the political bands which have connected them with another, and to assume among the Powers of the earth, the separate and equal station to which the Laws of Nature *and of Nature's God* entitle them, a decent respect to the opinions of mankind requires that they should declare the causes which impel them to the separation.
>
> We hold these truths to be self-evident, that all men are created equal, that they are *endowed by their Creator* with certain unalienable Rights, that among these are Life, Liberty, and the pursuit of Happiness. That to secure these rights, Governments are instituted among Men....

In other words, the fifty-six signers of the Declaration of Independence proclaimed that both the laws of nature and of God gave our country the right to become an independent nation. They claimed *divine authorization* for the very existence of the United States of America! Furthermore, the signers said that the purpose of government is to protect the rights that are given to people by God ("endowed by their Creator"). This is hardly "excluding religion" from government or important government publications.

The First Amendment to the Constitution likewise declared: "Congress shall make no law *respecting an establishment of religion*, or *prohibiting the free exercise thereof*; or abridging the freedom of speech." What they meant by "an establishment of religion" was an established state church, a government-sponsored or government-endorsed denomination or specific religion. But they did not intend this amendment to exclude all religious speech and activity from government building and activities, for our nation's early political leaders continued praying publicly to God at government events, even having church services in the Capitol for many years.

The phrase "separation of church and state" does not occur anywhere in the Constitution. It was first seen in a letter from Thomas Jefferson in 1802, in which he assured some Baptists in Connecticut (the Danbury Baptists) that the government would never interfere with the affairs of their church. The First Amendment was never intended to guarantee that government should be free from religion or religious influence. The only "freedom of religion" that was intended was freedom from government sponsorship of one particular religion or denomination.

2. It wrongly restricts freedom of religion and freedom of speech

The First Amendment also excluded any law "prohibiting the free exercise" of religion. This is directly opposed to the "exclude religion from government" view, which actually seeks to *prohibit* Christians and Jews and others from exercising their religious freedom when speaking or giving a prayer at a public event. Their free exercise of religion is taken away from them.

This view also wrongly restricts individual freedom of speech. Why should a high school valedictorian not be free to express his own viewpoint in his graduation speech? *Speaking* a religious opinion in public is not *compelling* people to accept that viewpoint!

3. It was never adopted by the American people

The "exclude religion" view was never adopted by the American people through any democratic process, but it is being imposed on our nation by the exercise of "raw judicial power" by our courts, and especially by the Supreme Court. This has been an increasing problem for the last several decades in America.

The Supreme Court decision *Lemon v. Kurtzman* (1971) was especially significant. In that case the court said that government actions "must not have the primary effect of advancing or inhibiting religion." It did not say "advancing or inhibiting *one particular religion*" but "religion" in general. (An earlier decision in 1947, *Everson v. Board of Education*, had said something similar.) This kind of "exclude religion" view was never adopted or approved by the American people but simply decreed by our Supreme Court, taking to itself powers it never legitimately had.

4. It removes from government God's teaching about good and evil

The Bible says that a government official is "God's servant for your good" (Rom. 13:4), but how can government officials effectively serve God if no one is allowed to tell them what they believe God expects of them? The Bible says that government officials are sent "to punish those who do evil and to praise those who do good" (1 Peter 2:14), but how can they do that if no spokesmen from any of the world's religions are allowed to give them counsel on what is "good" and what is "evil"?

Such a viewpoint has to assume that there is no God, or if there is, his moral standards can't be known. And by rejecting the idea of absolute standards that come from God, this viewpoint leads toward the moral disintegration of a society.

We see the payoff of this view in the rampant moral relativism among today's young adults who were taught as children in "exclude religion" schools, schools where "because God says so" could no longer be used as the strong foundation for moral conduct as it had been for the first 200 years of this nation.

C. WRONG VIEW #3: ALL GOVERNMENT IS EVIL AND DEMONIC

According to this third view, all use of government power is deeply infected by evil, demonic forces. The realm of government power is the realm of Satan and his forces, and therefore all governmental use of "power over" someone is worldly and not the way of life that Jesus taught.

1. Support from Luke 4:6

This viewpoint has been strongly promoted by Minnesota pastor Greg Boyd in his influential book *The Myth of a Christian Nation* (Grand Rapids: Zondervan, 2005). Boyd's views in this book have had a large impact in the United States, especially on younger evangelical voters.[1]

Boyd says that all civil government is "demonic" (p. 21). His primary evidence is Satan's statement to Jesus in Luke 4:

> And the devil took him up and showed him all the kingdoms of the world in a moment of time, and said to him, "To you I will give all this authority and their glory, *for it has been delivered to me*, and I give it to whom I will. If you, then, will worship me, it will all be yours" (Luke 4:5–7).

Boyd emphasizes Satan's claim that all the authority of all the kingdoms of the world "has been delivered to me" and then says that Jesus "doesn't dispute the Devil's claim to own them. Apparently, the authority of all the kingdoms of the world has been given to Satan."

Boyd goes on to say, "Functionally, Satan is the acting CEO of all earthly governments" (p. 22). This is indeed a thoroughgoing claim!

2. The mistake of depending on Luke 4:6

Greg Boyd is clearly wrong at this point. Jesus tells us how to evaluate Satan's claims, for he says,

> When he lies, he speaks out of his own character, for he is a liar and the father of lies (John 8:44).

Jesus didn't need to respond to *every* false word Satan said, for his purpose was to resist the temptation itself, and this he did with the decisive words, "It is written, 'You shall worship the Lord your God, and him only shall you serve'" (Luke 4:8).

And so we have a choice: Do we believe *Satan's words* that he has the authority of all earthly kingdoms, or do we believe *Jesus' words* that Satan is a liar and the father of lies? The answer is easy: Satan wanted Jesus to believe a lie, just as he wanted Eve to believe a lie (Gen. 3:4), and he wants us to believe a lie as well, that he is the ruler of earthly governments.

---

1. For example, echoes of Boyd's writing can be seen at various places in Shane Claiborne and Chris Haw, *Jesus for President* (Grand Rapids: Zondervan, 2008).

By contrast, there are verses in the Bible that tell us how we should think of civil governments. These verses do not agree with Satan's claim in Luke 4:6 or with Boyd's claim about Satan's authority over all earthly governments. Rather, these verses where *God* is speaking (not Satan) portray civil government as a gift from God, something that is subject to God's rule and used by God for his purposes. Here are some of those passages:

> *The Most High rules the kingdom of men* and gives it to whom he will and sets over it the lowliest of men (Dan. 4:17).

> Let every person be subject to the governing authorities. For *there is no authority except from God, and those that exist have been instituted by God....* For rulers are not a terror to good conduct, but to bad. Would you have no fear of the one who is in authority? Then do what is good, and you will receive his approval, for *he is God's servant for your good* ... the *authorities are the ministers of God* (Rom. 13:1–6).

Peter sees civil government as doing the *opposite* of what Satan does: civil governments are established by God "to *punish* those who do evil," but Satan *encourages* those who do evil! Civil governments are established by God "to *praise* those who do good" (1 Pet. 2:14), but Satan *discourages and attacks* those who do good.

The point is that Satan wants us to believe that all civil government is under his control, but that is not taught anywhere in the Bible. The only verse in the whole Bible that says Satan has authority over all governments is spoken by the father of lies, and we should not believe it. Greg Boyd is simply wrong in his defense of the view that "government is demonic."

D. WRONG VIEW #4: DO EVANGELISM, NOT POLITICS

A fourth wrong view about Christians and politics is promoted by evangelicals who essentially say, "We should just preach the Gospel, and that is the only way Christians can hope to change peoples' hearts and change our society." I call this the "do evangelism, not politics" view. It claims that the church is only called to "preach the Gospel," not to preach about politics.

1. God calls Christians to do "good works"

Of course, we must insist that people can never earn their salvation by doing "good works." The Bible insists that "all have sinned and fall short of the glory of God" (Rom. 3:23), and it also says, "by works of the law no human being will be justified in his sight" (Rom. 3:20).

But after people have trusted in Jesus Christ for forgiveness of sins, then what should they do? How should we live now as Christians? The Bible says we should be doing "good works." In fact, right in the place where Paul writes a magnificent proclamation of justification by faith alone, he adds an important sentence about good works. First he says,

> For by grace you have been saved through faith. And this is not your own doing; it is the gift of God, not a result of works, so that no one may boast (Eph. 2:9).

Then he immediately adds,

> For we are his workmanship, created in Christ Jesus *for good works*, which God prepared beforehand, that we should walk in them (Eph. 2:10).

In another place he says, "As we have opportunity, let us do good to everyone, and especially to those who are of the household of faith" (Gal. 6:10). Certainly that means that we should do good to others, as we have opportunity, by being a good influence on laws and government and by having a good influence on the political process.

Jesus left us here on earth in part because he wants to allow our lives to give glory to him in the midst of a fallen and sinful world: "Let your light shine before others, *so that they may see your good works* and give glory to your Father who is in heaven" (Matt. 5:16).

If a pastor teaches his people how to raise their children, that's "good works." If he teaches them how to have good marriages, that's "good works." If he teaches them to love their neighbors as themselves (Matt. 22:39), that's "good works."

Should churches teach their people how to do "good works" in families, in hospitals and in schools, and in businesses and in neighborhoods, but not in government? Why should that area of life be excluded from the influence of the "good works" of believers that will "give glory to your Father who is in heaven"?

2. Influencing government for good is a way to love our neighbors

Jesus' command, "You shall love your neighbor as yourself" (Matt. 22:39) means that I should seek *good laws* that will protect preborn children. It means that I should seek *good laws* that protect marriages and families. It means I should seek *good laws* that protect children from corrupting moral influences that want to use classrooms to teach that all kinds of sexual experimentation outside of marriage are fine and that there is nothing wrong with pornography.

In short, Jesus' command to "love your neighbor" means that I should seek the good of my neighbors in every aspect of society, *including government, by seeking to bring about good government and good laws.*

3. Obeying what God tells us is doing spiritual good because it glorifies God

I cannot agree with people who say that Christian political involvement will do "no spiritual good." If it is commanded in the Bible and it's what God tells us to do, then by definition it *is* doing spiritual good. "This is the love of God, that we keep his commandments" (1 John 5:3) — therefore, following his teachings regarding government is one way of showing love to him.

In addition, when Christian influence brings about good laws that do good for society, we should expect that some people will realize how good God's moral standards are and they will glorify God as a result. People will "see your good works and give glory to your Father who is in heaven" (Matt. 5:16). Even in the Old Testament, Moses told the people of Israel:

> [The other nations] when they hear all these statutes, will say, "Surely this great nation is a wise and understanding people" (Deut. 4:6).

4. Good and bad governments make a huge difference in people's lives, and in the church

When people say that the kind of government we have doesn't make any difference to the church or to the spiritual lives of Christians, I think of the difference between North Korea and South Korea. These countries have the same language, the same ethnic background, the same cultural history, and live in the same location of the world. The only difference between them is that South Korea is a robust, thriving democracy with free people and North Korea is a Communist country with the most repressive, totalitarian government in the world.

And what a difference that makes in people's lives. There is just a handful of Christians in North Korea, and they must exercise their faith in secret. Severe, persistent persecution has hindered the church so greatly that there is no missionary activity, no public worship, no publication of Christian literature. Millions of North Koreans are born, live, and die without ever hearing the Gospel of Jesus Christ. By contrast, the church in South Korea, where the government has allowed freedom of religion, is growing, thriving, and sending missionaries around the world. It has one of the highest percentages of evangelical Christians of any nation (around 25%).

What is the only difference? The kind of government they have. One country is free and one is totalitarian. And in between these extremes fall many other nations of the world, governments more or less free and more or less conformed to God's principles for government as taught in Scripture. Where God's principles are followed more fully and people are allowed more freedom, the church will often thrive and people's lives are better in hundreds of ways.

Governments do make a difference to the church and to the work of God's kingdom. This is why Paul urged that prayers be made "for kings and all who are in high positions, that we may lead a peaceful and quiet life, godly and dignified in every way" (1 Tim. 2:2). Good governments help people to live a "peaceful" and "godly" life, and bad governments hinder that goal.

Governments can allow churches to meet freely and evangelize or they can prevent these things by force of law (as in Saudi Arabia and North Korea). They can hinder or promote literacy (the latter enabling people to read a Bible). They can stop murderers and thieves and drunk drivers and child predators or allow them to terrorize society and destroy lives. They can promote and protect marriages or hinder and even destroy them. Governments do make a significant difference for the work of God in the world, and we are to pray and work for good governments around the world.

5. Christians have influenced governments positively throughout history

Historian Alvin Schmidt points out how the spread of Christianity and Christian influence on government was primarily responsible for outlawing infanticide, child abandonment, and abortion in the Roman Empire (in AD 374);[2] outlawing the brutal battles-to-the-death in which

---

2. Alvin Schmidt, *How Christianity Changed the World* (Grand Rapids: Zondervan, 2004; formerly published as *Under the Influence*, 2001), 51, 53, 59.

thousands of gladiators had died (in 404);[3] granting of property rights and other protections to women;[4] banning polygamy (which is still practiced in some Muslim nations today);[5] prohibiting the burning alive of widows in India (in 1829);[6] outlawing the painful and crippling practice of binding young women's feet in China (in 1912);[7] persuading government officials to begin a system of public schools in Germany (in the sixteenth century);[8] and advancing the idea of compulsory education of all children in a number of European countries.[9]

During the history of the church, Christians had a decisive influence in opposing and often abolishing slavery in the Roman Empire, in Ireland, and in most of Europe (though Schmidt frankly notes that a minority of "erring" Christian teachers have supported slavery in various centuries).[10] In England, William Wilberforce, a devout Christian, led the successful effort to abolish the slave trade and then slavery itself throughout the British Empire by 1840.[11]

In the United States, though there were vocal defenders of slavery among Christians in the South, they lost the argument, and they were vastly outnumbered by the many Christians who were ardent abolitionists, speaking, writing, and agitating constantly for the abolition of slavery in the United States. Schmidt notes that two-thirds of the American abolitionists in the mid–1830s were Christian clergymen who were preaching "politics" from the pulpit, saying that slavery should be abolished.[12]

The American civil rights movement that resulted in the outlawing of racial segregation and discrimination was led by Martin Luther King Jr., a Baptist pastor, and supported by many Christian churches and groups.[13]

There was also strong influence from Christian ideas and influential Christians in the formulation of the Magna Charta in England (1215)[14] and

---

3. Ibid., 63.
4. Ibid., 111.
5. Ibid., 115.
6. Ibid., 116–17.
7. Ibid., 119.
8. Ibid., 179.
9. Ibid., 179–80. Although this is not a matter of merely influencing laws, Schmidt also points out the immense influence of Christians on higher education: By the year 1932 there were 182 colleges and universities in the United States, and of that number, 92 percent had been founded by Christian denominations (p. 190).
10. Ibid., 274–76.
11. Ibid., 276–78.
12. Ibid., 279.
13. Ibid., 287–89.
14. Ibid., 251–52.

of the Declaration of Independence (1776) and the Constitution (1787)[15] in the United States. These are three of the most significant documents in the history of governments on earth, and all three show the marks of significant Christian influence in the foundational ideas of how governments should function. These foundations for British and American government did not come about as a result of the "do evangelism, not politics" view.

Schmidt also argues that several specific components of modern views of government had strong Christian influence in their origin and influence, such as individual human rights, individual freedom, the equality of individuals before the law, freedom of religion, and separation of church and state.[16]

As for the present time, Charles Colson's insightful book *God and Government*[17] (previously published as *Kingdoms in Conflict*) reports dozens of encouraging narratives of courageous, real-life Christians who in recent years, in causes large and small, have had significant impact for good on laws and governments around the world.

When I look over that list of changes in governments and laws that Christians incited, I think God *did* call the church and thousands of Christians within the church to work to bring about these momentous improvements in human society throughout the world. Or should we say that Christians who brought about these changes were *not* doing so out of obedience to God? That these changes made *no difference* to God? This cannot be true.

I believe those changes listed above were important to the God who declares, "Let justice roll down like waters, and righteousness like an ever-flowing stream" (Amos 5:24). God *cares* how people treat one another here on earth, and these changes in government listed above *do* have eternal value in God's sight.

If the Christian church had adopted the "do evangelism, not politics" view throughout its history, it would never have brought about these immeasurably valuable changes among the nations of the world. But these changes did happen, because Christians realized that if they could influence laws and governments for good, they would be obeying the command of their Lord, "Let your light shine before others, so that they *may see your good works* and give glory to your Father who is in heaven" (Matt. 5:16). They influenced governments for good because they knew that "we are his

15. Ibid., 253–58.
16. Ibid., 258–70.
17. Charles W. Colson, *God and Government: An Insider's View on the Boundaries between Faith and Politics* (Grand Rapids: Zondervan, 2007).

workmanship, created in Christ Jesus *for good works*, which God prepared beforehand, that we should walk in them" (Eph. 2:10).

6. Doesn't the Bible say that persecution is coming?

Sometimes people ask me, "Why should we try to improve governments when the Bible tells us that persecution is coming in the end times before Christ returns? Doesn't that mean that we should expect governments to become more and more anti-Christian?" (They have in mind passages like Matt. 24:9–12, 21–22; 2 Tim. 3:1–5.)

The answer is that we do not know if Christ will return next year or 500 years from now. What we do know is that while we have opportunity, God tells us not to give up but to go on preaching "the whole counsel of God" (Acts 20:27) and doing "good works" (Eph. 2:10) and loving our neighbors as ourselves (Matt. 22:39). That means we should go on *trying to influence governments for good* as long as we are able to do so.

If all the Christians who influenced governments for good in previous centuries had given up and said, "Persecution is coming and governments will become more evil, so there is nothing we can do," then none of those good changes in laws would have come about. Instead of giving in to such a hopeless attitude, courageous Christians in previous generations sought to do good for others and for governments, and God often blessed their efforts.

7. But won't political involvement distract us from the main task of preaching the Gospel?

At this point someone may object that while political involvement may have *some* benefits and may do *some* good, it can so easily distract us, turn us away from the church, and cause us to neglect the main task of pointing people toward personal trust in Christ.

Yet the proper question is not, "Does political influence take resources away from evangelism?" but, "Is political influence something God has called us to do?" If God has called some of us to some political influence, then those resources would not be blessed if we diverted them to evangelism — or to the music ministry, or to teaching Sunday School to children, or to any other use.

In this matter, as in everything else the church does, it would be healthy for Christians to realize that God may call *individual Christians* to different emphases in their lives. This is because God has placed in the church "varieties of gifts" (1 Cor. 12:4) and the church is an entity that has "many members" but is still "one body" (v. 12).

Therefore God might call someone to devote almost all of his or her time to the music ministry, someone else to youth work, someone else to evangelism, someone else to preparing refreshments to welcome visitors, and someone else to work with lighting and sound systems. "But if Jim places all his attention on the sound system, won't that distract the church from the main task of preaching the Gospel?" No, not at all. That is not what God has called Jim to emphasize (though he will certainly share the Gospel with others as he has opportunity). Jim's exclusive focus on the church's sound system means he is just being a faithful steward in the responsibility God has given him.

I think it is entirely possible that God called Billy Graham to emphasize evangelism and say nothing about politics and also called James Dobson to emphasize a radio ministry to families and to influencing the political world for good. Aren't there enough Christians in the world for us to focus on more than one task? And does God not call us to thousands of different emphases, all in obedience to him?

The whole ministry of the church will include many emphases. And the teaching ministry from the pulpit should do nothing less than proclaim "the whole counsel of God" (Acts 20:27). It should teach, over the course of time, on all areas of life and all areas of Bible knowledge. That certainly must include, to some extent, what the Bible says about the purposes of civil government and how that should apply to our situations today.

E. WRONG VIEW #5: DO POLITICS, NOT EVANGELISM

The fifth view says that the church should just try to change the laws and the culture and should not emphasize evangelism. I do not know of any responsible evangelical leaders or prominent Christian groups today who hold this view or say that Christians should just "do politics, not evangelism."

But this was a primary emphasis of the Social Gospel movement in the late nineteenth and early twentieth centuries, with its campaigns to get the church to work aggressively to overcome poverty, slums, crime, racial discrimination, and other social evils. These were good causes in themselves, but this movement placed little if any emphasis on the need for individuals to place personal trust in Christ as Savior or the need to proclaim the entire Bible as the Word of God and worthy of our belief. The Social Gospel movement gained followers primarily among liberal Protestants rather than among more conservative, evangelical Protestant groups.

Christians who encourage greater Christian involvement in politics today need to hear an important word of caution: If we (and I include myself here) ever begin to think that *good laws alone* will solve a nation's problems or bring about a righteous and just society, we will have made a huge mistake. Unless there is simultaneously an inner change in people's hearts and minds, good laws alone will only bring about grudging, external compliance with the minimum level of obedience necessary to avoid punishment. Good government and good laws can prevent much evil behavior, and they can teach people and show what society approves, but they cannot by themselves produce good people.

Genuine, long-term change in a nation will only happen (1) if people's *hearts* change so that they seek to do good, not evil; (2) if people's *minds* change so that their moral convictions align more closely with God's moral standards in the Bible; and (3) if a nation's *laws* change so that they more fully encourage good conduct and punish wrong conduct. Item 1 comes about through personal evangelism and the power of the Gospel of Jesus Christ. Item 2 takes place both through personal conversation and teaching and through public discussion and debate. Item 3 comes about through Christian political involvement. All three are necessary.

This "do politics, not evangelism" view is certainly wrong. The church must above all proclaim that "the wages of sin is death, but the free gift of God is eternal life in Christ Jesus our Lord" (Rom. 6:23). People definitely experience a change in their hearts when they believe in Christ: "Therefore, if anyone is in Christ, he is a new creation. The old has passed away; behold, the new has come" (2 Cor. 5:17).

What then? Is there a correct view that is different from these five wrong views? The view I propose next is "significant Christian influence on government." "Significant Christian influence on government" is not *compulsion* (view 1), it is not *silence* (view 2), and it is not *dropping out of the process* (views 3 and 4), nor is it thinking *the government can save people* (view 5). It is different from each of these wrong views, and I think it is much closer to the actual teaching of the Bible.

F. A BETTER VIEW: SIGNIFICANT CHRISTIAN INFLUENCE ON GOVERNMENT

In contrast to the five wrong views in the previous sections, I believe the Bible supports a sixth view: significant Christian influence on government. This "significant influence" view says that Christians *should* seek to influence civil government according to God's moral standards and God's purposes for government as revealed in the Bible (when rightly understood). But while Christians exercise this influence, they must simultaneously insist on protecting freedom of religion for all citizens.

1. Old Testament support for significant Christian influence

The Bible shows several examples of believers in God who influenced secular governments.

For instance, the Jewish prophet Daniel exercised a strong influence on the secular government in Babylon. Daniel said to Nebuchadnezzar,

> "Therefore, O king, let my counsel be acceptable to you: *break off your sins* by *practicing righteousness*, and your iniquities by *showing mercy to the oppressed*, that there may perhaps be a lengthening of your prosperity" (Dan. 4:27).

Daniel's approach is bold and clear. It is the opposite of a modern multicultural approach that might say something like this:

> "O King Nebuchadnezzar, I am a Jewish prophet, but I would not presume to impose my Jewish moral standards on your Babylonian kingdom. Ask your astronomers and your soothsayers! They will guide you in your own traditions. Then follow your own heart! It would not be my place to speak to you about right and wrong."

No, Daniel boldly told the king, "*Break off your sins* by practicing righteousness, and your iniquities by showing mercy to the oppressed."

At that time Daniel was a high official in Nebuchadnezzar's court. He was "ruler over the whole province of Babylon" and "chief prefect over all the wise men of Babylon" (Dan. 2:48). He was regularly "at the king's court" (v. 49). Therefore it seems that Daniel had a significant advisory role to the king. This leads to a reasonable assumption that Daniel's summary statement about "sins" and "iniquities" and "showing mercy to the oppressed" (Dan. 4:27), was probably followed by a longer conversation in which Daniel named specific policies and actions of the king that were either good or evil in the eyes of God.

The counsel that Jeremiah proclaimed to the Jewish exiles in Babylon also supports the idea of believers having influence on laws and government. This was a secular government, a pagan society in Babylon. But Jeremiah told these exiles, "*Seek the welfare of the city* where I have sent you into exile, and pray to the LORD on its behalf, for in its welfare you will find your welfare" (Jer. 29:7). But if believers are to seek to bring good to such a pagan society, that must include seeking to bring good to its government (as Daniel did). The true "welfare" of such a city will be advanced through governmental laws and policies that are consistent with God's teaching in the Bible, not through those that are contrary to the Bible's teachings.

Other believers in God also had high positions of governmental influence in non-Jewish nations. Joseph was the highest official after Pharaoh, king of Egypt, and had great influence in the decisions of Pharaoh (see Gen. 41:37–45; 42:6; 45:8–9, 26). Later, Moses boldly stood before Pharaoh and demanded freedom for the people of Israel, saying, "Thus says the LORD, 'Let my people go'" (Exod. 8:1). Nehemiah was "cupbearer to the king" (Neh. 1:11), a position of high responsibility before King Artaxerxes of Persia.[18] Queen Esther had a huge influence on the decisions of King Ahasuerus, risking her very life to save the Jewish people from destruction (see Esth. 5:1–8; 7:1–6; 8:3–13; 9:12–15, 29–32). Later, Esther's uncle Mordecai "was second in rank to King Ahasuerus" of Persia (Esth. 10:3; see also 9:4).

In addition, there are several passages in the Old Testament prophets that address the sins of foreign nations around Israel: see Isaiah 13–23; Ezekiel 25–32; Amos 1–2; Obadiah (addressed to Edom); Jonah (sent to Nineveh); Nahum (addressed to Nineveh); Habakkuk 2; Zephaniah 2. These prophets could speak to nations outside of Israel because the God who is revealed in the Bible is the God of *all peoples* and *all nations* of the earth. Therefore the moral standards of God as revealed in the Bible are the moral standards to which God will hold all people accountable. This includes more than the way people conduct themselves in their marriages and families, in their neighborhoods and schools, and in their jobs and businesses. It also concerns the way people conduct themselves *in government offices*. Believers have a responsibility to bear witness to the moral standards of the Bible by which God will hold all people accountable, including those people in public office.

2. New Testament support for significant Christian influence

A New Testament example of influence on government is found in the life of John the Baptist. During his lifetime the ruler of Galilee (from 4 BC to AD 39) was Herod Antipas, a "tetrarch" who had been appointed

---

18. "The position of cupbearer to the king was a high office and involved regular access to the king," ESV *Study Bible* (Wheaton, IL: Crossway, 2008), 825.

by the Roman emperor and was subject to the authority of the Roman Empire. Luke's Gospel tells us that John the Baptist rebuked Herod not only for the sin of taking his brother's wife (see also Matt. 14:4), but also for many other sins:

> [John the Baptist] preached good news to the people. But Herod the tetrarch, who had been reproved by him for Herodias, his brother's wife, *and for all the evil things that Herod had done,* added this to them all, that he locked up John in prison (Luke 3:18–20).

Certainly "all the evil things that Herod had done" included evil actions that he had carried out as a governing official in the Roman Empire. John the Baptist rebuked him *for all of them.* He boldly spoke to officials of the empire about the moral right and wrong of their governmental policies. In doing this, John was following in the steps of Daniel and many Old Testament prophets. The New Testament portrays John the Baptist's actions as those of "a righteous and holy man" (Mark 6:20). He is an excellent example of a believer who had what I call "significant influence" on the policies of a government (though it cost him his life: see Mark 6:21–29).

Another example is the apostle Paul. While Paul was in prison in Caesarea, he stood trial before the Roman governor Felix. Here is what happened:

> After some days Felix came with his wife Drusilla, who was Jewish, and he sent for Paul and heard him speak about faith in Christ Jesus. And *as he reasoned about righteousness and self-control and the coming judgment,* Felix was alarmed and said, "Go away for the present. When I get an opportunity I will summon you" (Acts 24:24–25).

The fact that Felix was "alarmed" and that Paul reasoned with him about "righteousness" and "the coming judgment" indicates that Paul was talking about moral standards of right and wrong and the ways in which Felix, as an official of the Roman Empire, had obligations to live up to the standards that are given by God. Paul no doubt told Felix that he would be accountable for his actions at "the coming judgment" and that this was what led Felix to be "alarmed." When Luke tells us that Paul "reasoned" with Felix about these things, the word (Greek *dialegomai*) indicates a back-and-forth conversation or discussion, and the verb tense (present participle) suggests a conversation that continued over time. It is not difficult to suppose that Felix asked Paul, "What about this decision that I made? What about this policy? What about this ruling?" It would be an artificial restriction on the meaning of the text to suppose that Paul *only* spoke with Felix about his "private" life and not about his actions as a Roman governor. Paul is thus another example of attempting to exercise "significant Christian influence" on civil government.

Clearly, examples of godly believers' influence on governments are not minor examples confined to obscure portions of the Bible, but are found in Old Testament history from Genesis (Joseph) all the way to Esther (the last historical book); in the canonical writing prophets from Isaiah to Zephaniah; and in the New Testament in both the Gospels and Acts. And those are just the examples of God's servants bringing "significant influence" to *pagan* rulers who gave no allegiance to the God of Israel or to Jesus in the New Testament times. If we add to this list the many stories of Old Testament prophets bringing counsel and encouragement and rebuke to the good and evil kings of Israel as well, then we would include the histories of all the kings and the writings of all the prophets—nearly every book of the Old Testament. In addition, we could add in several passages from Psalms and Proverbs that speak of good and evil rulers. Influencing government for good on the basis of the wisdom found in God's own words is a theme that runs through the entire Bible.

3. Romans 13 and 1 Peter 2

In addition to these examples, *specific Bible passages that teach about government* present an argument for "significant Christian influence." Why do we think God put Romans 13:1–7 and 1 Peter 2:13–14 and other related passages (as in Psalms and Proverbs) in the Bible? Are they in the Bible simply as a matter of intellectual curiosity for Christians who will read them privately but never use them to speak to government officials about how God understands their roles and responsibilities? Does God intend this material to be *concealed* from people in government and *kept secret* by Christians who would read it and silently moan about "how far government has strayed from what God wants it to be"?

Certainly God put such passages there not only to inform Christians about how *they* should relate to civil government, but also in order that *people with governmental responsibilities* could know what God himself expects from them. This also pertains to still other passages in the Bible that instruct us about God's moral standards, about the nature and purpose of human beings made in God's image, about God's purposes for the earth, and about principles concerning good and bad governments.

All of these teachings are relevant for those who serve in governmental office, and we should speak and teach about them when we have opportunity to do so.

4. The responsibility of citizens in a democracy to understand the Bible's teaching

There is still another argument for "significant Christian influence" on government that applies to anyone who lives in a democracy, because in a democracy a significant portion of the ruling power of government is entrusted to the citizens generally, through the ballot box. This means that all of the passages in the Bible that instruct "rulers" are directly relevant to every citizen in a democracy, for through the ballot box we all share in part of the "ruling" of our countries. Therefore all citizens who are old enough to vote have a *responsibility* before God to know what God expects of civil government and what kind of moral and legal standards he wants government to follow. But *how can citizens learn what kind of government God is seeking?* They can learn this only if churches teach about government and politics from the Bible.

I realize that pastors will differ in the degree of detail they wish to teach with regard to specific political issues facing a nation (for example, whether to teach about issues such as abortion, euthanasia, care for the poor, the military and national defense, use and care of the environment, or the nature of marriage). But surely it is a responsibility of pastors to *teach* on *some* of these specific policies in ways that go beyond the mere statement, "You have a responsibility to vote intelligently."

After all, who else is going to teach these Christians about *exactly how* the Bible applies to specific political issues? Would pastors think it right to leave their congregations with such vague guidance in other areas of life? Would we say, "You have a responsibility to bring up your children according to Christian principles," and then never explain to them what those Christian principles are? Would we think it right to say to people in the business world, "You have a responsibility to work in the business world according to Christian principles," and then never give them any details about what these Christian principles are? No, the responsibility of pastors is to give wise biblical teaching, *explaining exactly how the teachings of the Bible apply to various specific situations in life*, and that should certainly include instruction about some policy matters in government and politics.

In the United States since 1954 the Internal Revenue Service has had regulations that prohibit pastors or churches from explicitly saying that they support or oppose any candidates by name (though they are still allowed to take positions on moral issues that are part of an election campaign). The Alliance Defense Fund (www.telladf.org) believes this policy is an unconstitutional violation of freedom of speech and freedom of religion in the First Amendment, and I think they are right. They have launched a "Pulpit Freedom Sunday" initiative seeking to challenge the IRS in Federal court, and I think they will ultimately prevail. Pastors and churches, not the government, should control what is said in church pulpits.

But however that controversy is resolved, pastors in the United States today can easily teach on the moral issues that are at stake in any election without naming any specific candidate or even naming any political party, but simply saying that "Party A (or Candidate A) holds this view," and "Party B (or Candidate B) holds this view" and leaving it to the congregation to read and discover which party holds which view. That is completely legal now under current IRS policy. Pastors should at least be doing this.

G. FINAL THOUGHTS

1. I am not saying that Christians should only vote for Christian candidates

When I speak about "significant Christian influence" on government, I want to be clear that *I do not mean that Christians should only vote for other Christian candidates for office*, or even that Christians should generally prefer an evangelical candidate over others who are running. I would not support an evangelical Christian candidate who opposed most of the policies I support in this book, because I think that candidate would simply be mistaken in his political thinking. And I might choose to support a non-Christian candidate who followed generally conservative political positions. The relevant principle is this: Christians should support candidates who best represent moral and political values consistent with biblical teaching, no matter their religious background or convictions.

2. Without Christian influence, governments will have no clear moral compass

Try to imagine what a nation and its government would be like *if all Christian influence on government were suddenly removed*. Within a few years no one would have any moral absolutes beyond their individual moral sentiments and moral intuitions, which can be so unreliable. In addition, most people would have no moral authority beyond that of individual human opinion. Therefore, how could a nation find any moral guidance?

Consider the many political issues facing the United States (and other nations) that have significant moral components to them. For example: war, same-sex marriage, abortion, pornography, poverty, care for the environment, capital punishment, and public education. There are many other issues as well. The United States has a tremendous need for moral guidance, and I am convinced that Christians should study and discuss and then speak publicly about them.

If pastors and church members say, "I'll let somebody else speak about that," where will the nation's moral standards come from? Where will people learn about ethics? Perhaps from Hollywood movies? From friends at work or at the local bar? From professional counselors? From elementary school teachers? But where do *these* people learn about right and wrong?

The simple fact is that if Christians do not speak publicly about what the Bible teaches regarding issues of right and wrong, there aren't many other good sources for finding any transcendent source of ethics, any source outside of ourselves and our own subjective feelings and consciences.

As Christians, we need to remember that the entire world is locked in a tremendous spiritual battle. There are demonic forces, forces of Satan, that seek to oppose God's purposes and bring evil and destruction to every human being that God created in his own image, and also bring destruction to every human society and every nation. If pastors and church members say, "I'm going to be silent about the moral and ethical issues that we face as a nation," that will leave a moral vacuum, and it will not be long until the ultimate adversaries of the Gospel—Satan and his demons—will rush in and influence every decision in a way contrary to biblical standards.

3. The political obligations of all Christian citizens

I believe that every Christian citizen who lives in a democracy has at the very least a minimal obligation to be well-informed and to vote for candidates and policies that are most consistent with biblical principles. The opportunity to help select the kind of government we will have is a *stewardship* that God entrusts to citizens in a democracy, a stewardship that we should not neglect or fail to appreciate.

But in addition to that, I want to ask every Christian in the United States to consider whether he or she has a higher obligation than merely voting. The question is whether someone thinks it is morally right *to receive great benefits from a nation but to give almost nothing in return.* The great freedoms that citizens have in the United States came only as a result of great sacrifice on the part of millions of others. The original signers of the Declaration of Independence knew that they were publicly declaring themselves to be guilty of treason against Britain, and they knew they would be subject to the death penalty and to confiscation of their property if the British caught them or defeated them.[19] Nor could they have any great confidence that they would win a war against the most powerful nation on earth at that time. Therefore the last line in the Declaration of Independence says this:

> And for the support of this declaration, with a firm reliance on the protection of divine Providence, we mutually pledge to each other our lives, our fortunes, and our sacred honor.[20]

Independence from Britain did not come cheaply. In the War of Independence, approximately 4,500 Americans died. Later wars were even more costly. All told, hundreds of thousands of men (and many women as well) *sacrificed their lives* to protect the nation and preserve the freedoms we enjoy today. *Is it right that we simply enjoy these freedoms while giving back to our nation nothing in return?* Should we not participate at least at some level in giving money or giving time to support specific candidates and issues? Or writing letters or helping to distribute literature? Or even running for office or volunteering to serve in the military? Is it not right that all of us at least do *something* more than merely voting to preserve and protect our nation?

19. Pauline Maier, *American Scripture: Making the Declaration of Independence* (New York: Alfred A. Knopf, 1998), 59, 118, 125, 147, 152.
20. Declaration of Independence, adopted July 4, 1776. www.archives.gov/national_archives_experience/charters/declaration_transcript.html.

Chapter 2

ECONOMICS: FUNDAMENTAL PRINCIPLES

What should be the role of government regarding a nation's economic system?

This is a large question, and it involves many specific economic issues. This chapter will treat the following subtopics:

Private property

Economic development

Money supply

Free markets and regulation

The rich and the poor

Government and business

A. PRIVATE PROPERTY

According to the teachings of the Bible, government should both document and protect the ownership of private property in a nation.

The Bible regularly assumes and reinforces a system in which *property belongs to individuals*, not to the government or to society as a whole.

We see this implied in the Ten Commandments, for example, because the eighth commandment, "You shall not steal" (Exod. 20:15), assumes that human beings will own property that belongs to them individually and not to other people. I should not steal my neighbor's ox or donkey because *it belongs to my neighbor,* not to me and not to anyone else.

The tenth commandment makes this more explicit when it prohibits not just stealing but also *desiring* to steal what belongs to my neighbor:

> "You shall not covet your neighbor's house; you shall not covet your neighbor's wife, or his male servant, or his female servant, or his ox, or his donkey, or anything that is your neighbor's" (Exod. 20:17).

The reason I should not "covet" my neighbor's house or anything else is that *these things belong to my neighbor,* not to me and not to the community or the nation.

This assumption of private ownership of property, found in this fundamental moral code of the Bible, puts the Bible in direct opposition to the communist system advocated by Karl Marx. Marx said:

> The theory of the Communists may be summed up in the single sentence: abolition of private property.[1]

The reason why communism is so incredibly dehumanizing is that when private property is abolished, government controls all economic activity. And when government controls all economic activity, it controls what you can buy, where you will live, and what job you will have (and therefore what job you are allowed to train for, and where you go to school), and how much you will earn. It essentially controls all of life, and human liberty is destroyed. Communism enslaves people and destroys human freedom of choice. The entire nation becomes one huge prison. For this reason, it seems to me that communism is the most dehumanizing economic system ever invented by man.

Other passages of Scripture also support the idea that property should belong to individuals, not to "society" or to the government (except for certain property required for proper government purposes, such as government offices, military bases, and streets and highways). The Bible contains many laws concerning punishments for stealing and appropriate restitution for damage of another person's farm animals or agricultural fields (for example, see Exod. 21:28–36; 22:1–15; Deut. 22:1–4; 23:24–25). Another commandment guaranteed that property boundaries would be protected: "You shall not move your neighbor's landmark, which the men of old have set, in the inheritance that you will hold in the land that the LORD your God is giving you to possess"

---

1. Karl Marx, *Communist Manifesto* (New York: International Publishers, 1948), 23.

(Deut. 19:14). To move the landmark was to move the boundaries of the land and thus to steal land that belonged to one's neighbor (compare Prov. 22:28; 23:10).

Another guarantee of the ownership of private property was the fact that, even if property was sold to someone else, in the Year of Jubilee it had to return to the family that originally owned it:

> It shall be a Jubilee for you, when *each of you shall return to his property* and each of you shall return to his clan (Lev. 25:10).

This is why the land could not be sold forever: "The land shall not be sold in perpetuity, for the land is mine. For you are strangers and sojourners with me" (Lev. 25:23).

This last verse emphasizes the fact that private property is never viewed in the Bible as an *absolute* right, because all that people have is ultimately given to them by God, and people are viewed as God's "stewards" to manage what he has entrusted to their care.

> The earth is the LORD's and the fullness thereof, the world and those who dwell therein (Ps. 24:1; compare Ps. 50:10–12; Hag. 2:8).

Yet the fact remains that, under the overall sovereign lordship of God himself, property is regularly said to belong *to individuals*, not to the government and not to "society" or the nation as a whole.

When Samuel warned the people about the evils that would be imposed upon them by a king, he emphasized the fact that the monarch, with so much government power, would "take" and "take" and "take" from the people and confiscate things for his own use:

> So Samuel told all the words of the LORD to the people who were asking for a king from him. He said, "These will be the ways of the king who will reign over you: he will *take* your sons and appoint them to his chariots and to be his horsemen and to run before his chariots. And he will appoint for himself commanders of thousands and commanders of fifties, and some to plow his ground and to reap his harvest, and to make his implements of war and the equipment of his chariots. He will *take* your daughters to be perfumers and cooks and bakers. He will *take* the best of your fields and vineyards and olive orchards and give them to his servants. He will *take* the tenth of your grain and of your vineyards and give it to his officers and to his servants. He will *take* your male servants and female servants and the best of your young men and your donkeys, and put them

to his work. He will *take* the tenth of your flocks, *and you shall be his slaves*. And in that day you will cry out because of your king, whom you have chosen for yourselves, but the LORD will not answer you in that day" (1 Sam. 8:10–18).

This prediction was tragically fulfilled in the story of the theft of the vineyard of Naboth the Jezreelite by Ahab the wicked king and Jezebel, his even more wicked queen (see 1 Kings 21:1–29). The regular tendency of evil human governments is to seek to take control of more and more of the property of a nation that God intends to be owned and controlled by private individuals.

One of the primary reasons why God establishes a system of ownership of property among human beings is our creation "in the image of God" (see Gen. 1:27). God placed human beings on the earth as his representatives, and he wants us to be like him and to imitate his character in many ways: "Therefore be imitators of God, as beloved children" (Eph. 5:1). When we own possessions, he gives us many opportunities to imitate God's attributes and thus reflect something of his excellence (his "glory") on the earth.[2]

For example, just as God is sovereign over the whole universe, so he gives us opportunity to be sovereign over a small portion of land, or a car, or clothing and books, and so forth. In our stewardship of these possessions we have opportunities to imitate God's wisdom, his creativity, his love for other people, his justice and fairness, his mercy, his knowledge, and many other attributes. Ownership of possessions also provides many opportunities to test what is in our hearts and gives us opportunities to give thanks to God for what he has provided to us (see Col. 3:15; 1 Tim. 6:17).

Unfortunately, it is not only communist countries that make it impossible for individual people to own private property. In many other supposedly "capitalist" countries there is no effective free market system regarding ownership of private property either, because nearly all property is controlled by a few wealthy individuals, and they have enough influence that government laws are set up to prevent ordinary people from owning property themselves. Therefore most of the people cannot legally own property and as a result are trapped in poverty.

The Peruvian economist Hernando de Soto attempted, as an experiment, to register a small business in Peru, using some graduate students as a research team. They tried to open a small garment workshop (with one worker) on the outskirts of Lima, the capital. They worked at the

---

2. See a further discussion of this idea in Wayne Grudem, *Business for the Glory of God: The Bible's Teaching on the Moral Goodness of Business* (Wheaton, IL: Crossway, 2003).

registration process for six hours a day, and it took them 289 days! The cost was the equivalent of $1,231 US dollars, or thirty-one times the monthly minimum wage (approximately three years' salary for an ordinary person in Peru). De Soto then explained what happened when they tried to get permission to build a house:

> To obtain legal authorization to build a house on state-owned land took six years and eleven months requiring 207 administrative steps in 52 government offices.... To obtain a legal title for that piece of land took 728 steps.[3]

De Soto and his team document similar roadblocks to ownership of property and small businesses in other countries such as Egypt, the Philippines, and Haiti. They conclude that *legal ownership of property or a business is effectively impossible for the vast majority of the population in many Third World countries.* Thus citizens are trapped in poverty every bit as much as they would be if they were living in a communist society.

If people can never *own* property or *own* a business, they cannot *build* a business and become even moderately well-off; they can never acquire rental property as a source of additional income; they can never take a second mortgage on a house as a means of starting a business; and they will find it nearly impossible to obtain anything more than a very tiny amount of credit to invest in building a business (because they have no permanent address).

This is why DeSoto has argued — I think persuasively — that one of the most important factors for economic development of a nation is a system where ownership of private property is *easily documented* and *publicly known.*

The issue of private ownership of property also has practical application to the United States today, because threats to private ownership of property are increasing at the highest level of government. In the early months of 2009 (the opening months of the Obama administration), the federal government took unprecedented steps to acquire a near-controlling interest in some of the nation's largest banks, including Citigroup and Bank of America.[4] It forced Chrysler Corporation into

---

3. Hernando de Soto, *The Mystery of Capital: Why Capitalism Triumphs in the West and Fails Everywhere Else* (New York: Basic Books, 2000), 19 – 20.

4. Mike Allen and Craig Gordon, "Treas. and the Citi: Deal Announced," *Politico.com* (Feb. 27, 2009), www.politico.com/news/stories/0209/19401.html; and Binyamin Appelbaum and David Cho, "White House Banking on Nationalization," *Washington Post* (Feb. 24, 2009), www.cbsnews.com/stories/2009/02/24/politics/washingtonpost/main4823573.shtml?sourc e=RSSattr=Politics_4823573.

accepting an agreement by which a large share would be bought by Fiat and a controlling interest in the company would be held by the autoworkers union, the United Auto Workers (UAW).[5] It effectively acquired a controlling interest in General Motors as well, so that one day President Obama could announce that he thought that the president of General Motors, Rick Wagoner, needed to resign, and immediately the company's president was gone.[6] It was previously unheard-of in America—and thought to be impossible—for the US President to be able to "fire" the president of one of America's largest corporations. But now government control of the nation's property has extended even to this action.

In addition, the Democratic majority in Congress in early 2010 passed legislation that gives the federal government significant control of the nation's health care system, which comprises approximately 17.6% of the nation's gross domestic product (GDP).[7] The bill calls for large segments of the American economy to be taken over by the federal government and essentially become *owned* by the government rather than by shareholders or private individuals.

In another area, in 2005, the US Supreme Court decided that government could use the power of eminent domain to transfer *private* land to another *private* owner.[8]

Yet another source of threats to private ownership of property comes in the increasingly burdensome weight of government regulations on how people can use their property. Homeowners in sections of California that are prone to forest fires have been prohibited by environmental regulations from cutting down the trees that grow close to their homes, sometimes resulting in fires that needlessly destroy their homes.

For example, homeowners near Santa Cruz, California (about ninety miles south of San Francisco) have faced so many environmental regulations that it has become cost prohibitive for them to do the things necessary to protect them. One woman who had intended to clear some fire-prone eucalyptus from her six-acre property found out that she had to pay a county planner between $1,300 and $1,500 to survey her prop-

5. "UAW, Chrysler, and Fiat Reach Concession Deal," *ABCNews.com* (August 26, 2009). http://abcnews.go.com/Business/wireStory?id=7435524.

6. Dan Strumpf, "GM CEO Wagoner Forced Out," Associated Press (March 30, 2009). www.myfoxdc.com/dpp/news/dpg_GM_Rick_Wagoner_Out_fc_200903302343214.

7. A. Siska et al., "Health Spending Projections Through 2018: Recession Effects Add Uncertainty to the Outlook," *Health Affairs* 28, no. 2 (March/April 2009), p.w 346-w357: cited in "Health Care Costs: Costs," National Coalition on Health Care (July 2009), www. nchc.org/documents/Fact%20Sheets/Fact%20Sheet%20-%20Cost%208–10–09.pdf.

8. *Kelo et al. v. City of New London et al.*, 545 U.S. 469, (2005).

erty before altering the landscape, without any certainty that she would get permission to cut the trees down.

One neighbor said, "You will go through this misery of trying to get a plan approved. If you're one of these citizens who wants to stay on the correct side of the law, you could really be off to the races with your checkbook."

The homeowner decided to forego removing the trees, and her 2,800-square-foot home eventually burned down.

These were *her* trees on *her* property, and she could not cut them down!

The county planning department was sympathetic to her plight, but said they were forced to enforce state and federal environmental laws. The planning director, Tom Burns, said, "There's got to be a balance between environmental protections and allowing people to protect their houses."[9]

In 2007, columnist Michelle Malkin reported on how environmental lawsuits kept the government from being able to proceed with procedures to stop wildfires:

> The government accounting office (GAO) examined 762 U.S. Forest Service (USFS) proposals to thin forests and prevent fires during the past two years. According to the study, slightly more than half the proposals were not subject to third-party appeal. Of those proposals subject to appeal, third parties challenged 59 percent. Appeals were filed most often by anti-logging groups, including the Sierra Club, Alliance for Wild Rockies, and Forest Conservation Council. According to the GAO, 84 interest groups filed more than 400 appeals of Forest Service proposals. The appeals delayed efforts to treat 900,000 acres of forests and cost the federal government millions of dollars to address.[10]

Dana Joel Gattuso, writing in National Policy Analysis, concurs:

> Appeals and lawsuits, along with regulations under the National Environmental Policy Act (NEPA) requiring the Forest Service

---

9. Kurtis Alexander, "Environmental Regulations Blamed for Compromising Fire Safety of Homeowners," *Santa Cruz Sentinel* (June 30, 2008). www.santacruzsentinel.com/fire/ci_9744744.

10. Michelle Malkin, "Wildfires and Environmental Obstructionism," *MichelleMalkin,com* (Oct. 23, 2007). http://michellemalkin.com/2007/10/23/wildfires-and-environmental-obstructionism/.

to perform extensive environmental impact analyses before undertaking fuel reduction projects, all divert time, effort and dollars away from fire prevention. NEPA, for example, requires the Forest Service to consider between six and nine alternatives for each treatment plan proposed, each costing approximately $2 million. These costs, along with the expense of appeals and lawsuits, typically consume 30 to 45 percent of the agency's budget earmarked for fire prevention.[11]

After one destructive forest fire, Forest Ranger Kate Klein said, "If we had done all the thinning we wanted to over the years, we could have kept this fire from exploding, and we could have saved the towns it burned through."[12]

In still other situations, developers acquire land to build residential or commercial buildings and then find that oppressive environmental regulations and lawsuits keep them from developing the land for many years and greatly increase their building costs. But this is their own land!

Michael H. Schill, dean of the UCLA Law School, wrote:

> Government rules requiring developers and/or public entities to undertake environmental impact analyses ... are likely to generate higher costs and lead to a diminished supply of housing for two reasons. First, the review itself and the possible resulting environmental impact statement could be very costly. Second, potential lawsuits from neighbors or environmental activists challenging the review could be even more problematic. In addition to assuming the costs of defending the case, the developer would have to factor into the project the costs of delay and settlement. In some instances, this uncertainty actually may deter builders from undertaking projects, thereby reducing the overall supply of housing and increasing price.[13]

In the Pacific Northwest the entire logging industry has been destroyed by environmental regulations regarding logging and species such as the spotted owl, and such regulations prevent owners from cut-

11. Dana Joel Gattuso, "Signs of New Growth in Forest Debate?" *National Policy Analysis* (Oct. 2003), www.nationalcenter.org/NPA491.html. Gattuso cites Molly Villamana, "Forests," *Environment and Energy Daily* (July 25, 2003), and David Rogers, "Timber Rivals Rally in Name of Wildfires," *Wall Street Journal* (Aug. 11, 2003).

12. Kate Klein: quoted in Paul Trachtman, "Fire Fight," *Smithsonian* (Aug. 2003), 46.

13. Michael H. Schill, "Regulations and Housing Development: What We Know," *Cityscape: A Journal of Policy Development and Research* 8:1 (2005), 10. www.huduser.org/periodicals/cityscpe/vol8num1/ch1.pdf.

ting down trees and taking lumber *from their own land*! In 1992 the National Center for Public Policy Research reported:

> Recovery efforts for the Pacific Northwest Spotted Owl will cost an estimated 50,000–100,000 timber industry jobs. In 1990, the Northwest's Spotted Owl was listed as a "threatened species" under the Endangered Species Act even though it is virtually indistinguishable from the California Spotted Owl—an owl in abundant supply. Since 1990, 100 wood products mills, employing some 8,000 workers, have been closed in the Pacific Northwest.[14]

Dick Hammer, vice president of A.L.R.T. Corporation, a timber, logging, road, and trucking company in Washington state, said, "It doesn't cause me any pain to cut down a tree because I know when I cut down a tree I am going to plant a number of trees to take its place."[15] But despite the fact that logging companies replace the trees they cut down, environmental regulations have put many of these companies out of business.

Of course, I agree that we need some regulations to protect the environment from harmful and destructive uses. (One has only to travel to large cities in Third World countries to experience the human health costs of unrestrained pollution, for example.) The restrictions I am objecting to are not done for the benefit of human beings, however, but primarily to prevent *even the wise use of natural resources*. An attitude that disregards the importance of private property rights and sees all property as ultimately belonging to the state will demand excessive environmental regulations that ignore the substantial costs in terms of loss of personal freedom and the right to use one's own property for one's own benefit.

Another erosion of the right to private property came under President Clinton when he, by executive order, classified millions of acres of private property in the western United States as protected land that could not be bought or sold or developed. Under Executive Order 13061, then-President Clinton designated fourteen rivers—with the authorization to subsequently add ten rivers per year—as federal property—regardless of whether they ran through private property.[16] The same thing has already begun to happen under President Obama, with

---

14. "It's Not Easy Being Green: Excessive Environmental Regulations Hurt Working Class Americans," *Talking Points on the Economy: Follies of Regulation #2*, National Center for Public Policy Research (Feb. 26, 1992). www.nationalcenter.org/TPRegulations.html.

15. Dick Hammer: Quoted in Richard Quest, "Environment Meets Politics Amid Firs," *CNN.com* (Aug. 13, 2004). http://edition.cnn.com/2004/ALLPOLITICS/08/13/quest.trees/.

16. Executive Order 13061. http://clinton6.nara.gov/1997/09/1997–09–11-executive-order–13061-on-american-heritage-rivers.html.

millions of additional acres of land being confiscated by Congress and effectively removed from private use forever.[17]

In all of these ways and many others, the federal government today is behaving in much the same way that Samuel warned that the king in Israel would behave when he acquired too much power: "He will *take*.... He will *take*.... He will *take*.... He will *take*" (see 1 Sam. 8:10–18).

Whenever government takes over private companies and private property in this way, more personal freedom is lost. The people who work in the company or live on the land increasingly become servants of the government, subject to the government's dictates and controls. Their freedom to do *as they think best* with their companies or their property is taken away.

If this happens to the health care system in the United States, for example, then private doctors, nurses, pharmacies, hospitals, medical labs, medical employees, and medical supply companies will essentially become employees of the federal government. In effect, they will become its servants, and a huge amount of human freedom will be lost.

The fundamental issue at stake in the battle for ownership of private property in a nation is the issue of human liberty — liberty to be free to choose to obey God or disobey him in our roles as stewards of what he has entrusted to us. When the government takes over more and more of people's property, such liberty is increasingly forfeited.

B. ECONOMIC DEVELOPMENT

Government should promote healthy economic development in a nation.

Is it any part of a government's responsibility to seek to promote conditions that will lead to economic growth and development in a nation? Should governments seek to increase the standard of living and the annual per capita income in a nation? Or is that kind of thing just promoting a wrongful type of "materialism"?

I believe that government *should* promote economic growth in a nation. This is because one of the primary responsibilities of government is to act as God's servant to "do good" for the citizens of a nation (see Rom. 13:4) or, in the words of the US Constitution, to "promote the general welfare" of a nation.

Sometimes people assume that "Christians should not promote economic growth because that is materialism, and materialism is evil." But

---

17. "Congress votes to expand wilderness in 9 states," Associated Press (March 26, 2009). www.usatoday.com/news/washington/legislative/house/2009 – 03 – 25-wilderness_N. htm?csp=34.

I disagree. I do not believe that economic growth *in itself* is morally evil or simply the result of wrongful "materialism." Nor do I believe that economic growth is something that is morally "neutral." Rather, I believe that economic growth is, in itself, morally good and part of what God intended in putting human beings on the earth. It is right that government should promote it.

One of God's original purposes for human beings was to make the earth productive:

> And God blessed them. And God said to them, "Be fruitful and multiply and fill the earth and *subdue it* and *have dominion* over the fish of the sea and over the birds of the heavens and over every living thing that moves on the earth" (Gen. 1:28).

The word translated "subdue" is the Hebrew term *kâbash*, meaning "to subdue, dominate, bring into servitude or bondage." This same term is used of "subduing" the land of Canaan so it would serve and provide for the people of Israel (Num. 32:22, 29; Josh. 18:1) and of David "subduing" the nations that he conquered so that they would bring tribute to him (2 Sam. 8:11). This expression in God's original command to Adam and Eve implies that he wanted them to investigate, understand, use, and enjoy the resources of the earth. They were to do this as God's image-bearers and with thanksgiving to God.

This implies that *developing and producing more and better goods from the earth* is not simply a result of sin or greed or wrongful "materialism," but something that God planned for human beings to do from the beginning. It is an essential part of how he created us to function.

Throughout the rest of the Bible, one of God's blessings is the blessing of increased productivity from the earth, and one of his curses on people who sin is that he will hinder their productivity, make their work painfully laborious, and ultimately send famine on them when a desolate earth will not bear its fruit: "Cursed is the ground because of you; in *pain* you shall eat of it all the days of your life; *thorns and thistles* it shall bring forth for you.... By *the sweat of your face* you shall eat bread, till you return to the ground" (Gen. 3:17–19; see also the curses promised in Deut. 28:15–68).

By contrast, God often promised to give material abundance as a blessing to those who trust and obey him:

> For the LORD your God is bringing you into a good land, a land of brooks of water ... a land of wheat and barley ... a land of olive trees and honey, a land in which *you will eat bread without*

scarcity, in which *you will lack nothing....* And you shall eat and be full, and you shall bless the LORD your God for the good land he has given you (Deut. 8:7–10; see also 11:10–17; 28:1–14).

In fact, some places in the prophets foretell a future time of even greater productivity with much material blessing (see Isa. 35:1–2; Joel 3:18). Greater productivity will accompany times of greater blessing from God.

Another indication that *material productivity is good* is found in the New Testament reminders to help the poor. These imply that poverty is not something desirable but something that we need to work to overcome (see Gal. 2:10; 1 John 3:17).

Jesus himself practiced his trade as a carpenter (see Mark 6:3) and Paul did the same as a tent maker (see Acts 18:3; 2 Thess. 3:7–8), thus showing that an occupation of producing and selling goods from the earth is not in itself "greedy" or "materialistic," but something that is right and pleasing in the sight of God.

The New Testament also looks forward to a time when the earth will be renewed and will regain an amazing productivity and the rich fruitfulness that it had in the garden of Eden before God placed a curse on the earth. Paul writes that "the creation itself will be set free from its bondage to decay and obtain the freedom of the glory of the children of God" (Rom. 8:21). Also, the book of Revelation contains pictures of the age to come that portray it as a time of immense material abundance beyond anything we can imagine (see Rev. 21:10–26).

To summarize: One of God's purposes for human beings from Genesis to Revelation has been that we should *produce useful things from the earth*—things that we *enjoy* and for which we therefore give thanks to God. Therefore material things are not in themselves "unspiritual," but are gifts from God. We can and should use them with a clear conscience and with thanksgiving to God for the things he has provided to us. "For everything created by God is good, and nothing is to be rejected if it is received with thanksgiving" (1 Tim. 4:4; cf. 6:17).

Of course, there are temptations that accompany the production and ownership of material goods (such as pride, envy, selfishness, lack of love for one's neighbor, and laziness from having excessive possessions). The greatest temptation is setting our hearts on material things rather than the God who gives them: "You cannot serve God and money" (Matt. 6:24). But these *temptations to sin* must not cause us to think that material goods are evil in themselves, and surely it is not evil but *good* for a nation to continually *increase* its production of goods and services, for this is what God intended human beings to do on the earth, and that is the only long-term solution to poverty in a nation.

It is not surprising, therefore, that God has created us with a strong internal desire to create, develop, and produce things from the earth, whether this happens in gardening or cooking or carpentry or car repairs or many other crafts and hobbies as well as in producing many manufactured products.

When the wealth of a nation increases, it becomes easier for people to fulfill many of God's other commands, such as raising children, spreading the Gospel at home and abroad, caring for those in need, building up the church, even meeting together as a church in a suitable building. Even though the Bible says that God has "chosen those who are poor in the world to be rich in faith" (James 2:5), it never encourages people to *seek* to be poor or to make others poor, but just the opposite: we should help and care for those who are poor (see Gal. 2:10; 1 John 3:17), and seek to help them come out of poverty.

Therefore there are many reasons why it is morally *right* for governments to seek to increase the economic productivity of a nation. It helps people fulfill one of the purposes for which God put us on the earth; it enables people more effectively to obey many other commands of Scripture; it enables people to fulfill the desire to be productive that God has put in their hearts; it enables people to work and support themselves and so obey New Testament commands (see 2 Thess. 3:6–12); it enables many people to overcome poverty for themselves; and it provides many opportunities for giving thanks to God.

C. THE MONEY SUPPLY

Government should establish and maintain an effective money supply for a nation.

The Bible never says that money is evil, but rather it says that "*the love of money* is the root of all kinds of evils" (1 Tim. 6:10).

Money in fact is *good in itself* because it enables people to buy the goods they need and sell the goods they produce on the basis of a standard item (money, such as an American dollar or a British pound or a Euro) on which everybody agrees about the value. If we didn't have money, we would have to barter with one another, exchanging eggs or bags of apples or other such things, and most modern business transactions would effectively become impossible. (How many eggs would you trade for a new car?)

But since very few people now are able to produce everything they need for themselves (only subsistence farmers in primitive societies do that), *we need money to buy and sell* and thus enjoy the benefits of things that other people produce. This is a wonderful process because it forces us into personal interactions with others in which friendship and a level of trust can be developed, and honesty and integrity can be demonstrated.

Thus, money is a *measure of value*, and money itself *carries value* until we use it to purchase something else of value.[18]

But who can provide people with the money they need to buy and sell things? The best solution is that the government of each nation should have a currency that is known and accepted and that has a standard value across the nation (such as a dollar in the United States, a peso in Mexico, or a pound in the United Kingdom).

Yet, in order for the system to work, *the value of a currency must remain stable over time.* To take an extreme example, imagine this: Let's say that a painter agrees to paint a room in my house for $200. One week later, he comes and paints the room, and I pay him $200. Everything works just fine if the value of $200 has remained the same. But in some countries, inflation changes the value of money and effectively changes the rules in the middle of the game.

For example, suppose that when I agreed to pay him $200 for painting my room, a loaf of bread cost $4 and a gallon of gas to drive the painter's truck cost $2. His monthly rent was $800. Knowing all this, he agreed to paint my room for $200. But after he made the agreement, suppose that unrestrained inflation set in, and the price of a loaf of bread went to $40 and then to $400! A gallon of gas all of a sudden would cost $200, and his rent would cost $80,000 per month!

Some examples of terrible hyperinflation include:

Hungary—July 1946: 207% daily inflation rate. Prices would double within 15 hours.

Zimbabwe—November 2008: 98% daily inflation rate. Prices would double within 24.7 hours.

Yugoslavia—January 1994: 64.6% daily inflation rate. Prices would double within 1.4 days.

Germany—October 1923: 20.9% daily inflation rate. Prices would double within 3.7 days.

18. See further discussion of the moral goodness of money in Grudem, *Business for the Glory of God*.

Greece—October 1944: 17.9% daily inflation rate. Prices would double within 4.3 days.

China—May 1949: 11% daily inflation rate. Prices would double within 6.7 days.[19]

When inflation like this occurs, then I might still pay the painter the $200 that I agreed on, but instead of buying fifty loaves of bread, it won't even buy him one loaf of bread! The government allowed the rules to change in the middle of the game, and all of a sudden *everybody is robbed* of the value of the money they have worked for. No one will want to make contracts any more because no one will know what a dollar will be worth in a week or two or a month. The entire economic system will break down, and people will be reduced to bartering with precious metals or jewelry or other such things. Inflation like this will absolutely destroy an economy and a nation.

If inflation occurs at 10 or 15% a year, people might not notice it quite so abruptly, but the sinister, destructive effects will still be felt. They are still being robbed of 15% of the value of their money and their contracts each year! Therefore it is necessary for good governments to maintain a relatively stable currency over time.[20] This can even be understood as an issue of fairness. (That is, will people who make future commitments be treated fairly in the value they have agreed on to buy or sell something?) It can also be seen as an issue of truthfulness in the economic system as a whole. (That is, can people depend on the fact that "one dollar" in an agreement will truthfully reflect the value that they reasonably expected "one dollar" to have in the future?)

To put it another way, the *value of a currency* is the *standard* by which business transactions are evaluated, something like the "weights and measures" that a merchant would use in a transaction. But if the value of a currency is constantly fluctuating, there is no dependable standard by which people can evaluate what they are buying and selling. Therefore this verse in Proverbs is appropriate:

> Unequal weights and unequal measures are both alike an abomination to the LORD (Prov. 20:10).

---

19. Steve H. Hanke and Alex K. F. Kwok, "On the Measurement of Zimbabwe's Hyperinflation." *Cato Journal* 29:2 (Spring/Summer 2009). www.cato.org/pubs/journal/cj29n2/cj29n2-8.pdf.

20. I say "relatively stable" because many economists would say that a moderate rate of inflation (such as 2 or 3% per year) is characteristic of a healthy, growing economy where productivity is increasing by about that much each year. But my concern here is inflation substantially in excess of that amount.

To conclude: Government should establish and maintain an effective money supply for a nation, and that means one in which the value of the currency is relatively stable over time.

What causes excessive inflation? An excessive increase in the money supply in a nation. (In the United States this would be an increase in the total number of dollars in the economy.) To illustrate this, imagine some people playing the board game *Monopoly*. Let's say that most of the property has been sold and several players are bidding for the property "Atlantic Avenue," trying to get the player who has it to sell it. Tom looks at the cash he has and offers $1,200, Dick offers $1,250, and Harry offers $1,100 now and $200 more after he passes "Go." But now imagine that some outside authority (like a parent) comes along and suddenly doubles the amount of money each player has! All at once the bids go up: Tom might offer $2,400, and Dick $2,500, and Harry $2,200 plus $200 for the next two times he passes "Go"! The money supply in their "country" doubled, and Atlantic Avenue was still for sale, so all of a sudden the offered price doubled!

Inflation happened because the money supply increased excessively. This process gave rise to Nobel Prize–winning economist Milton Friedman's classic dictum, "Inflation is always and everywhere a monetary phenomenon."[21]

For this reason, the monetary policies of the Federal Reserve Board under the first few months of the Obama administration in 2009 were troubling. They decided to pump reserves into the financial system by purchasing $1.2 trillion in assets, including $750 billion in mortgage-backed securities from companies like Fannie Mae and Freddie Mac.[22] Banks then had huge amounts of additional money in their reserves. While such bank reserves are *not yet* part of the money supply, narrowly defined,[23] they are counted as part of what is called "the monetary base" and can be turned into new money added to the economy through future bank lending. The current level of the money supply was $8.5 trillion in January 2010,[24] so this increase in bank reserves is ready

21. Milton Friedman. *Money Mischief: Episodes in Monetary History* (Boston: Houghton-Mifflin/Mariner Books), 104.

22. Neil Irwin, "Fed to Pump $1.2 Trillion into Markets," *Washington Post* (March 19, 2009). www.washingtonpost.com/wp-dyn/content/article/2009/03/18/AR2009031802283.html?hpid=topnews.

23. The Federal Reserve defines the money supply as "M2," which includes currency, bank deposits, and money market mutual funds. See footnote 2 in www.federalreserve.gov/releases/h6/current/h6.htm.

24. Federal Reserve H6 release, www.federalreserve.gov/releases/h6/current/h6.htm.

to become a 14% or more jump in the money supply when the economy starts to recover and banks are able to use these funds to increase their lending.[25] This is why Ben Bernanke, the Federal Reserve chairman, recently had to explain to Congress his "exit strategy":

> In due course, however, as the expansion matures the Federal Reserve will need to begin to tighten monetary conditions to prevent the development of inflationary pressures.... Although at present the U.S. economy continues to require the support of highly accommodative monetary policies, at some point the Federal Reserve will need to tighten financial conditions by raising short-term interest rates and reducing the quantity of bank reserves outstanding.[26]

But will the Federal Reserve do this and put the brakes on economic growth when it begins to heat up? With such record-setting government expenditures made in 2009 and projected for 2010 and later, the temptation will be simply to finance this government spending by pumping more and more dollars into the system, leading to increased inflation and thereby robbing everyone in society of the value of their dollars and their contracts. And out-of-control government spending promotes this behavior.

Richard Rahn, a senior fellow at the Cato Institute and chairman of the Institute for Global Economic Growth, wrote:

> What is particularly frightening is that neither political party has offered a serious plan to defuse the debt bomb. The Democrats are just piling up more debt as if there were no limit, and the Republicans, to date, are only proposing measures to reduce the increase, rather than reverse it. When the debt bomb explodes—within the next one to three years—expect to see record high interest rates and/or inflation, coupled with the collapse of many "entitlements." It will be like the neutron bomb, the buildings will be left standing, but the people will not.[27]

---

25. The increase in the money supply would be more than 14% if the money multiplier comes into play, which is when banks lend out the same dollar more than once, knowing that these dollars will generally not all be used at the same time.

26. Testimony of Chairman Ben S. Bernanke before the Committee on Financial Services, US House of Representatives, Washington, DC (Feb. 10, 2010). www.federalreserve.gov/newsevents/testimony/bernanke20100210a.htm.

27. Richard W. Rahn, "The Growing Debt Bomb," Cato Institute (Sept. 22, 2009). www.cato.org/pub_display.php?pub_id=10563.

Such irresponsible spending is morally wrong because it is theft—it is robbing our children and grandchildren for generations to come. A biblical view of government would demand that politicians take responsibility for this problem today, no matter who created it. "The wicked borrows but does not pay back" (Ps. 37:21). Voters need to demand that nations, like families, must live within their means.

D. FREE MARKETS AND REGULATION

All modern societies have come to agree that we need some government regulations to prevent fraud and injustice in business transactions. It is necessary, for example, for government to enforce contracts (so that people have to keep the agreements they make). And it is necessary for governments to impose some health and safety standards on the sale of medicines and foods or other products such as bicycles and cars. It is necessary for government to enforce health and cleanliness regulations on public restaurants. And some government regulation is necessary for weights and measures, so that the gasoline pump really does put one gallon of gasoline in my car when one gallon registers on the dial, and so that a gallon of milk really does contain one gallon of milk. Such regulations and others like them are necessary because it would simply be impractical, if not impossible, for individuals to attempt to check all such things for themselves before buying an item. (Therefore I differ with "libertarian" views of government that make human freedom of choice their ultimate standard of good rather obedience to God's moral principles in the Bible, and fail adequately to recognize that governments should do "good" for people [Rom. 13:4], not merely protect their freedom.)

For similar reasons, most people in modern societies would also agree that it works well for government to provide certain other goods that nearly everyone uses, such as roads, traffic regulation, supporting an army and police force and a fire department, and perhaps a postal service.

But beyond that point there is a large difference of opinion. Some people favor a "free market" approach to the rest of the economy, while others think a "socialist" system is preferable (where the government owns and controls most of the businesses and factories, what economists call the "means of production"). Still others have argued that a "communist" system is better (where the government owns and controls not only the means of production but also all property, so that there is no private ownership of property even for homes or apartment buildings or farms, but all is owned by the government).

In 2009 this question came up in many areas: Should the federal government own the US banking system and control every detail of it? Should the federal government run the nation's entire health care system? Should it run automakers General Motors and Chrysler, as it apparently began to do in April and May 2009? Should it begin to set wage levels for everyone in the banking and financial service industries, as the Obama administration seemed to suggest in mid-May of 2009?[28]

Several factors support the idea that the *free market* is almost always a better way of solving an economic problem than government ownership or control.

(1) The Bible's teaching on the role of government gives support to the idea of a free market rather than socialism or communism. This is because nothing in the Bible's teachings on the role of government would give the government warrant to take over ownership or control of private businesses, which would have included farms and traders and small shops in the ancient world. The government is to punish evil and reward those who do good and enforce order in society. It is not to own the property or businesses of a nation.

(2) The Bible gives repeated warnings against a ruler who would use his power to "take" what rightfully belongs to the people, including their fields and vineyards, for example. These are the ancient parallels to modern factories and companies.

(3) The Bible's teaching about private property indicates that property rightfully belongs to individual people, not to the government (and businesses are one form of property). (See discussion of private property above, pp. 37–46.)

(4) The Bible's emphasis on the value of human liberty (see above, p. 46) also argues for a free market system rather than a socialist or communist system. A free market allows *individuals* to choose where they work, what they buy, how they run a business, and how they spend their money. But a government-controlled economy makes these decisions for people rather than allowing people freedom to make them for themselves.

(5) History demonstrates time and again that the free market brings better results than a government-controlled economy or government control of any section of the economy.

---

28. "U.S. Eyes Bank Pay Overhaul," *Wall Street Journal* (May 13, 2009), 81.

Here is what I mean by a free market:

> A wonderful, God-given process in human societies through which the goods and services that are *produced* by the society (supply) continually adjust to exactly match the goods and services that are *wanted* by the society (demand) at each period of time, and through which the society assigns a measurable value to each good and service at each period of time, entirely through the free choices of every individual person in the society rather than through government control. (But this process needs some government regulation to prevent wrongdoing such as theft, fraud, and breaking of contracts.)

The better results of a free market are seen in several ways:

(a) A free market is better than government control at producing goods and services. The economic "goods" that the free market produces are of better quality, at a lower price, and are the goods that people *actually want* rather than the goods that some government agency tells them they *should* want. This can be seen by numerous examples in recent history.

In 1985–86 I spent an academic year doing research and writing in England, and near the end of that time our family traveled to several countries in Europe. We made a point of crossing from West Berlin to East Berlin because I wanted my children (who were twelve, nine, and six) to see the difference between a free market economy and a state-controlled communist economy. West Berlin was prosperous, energetic, bright, modern, and teeming with all sorts of evidence of economic prosperity everywhere you looked. But as soon as we crossed the Berlin Wall (which was still there at that time) we entered into a gloomy world of brown and gray buildings, empty streets, and colorless shops with little to offer the East German people. It looked as if the life had been drained out of the city. The people were trapped in poverty. That was why they had to build the Berlin Wall—to keep people from leaving East Berlin.

What was the difference? The only difference was the economic system. Both halves of the city were filled with German people from the same ethnic and cultural and linguistic background. But one half had fallen under communist control at the end of World War II, and the other half had remained free.

We saw the same contrast a year later when we took a bus from Helsinki, Finland, to Leningrad (now St. Petersburg), Russia. The bus ride took only four hours (and part of that was spent at the border crossing), because the two cities are in the same geographic region of the world. The markets in Helsinki were brimming with an abundance of beautiful fruits and vegetables and meats produced by a free market economy. In Leningrad we wandered through the stores and saw rows of the same style of drab brown winter coat that no one wanted but had been produced in excess. We watched as women lifted up one milk bottle after another, hoping to find one that had not gone sour. We saw nearly empty shelves with a few cans of canned vegetables produced by a government cooperative with no competition from other brands, no incentive to produce quality goods, and no incentive to produce what people really wanted to buy. Peoples' faces appeared to be drained of hope or any joy in life. Helsinki and Leningrad had the same climate, and both had access to the shipping lanes in the Baltic Sea, but one city was wealthy and the other was poor. Why? Because government control destroys economic productivity.

(b) A free market allows people freedom to work at the jobs they choose (rather than being assigned to a job by the government) and encourages people to get better training for the jobs they seek and to perform better when they know they will be rewarded for better quality work. All of this provides much greater job satisfaction.

(c) A free market gives an employer the benefit of being free *to hire* the employees that he or she thinks are best-suited for the job, and *not* to hire (or else to fire) those whose work is not providing adequate value to the company. This process improves the economic productivity of individual businesses and the nation as a whole.

(d) A free market offers the great benefit of consumer satisfaction by producing the goods and services that people actually want.

(e) A free market — unlike any government agency, no matter how large — is able to have enough information to predict accurately the economic wants of millions of people at any day in the future and then to plan effectively to meet those wants. The free market does this by itself, without anybody overseeing it, because decisions are made according to the "feet on the ground" instincts and experience of many thousands of people, each using the accumulated wisdom gained by trial and error over many years to decide how many eggs or gallons of milk will be purchased at each corner grocery store for each day of the year. If stores buy too much, they waste money and the product spoils. If they buy too little, they lose potential sales and waste their investment in empty shelf space, and they find that customers won't return to a store that does not have what they came for. But — with no direction from any government planning committee — somehow it all works! In a free market economy, the successful corner stores know how to order the right amount.

Day and night, year after year, dozens of delivery trucks come and go, supplying each convenience store, restaurant, gas station, and department store with *just enough* of each product to meet consumer demand in that neighborhood for that day. It happens tens of thousands of times every day in every city in a free market society. But how does it happen? *Nobody* tells all these suppliers and shop owners how much they should order or deliver. If we could observe this process for just one local convenience store from the air, it would seem nearly miraculous. No person or government agency or planning board directs all this activity, yet it all gets done!

Another example of the amazing working of the free market system can be seen even in a manufactured product as simple as a lead pencil. Consider the thousands of individual decisions that had to be made (in logging companies, rubber factories, paint companies, graphite factories, trucking firms, and so forth) in order to produce this pencil, and yet it happened with no central planning agency and no government control ordering it to be produced. Yet I can walk into any grocery store in the United States and buy a yellow pencil with a rubber eraser at the end, and I think nothing of it. The free market has anticipated my needs and provided for those needs (and thousands of other needs), all without any central direction. It "just happened" because the individuals who produce, supply, and sell these pencils have found that it is in their self-interest to estimate accurately and then provide for the economic wants of each segment of the population at each time of the year — and those who do it best are in the companies that best survive and thrive economically. They seek their own self-interests, but in a free market that is achieved by best providing for the interests of others.

(6) Application to current controversies:

As indicated above, several principles of the Bible as well as the superior results indicate that the free market is a much better solution than government control for many controversial areas of policy today. A government-controlled automobile industry would produce more and more cars that few people want to buy and would fail to produce other cars that consumers really want. (This will be evident when the government has to add large cash "rebates" or tax benefits to people who buy the government-mandated small, high-mileage cars or poorly made cars — essentially paying people a lot of money to buy a car they would not otherwise choose.) Such a policy of government-run companies failing to be sensitive to consumer demand will also shift people to buying the cars they actually want from foreign companies, even if they have to pay more. The government will then respond by slapping huge tariffs on foreign cars, again denying consumer choice and attempting to force people either to spend much more or to buy cars they don't want.

Similarly, a government-controlled health care system would fail to provide enough of the services that people want, leading to the rationing of health care by which some government agencies would determine which kinds of patients are eligible to receive various kinds of care, and leading also to long waits for certain services (as is seen in the government-run health care systems of Canada or England, for example).

Governmental distortions of the free market mean that market prices are no longer a good signal of consumer demands or producer supplies. Therefore supply and demand will not match, and the market will not naturally "clear." Overproduction and waste of some things and underproduction and rationing of other things necessarily result. Both waste and rationing are very costly to an economy. Waste costs the public more tax dollars and the freedom to spend those dollars, since they have to pay for the government-caused waste. Rationing costs the public more time and personal freedom, as people have to wait on a list rather than be able to purchase the things they want or need.

E. THE RICH AND THE POOR

1. Government and the rich

Today I often hear comments in the media — or in conversation with people — that simply *assume* that rich people have somehow gotten their wealth unjustly, so it is right for government to take some of their wealth from them. This is seen in remarks such as, "It is time for folks like me who make more than $250,000 to pay our fair share"[29] — a comment by Barak Obama during the 2008 campaign that simply *assumes* (without argument) that whatever "fair" is, it must somehow be *more taxes* than what rich people are currently paying! Or people might say things like, "They can afford it," or "It won't hurt them."

But the Bible does not reflect this kind of thinking, nor is there any suggestion that governments have the right to take money from wealthy people *simply because they are wealthy*.

The emphasis in the Bible is on treating both rich and poor *fairly and justly*. If they have done wrong, they should be penalized, but if they have not done wrong, they should not be punished.

---

29. William McGurn, "For Obama, Taxes Are about Fairness," *Wall Street Journal* (Aug. 19, 2008). http://online.wsj.com/article/SB121910117767951201.html?mod=todays_columnists.

In some places the Bible warns against treating the poor unjustly: "You shall not pervert the justice *due to your poor* in his lawsuit" (Exod. 23:6). But at other times it warns against favoring the poor (and thus presumably having a bias against those who are rich): "Nor shall you be partial *to a poor man* in his lawsuit" (Exod. 23:3).

The question is not whether someone is rich or poor, but whether someone has done good or evil. It is wrong to punish those who have not done evil:

> To impose a fine on *a righteous man* is not good, nor to strike the noble for their uprightness (Prov. 17:26).

This is consistent with what the Bible teaches about the role of government: "to punish those who do evil and to praise those who do good" (1 Peter 2:14).

Of course, there are some wealthy people in the world who do evil. There are also middle-class people who do evil, and there are poor people who do evil. Wealth or poverty do not by themselves accurately indicate the morality of a person's conduct in society.

Those who break the law should be punished by the government, whether they are rich or poor or somewhere in between. But it is unfair — and contrary to the teaching of Scripture — to stereotype all rich people as "evil" or "probably evil," or to assume that they have somehow exploited other people and made their money in unjust ways.

Rather than thinking about "the rich" as a vague category to be viewed with suspicion, it might help to think of *specific wealthy people* and ask whether we think they have done something evil to get their money. (Perhaps readers now can actually think of someone who is wealthy in their own church or community, as a concrete example.) As I write this, I am thinking of three of four people whom I have known in Christian circles and are "wealthy." Yet, in every case they seem to spend most of their time doing good for other people, and they are men of high integrity who would not consciously or willfully do anything wrong.

In March 2009, *Forbes* magazine published a list of all 793 billionaires in the world, including photos and a bit more information about the top twenty. Do we really want to think of these people as evil? Here are some of their names, with a number indicating where they rank among the wealthiest people in the world: (1) Bill Gates, Microsoft Corporation; (2) Warren Buffet, Berkshire Hathaway (including many companies such as GEICO Insurance); (4) Larry Ellison, Oracle Corporation (producer of software for managing databases for business); (5) Ingvar Kamprad, Sweden, Ikea Stores (discount furniture); (6) Karl Albrecht, Germany,

Aldi Supermarkets (discount food stores); (9) Theo Albrecht, Germany, Trader Joe's (grocery store chain); (11) Jim Walton, Wal-Mart; (12) S. Robson Walton, Wal-Mart; (13) Alice Walton, Wal-Mart; (14) Christy Walton, Wal-Mart.[30]

As I looked at this list, I realized that I have helped make many of these people rich! I have bought many Microsoft computer programs. I have bought automobile insurance for many years from GEICO. My wife and I shop at Trader Joe's from time-to-time. And we shop at Wal-Mart.

Do I think that these people have gotten rich by "exploiting" other people or violating the law in some way? No. I think they have become wealthy by providing products and services that people want at a good price and with reliable quality. They have competed in the free market, and consumers have wanted more and more of their products, and they have become wealthy.

So what do I think of Bill Gates with his $40 billion in net worth? I think that consumers around the world have decided that Microsoft's products are worth $40 billion more than it cost Gates to produce them, so he ended up with that much wealth. By "voting" with their dollars, consumers have said that Bill Gates *added $40 billion of value to the world* with his software.

Or what do I think of the four members of the Walton family who together have a net worth of $70.6 billion? I think that shows that 200 million customers in 7,200 Wal-Mart stores have collectively "voted" freely to say that the Wal-Mart family has *provided them with value that is $70 billion greater than what it cost the Waltons* to purchase these goods to sell. Without any compulsion from anyone, but in a free market system, the Waltons have "added value" to the world in the amount of more than $70 billion, and this is in addition to all the 1.1 million jobs that Wal-Mart provides.[31] Wal-Mart has also supported millions of other employees of the companies who *made* the products that are sold at Wal-Mart. Have the Waltons done "evil" by finding quality goods and selling them at lower prices than others were doing? It seems to me that they have done something *good* for society, and everyone who shops at Wal-Mart is "voting with dollars" in agreement with that evaluation. (Some people object that Wal-Mart drives smaller stores out of business, but those who make this objection fail to take account of the benefit to *the*

30. "The World's Billionaires,"*Forbes* (March 11, 2009). www.forbes.com/2009/03/11/worlds-richest-people-billionaires–2009-billionaires_land.html.

31. Lorrie Grant, "Retail Giant Wal-Mart Faces Challenges on Many Fronts," *USA Today* (Nov. 10, 2003). www.usatoday.com/money/industries/retail/2003–11–10-walmart_x.htm.

whole society that comes when *everybody* can buy goods for less money and therefore have more of their own money left over. *Every* consumer benefits from this, because of the downward pressure on prices. If people want to shop at smaller, more expensive stores that provide more per- sonal service, they are free to do so — and sometimes I do that! — but they should not try to force everyone to spend their money that way.)

What should we think about the rich, and how should it affect our ideas about the role of government? My conclusion is that most rich people today got their money fairly and honestly, and government has no inherent right to take it from them *unless it can be shown that they got it through criminal activity of some sort*. We should not immediately assume that "the rich" are evil.

What about the attitude that says that money should be taken from the rich because "they can afford it" or because "it won't hurt them"? The teaching of the Bible is this: "You shall not steal" (Exod. 20:15). It is not right to steal from the poor, nor is it right to steal from the rich. If I were ever to visit the home of Bill Gates and see a few dollar bills lying out in some room, *it would still be wrong* in the sight of God to steal even one dollar from the $40 billion that Gates owns. It does not matter one bit whether I might think "he can afford it" or "it won't hurt him," because the dollar *belongs to him*, not to me. It is his property. It would be morally wrong to take the dollar, because God says, "You shall not steal."

2. Government and economic equality

Should it be the rule of government to "take from the rich and give to the poor"? Should government try to equalize the amount of income or possessions that people have, or at least take actions that move in the direction of equality?

Before answering that question directly, I need to make clear that I think there is some need for government-supported welfare programs *to help cases of urgent need* (for example, to provide a "safety net" to keep people from going hungry or without clothing or shelter).

I also think it is appropriate for government to provide enough fund- ing so that everyone is able *to gain enough skills and education to earn a living.* So with regard to some basic necessities of life (food, clothing, shelter, and some education) I think it is right for government to "take from everybody else and give to the poor." Such assistance can be pro- vided from general tax revenues.

Those convictions are based on the purpose of government *to pro- mote the general well-being of the society,* or as the US Constitution says in its preface, "to promote the general welfare." That includes enabling every citizen to live adequately in the society. It is not based on any vague instinct that it would be "more just" to reduce the differences between rich and poor.

But apart from those basic requirements for government, I cannot find any justification in Scripture for thinking that government, as a matter of policy, should attempt to take from the rich and give to the poor. I do not think that government has the responsibility or the right to attempt to equalize the differences between rich and poor in a society. When it attempts to do so, significant harm is done to the economy and to the society.

In a free society, with no government confiscation of wealth, the amount of money that people earn will vary widely. This is because people have different abilities, different interests, and different levels of economic ambition. Only a very few people are able to become skilled surgeons or highly paid professional athletes or write best-selling novels or invent some amazing new computer software or start a small business and lead it to become highly profitable. Therefore, *if people are free from government intervention*, some will become very wealthy, others will have a comfortable level of income, and some will remain relatively poor. If the economic system is relatively free, and if people are allowed to be paid fairly for the different kinds of work they do, this is simply going to happen.

And even if, through some kind of social experiment, everyone in some city were given $100,000 cash to start with, after a few weeks some would have spent it all, some would have saved most of it, and some would have invested it in activities that would produce more income. After a few months there would be significant inequalities all over again. This is inevitable as long as people are allowed to be free.

If such an experiment continued, how could any government force people to have equal amounts of possessions? Only by continually redistributing money over and over again each year, taking from those who have been most frugal and most productive, and giving to those who have been least productive or who have simply wasted their money. In other words, equality of possessions could not be maintained apart from *penalizing good habits* (hard work, productivity, frugality) and *rewarding bad habits* (profligate spending, wastefulness, frittering time on unproductive activities). The longer such "redistribution of wealth" continued in this hypothetical city, the more the productive people would just decide to give up (for they cannot enjoy the fruits of their labor) and the society would spiral downward into poverty and despair.

It works in the same way, but to a lesser degree, when government attempts to equalize differences in *income* levels (rather than total possessions). Governments can use their power to *impose* income equality on a population, but wherever this happens, it is brought about through severe restrictions on human freedom, and the result is to trap most of the nation in the "equality" of poverty.

Another result of attempting to impose economic equality on a nation is that, even if people are equal in their *economic possessions*, they will inevitably be unequal in terms of *political power* and government-allocated *privilege*. This has been seen historically in communist countries such as the former Soviet Union, where high-ranking political officials had access to limousines, fancier homes, and opportunities for vacations on the Baltic Sea that were not available to anyone else. They could also buy desirable Western goods through private channels to which only they had access. If *economic inequality* is removed, it is simply replaced by any *inequality in privilege* and vast benefits that come from high political power.

The conclusion is that it should not be the role of government to attempt to equalize income or possessions among people in a society.

3. Government and poverty

Several verses in the Bible command people to help the poor. For example:

> At present, however, I am going to Jerusalem *bringing aid to the saints*. For Macedonia and Achaia have been pleased to make some contribution for the poor among the saints at Jerusalem (Rom. 15:25–26; see also 2 Cor. 8–9).

> Only, they asked us *to remember the poor*, the very thing I was eager to do (Gal. 2:10).

> But if anyone has the world's goods and sees *his brother in need*, yet closes his heart against him, how does God's love abide in him? (1 John 3:17).

Therefore it is right for Christians to do what they can to help those who are poor. Yet I am surprised to discover that few people seem to realize that these verses say *nothing* about civil government overcoming individual citizens' poverty! In fact, I do not think there is any passage in Scripture that justifies the idea that *government* has the right to *compel* rich people to help the poor or to "take from the rich and give to the poor," apart from using general tax revenue (from all taxpayers) to provide for very basic needs (see discussion above, pp. 62–63).

But we must remember that such government handouts of money are *never* going to solve the problem of poverty. These handouts simply have to be repeated month after month and year after year, and the recipients are still poor. The only long-term solution to poverty comes when people have enough skills and discipline to get *economically productive jobs* and keep them.

The government itself cannot provide people with economically productive jobs (except for some government-funded jobs such as police and fire protection, the military, highway maintenance, and teachers in the educational system). By far the largest number of *economically productive jobs*—jobs that actually contribute something new of value to a society—are found in the private sector, in the business world. Someone working for a bakery bakes new loaves of bread each day and creates that amount of new wealth in the society. Someone working in an automobile factory creates new automobiles and thus adds economic wealth to the society. In the service industries, a plumber repairs a leaky faucet and thereby adds the value of one working faucet to the society. A landscaper trims trees and bushes and adds the aesthetic value of beautiful trees and bushes to the society. In this way, *every successful business gives people economically productive jobs* for which they are paid, and in that way it contributes value to the society. The poor person working at such a job is paid according to that added value, and thus begins to climb out of poverty.

This is what should happen, for God intends people to be economically productive. He put Adam in the Garden of Eden "to work it and keep it" (Gen. 2:15) before there was any sin or evil in the world, which shows that the need to work in a productive way is an essential part of how God created us as human beings. Therefore Paul could command the church in Thessalonica to "work with your hands, as we instructed you, so that you may live properly before outsiders and be dependent on no one" (1 Thess. 4:11–12). He also said, "If anyone is not willing to work, let him not eat" (2 Thess. 3:10). God actually created us with a need for food to survive, at least in part because this provides an incentive to regular work: "A worker's appetite works for him; his mouth urges him on" (Prov. 16:26).

Therefore, for those who desire to help the poor and overcome the problem of poverty, their *primary goal* should *not* be to increase and prolong government handouts of money to those who are poor, but to provide incentives and appropriate conditions for privately-owned businesses to grow and thrive and thus provide the jobs that will be the only long-term solution to poverty and the only way for the poor to gain the dignity and self-respect that comes from supporting themselves.

It is important, therefore, that government not hinder the development and profitability of businesses, but rather encourage them. Such encouragement would include a free market with a functioning price system that will guide the allocation of resources, a stable system of money, and a government that effectively punishes crime, enforces contracts, and enforces patent laws and copyrights and that documents and protects private ownership of property. It would also include a fair court system that is not partial to the rich or poor, or to the powerful or the weak. Relatively low levels of taxation, an effective educational system, and a trustworthy banking system, are also needed. When such factors are implemented by governments, then businesses can grow and thrive and provide the jobs that alone will lift people permanently out of poverty.

F. GOVERNMENT AND BUSINESS

As explained above, businesses should be encouraged and not penalized by government. This is because private businesses are the primary creator of wealth and productive jobs in a society. Businesses continue producing goods year after year and continue providing jobs and paying wages year after year.

Because businesses need to compete with one another to produce better goods at lower prices, the competitive free market *continually rewards those who improve their productivity and the quality of their products.* Thus, economically beneficial activity is encouraged and rewarded in a free market economy.

Unfortunately, too many Christians in contemporary society are suspicious of economic competition. They think it is somehow "unspiritual" or "unchristian." I do not agree with that at all. Competition is simply a system that encourages people to strive for excellence in their work. Even people who say they dislike competition still encourage it by shopping for less expensive places to buy the same product or through buying the healthier strawberries and tomatoes at a farmer's market. In doing this, they are encouraging the more efficient, more effective farmer who produces a higher quality of product. People who read *Consumer Reports* to find the best brand of computer or washing machine or bicycle are also encouraging competition, because they are looking for a higher quality product that is a "best buy," that is, one produced at a more economical price. Therefore even those who say they dislike competition continually support it by their shopping habits! If Christians are going to be good stewards of their money, they have to act in ways that support healthy economic competition.

But the competition of the free market that continually improves products and prices is far different from what government does. Whatever government does, it is the only government in power at that time, and therefore it has a monopoly, both on the ability to collect taxes and on the ability to require people to buy its goods. (The US Postal Service is a government monopoly, for example, for the delivery of first class mail.)

Because government does not have to compete for customers, government in general is a poor creator of wealth in an economy. In fact, it is difficult to think of any goods or services that a government might produce that could not be produced better by private companies.[32]

---

32. I realize of course that some services and products needed by the entire society are best provided by government, such as the judicial system, the enforcement of laws, police departments, national defense, and roads and highways. These are not ordinary consumer goods.

Chapter 3

ECONOMICS: TAXES, SOCIAL SECURITY, HEALTH CARE, AND RECESSIONS

Building on the previous discussion of economic fundamentals, this chapter covers specific topics of intense debate in recent years, namely:

Taxes

Social Security

Heath Care

The best cure for recessions

A. TAXES

1. Does government have the right to collect taxes?

Taxes were a controversy even in Jesus' day. Some of Jesus' enemies came and asked him, "Is it lawful to pay taxes to Caesar, or not?" (Matt. 22:17). But Jesus, taking a denarius (a common coin) and noting that Caesar's likeness was on it, said, "Therefore *render to Caesar the things that are Caesar's*, and to God the things that are God's" (Matt. 22:21). Jesus thus endorsed the legitimacy of paying taxes to a civil government, for the coin that he held had Caesar's inscription and that coin was used for paying the tax (see v. 19).

Paul also told the Christians in Rome that the civil authority "is the servant of God" and then said,

> For the same reason you *also pay taxes*, for the authorities are ministers of God, attending to this very thing. *Pay to all what is owed to them: taxes to whom taxes are owed*, revenue to whom revenue is owed, respect to whom respect is owed, honor to whom honor is owed (Rom. 13:6–7).

Therefore it is right to pay taxes to the civil government, and it is right for government to collect taxes to carry out its responsibilities (including the provision of basic needs to those who are poor).

But as I explained in the last chapter, it does not seem to me that the Bible gives any support for the idea that governments should use taxes simply to redistribute income from the "rich" to the "poor." The Bible's teaching about the purpose of civil government, about private property, and about economic productivity does not support this idea. Such redistribution of income (which is different from basic support of the very poor) is not part of punishing evil and rewarding good, and it is not part of impartially enforcing justice; rather, it is carrying out an additional social agenda that the Bible does not support.

2. Should tax rates be high or low in an economy?

Taxes are a powerful tool that can either help or hinder economic growth. They also have enormous effect on individual lives, and tax rates can either significantly hinder or significantly help individual liberty within a nation.

This is seen if we take the two extremes that are possible. If the tax rate is 0%, then the government has no money to support its functions, and it cannot carry out its responsibilities. On the other hand, if the tax rate is 100%, then government controls all economic life, and no one has freedom to invest or build or create anything, or even to give to others. So the proper solution is somewhere in between.

But every increase in taxes takes away that much more human freedom. If my taxes increase by $100, then I have $100 less to buy some new shoes or clothing, to take my wife to a movie or restaurant, to give to some missions program at my church, to buy books for additional research, to send as a gift to my children, or to do any of a thousand other things. My *freedom* to decide what to do with that $100 has been taken from me when the government collects another $100 in tax.

So it is every time that taxes increase: A little more freedom—another small portion of everyone's life—has been taken away by the government.

Now let's say that the government taxes me $100 and then *gives me back some kind* of benefit. Perhaps it subsidizes a public transit system so that I get a cheaper ride on the train. Or perhaps it decides to give additional welfare payments to those beneath the poverty line, so that I get the benefit of knowing that my society is helping a poor person. Or perhaps the government uses the money to build a new bridge on a new highway somewhere in Missouri; then (if I ever travel to Missouri) I get the benefit of being able to drive on that new bridge. But in all these cases *the choice of what to do with that $100 has been taken away from me,* and the choice has been made for me by the government. I have lost that much freedom.

In addition, governments all over the world are notorious for waste and inefficiency. Even if a government promises to give $100 in benefits for the $100 in increased taxes, I know that a good share of that $100—maybe $50 or so!—will go to pay numerous government employees who don't have to compete in the free market, so the society will never get back the same amount of value that it would have received if people had been free to spend the $100 for themselves and to watch carefully how it was spent.

3. The benefit of lower taxes

Several economic studies have demonstrated that when a government lowers its tax rates, it actually ends up collecting more money! How can this be? It is because the lower tax rates bring economic benefits in the following way:

(1) When tax rates are lowered, this encourages businesses to invest and grow.

(2) This provides more jobs and lower prices, both of which are beneficial for the economy, and both of which encourage overall economic growth.

(3) As the economy grows, businesses and individuals earn higher incomes.

(4) These higher incomes are taxed at the lower tax rate, but *more* tax money still flows into the government coffers because people are paying taxes on so much more income.

For example, if in 2009 Mr. Smith earned $80,000 and paid 25% in taxes, he would pay $20,000 in taxes. But if the tax rate drops to 20%, it provides an incentive for businesses to invest and grow, and people also work harder, knowing they can keep more of their money. Then perhaps in 2010 Mr. Smith's income will be $110,000. At the new tax rate of 20%, he ends up paying $22,000 in taxes. The government has lowered the tax rate, helped the economy, and collected more money in taxes! (And Mr. Smith has $88,000 left for himself instead of $60,000.) Everyone is better off.

In addition, there is a great benefit to society because lower taxes have increased peoples' personal freedom to do what they want with more of their own money.

Of course, there is a lower limit to how far tax rates can drop and still result in a total increase in taxes paid to government. Beyond a certain point, lowering taxes cannot stimulate enough economic growth to make up for the smaller percentage of income that is collected. (At a tax rate of 0%, the government would collect zero dollars.) The graph of how this works is called the "Laffer Curve," after Arthur Laffer, the economist who first explained this concept to President Ronald Reagan and persuaded him that he could cut tax *rates* and help the economy and still collect more actual tax dollars. The idea is not very controversial, because at a 100% tax rate nobody will want to work (all their pay would be taken away) and so the government would also collect zero dollars. At some point in between is the best rate for governments to maximize the tax money they collect.

Arguments occur over just where that maximum point lies. Let's look at an example of the Laffer Curve. ("Tax Revenue" refers to the total amount of money that the government collects in taxes, and "Tax Rate" refers to the percentage of people's income that they have to pay to the government in taxes.)[1]

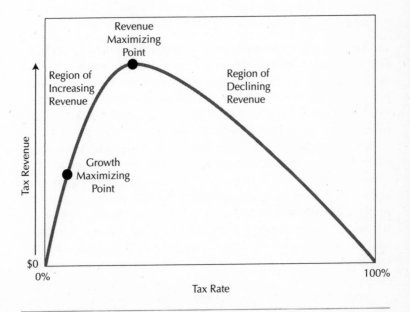

1. This graph is taken from Daniel J. Mitchell, "The Correct Way to Measure the Revenue Impact of Changes in Tax Rates," Heritage Foundation (May 3, 2002). www.heritage.org/Research/Taxes/BG1544.cfm (accessed Feb. 12, 2010).

It should also be remembered that the "Revenue Maximizing Point" might be best for the government's treasury but not best for the country. A lower tax rate might lead to more economic growth (as illustrated on this graph by the "Growth Maximizing Point").

This phenomenon of lower tax rates leading to a growing economy and therefore higher tax revenue for the government has actually happened more than once in recent US history. It happened with the Reagan tax cuts of 1981. In 1980, the year before the tax cuts, federal revenue was $956 billion (measured in 1996 dollars). By 1985, even with a much lower tax rate, the federal government took in more than $1 trillion in revenue. At the end of Reagan's term in 1988, government revenue was $1.1 trillion.[2]

Then it happened again with the Bush tax cuts of 2001 and 2003, which brought a huge boost to the economy. Author Steven Moore wrote in the *Wall Street Journal*:

> Federal tax revenues surged in the first eight months of this fiscal year by $187 billion. This represents a 15.4% rise in federal tax receipts over 2004. Individual and corporate income tax receipts have exploded like a cap let off a geyser, up 30% in the two years since the tax cut. Once again, tax rate cuts have created a virtuous chain reaction of higher economic growth, more jobs, higher corporate profits, and finally more tax receipts.[3]

Therefore, when Christians are thinking whether they should favor higher or lower taxes in a state or nation, the question is whether, on the one hand, they want to *increase human freedom* and *also raise more money for government needs* and *also help the economy*, or on the other hand, they think that taking more money from the "wealthy" is *more important than all of these other three goals*.

When political leaders are asked about such choices, their answers can sometimes reveal their underlying economic beliefs. For example, when presidential candidate Obama was asked a question like this during one of the 2008 debates, he affirmed his conviction that his idea of "fairness" would still be a reason to raise taxes, even if it meant collecting *less* tax revenue for the government. In the April 17, 2008, presidential debate, ABC News' Charles Gibson cited the fact that when the capital gains tax rate dropped from 28 to 20% and then to 15%, "revenues from the taxes

---

2. Andrew Olivastro, "Tax Cuts Increase Federal Revenues," *Heritage Foundation Web Memo* #182 (Dec. 31, 2002). www.heritage.org/Research/Taxes/wm182.cfm?renderforprint=1.

3. Stephen Moore, "Real Tax Cuts Have Real Curves," *Wall Street Journal* (June 19, 2005). www.opinionjournal.com/extra/?id=110006842.

increased," but "in the 1980s, when the tax was increased to 28%, the revenues went down." So Gibson asked candidate Obama, "So why raise it at all, especially given the fact that 100 million people in this country own stock and would be affected?" Obama replied, "Well, Charlie, what I've said is that I would look at raising the capital gains tax for purposes of fairness."[4]

That conviction reflects the mentality of many in the Democratic Party today—as well as quite a few others in society who don't normally consider themselves Democrats. It seems that envy of the rich, or animosity toward the rich, is such a deeply engrained characteristic in many peoples' minds that they are not willing to let the rich keep more of their money *even if* this would mean collecting more government money in taxes *and* helping the economy *and* increasing personal freedom in society as a whole. The most important thing is thought to be taking more money from the "wealthy," who presumably are thought to have gotten their money unjustly or are thought not to deserve the money that they have earned.

4. Taxes on corporations

Another misconception that people have today is the assumption that *imposing high taxes on corporations* is just another way of taking money from the rich that really doesn't affect ordinary people much at all. But this is an incorrect assumption. Higher taxes on corporations are just passed on to consumers in the form of higher prices, so *the entire society* actually pays this tax as a hidden part of the higher cost of the goods that the corporation produces. For example, if the corporate tax rate goes up 5%, then all the grocery stores in Arizona have to pay the government 5% more of their income. What will the stores do? Will they just say, "Well, our costs have just gone up by 5% of our income! But that doesn't matter to us. We will keep all our prices just the same!" Of course they will not do that. If their costs go up, their prices have to go up or they will begin to lose money and eventually go out of business. So they raise the prices of groceries, and the whole society pays this "invisible" tax.

This false idea that high taxes on corporations don't hurt ordinary people is the mistake that has allowed our corporate tax rate in the United States to climb to an astounding 39.3% (average combined federal and state taxes on corporations).[5] This is the second highest cor-

---

4. Charles Gibson and President Obama: quoted in Gerald Prante, "Obama and Gibson Capital Gains Tax Exchange," *The Tax Foundation* (April 17, 2008). www.taxfoundation.org/blog/show/23137.html.

5. Scott A. Hodge, "U.S. Leads the World in High Corporate Taxes," *The Tax Foundation Fiscal Facts* (March 18, 2008). www.taxfoundation.org/publications/show/22917.html.

porate tax rate *in the world* (only Japan is slightly higher), and in some states (California, Iowa, New Jersey, and Pennsylvania) the combined corporate tax rate is the highest in the world.[6] The *Wall Street Journal* notes that "over the past eighteen months, nine of the thirty most developed nations … from Israel to Germany to Turkey—have cut their corporate tax rates. Nations are slashing rates to attract capital and jobs from the United States, and the tragedy is that our politicians keep making it easy for them."[7] In fact, the average European nation now has corporate tax rates *ten percentage points less* than the United States.[8]

Nevertheless, Democratic politicians continue their campaign of demonizing big corporations. For example, US Sen. Byron Durgan of North Dakota announced a new report showing that 28% of large corporations paid no income tax in 2005. "It's time for big corporations to pay their fair share," Durgan roared, according to the *Wall Street Journal.*[9] But on further investigation the *Journal* discovered what Senator Durgan conveniently failed to mention: among those large corporations that paid no taxes, the vast majority of them (85%) also made no profits that year.[10] No wonder they paid no taxes!

To restore competitiveness in the world economy, encourage business investment, and truly stimulate the economy, and bring about lower prices for goods produced in the United States, we should lower the corporate tax rate so that it is no higher than 20% (combined federal and state tax). This would attract much more foreign investment to the United States as well as encourage our own corporations to invest more here rather than abroad. Where would government get the money to make up for the "lost" taxes from the lower tax rate? A growing economy would soon provide even more *tax revenues* than before, both through corporate taxes and through higher collections of income taxes as people who work for these corporations earn more income.

5. Capital gains tax

The capital gains tax is a tax paid on the increase in the value of an asset that is held over a period of time. If I buy an apartment building

---

6. "America the Uncompetitive," *Wall Street Journal* (Aug. 15, 2008), 814. http://online.wsj.com/article/SB121875570585042551.html?mod=opinion_main_review_and_outlooks.
7. Ibid.
8. Ibid.
9. Ibid.
10. Ibid.

for $800,000 and sell it two years later for $900,000, I have $100,000 in capital gains and have to pay a tax on that amount. In the United States, the most important capital gains tax rate is on long-term capital gains, which applies to assets that someone holds for more than a year. In 2003, with President Bush's tax cuts, the capital gains tax was reduced to 15%.[11] (Many Republicans wanted to abolish it completely.) However, this reduction is set to expire in 2010, after which the rate will revert to 20%.[12] What would be the outcome of the increase in that tax? The Heritage Foundation put out this sobering prediction:

- Increasing capital gains and dividend tax rates would reduce the capital stock by $12 billion (in constant 2000 dollars) by 2012.
- Potential employment would drop by 270,000 in 2011 and 413,000 in 2012.
- Personal incomes would decline by $1,675 (in 2000 dollars) for a family of four in 2012.
- The broadest measure of economic activity, GDP after inflation, would decline steadily over the forecast period of 2011 through 2018.
- In 2011, GDP would be $44 billion below where it would be if the tax cuts were not made permanent. That figure would rise to $50 billion in 2012.
- Annual GDP after inflation losses would average $37 billion below baseline over that seven-year period.[13]

It is important to remember that this is a tax on the *increased value* of something purchased *as an investment* (for example, a rental property or an apartment building). Given that the owner already pays taxes on the income that is produced each year from that investment, should he also pay taxes on the increase in value on that property?

A strong argument can be made that the capital gains tax should be completely abolished, to encourage investment in the economy. At any rate, it is economically beneficial to the nation to have this rate be very low, since that encourages more investment, which helps an economy to grow. (This is based on the principle, "If you penalize something you get less of it, and if you reward something you get more of it.")

11. Moore, "Real Tax Cuts Have Real Curves."
12. William W. Beach, Rea S. Hederman Jr., and Guinevere Nell, "Economic Effects of Increasing the Tax Rates on Capital Gains and Dividends," *Heritage Foundation Web Memo #1891* (April 15, 2008). www.heritage.org/Research/Taxes/wm1891.cfm.
13. Ibid.

6. Income tax rates

The tax laws of the United States are set up so that the income tax rate a person pays increases according to the amount of income that person earns in a calendar year. To get an idea of such rates, here are the 2009 rates for income for a single person and for a married couple filing their tax return jointly in the United States:

Marginal Tax rate	Single	Married Filing Jointly
10%	$0 - $8,350	$0 - $16,700
15%	$8,351 - $33,950	$16,701 - $67,900
25%	$33,951 - $82,250	$67,901 - $137,050
28%	$82,251 - $171,950	$137,051 - $208,850
33%	$171,951 - $372,950	$208,851 - $372,950
35%	$372,951 +	$372,951 +

"Marginal tax rate" means the rate of tax *for each additional dollar* that is earned within a person's highest tax bracket. For example, if a married couple earned $46,700, they would pay 10% tax on the first $16,700, and then they would pay 15% tax on the remaining $30,000 of income. (They would not pay 15% on the entire $46,700.) Their *marginal tax rate* is 15%. The marginal tax rate is the rate that most affects people's economic behavior (because people use it to calculate how much they will be able to keep from any additional work they might do).

However, other factors go into calculating the amount on which tax is paid. For example, in 2009 there was a *personal exemption* of $3,650 per person, or $7,300 per couple. In addition, taxpayers were allowed a *standard deduction* from their income, which was $11,340 for a married couple filing jointly in 2009. This is a total of $18,640 of income that is not subject to income tax. Therefore, if a couple earned $28,640, they would pay no income tax on the first $18,640 and would pay 10% on the remaining $10,000 (that is, they would pay $1,000 in tax).

Single taxpayers are allowed a deduction of $5,700 and a personal exemption of $3,650, which means the first $9,350 of income is exempt from income tax for a single person. The term economists use to describe an income tax system where the rates increase at higher levels of income is "progressive." The US tax system is "progressive" in the sense that income tax rates "progress" to higher levels as one's income increases.

Now the question is, is such a system of tax rates *fair*?

In the Old Testament, all the people of Israel were required to pay a "tithe," by which they were to give 10% of their income to the Lord:

> You shall tithe all the yield of your seed that comes from the field year by year. And before the LORD your God, in the place that he will choose, to make his name dwell there, you shall eat the tithe of your grain, of your wine, and of your oil, and the firstborn of your herd and flock, that you may learn to fear the LORD your God always (Deut. 14:22–23).

> Every tithe of the land, whether of the seed of the land or of the fruit of the trees, is the LORD's; it is holy to the LORD.... And every tithe of herds and flocks, every tenth animal of all that passes under the herdsman's staff, shall be holy to the LORD (Lev. 27:30–32).

A "tithe" was exactly 10%. This system, therefore, was a like a "flat tax" because everyone paid the same percentage. There was no increase in the amount that had to be given by the wealthy and no decrease for those who were poor.

In such a system the wealthy would still pay much more than the poor in absolute terms. To use modern American equivalents, a farmer whose one-year crops were worth $30,000 would pay $3,000 for his tithe, while the farmer whose crops were worth $300,000 would pay $30,000 for his tithe. The wealthy man would pay ten times as much as the poor man.

The people of Israel also had a census tax that was imposed on every person in the amount of half a shekel:

> Each one who is numbered in the census shall give this: *half a shekel* according to the shekel of the sanctuary (the shekel is twenty gerahs), half a shekel as an offering to the LORD. Everyone who is numbered in the census, from twenty years old and upward, shall give the LORD's offering. *The rich shall not give more, and the poor shall not give less, than the half shekel,* when you give the LORD's offering to make atonement for your lives (Exod. 30:13–15).

Each person had to pay exactly the same amount in this case, which economists would call a "head tax," because the exact same amount was collected from each person (each "head") in a nation.

From this material on taxes and tithes, I can see no justification in the Bible for a "progressive" tax rate. Many societies and nations have adopted a progressive tax rate, but the justification for it will have to come from somewhere other than the explicit patterns of taxes and tithes found in the Bible.

7. But isn't it "fair" for the rich to pay a higher percentage?

This brings us back to the question about what is "fair" with regard to taxes. On what basis can we decide what is fair? People may have subjective preferences or emotional preferences for one rate or other being "fair," but those preferences will often be influenced strongly by self-interest rather than by some objective standard of fairness. Just using round numbers for convenience, imagine a case with Taxpayer A and Taxpayer B:

Taxpayer A has $50,000 in taxable income.
Taxpayer B has $500,000 in taxable income.

If we assume a tax rate of 20%, they pay the following taxes;

Taxpayer A pays 20% of $50,000, equaling $10,000.
Taxpayer B pays 20% of $500,000, equaling $100,000.

Would that be *fair*? If we ask Taxpayer A, he would probably say that what is truly "fair" is for him to pay $0 and for Taxpayer B, who is wealthy, to pay not $100,000, but $110,000!

But if we ask Taxpayer B, he might say that he is paying *far more* than his fair share even with a "flat tax" of 20%. He might say, "Why should I pay $100,000 to receive the same benefits as Taxpayer A when he only pays $10,000? We both get the same fire and police protection, we both use the same highways, we both benefit from the same military protection of our country, we both breathe the same air that is maintained by pollution-control standards enforced by the government, and so forth. We receive *exactly the same benefits* from the government, but I pay *ten times as much as taxpayer A* for these benefits! How can that be *fair* for one person to pay ten times more than someone else for the same things?"

Then a third person, Taxpayer C, might think Taxpayer B should pay *even more* than $110,000 because, even if he pays more, he still has more money left to live on. If they both pay 20% of their income, then Taxpayer A, after paying $10,000 in tax, only has $40,000 left to live on, yet Taxpayer B, after paying $100,000 in tax, still has $400,000 left to live on.

But there is a questionable assumption underlying that argument. The assumption is that Taxpayer B for some reason *does not deserve* to have $400,000 left to live on. In fact, he only *deserves* to have $300,000 left to live on. And we could go further and say that he doesn't even deserve $300,000 to live on. He should pay the tax for twenty more taxpayers in the same situation as Taxpayer A. He should pay another $100,000 in tax so that he has only $200,000 left to live on! And so on.

It is very easy for people in Taxpayer A's position or Taxpayer C's position to assume that they have some kind of superior moral judgment that is able to decide how much Taxpayer B "really deserves" to live on.

But the question then must be asked, how do we decide what someone *deserves*? Do we really believe everybody somehow *deserves* the same amount of money to live on in the end? Of course, that would be a communist totalitarianism of the worst kind, placing everybody in the nation at the same income level and destroying incentives for work and excellence and productivity.

There is a far better solution to the question of what each person "deserves." The solution is this: Each person deserves *what he has legally earned* in each year. "The laborer deserves his wages" (Luke 10:7). Even in the calculation of heavenly reward from God, Paul says, "He who plants and he who waters are one, and each will receive his wages according to his labor" (1 Cor. 3:8). In Jesus' parable of the ten servants who each received one mina to use in "business" (Luke 19:13), the servant who said, "Your mina has made ten minas more," was commended by the master and given great reward. The master said,

> "Well done, good servant! Because you have been faithful in a very little, you shall have authority over ten cities" (Luke 19:17).

In this parable, the master (who stands for Jesus) rewards the servants according to what they had done with what they had been given. What they "deserved" was what they had earned, even though it varied greatly from servant to servant (see also the parable of the talents in Matt. 25:14–30).

So it seems to me that the answer to the question, "What does each person deserve?" is, "Each person deserves what he has legally and fairly earned."

Then how much tax should each person pay? Again, the principle of a 10% tithe in the Bible would give some support to the idea of a "flat tax" by which each person pays a certain percentage of what he earns, whether 15 or 18 or 20% or whatever the society decides is the best rate of taxation to support the functions of the government.

It is very important to note that the "fair" or appropriate rate of taxation *does not depend on how much each person has left after paying taxes.* It is of no concern to the government how much Taxpayer B has left after he pays his taxes, because that money does not belong to the government or to society; it belongs to Taxpayer B.

This idea is based on the biblical teaching about private property, which we discussed above (see pp. 37–46). The reason God commands people, "You shall not steal" (Exod. 20:15), is that a person's property belongs to that person, not to the government or to society or to that person's neighbor. Therefore, if Taxpayer B has $500,000 in taxable income and pays $100,000, then the remaining $400,000 belongs to Taxpayer B. He deserves it because he has earned it fairly and legally, and so it is his.

Now someone might object that "nobody in society should be able to earn $500,000. That is just too much for any one person."

But the reason Taxpayer B has earned $500,000 is that the society as a whole, through individual decisions about how to spend their money, has "voted" with their dollars how much it wants to give Taxpayer B. If he is an executive at Wal-Mart, then people who shop at Wal-Mart have freely decided to shop at Wal-Mart enough to hire him at that rate. If he is a professional athlete, then people who watch sports on TV have freely voted with their viewing habits to watch his team enough that they can pay him that amount. If he is a Hollywood movie star, then people who watch his movies have freely chosen for him to be paid that much. Salaries are determined according to the varying market demand for certain skills and abilities. If we don't like it, the way to change it is to change the viewing habits and spending habits of the society. Society gets what it decides to pay for.

8. It is good for society if everyone who earns income pays some taxes, and it is destructive to society if most people who earn income pay little or no taxes

If everyone who earns income in a society pays at least some amount of tax, then the government is accountable to the broadest possible base of society for how it spends money. If the government raises taxes unnecessarily, or if it wastes taxpayers' money, then every wage-earner is thinking, *"They are wasting my money!"* Then it is likely that those elected representatives will be voted out of office at the next election.

Of course, I agree that some provision should be made so that people who earn a very small amount of income will pay only a small amount of tax. Even in the law code of ancient Israel, where a sacrifice of a lamb was required after the birth of a child (see Lev. 12:6), there was a provision for people who could not afford this:

> And if she cannot afford a lamb, then she shall take two turtle-doves or two pigeons, one for a burnt offering and the other for a sin offering ... (Lev. 12:8).

But even people who earn very little should be required to pay *some tax* (even if very small), so that there will be a sense of responsibility to pay for the services of the government and a sense of accountability on the part of the government for how these taxes are used.

However, in the United States in 2009, after endless tinkering with the tax code, the government has now put us in a position where nearly half (47%) of the adult citizens *pay no federal income taxes at all*—71 million people![14] This is because people can earn quite a bit of money and still claim deductions for retirement accounts, education accounts, interest paid on a home mortgage, child and dependent care, charitable giving, care for the elderly and disabled, health savings accounts, and several other things.

But this means that *nearly half of the voters in the United States* do not really care whether the government doubles or triples the tax rate, because they don't see taxes really affecting their pocketbook. When a politician such as President Obama promises *trillions* of dollars in new government spending, half of the population doesn't think it matters at all, because they don't think it will cost them a dime. In this way the government is cut loose from accountability to the voters, and it can decide to tax and spend the nation into oblivion, with little fear that the majority of the population will care at all—until it is too late. The US national debt accumulated by massively increased spending will take a dreadful toll on the future economic health of the nation. By June 1 of 2009 alone, the spending that President Obama committed and that was approved by Congress increased the national debt over the next decade by more than $4 trillion compared with what it was on January 20, 2009, when Obama was inaugurated.[15] That is a future tax obligation of $38,943 for every one of the 307,000,000 people (every man, woman, and child) now living in the United States.[16] To put it another way, President Obama's huge spending increases have resulted in an *increased* obligation of $110,023 for every person who is now paying income taxes in the United States.[17]

There was no outcry because the near-majority of the population, who now pay no income taxes at all, simply thought, "So what? It won't hurt me!" And the mainstream press, which overwhelmingly supported President Obama, was passive.

---

14. Jeanne Sahadi, "47% Will Pay No Federal Income Tax," *CNN.com* (Sept. 30, 1999). http://money.cnn.com/2009/09/30/pf/taxes/who_pays_taxes/index.htm?postversion=2009093012.

15. Richard W. Rahn, "The Growing Debt Bomb," Cato Institute (Sept. 22, 2009).

16. See www.usdebtclock.org/index.html.

17. Ibid.

9. Who is paying most of the taxes in the United States today?

Another way to look at the present skewing of the tax burden in the United States is to ask who pays most of the taxes today. The truth is, the top 50% of wage earners paid 97% of all the taxes in 2006, and the bottom half of those who earned income paid less than 3%. The top 1% of wage earners paid 40% of the income taxes in 2006. (They earned 22% of the income reported.)[18] Although the government also collects money from corporate income taxes, estate taxes, and other sources, the *2009 Economic Report of the President* estimated that in 2008 income taxes accounted for 70.6% of federal revenues (excluding Social Security and Medicare). But this means that just 1% of the population is paying for 28% of the expenses of the federal government.

This shows a significant change over the previous fifteen years. In 1990, the richest 1% in the United States paid not 40%, but 25% of income tax revenue. By the year 2000, they were paying 37% of these taxes,[19] and then in 2006 they paid 40% of the taxes (see above).

Is such a system truly *fair*? On the principle that money does not belong to government or society but to individuals who earn it, and on the principle that it is healthy when everyone pays something in taxes, such a system does not at all seem to be *fair*. It is steeply "progressive" and had become more "progressive" over those fifteen years.

But now that people who pay almost no taxes have become a majority of the voters in the United States, the stage is set for this situation to continue in the same direction, so that a greater and greater share of the total tax burden will be borne by a smaller and smaller percentage of the population. I can see no justification for such a system in the pages of the Bible.

10. The economy as a whole, all the people in the nation, and the government all gain benefits from lower taxes on the rich

At first it seems hard to understand how it could bring a benefit to the economy as a whole to *lower* the current US tax rates for those who are wealthy. What good could that do for everyone else or for the economy? And what good could that do for the government?

But here is a situation where the study of economics provides greater insight that helps us understand what happens. This can be explained in a way that someone who is not an economist can understand quite easily.

---

18. "Their Fair Share," *Wall Street Journal* (July 21, 2008), A12.
19. "Fact Sheet: Who Pays the Most Individual Income Taxes?" U.S. Department of Treasury Fact Sheet (April 1, 2004). www.ustreas.gov/press/releases/js1287.htm.

For example, consider Taxpayer D who has a *taxable* income of $250,000, which puts him in the top 2% of American taxpayers.[20] Using round numbers for simplicity, let's assume that at the current tax rates he pays a total of $62,500 in taxes (or 25% of his taxable income). After taxes, he has $187,500 left for himself.

Now what would be the effect on the economy if his tax rate were *reduced* from 25 to 20% of his income? His tax would drop to 20% of $250,000, or $50,000. Instead of having $187,500 left over after taxes, he would have $200,000 left over. What will he do with the extra $12,500 that the government does not take away from him in taxes?

(1) The first result is that no matter what he does with the extra money, it will quickly begin to help others as well as himself. He has only three choices of what to do with it: he can (a) save it, (b) spend it, or (c) give it away.

(a) If he *saves* his $12,500, he could put it in the bank and earn interest, and the bank will then quickly loan out most of the $12,500 to someone else who wants to buy a house or start a business. So the $12,500 that the wealthy Taxpayer D puts in the bank will quickly begin doing good for other people too. But instead of putting it in the bank, it is likely that he will look for a place to invest it so it will earn him *more* money than just a savings account in a bank. In fact, wealthy people like Taxpayer D look for the *highest rate of return* on their money, within the range of risk that they are willing to tolerate. Some people like Taxpayer D will invest it in a new business, while others will invest it in expanding their business, both of which create new jobs and new productivity in the economy. Or Taxpayer D may buy stocks with it, which is simply a way of investing it in someone else's company so that that company can expand and produce more and provide more jobs. The important point is that what Taxpayer D "saves" does not sit idle in a cookie jar in the kitchen pantry, but is put to use in ways that bring economic benefit.

(b) If Taxpayer D *spends* some of this $12,500, it will also bring economic benefit in the private sector. If he goes out to eat at a restaurant, it brings benefit to the waiters, the cooks, the food suppliers, the truckers who brought the food, and the farmers who produced the food. If he uses it to buy a new car, it brings benefit to the car dealer, the sales force, the window washers who keep the windows clean, the gas station attendants where he buys gas for his car, the auto workers who produced the car, the vendors who supply the auto factory, and so forth.

---

20. See www.factcheck.org/askfactcheck/what_percentage_of_the_us_population_makes.html.

All of these results that come from saving or spending are *far more helpful to the economy* than turning the $12,500 over to some government agency that will waste much of it and use it to pay government workers to file endless forms in triplicate in a cavernous building in Washington, DC. (I am not saying that government workers contribute no value to society, for certainly many government functions are necessary and beneficial, but because government is not accountable to the competitive forces of the free market, it will never use money as productively or efficiently as the private sector will.)

(c) The third option for Taxpayer D is that he could *give away* his $12,500. If he gives it to people who need it for daily necessities, that helps society and also helps the economy because these people will spend it at the grocery store or buy clothing or shoes and so forth. No matter where he gives the money, if he does not give it to government but to a private charity, they will in turn spend the money in the private sector and more economic benefit will result. All three of these results seem to me to bring more benefit to the economy than giving the money to the government.

(2) There are still further benefits that come from lowering Taxpayer D's tax rate. With a lower rate he now has a greater incentive to work and be more productive next year, because he knows he will be able to keep more of his hard-earned money. Lower taxes *increase the incentives to work and be productive*, and when they increase incentives among the most economically productive members of society—those with the highest earnings—they bring the added benefit of more productivity that comes from the skilled work of Taxpayer D.

(3) There is still more benefit to the economy. As Taxpayer D invests more (because he has more money to invest) and works more (because of a higher incentive to work), he is going to *earn* more money next year as well. In fact, when the *permanent* tax rates in the United States have been reduced (so that people can plan for lower taxes next year *and the years following* as well), the result has been an amazing increase in personal income in the country.

For example, let's say that after two years, Taxpayer D's taxable income has grown from $250,000 to $320,000. Now, at this 20% tax rate he pays $64,000 in taxes—which is $1,500 more than he was paying at the higher 25% rate! The government has suddenly collected *more* money from Taxpayer D than it did before. And yet he is better off as well, because even after paying $64,000, he still has $256,000 left for himself. And it is not only Taxpayer D who has decided to earn more, but the entire population in general has decided to invest more and work more because they can keep a higher percentage of their income. So the entire economy is growing. And the amount of taxes collected by the *government is also growing at this lower tax rate!*

The results we saw with Taxpayer D do not happen only with rich people whose tax rates are reduced. The same results also happen to some degree for lower-income taxpayers, except that they will tend to spend more and save and invest less, and it is the savings and investment that have the largest positive influence on growing an economy.

This is not wishful thinking, but is what actually happened, both with the Reagan tax cuts in 1981 and with the Bush tax cuts in 2001 and 2003.

According to William Niskanen and Stephen Moore of the Cato Institute, the Reagan tax cuts had these results:

1. Real economic growth averaging 3.2% versus 2.8% during the Ford-Carter years, and 2.1% during the Bush I-Clinton years.
2. Real median family income growing by $4,000 during the Reagan period, compared to no growth during the pre-Reagan years, and a loss of approximately $1,500 in the post-Reagan years.
3. Interest rates, inflation, and unemployment falling faster under Reagan than they did immediately before or after his presidency.[21]

Niskanen and Moore reported that family incomes plummeted 9% under Jimmy Carter, but rose 11% under Ronald Reagan.[22]

With regard to the Bush tax cuts, the National Center for Policy Analysis reported:

1. In the third quarter of 2003, the gross national product (GNP) grew at a 7.2% annual rate. The real annual GDP growth rate increased from 0.3% in 2001 to 2.5 in 2002.
2. 2003 and 2004 economic growth levels resulted in $300 billion of greater than expected growth, or roughly $2,500 per household.
3. 1.4 million jobs were added in the nine months after August 2003.[23]

Finally, according to one analysis, instead of costing the government $27 billion in revenues, the tax cuts actually *earned* the government

21. William A. Niskanen and Stephen Moore, "Supply-Side Economics and the Truth about the Reagan Economic Record," *CATO Policy Analysis* (Oct. 22, 1996). www.cato.org/pub_display.php?pub_id=1120&full=1.
22. Ibid.
23. "Are the Bush Tax Cuts Working?" http://taxesandgrowth.ncpa.org/news/are-the-bush-tax-cuts-working.

$26 billion extra. Donald Luskin, the chief investment officer of Trend Macrolytics, an independent economics and investment research firm, explains how this occurred:

> The 2003 tax cut on capital gains has entirely paid for itself. *More* than paid for itself. *Way* more. To appreciate the story, we have to go back in time to January 2003, before the tax cut was enacted. Table 3–5 on page 60 in CBO's *Budget and Economic Outlook* published in 2003 estimated that capital-gains tax liabilities would be $60 billion in 2004 and $65 billion in 2005, for a two-year total of $125 billion.
>
> Now, let's move forward a year, to January 2004, after the capital gains tax cut had been enacted. Table 4–4 on page 82 in CBO's *Budget and Economic Outlook* of that year shows that the estimates for capital gains tax liabilities had been lowered to $46 billion in 2004 and $52 billion in 2005, for a two-year total of $98 billion. Compare the original $125 billion total to the new $98 billion total, and we can infer that CBO was forecasting that the tax cut cost the government $27 billion in revenues.
>
> Those are the estimates. Now's let see how things really turned out. Take a look at Table 4–4 on page 92 of the *Budget and Economic Outlook* released this week. You'll see that actual liabilities from capital gains taxes were $71 billion in 2004, and $80 billion in 2005, for a two-year total of $151 billion. So let's do the math one more time: Subtract the originally estimated two-year liability of $125 billion, and you get a $26 billion upside surprise for the government. Yes, instead of costing the government $27 billion in revenues, the tax cuts actually earned the government $26 billion extra.[24]

(4) There is yet another benefit from lower taxes, one of gigantic significance. When taxpayers are allowed to keep more of their own money, there is an increase in the amount of *personal liberty* in the society. This is because *individuals*, not the government, are deciding how

---

24. See Donald Luskin, "The 2003 Tax Cut on Capital Gains Entirely Paid for Itself, I'm Not Just Saying It—CBO Is," *National Review Online* (Jan. 27, 2006), www.nationalreview. com/nrof_luskin/luskin200601270946.asp; and "Are the Bush Tax Cuts Working?" *National Center for Policy Analysis*, http://taxesandgrowth.ncpa.org/news/are-the-bush-tax-cuts-working: citing Congressional Budget Office, "The Budget and Economic Outlook: Fiscal Years 2007 to 2016," Congressional Budget Office (Jan. 2006). Table 4–4, pg. 92. www.cbo. gov/ftpdocs/70xx/doc7027/01–26-BudgetOutlook.pdf.

that amount of money will be spent. Even a low-income taxpayer who keeps $120 more of his own money now has the freedom to decide if he wants to spend that $120 on buying healthier food at the grocery store, buying a new program for his computer, taking his family to a baseball game, giving it to some missionaries, or doing any of thousands of other things. The decision is wholly up to him because the money is still his and the government is no longer taking it and deciding for him how it should be spent. So it is with *every* taxpayer who is able to keep more of his own money.

To summarize, the benefits of lowering the permanent tax rates in a nation, and especially the benefits of lowering the tax rates on the wealthier members of society, are these:

(1) It means that each taxpayer is able to keep more of his own money, which not only helps him but also, because the money is quickly put to work, helps others in the economy, and the economy grows.
(2) It gives more incentive for people to work and to be productive, and this also means that the economy will grow.
(3) The government will collect more money in taxes.
(4) There will be a significant increase in personal liberty in the nation.

Once we understand this, and understand the tremendous benefits that came to the nation from the Bush tax cuts of 2001–2003, we would hope that there would be a unanimous vote in Congress to extend these tax cuts beyond the date when they are set to expire at the end of 2010. But President Obama and the Democratic Party are adamantly opposed to extending these tax cuts. The only thing they can say about them is that they bring too much benefit to "the rich."

The truth is that the tax cuts bring benefit to every taxpayer, including rich taxpayers. But if these tax cuts are not extended, then the tax rates in the United States will go back to their harmful, pre–2003 levels. The Heritage Foundation reports that when the tax cuts expire in 2010:

- Tax rates will rise substantially in each tax bracket, some by 450 basis points [= 4.5%];
- Low-income taxpayers will see the 10-percent tax bracket disappear, and they will have to pay taxes at the 15-percent rate;
- Married taxpayers will see the marriage penalty return;
- Taxpayers with children will lose 50% of their child tax credits;
- Taxes on dividends will increase beginning on January 1, 2009;

- Taxes on capital gains will increase, also beginning on January 1, 2009; and
- Federal death taxes will come back to life in 2011, after fading down to nothing in 2010.[25]

The result of this is going to be the opposite of what we saw above when taxes were cut. These tax increases will harm the economy (by giving more of peoples' income to the government), will take away the incentive of people to work and be more productive, will cause the economy to contract and therefore government will collect less money in taxes, and these tax increases will decrease personal liberty by taking away peoples' freedom to decide what to do with their own money.

So the question is a simple one: What do we want to do? Do we want to (a) help the economy, help people at every income level from poor to rich, help society, increase government tax revenue, and increase liberty, or do we want to (b) take a higher percentage of money from the rich, harm the economy, harm everybody in society from poor to rich, harm society, decrease taxes received by the government, and decrease liberty? Astoundingly, the Democratic Party is unanimously in favor of option (b).

Does the teaching of the Bible give us any guidance on these options? As we have indicated in previous sections, the biblical teachings (a) that property belongs to individuals, not to society and not to the government, (b) that governments should not take excessive amounts of money for itself, (c) that government should seek to bring economic benefit and economic growth to a society, and (d) that government should protect and safeguard individual liberty, all argue in favor of lower tax rates than we now have, especially on those who are in the higher categories of income earners in the society.

11. But are the rich getting richer and the poor getting poorer?

One argument commonly heard in support of higher taxes on the rich is that "the rich are getting richer and the poor are getting poorer." Therefore, it is said, we should tax the rich more to make life more "just" (which these people take to mean "more equal in wealth").

There are several mistakes with this argument. First, it is factually wrong. The poor are not "getting poorer" in the United States nor in any developed country.

---

25. William W. Beach and Rea S. Hederman Jr., "Make The Bush Tax Cuts Permanent," *Heritage Foundation Web Memo #956* (Jan. 5, 2006). www.heritage.org/Research/Taxes/wm956.cfm.

U.S. INCOME MOBILITY: Percentage change in Median Income
from 1996 to 2005, by 1996 Income Quintile, in 2005 Dollars

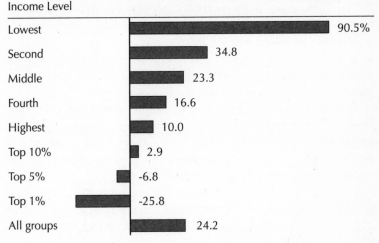

Income Level

Lowest	90.5%
Second	34.8
Middle	23.3
Fourth	16.6
Highest	10.0
Top 10%	2.9
Top 5%	-6.8
Top 1%	-25.8
All groups	24.2

Source: US Treasury Dept., 2007

This chart taken from data published by the US Treasury Department shows that from 1996 to 2005 the greatest percentage of economic growth has occurred with those who were at the lowest end of the income scale in 1996. In fact, nearly 58% of the tax filers in the poorest income group in 1996 had moved into a higher income category ten years later. Nearly 25% moved into the middle- or upper-middle-class income groups. The report said that the only group that saw their median income *decline* over that period was people who were in the top 1% of taxpayers in 1996 — because quite a few people have very high income only for a few years and then it suddenly declines.[26] As the US economy grows, yes, many of the rich are getting richer. (Bill Gates was worth $58 billion in 2008,[27] but the world's richest man in the late 1960s was Bunker Hunt, whose net worth was estimated to be between $8 and $16 billion.[28]) But *the poor are also getting richer*, because as the economy grows, people *at every level of income* generally benefit.

26. "Movin' On Up," *Wall Street Journal* (Nov. 13, 2007). www.opinionjournal.com/editorial/feature.html?id=110010855.

27. See www.forbes.com/lists/2008/10/billionaires08_William-Gates-III_BH69.html.

28. Doug J. Swanson, "Once World's Richest Man, Bunker Hunt Has 'No Regrets,' 29 Years After Silver Collapse," *Dallas Morning News* (March 22, 2009). www.dallasnews.com/sharedcontent/dws/dn/latestnews/stories/032209dnprobunkerhunt.3d93ff8.html.

It is a mathematical fact that when the economy grows by 10%, if everybody in the economy gains 10%, the rich will gain more in total dollars. To use round numbers, if Bill Gates would increase his net worth by 10% from $60 billion to $66 billion, he is $6 billion richer. But if a poor person whose net worth is $40,000 also increases 10% to $44,000, he is only $4,000 richer. Bill Gates has gained wealth at a faster pace, and he is now $5,999,996,000 farther "ahead" of the poor person. *That is inevitable if an economy grows and everyone benefits.*

It is simple mathematics that a 10% gain on a large amount is more than a 10% gain on a small amount. That will be true forever, and therefore as long as economies continue to grow, the rich will continue to get richer and the poor will continue to get richer, but at a slower rate. *The important point is that everybody is better off.*

The only way to prevent this is for government to confiscate $5,999,996,000 of the extra money Bill Gates makes, so that both he and the poor person each gain $4,000. But if that happens, then Bill Gates will decide to work less (why work when the government takes more than 99% of what you earn?) and thus will produce less and help the economy less. The rich person also might just decide to move to another country where government lets him keep more of what he earns (as many highly skilled, wealthy people have done in other countries when tax rates increase significantly).

In other words, government, by massive use of its tax power, can *force* everyone to live in *equality of poverty* (as in communist nations), but it is impossible to force everyone to live in equality of riches, or to live in equality of income in a healthy, growing economy.

There is another reason why we should not think that "the rich are getting richer and the poor are getting poorer." Many people who are poor one year actually start becoming wealthier the next year. If we divide the US population into five groups, with 20% of the people in each (5 quintiles) and study what happened to each group from 1975 to 1991 (a period of 16 years), 98% of those in the lowest income group had moved to a higher group! In the next-lowest income group, 78% had moved to a higher income group, while 58% of those in the third group had moved to a higher group. On the other hand, 31% of those in the top income group had moved to a lower group, as had 24% of those in the second-highest group. The following graph shows these changes: [29]

---

29. "Income mobility 1975–91," in Stephen Moore and Julian Simon, *It's Getting Better All the Time: Greatest Trends of the Last 100 Years* (Washington, DC: Cato Institute, 2000), 79.

INCOME MOBILITY 1975–91

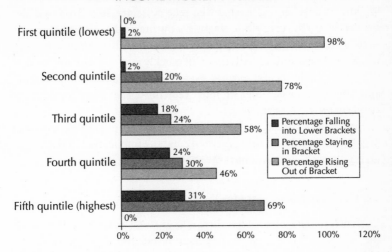

Such patterns have also been seen in more recent studies. A study on income mobility for 1996–2005 found that for those in the lowest income brackets, median pre-tax income rose 77.2% for 1996–2005, compared with 67.8% for the previous period.[30] Another study done by the Department of the Treasury found that roughly half of the taxpayers who began in the bottom quintile in 1996 had moved to a higher tax bracket by 2005. The study also found that among those with the very highest incomes in 1996—the top 1/100 of 1%—only 25% remained in this group in 2005. In addition, their median real income dropped during this period as well.[31]

In other words, various measures show that there is tremendous income mobility over time in the United States.

One example of such movement would be a poor medical school student who suddenly graduates and moves at once from "low income" status to "moderate/high income" status in one year and soon after that to "high income" status. A similar thing happens, in general, to poor college students once they begin climbing their career path. And it happens to poor immigrant families who are just learning the language and looking for business opportunities at which they will soon begin to

---

30. "Income Mobility in the United States: New Evidence from Income Tax Data," *National Tax Journal* LXII:2 (June 2009), 315.

31. "Income Mobility in the United States: 1996–2005," US Department of the Treasury (Nov. 13, 2007), 2.

succeed.[32] This shift from "low income" to "high income" also happens to "low income" entrepreneurs who take no salary and live off savings for two or three years while starting a business; they show up as "the poor" in national income distribution charts (they have $0 income), but when the business does well, they will quickly join the ranks of middle- or upper-middle-income earners. So when people talk about "the poor" and "the rich" over time, we must remember that *there are different people in the groups over time.*

Finally, as I argued in the previous section, taxing the rich less will help the economy and help everybody, but the implication of this is that taxing the rich more will hurt the economy and hurt everyone as well.

12. The death tax (estate tax)

Currently in the United States there is a very high estate tax (often called the "death tax") on the value of a person's estate above a certain amount. This is a tax that has to be paid by a person's estate after the person dies.

Should a person's property be subject to a tax when he or she dies? At present, any value of an estate above a certain "exclusion amount" is taxed at a fairly significant rate before any of it can be given to the deceased person's heirs.

The actual tax has been changing in recent years, but here is a table of the rates from 2001 to 2011 (unless Congress passes a law that changes the 2011 rate):

Year	Exclusion Amount	Max / Top Tax Rate
2001	$675,000	55%
2002	$1.0 million	50%
2003	$1.0 million	49%
2004	$1.5 million	48%
2005	$1.5 million	47%
2006	$2.0 million	46%
2007	$2.0 million	45%
2008	$2.0 million	45%
2009	$3.5 million	45%
2010	Repealed	0%
2011	$1.0 million	55%

32. For numerous examples see Thomas J. Stanley, Ph.D., and William D. Danko, Ph.D., *The Millionaire Next Door* (New York: Pocket Books, 1998).

As this table shows, according to important changes passed in the Bush tax cuts of 2001 and 2003, the amount of an estate that was excluded from the taxable value has been increasing regularly since 2003, and the tax rate on the size of the estate over that amount has been decreasing. But *unless Congress passes another law*, in 2011 the estate tax will go back to a higher rate than it has been since 2001.

For example, if Taxpayer E dies in 2011 and owns a house worth $600,000 and a hardware store that he has built as a small business worth $1 million, and if he also has $400,000 in savings, then his estate is worth $2 million. One million would be excluded, but the estate would have to pay 55% on the other $1 million, or $550,000 in taxes.

Suppose Taxpayer E has four children, and he wishes to leave an inheritance to them in four equal amounts. If there were no estate tax, he would split his $2,000,000 four ways and leave them $500,000 each. But with the 2011 rates that are scheduled to take effect with the estate tax, his children would first have to pay $550,000 in tax out of the estate. The $400,000 in savings does not provide enough cash in the estate to pay this tax, so they will have to sell the house at once or sell the business at once, just to raise enough cash to pay the tax. In many such situations a family business or a family farm just has to be sold.

Now the question is this: Is it right for the government to take $550,000 from the estate of Taxpayer E before he can give it to his children?

The first question is, *whose money is this $2 million?* Does it belong to Taxpayer E so that he should be free to do what he wants with it (assuming he has earned it legally)? Or does it belong to society or to the government? As indicated above, the principles of the Bible indicate that private property belongs to individuals, not to society and not to the government. Therefore the $2 million belongs to Taxpayer E. Why should the government have any right to take away money that he has honestly earned?

In addition, when Taxpayer E acquired this wealth through productive work and saving, he *already paid* income tax on that amount as he was earning it. Why should his estate be taxed *again* on that same money?

Economists have argued that the estate tax is a strong disincentive to entrepreneurship, that is, to investing in a business that one owns. If the business grows and the government is simply going to take away 55 cents on every additional dollar that the business is worth when the owner dies, then why should the owner work very hard at trying to build the business? Over half of his work is going to go to the government anyway, rather than any family members or charity to which he wishes to give the money.

Who benefits? Large corporations often buy small businesses that have to be sold because of this estate tax, as was shown in a study by economists Antony Davies and Pavel Yakovel of Duquesne University, as reported in the *Wall Street Journal*:

> The estate tax "impacts small firms disproportionately versus large firms" by encouraging well-capitalized companies to gobble up smaller ones at the owner's death. The study shows the result is to "promote the concentration of wealth by preventing small businesses from being passed on to heirs."[33]

Economists Patrick Fleenor and J. D. Foster of the Tax Foundation wrote about the disincentive effect of the estate tax:

> Because the estate tax is a tax on wealth that has been accumulated over an individual's lifetime, it is often assumed to have little or no effect on that person's economic decision making. This is a specious notion. An individual's decision to work and save is part of a life-long, forward-looking process. High effective estate tax rates, such as those currently in effect, cause people to reduce productive effort and lower the size of their targeted estates.[34]

Fleenor and Foster ran several simulations of how the estate tax (at the minimum rate of 17% for estates under $10,000 to the maximum rate of 55% for estates over $3 million, to which it will return in 2011) negatively impacts entrepreneurs and, as a result, economic growth. They wrote:

> The various simulations conducted using this model showed that the estate tax has roughly the same effect on entrepreneurial incentives as a doubling of income tax rates. In other words, income tax rates would need to be nearly twice their current levels, or roughly 70 percent, to produce the same disincentive effects as the current estate tax.
>
> Furthermore, given the progressivity of the estate tax, the increase in income tax rates is greater as the size of the estate increases. Given the fact that the estate tax raises only about 1 percent of federal revenue, it is clear that the disincentive effects

---

33. "The Tax That Won't Die," *Wall Street Journal* (Dec. 11, 2009), A20.

34. Patrick Fleenor and J. D. Foster, "An Analysis of the Disincentive Effects of the Estate Tax on Entreprenurship," *Tax Foundation Background Paper #9,* Tax Foundation, Washington, DC (June 1, 1994), 17. www.taxfoundation.org/files/bp9.pdf.

of the tax are well out of proportion to the revenues associated with the estate tax.[35]

Fleenor and Foster concluded:

> Because many business endeavors require the accumulation of large amounts of business assets, high effective estate tax rates have a particularly deleterious effect on entrepreneurship.... The estate tax is a heavy burden to place on the nation's most productive citizens.[36]

13. The "fair tax"

Several proposals have been made to simplify the horribly complicated tax system in the United States. One such proposal is called the "fair tax," which would be a national sales tax (or "consumption tax") on retail sales. One current proposal would be to enact such a "fair tax" and simultaneously abolish personal income taxes, corporate income taxes, capital gains taxes, Social Security and Medicare taxes, other payroll taxes, gift taxes, and estate taxes. I have to admit that the first time anyone looks at that list, a proposal to abolish all those taxes has some initial appeal.

But would it really be a good idea? Such a national sales tax, as proposed, faces some serious objections. First, while it is sometimes promoted as a 23% tax, the way it is defined shows that it is different from current sales taxes, because the 23% in this proposal is calculated *on the basis of the entire amount paid including the tax*. For example, if someone bought an item for $77.00, this "fair tax" on top of that would be $23.00, making a total expenditure of $100.00. But $23.00 added onto a $77.00 item *is really a 30% tax, as people ordinarily calculate sales tax today* (because 23/77 = .299). So the first question that has to be asked is whether people really want a 30% national sales tax, and the first objection is (1) the huge size of the sales tax.

Another objection is (2) tax creep from adding a new kind of tax. That is, because of the never-ending governmental desire for power, once there is a national sales tax, Congress will find it easy to let these other taxes creep back in as well—on top of the 30% sales tax—so soon there would be a 1% national income tax, then 2%, then up and up it would go. And a corporate income tax would probably also come back in. Soon this new kind of tax would be just another tax among many.

---

35. Ibid., 2.
36. Ibid., 17.

Of course, one way to prevent such a reimposition of income taxes would be to repeal the 16th Amendment to the Constitution, which empowers the government to "collect taxes on incomes." But it is exceptionally difficult to pass a constitutional amendment, and it is doubtful that this would ever happen. Such a proposal is basing an argument on wishful thinking, not on reality.

Another objection is that (3) it would place a much greater tax burden on poor people than the current tax system, because everything they buy would be taxed, whereas many of them now pay no tax. (It would burden them more even if a substantial tax rebate were given to the poorest segments of society, at least for people who were just above the "rebate line.")

Still another objection is that (4) charitable organizations might not support the loss of tax benefits that come in the present system for charitable contributions. (That is, if there is no income tax, then of course there would be no deductions from income taxes for charitable contributions.) Another objection is that (5) a huge "black market" would swallow up large segments of the economy because people would simply make transactions in cash and keep no records, thus avoiding a 30% sales tax, which is a huge incentive for tax avoidance on transactions that are almost impossible to trace! Therefore (6) the revenue generated by such a tax might be far less than what is projected, and (7) the increase in tax evasion through cash transactions would have a corrosive effect on society in terms of obedience to law.

Proponents of the "fair tax" have responses to these objections, and I do not deny that the idea has some initial attractiveness. But it seems to me that some of these objections are extremely persuasive, so I cannot support this "fair tax" proposal. It seems to be unrealistic.

But I admit that my evaluation here is based much more on a set of practical concerns rather than on any clear principles from the Bible. (Note also some biblical considerations in favor of a "flat tax" in section 7 above [pp. 78–80], a proposal that seems to me to have much more to commend it than the "fair tax" proposal.)

14. The Bible's teaching on inheritance

In ancient Israel, giving property and possessions to children through inheritance was a normal practice:

> A good man leaves an inheritance to his children's children (Prov. 13:22).

> House and wealth are inherited from fathers, but a prudent wife is from the LORD (Prov. 19:14).

It is interesting that the Lord gave to Moses specific directions regarding inheritance:

> And you shall speak to the people of Israel, saying, "If a man dies and has no son, then you shall transfer his inheritance to his daughter. And if he has no daughter, then you shall give his inheritance to his brothers. And if he has no brothers, then you shall give his inheritance to his father's brothers. And if his father has no brothers, then you shall give his inheritance to the nearest kinsman of his clan, and he shall possess it. And it shall be for the people of Israel a statute and rule, as the LORD commanded Moses" (Num. 27:8 – 11).

Notice that *in no case is any percentage of this inheritance taken by the government* in any kind of "estate tax." It is left to the deceased persons' descendents, and if he has no descendents, it is left to others who are the next of kin.

In fact, the prophet Ezekiel reported God's words prohibiting a ruler from taking away the "inheritance" of people that they would then be unable to pass it down to their heirs:

> *The prince shall not take any of the inheritance of the people,* thrusting them out of their property. He shall give his sons their inheritance out of his own property, so that none of my people shall be scattered from his property (Ezek. 46:18).

One argument in favor of the estate tax is that it prevents "excessive" amounts of wealth from accumulating in the hands of a few families. But who is to decide what is "excessive"? Are we to assume that wealthy people are more likely to misuse their money or use it in socially harmful and destructive ways? If they use it in illegal ways, they will be punished by the government. But if they do not use it in illegal ways, why should it be taken away from them?

The other side of this argument is that an estate tax simply accumulates more and more power for the government. A good argument could be made that a more powerful, increasingly wealthy government is *more* harmful to a nation than a lot of wealthy families, many of whom often do much good for the nation through wise investments and business and through immense charitable donations (neither of which are normally done by government agencies).

So the questions about an estate tax ultimately boil down to the matter of who ultimately owns the property of a nation: individuals or the government? The Bible clearly takes the side of individual ownership of property.

My conclusion is that the estate tax should be permanently repealed.

B. THE SOCIAL SECURITY SYSTEM

1. Overview of Social Security

The term "Social Security" in the United States is used as the common term to refer to the entire federal program officially called the Old-Age, Survivors, and Disability Insurance program (abbreviated OASDI). The taxes to support Social Security are called FICA taxes because they are collected under the Federal Insurance Contribution Act. Currently, employees pay 6.2% of their income in Social Security tax and 1.45% in Medicare tax, for a total of 7.65% of income. Employers have to pay an equal amount, making the total contribution equivalent to 15.3% of an employee's income collected as FICA tax. Self-employed people pay the entire 15.3% themselves. No FICA tax is collected on earnings over $102,000 in a year.

The first Social Security act was signed by President Franklin D. Roosevelt on August 14, 1935. Prior to that time, the United States had no governmental provision to care for those who had retired with no ongoing income, or those who were disabled and could no longer work, or those who were unemployed. The idea was that people would pay into the Social Security fund during their working life and then collect monthly benefits after they retired, until they died.

The system collected only a very small percentage of income at the beginning (equivalent to 2%), half from the employee and half from the employer, and the system worked very well at first. That figure has now risen to 12.4% of income.[37] That growth came because Congress began giving away more and more money. They were able to do this at first because many people were paying into the system and very few people had retired (approximately 6% of the population in 1930 was sixty-five and over).[38] So in the late 1930s and through the 1940s and 1950s, the program had a surplus of funds and Congress repeatedly increased the benefits, which was a popular action and tended to gain them votes.

---

37. "Legislative History: Social Security Act of 1935," United States Social Security Administration, www.ssa.gov/history/35act.html; and "The 2008 Annual Report of the Board of Trustees of the Federal Old-Age and Survivors Insurance and Disability Insurance Trust Funds" (March 28, 2008). www.ssa.gov/OACT/TR/TR08/tr08.pdf.

38. See "65+ in the United States," United States Census Bureau (Dec. 2005), 9. www.census.gov/prod/2006pubs/p23–209.pdf.

But eventually many millions of people retired at age sixty-five, and then they continued to collect benefits for twenty or even thirty or more years beyond that time. According to US Census Bureau projections, a substantial increase in the number of older people will occur during the 2010 to 2030 period, after the first Baby Boomers turn sixty-five in 2011. The older population in 2030 is projected to be twice as large as in 2000, growing from 35 million to 72 million. [39] This worker-beneficiary ratio is projected to continue to fall to 2.2 workers to beneficiary by 2030 as well.[40] In 1945, the ratio was 41.9 to 1.[41] In addition, medical care benefits were added in 1965 under the Medicare and Medicaid programs. Now Social Security and Medicare *are the largest expenditures in the federal budget.*[42] In the 2010 fiscal year, Social Security payments will constitute 18.6% of the federal budget, and Medicare/Medicaid will constitute an additional 19.6%, for a total of 38.2% of government expenditures. This is a program of immense size, equal to 10% of the gross domestic product (GDP) of the United States (that is, the total economic value of all goods and services produced in the United States in a year).[43] The other large component of the federal budget is defense, which accounts for 19% of the budget.[44] By 2050, spending on Social Security, Medicare, and Medicaid is projected to be 16% of GDP (not 16% of all government spending, but 16% of all the economic wealth produced in the entire nation in one year!), more than twice as much as spending on all other government programs.[45] And all this to make payments to people who are retired and still consuming, but are not necessarily contributing any economically productive benefits to the economy.

2. Concerns about insolvency

The largest concern today about Social Security is that it is quickly running out of money.

Current projections are that by the year 2016 the Social Security Trust Fund will be paying out more than it is taking in. At that point, the federal government, which is required by law to pay back with interest the

---

39. Ibid., 1.

40. Ibid., 97: citing www.ssa.gov/OACT/TR/TR03/IV_Lrest.html.

41. "The 2008 Annual Report of the Board of Trustees of the Federal Old-Age and Survivors Insurance and Disability Insurance Trust Funds," op. cit. See also the 2009 report, 2. www.ssa.gov/OACT/TR/2009/tr09.pdf.

42. "Mid-Session Review Budget of the U.S. Government: Fiscal Year 2008," Office of Management and Budget, 4. www.whitehouse.gov/omb/budget/fy2008/pdf/08msr.pdf.

43. Ibid., 6.

44. Ibid., 4.

45. Ibid., 6.

loans that it takes from the Social Security Trust Fund, will owe $3.5 trillion to the Social Security program, or $10,400 for every man, woman, and child in America.[46] By 2041, it is projected that the trust fund will be exhausted. The Social Security Administration estimates that payroll taxes would have to increase by 28% to cover the projected deficit in 2041.[47] Because people are living longer and collecting so much in benefits, Social Security by 2080 will swamp the federal budget and require 20% of the gross domestic product simply to keep the payments going.[48] To solve this problem, many conservative political leaders have argued that Social Security should be gradually "privatized." This would mean that employees could decide that a small percentage of their Social Security tax, instead of going into government coffers, could be put in *private investments*, which the federal government would require them to do, but which they would individually own. The argument is that private investments would gain a much higher rate of return than giving the money to the government.

In fact, social security programs have successfully been privatized in other countries. Chile is a notable example. In 1981 the Chilean government instituted a social security personal ownership program. The contribution rate, including fees and taxes, is 14.4%. Each participant had an individual account in which their contributions were deposited, and they were then given the choice of five government-approved investment funds for investing the monies. The average yield on the accounts from 1981 to 2002 was 10.7% above the rate of inflation, and the program is self-funded and carries no deficit.[49] It is not hard to imagine that any kind of private investment would give a better rate of return than giving to the government. In fact, current estimates for a fifty-year-old show that he will receive back a rate of return of 0.24% on what he has paid into Social Security over his lifetime.[50] If that same person had been able to invest his money in a Personal Retirement Account, he could conceivably receive

46. "The 2008 Annual Report of the Board of Trustees of the Federal Old-Age and Survivors Insurance and Disability Insurance Trust Funds," op. cit.

47. Ibid.

48. "Mid-Session Review Budget of the U.S. Government: Fiscal Year 2008," op.cit., 6.

49. See Barbara Kritzer, "Social Security Privatization in Latin America," *United States Social Security Administration* 63:2 (Dec. 2000), www.socialsecurity.gov/policy/docs/ssb/v63n2/v63n2p17.pdf.; and "The Chilean Pension System: Fourth Edition," *Superintendencia de Administradoras de Fondos de Pensiones* (Superintendent of the Chile Pension Fund Administration), (May 2003). www.safp.cl/573/articles-3523_chapter6.pdf.

50. Rate of return can be calculated at http://site.heritage.org/research/features/socialsecurity/SSCalcWelcome.asp.

$6,000 a month *more* than he will receive from Social Security once he retires. (That is, a private retirement investment would pay him, when he retires, about $8,400 per month rather than $2,300 per month *for the rest of his life!*)

3. Conclusions regarding Social Security

There appears to be at least six conclusions we can draw from the current Social Security system.

(1) The root cause of the problem with Social Security is that, for the most part, it is wastefully paying healthy, potentially productive people not to work. This simply drains the life and vitality out of any economy. The idea that healthy, productive people should retire at age sixty-five and contribute no further productive work to an economic system is found nowhere in the Bible. In fact, as long as people are able to do so, the Bible tells them that they should work:

> But we urge you, brothers ... to aspire to live quietly, and to mind your own affairs, and to work with your hands, as we instructed you, so that you may live properly before outsiders and be dependent on no one (1 Thess. 4:10–12).

> Now we command you, brothers, in the name of our Lord Jesus Christ, that you keep away from any brother who is *walking in idleness* and not in accord with the tradition that you received from us. For you yourselves know how you ought to imitate us, because *we were not idle when we were with you*, nor did we eat anyone's bread without paying for it, but with toil and labor we worked night and day, that we might not be a burden to any of you. It was not because we do not have that right, but to give you in ourselves an example to imitate. For even when we were with you, we would give you this command: *If anyone is not willing to work, let him not eat.* For we hear that some among you walk in idleness, not busy at work, but busybodies. Now such persons we command and encourage in the Lord Jesus Christ *to do their work quietly and to earn their own living* (2 Thess. 3:6–12; see discussion above, pp. 46–49, on the value of productive work).

There is nothing wrong with the original idea behind Social Security as it was founded in 1935. It is appropriate to have some system of support for people who are no longer *able* to work due to old age or disability or involuntary unemployment. But it is completely foolish for any society to pay billions of dollars a year for retirement and medical benefits for people who are perfectly healthy and skilled and experienced and thus are perfectly able to do productive work and bring benefit to the economy for many years after age sixty-five. Therefore the entire system is now burdened by a flawed idea that is economically invalid and theologically unjustifiable. And it is now maintained by the government because the voting block of those who receive such benefits is so large that anyone who questions the idea is unlikely to be re-elected to office.

(2) The system is deceptive at its core. While it was originally set up as a means by which people could pay into a fund *that would accumulate savings for them,* so that they would have retirement funds when they were unable to work, it quickly shifted to a "pay as you go" system by which current workers are supporting not *their own future* retirement but *present* retirees.

I saw this in my own family, because for many years I was paying thousands of dollars in Social Security tax while my father was receiving Social Security payments. But because of retirement savings and investments, he had a higher annual income than I did! I failed to see why I, with a lower income, while working at economically productive tasks that brought benefit to the economy, should be paying thousands of dollars that went to him, who had a higher income than I did. What is the sense of that? It certainly was not saving for my own future, because the system is projected to be insolvent before I am able to draw any benefits from it.

(3) Therefore the entire Social Security system contains massive wasteful transfers of money from hard-working people to non-working people, many of whom have no need for this money.

(4) I want to reaffirm that I believe that it is right that government provide *some* kind of guarantee of support for those who are genuinely no longer able to work due to old age, disability, or involuntary unemployment. And it would of course make sense to provide provisions for *partial* benefits to be paid to people who wanted to take semi-retirement and then ease gradually into full retirement.

(5) There would be many benefits to a gradual privatization of Social Security:

    (a) It would bring the system back into financial solvency, so that it doesn't bankrupt the federal government.

    (b) It would give individuals instead of the government control over their retirement funds, which would increase individual liberty and responsibility.

(c) It would decrease government power over the population of the United States, which would again increase individual liberty.

(6) Why, then, do politicians not change the system? The opposition to change has come primarily from Democrats who have retained enough power in Congress to block any reforms. And they have been supported by some Republicans who are fearful of losing re-election if they alienate the vote of the senior citizens in their district.

But we can wonder about the possibility of mixed motives here. Do the Democrats who support Social Security in its present form and refuse to privatize it have as their primary motive only the protection of people's future income in retirement? Or do they see it not as a scheme for the needy but *as a means of retaining government power* and government control over more and more of peoples' money and therefore people's lives — an idea that is often a primary (but unspoken) goal of those who continually seek to expand the power of government. As long as politicians continue to argue for maintaining or increasing benefits, it helps to guarantee that they will get a significant portion of senior citizens' votes, and thus they can retain their political power. But they are not seeking what is best for the nation or even what is necessary to put our financial house in order.

C. HEALTH CARE

The basic health care question that has faced the United States several times in the recent past is whether or not it should be provided by and managed by the federal government or controlled by individuals and private health care providers.

The health care proposals that came from President Obama and Democrats in Congress in late 2009 were based on the philosophy that the federal government should ultimately control all medical care in the United States. These proposals resulted in the Patient Protection and Affordable Care Act, which was ultimately signed into law by President Obama on March 23, 2010.

One objection to such a plan is that government is never an efficient provider of economic goods, because it does not have to face the competitive incentives of the free market. Therefore other objections follow naturally. Federal government control of health care will inevitably mean a steep increase in costs, a decline in quality, a decline in freedom of choice, and a decline in the availability of certain kinds of medical care.

Most critics of the Democratic plans believed (I think rightly) that experience in other nations shows one thing clearly: If a nation's government controls health care, then *some rationing system will be necessary* to decide who gets treatments and who does not, and there will be widespread instances of denial of care (for a government simply cannot supply an infinite supply of care for everyone who asks for it). While the quality of medical care in the United States in 2009 was the best that was available in the entire world (which is why foreign people who can afford to do so often come to the United States for specialized medical care), critics fear that Obama's plan will lead to rapid decline in the quality of care.

Peter Ferrara, director of entitlement and budget policy for the Institute for Policy Innovation, writes:

> The combination of several elements of the Obama health plan would lead to government rationing of health care.... The first factor will be the low reimbursements to doctors and hospitals that would prevail under the Obama health plan. We see this already in Medicare, which pays doctors and hospitals 20 to 30 percent less than market rates for the care and services they provide under the program. Doctors are dropping out of the Medicare program or refusing to accept more patients.[51] The situation is even worse under Medicaid, which pays doctors and hospitals 30 to 40 percent less than Medicare does. In 2008, over 33 percent of physicians had closed their practices to Medicaid patients and 12 percent had closed their practices to Medicare patients.[52] This restricts access to health care for the poor and the elderly served by the programs, who must scramble for short and hurried appointments with available doctors or wait for emergency hospital care. The lower quality of care provided to Medicaid patients results in poorer health outcomes, including more and earlier deaths from heart disease and cancer compared to privately insured patients.[53]

---

51. Peter Ferrara, "The Obama Health Plan: Rationing, Higher Taxes, and Lower Quality Care, *The Heartland Institute*, no. 123 (Aug. 2009), 8–9: www.heartland.org/custom/semod_policybot/pdf/25813.pdf: citing The Physicians Foundation, "The Physicians' Perspective: Medical Practice in 2008," *Survey Key Findings* (Nov. 18, 2008), www.physiciansfoundations.org/news/news_show.htm?doc_id=728872.

52. Ibid.

53. Ferrara, op.cit., 9: citing Jeet Guram and John S. O'Shea, MD, "How Washington Pushes Americans into Low-Quality Health Care," *Heritage Foundation Backgrounder #2664* (April 24, 2009). www.heritage.org/Research/Healthcare/bg2264.cfm.

Ferrara continues:

> This underpayment would have a powerful effect on invest-
> ment in the health care industry. Investors are not going to
> finance acquisition of the latest, most advanced equipment
> and technologies if the government slashes compensation for
> the services such technologies provide. Investors won't finance
> new or expanded hospital facilities or clinics, or even the full
> maintenance of existing ones. This is how the long waiting
> lines for diagnostics, surgery, and other referrals begin to
> develop in countries with socialized health care. It is why hos-
> pitals and other medical facilities in those countries are often
> old and deteriorating.[54]

By contrast, Republicans proposed several alternative plans. They
recognized the need to provide health care coverage for those who
want it and are unable to obtain it, but argued that this is only a small
percentage of the population. In 2009, it was estimated that 18.8 million people were truly financially unable to purchase health insurance,
approximately 6.1% of the total population of the United States.[55] But
if the problem is that 6% of the population needs a way to get health
insurance, why have the government take over health care for the other
94%? This does not make sense (unless the real goal is more government control over people's lives). Some reforms that seem sensible to
me include these:

(1) A *tax credit* for people to use to purchase health insurance on
their own—which was one Republican proposal—would preserve the
private health care system in the United States and also preserve freedom of individual choice. This would guarantee coverage for those who
need it and would protect the free market and the quality of health care
as well as freedom of choice. People would keep their own money to use
for health care in the way that they think most wise.

(2) Individuals should be able to join together in voluntary groups in
order to obtain the preferable insurance rates now available to people in
larger companies.

(3) Congress should pass a law prohibiting individual states from
forcing companies to cover high-risk people at the same rate as everyone else, thus increasing costs for everyone in the state. (Unfortunately,
this expensive state practice just became national law under President

---

54. Ibid.
55. Ibid., 28.

Obama's plan.) In addition, the law should allow people to purchase health insurance from any company in any state, thus nullifying the terribly expensive costs of insurance that have been imposed by states such as New York, with their extensive requirements for the "Cadillac" plans that they mandate that insurance companies have to provide.

(4) Congress should pass medical malpractice reform (tort reform) that would bring immense savings in medicine by limiting the awards that can be given in lawsuits for medical malpractice. Such reform should also institute expert panels that would pre-qualify malpractice lawsuits so that frivolous, time-wasting lawsuits could be weeded out and prevented from clogging the system. With such tort reform, estimates from the Congressional Budget Office are that $5.4 billion could be saved each year out of the $35 billion that the nation spends on health care.[56]

(5) Some provision should be made to care for those who truly cannot afford medical insurance. The solution that seems most helpful to me would be some kind of pooling of high-risk patients to be covered by funds in individual states as their legislatures decide, and also some kind of fund that would enable the truly poor to obtain a basic health insurance policy.

Unfortunately, none of these reforms were included in the 2010 health care reform plan that was passed by Democrats without any Republican support.

D. WHAT IS THE BEST CURE FOR RECESSIONS?

When President Obama took office in January 2009, the nation was facing a severe economic crisis. Many banks and other financial firms were facing insolvency because they had accumulated a large number of home loans that were made to people who had no ability to repay them. The downturn in the real estate market meant that many homeowners owed more on their home than it could be sold for, and they found that they were unable to continue making payments on their mortgages. Large manufacturing companies such as General Motors and Chrysler were facing bankruptcy. Unemployment was 7.6% in January,[57] climbed to

---

56. According to the Congressional Budget Office in an October 9, 2009, letter to Senator Orrin Hatch, $54 billion would be saved over a ten-year period (or $5.4 billion per year) if caps were placed on non-economic damages at $250,000, a cap on punitive damages at $500,000, and the statute of limitations for filing lawsuits were shortened. www.cbo.gov/ftpdocs/106xx/doc10641/10–09-Tort_Reform.pdf.

57. US Bureau of Labor Statistics. http://data.bls.gov/PDQ/servlet/SurveyOutput Servlet?series_id=LNS14000000&data_tool=XGtable.

9.8% by September 2009,[58] and eventually to over 10%. Such a widespread recession in the economy required some response, lest it continue spreading to more and more sectors of the economy and become a deeper and deeper recession.

What should the solution be in such a situation? There are two views. One view is that the government should spend a lot more money to "stimulate" the economy. That strategy is called the "Keynesian" view after British economist John Maynard Keynes (1883–1946), who advocated much new government spending to overcome recessions. The other strategy is called the "free market" view, because it emphasizes cutting taxes to let people keep more of their own money and then allowing the free market to overcome the recession. (This view was most famously advocated by economist Milton Friedman [1912–2006] and his colleagues at the University of Chicago.)

I will examine the 2008–2009 situation in some detail, but the principles explained here are applicable much more broadly.

The option favored by President Obama was to begin a program of massive government spending. The spending programs that he favored and that the Democratic-controlled Congress passed were far beyond anything any government has ever spent in the history of the world.

According to Michael J. Boskin, a professor of economics at Stanford University and a senior fellow at the Hoover Institution, in the first year of the Obama administration the present and future debt commitments of the United States government increased *more than all previous presidents combined in the entire history of the United States.* [59] On Obama's inauguration day, the national debt was $10,626,877,048,913. On February 11, 2010, a little more than a year later, the national debt had climbed to $12,349,324,464,284, an increase of $1,722,447,415,371.[60] Columnist Robert Samuelson of the *Washington Post* wrote for RealClearPolitics.com:

> From 2010 to 2019, Obama projects annual deficits totaling $7.1 trillion; that's atop the $1.8 trillion deficit for 2009. By 2019, the ratio of publicly held federal debt to gross domestic product (GDP, or the economy) would reach 70 percent, up from 41 percent in 2008. That would be the highest since 1950 (80 percent). The Congressional Budget Office, using less optimistic economic forecasts, raises these estimates. The 2010–19

---

58. US Bureau of Labor Statistics. www.bls.gov/eag/eag.us.htm.
59. Michael J. Boskin, "Obama's Radicalism Is Killing the Dow," *Wall Street Journal* (March 6, 2009). http://online.wsj.com/article/SB123629969453946717.html.
60. See www.theobamadebt.com/.

deficits would total $9.3 trillion; the debt-to-GDP ratio in 2019 would be 82 percent.

But wait: Even these totals may be understated. By various estimates, Obama's health plan might cost $1.2 trillion over a decade; Obama has budgeted only $635 billion. Next, the huge deficits occur despite a pronounced squeeze of defense spending. From 2008 to 2019, total federal spending would rise 75 percent, but defense spending would increase only 17 percent. Unless foreign threats recede, military spending and deficits might both grow.[61]

On January 28, 2010, Congress voted to raise the debt ceiling to $14.3 trillion, which translates to about $45,000 for every American.[62]

Where was all this money going to come from? No one gave any clear answers, but the fact is, there are not many choices for how the government can get money. If the money were simply borrowed from investors around the world who wanted to loan money to the United States Government through the purchase of Treasury bills, notes, and bonds, then it would have to be repaid by enormously increased tax burdens, extending to future generations.

What if America's creditors become concerned about our soaring deficits? They could demand higher interest rates and make the debt problem worse. Len Burman, Syracuse University professor and former director of the Tax Policy Center, wrote, "Taxes would rise to levels that would make a Scandinavian revolt. And the government would not be able to provide anything but the most basic public services. We would no longer be a great power (or even a mediocre one) and the social safety net would evaporate."[63] According to Burman, writing in 2005, even before President Obama's deficit explosion:

> I'm looking through the Congressional Budget Office's crystal ball into the future, and what I see is scarier than Oz's Wicked Witch. If federal spending follows its historical pattern of the last 40 years, by 2050, the government would spend almost one-third of our gross domestic product — not counting inter-

61. Robert Samuelson, "Obama's Dangerous Debt," *RealClearPolitics.com* (May 18, 2009). www.realclearpolitics.com/articles/2009/05/18/obamas_dangerous_debt_96539.html.

62. "Senate Lifts Debt Ceiling by $1.9 Trillion," Associated Press (Jan. 28, 2010). www.foxnews.com/politics/2010/01/28/senate-lifts-federal-debt-ceiling-trillion/.

63. Len Burman, "Catastrophic Budget Failure," *Washington Times* (July 14, 2009). http://www.washingtontimes.com/news/2009/jul/14/catastrophic-budget-failure.

est on the debt. (Government spending would explode mainly because the baby boomers will retire and health care costs will keep rising, which would swell the costs of the government's Medicare and Medicaid programs.) By comparison, in 2004, the federal government raised about 16% of GDP in taxes— half as much as we would need under this scenario.

To balance the budget under the CBO's innocently named "Scenario 1," all taxes would have to double. The average income tax bill would increase by almost $7,000 at today's income levels. And that's only the start.

Imagine losing twice as much of your paycheck to Social Security and Medicare taxes, and twice as much to the excise taxes on beer, gas and wine. And if, despite these taxes, you managed to die with your nest egg intact, your estate might face a super-sized estate tax.

To cover all of the additional spending with income taxes alone, they'd have to more than triple from today's levels. Tripling rates wouldn't work because the top rate would be more than 100%.

To raise that much, the government would have to slash deductions and credits. (No deductions for kids, pensions, mortgage interest, state taxes or charity—and no child credits.) Even then, rates would have to increase by at least 70%. The top income tax rate would soar to 59% (compared with 35% now). A family of four with an annual income of $75,000 would pay more than $16,000 in additional taxes.[64]

However, instead of borrowing money, there was another way to finance this massive debt of 2009. The federal government (through the Federal Reserve Board) could simply begin *printing more money*, pouring billions of new dollars into the economy. And that is also what the Obama administration and the Federal Reserve Board decided to do.[65] (The actual mechanism was complex and involved some special financial procedures carried out by the Federal Reserve Board and the Treasury Department, but the net effect was the same as if the United States Mint just began printing billions of dollars in additional money.)

---

64. Leonard E. Burman, "If You Think Taxes are a Pain Now ...," Tax Policy Center, Urban-Brookings Institute (April 15, 2005). www.taxpolicycenter.org/publications/url.cfm?ID=900801.

65. Irwin, "Fed to Pump $1.2 Trillion into Markets."

What is the problem with the government simply printing billions of dollars of additional money to pay its bills? The problem is that *these new dollars do not represent any increase in the economic wealth of a nation.* They do not represent any real goods and services that people can use. If a baker bakes a loaf of bread or an automobile factory produces a car, then there is *added wealth* in the nation—one more loaf of bread or one more car. If a teacher teaches a class or a popular singer performs a concert, that also adds wealth in the nation—the added value of the education people got in school or the entertainment they enjoyed. However, putting more dollar bills into banks doesn't contribute any value to the economy in the way that these things do. So what does it do?

When the money supply is expanded rapidly like this, it increases the probability of significant inflation in future years (see above the illustration of a *Monopoly* game, p. 52). This is because there is more money in the system but the same amount of goods and services, so the money will be used to bid prices up above what they otherwise would have been.

As for the Obama stimulus plan itself, much of it was designated not to genuinely "stimulate" the economy, but simply to promote social change of the sort favored by Democrats. For example, building a new bridge may temporarily provide jobs for construction workers, yet it is not economically as beneficial as starting a new private business, because after the bridge is built, it doesn't employ anyone any longer. But a new business that is started continues to employ people and continues to produce economic benefit for the nation.

Was there any other solution to the economic crisis of 2009? An alternative proposal, one favored by many Republicans, was that the government should have enacted *huge tax cuts.*

For example, instead of increasing the national debt by having the government *spend* $800 billion in a "stimulus program," if the government had simply *cut taxes by $800 billion*, it would have left that much more money back in the hands of private individuals in the economy. What would they have done with it? People at the lower end of the economic spectrum probably would have spent most of it right away, but the benefit of that would be that these individuals, rather than the government, would be deciding where the money would be spent, and thus individual liberty would be advanced and there would be an increase in the competitive benefits that come from the free market economy. People at the higher end of the economic spectrum would probably have invested more of that money in expanding their businesses or in starting new businesses. As explained above, a decrease in marginal tax rates is a huge incentive for entrepreneurship—the act of investing money and taking risk in order to build a business. And these businesses would then employ more people in more jobs, and the economy would begin to work its way out of the recession quite quickly. Rather than increasing unemployment to around 10% as the Obama "stimulus plan" did, this would rapidly provide many new jobs in the economy, and people would be working again.

In other words, if the government is going to go into debt one way or another, it is far better for it to go into debt by cutting taxes than by increasing government expenditures. That is because money given to private individuals to use in the free market economy is always better in terms of economic growth, and better in terms of increasing individual liberty, than money given into the hands of the government that will use much of the money wastefully and use it to increase government control over everyone's life.

Chapter 4

THE ENVIRONMENT: BIBLICAL TEACHING AND THE STATE OF THE EARTH'S RESOURCES

What policies should governments adopt concerning the use and care of the environment?

A. BIBLICAL TEACHING

At this point I need to explain in detail some of the main biblical principles concerning the creation.

1. The original creation was "very good"

When God first completed his work of creation, "God saw everything that he had made, and behold, *it was very good*" (Gen. 1:31). This was a world in which there was no disease and no "thorns and thistles" (see Gen. 3:18) to harm human beings. It was a world of great abundance and beauty, far beyond anything we can imagine today. Moreover, Adam and Eve were included in the pronouncement "very good," so they were perfectly free from sin. In addition, they were not subject to disease or aging or death (see Rom. 5:12; also Eccles. 7:29).

But even in this perfect world, God gave Adam and Eve work to do in caring for the garden: "The LORD God took the man and put him in the

Garden of Eden *to work it and keep it*" (Gen. 2:15). God also set before Adam and Eve the entire created earth and told them to develop it and make it useful, with the implication that they would enjoy it and give thanks to him: "And God said to them, 'Be fruitful and multiply and fill the earth *and subdue it and have dominion* over the fish of the sea and over the birds of the heavens and over every living thing that moves on the earth'" (Gen. 1:28).

2. Because Adam and Eve sinned, God placed a curse on the entire natural world

The current state of the "natural world" is not the way God created it. After Adam and Eve sinned, one of the punishments that he imposed was to change the functioning of the natural world so that it was no longer an idyllic garden of Eden, but a much more dangerous and difficult place for human beings to live:

> And to Adam he said,
> "Because you have listened to the voice of your wife
> and have eaten of the tree
> of which I commanded you,
> 'You shall not eat of it,'
> cursed is the ground because of you;
> in pain you shall eat of it all the days of your life;
> thorns and thistles it shall bring forth for you;
> and you shall eat the plants of the field.
> By the sweat of your face
> you shall eat bread,
> till you return to the ground,
> for out of it you were taken;
> for you are dust,
> and to dust you shall return" (Gen. 3:17–19).

At that point early in the history of mankind, God caused a tremendous change in the beautiful creation that he had made. He "cursed" the ground so that rather than being a place from which Adam could eat food in overwhelming abundance, raising crops would require "pain" (v. 17) and hard toil, for "by the sweat of your face you shall eat bread" (v. 19).

a. The earth would now contain "thorns and thistles" and many other dangerous and harmful things

God's words to Adam told him that now there would be danger and harm on the earth, for "thorns and thistles" (Gen. 3:18) would come forth. Here the expression "thorns and thistles" functions as a kind of poetic image, a specific, concrete example that represents a multitude of things—such as hurricanes, floods, droughts, earthquakes, poisonous plants, poisonous snakes and insects, and hostile wild animals—that make the earth a place in which its natural beauty and usefulness are constantly mixed with other elements that bring destruction, sickness, and even death. Nature is not now what it was created to be, but is "fallen."

This component of a Christian worldview has significant implications for how people view the environment today. The creation is *not now perfect,* as it someday will be. At present, nature still exists in a "fallen" state. Therefore *what we think of as "natural" today is not always good.* We must protect children from putting their hands on the hole of a cobra or an adder, and we must build floodwalls and levies to protect against hurricanes, for example. We heat our homes in winter and air-condition them in summer rather than living all the time in "natural" temperature. We irrigate fields to grow crops where "nature" did not decide to grow them. We put screens on windows or spray insect repellant to keep "natural" mosquitoes from biting us. *Fallen nature today is not the garden of Eden!* We improve on nature in thousands of ways, to make it a more suitable place to live.

The fact that nature is not perfect today has many other implications. It means that people with a Christian worldview may decide that it is morally right to use insecticides to kill malaria-bearing mosquitoes, for example. They may decide it is right to clear flammable dead branches in national parks so as to prevent huge forest fires, and to cut down dry trees next to homes so that the homes are not consumed in the next flash forest fire. It means that it can be morally right, and even pleasing to God, to breed seedless grapes (that are not "natural") and seedless oranges and watermelons, or to use biological research and selective breeding of plants to develop varieties of rice or corn that are resistant to insects and mold, even though all of these things are somehow "tampering with nature." They are tampering with *fallen* nature, making natural products better. *That is what God intends us to do.* Part of our God-given task of subduing the earth and having dominion over it (Gen. 1:28) is inventing various measures to overcome the way in which nature is sometimes harmful to man and sometimes less than fully helpful. (Even in the unfallen world God told Adam and Eve to "subdue" it, implying that God wanted them to *improve on* nature as it was originally created—that is, God created it to be investigated and explored and developed!)

Of course, people can make mistakes in their attempts to subdue the earth, and there can be harmful results. But evaluating whether those attempts are "helpful" or "harmful" is *merely a matter of assessing the resulting facts*, not something to be dismissed merely because they are "tampering with nature." Attempting to make such modifications to what is "natural" is, in general, morally right and part of what God wants human beings to do with the earth. It is not an area in which Christians should automatically assume that what is "natural" is probably or always better. It is merely a matter of evaluating the measurable results.

By contrast, some people today, especially among the more radical environmental movements, do not understand the "fallen" status of the natural world but think that what is "natural" is the ideal, and therefore they regularly oppose ordinary, beneficial human efforts to improve on the way things exist in the natural world. This tendency leads some people to oppose every new factory, dam, or residential development project—no matter how carefully constructed and how sensitive it is to protecting the surrounding environment—all because their highest good—their "god" in some sense—is the earth *in its untouched natural state*. Thus they oppose everything that "tampers" with the earth, everything that changes an animal habitat or a growth of trees. This is making nature to be God, and it is not consistent with a biblical worldview.

It is not wrong *in principle*, as many environmentalists think it is, for human beings to modify the world, from the macro scale (such as hydroelectric dams and river-taming projects) to the micro scale (genetically modified organisms). God created the earth to be occupied and developed by human beings made in his image. Isaiah says that God "formed the earth and made it (he established it; he did not create it empty, *he formed it to be inhabited!*)" (Isa. 45:18).

b. God did not destroy the earth, but he left much that is good in it

A biblical worldview also recognizes that God did not *completely destroy* the earth, nor did he make it *entirely evil and harmful* (not all plants are poisonous, for example). He simply changed it so that it is not perfect now. The earth that God created is still "good" in many ways. It is *amazingly resourceful* because of the great treasures that he has placed in it for us to discover, enhance, and enjoy.

God did not tell Adam and Eve that they would be *unable* to eat of the ground, but that their existence on it would be *painful*, and in the same verse in which he said, "thorns and thistles it shall bring forth for you," he added, "and *you shall eat* the plants of the field" (Gen. 3:18).

This implies that there would still be much good for human beings to discover and use and enjoy in the earth.

In fact, many times in the Old Testament God promised abundant blessings on crops and livestock as a reward for the obedience of his people (see Deut. 28:1–14). With regard to various kinds of food, Paul could say, "*Everything created by God is good*, and nothing is to be rejected if it is received with thanksgiving, for it is made holy by the Word of God and prayer" (1 Tim. 4:4–5). Paul also said that God "richly provides us with everything to enjoy" (1 Tim. 6:17). This implies that human beings should feel free to use the earth's resources with joy and thanksgiving to God.

c. God promises a future time when the abundant prosperity of Eden will be restored to the earth

The Bible predicts a time after Christ's return when "the creation itself will be *set free* from its bondage to decay and obtain the freedom of the glory of the children of God" (Rom. 8:21). In that day,

> The wolf shall dwell with the lamb,
> and the leopard shall lie down with the young goat,
> and the calf and the lion and the fatted calf together;
> and a little child shall lead them....
> The nursing child shall play over the hole of the cobra,
> and the weaned child shall put his hand on the adder's den.
> They shall not hurt or destroy
> in all my holy mountain;
> for the earth shall be full of the knowledge if the LORD
> as the waters cover the sea (Isa. 11:6–9).

Therefore the prophet Amos could say that in this future time, crops will spring up and grow suddenly, just as soon as they are planted, and agricultural land will need no time to lie fallow and recover its productive abilities, because,

> "Behold the days are coming," declares the LORD,
> "when the plowman shall overtake the reaper
> and the treader of grapes him who sows the seed;
> the mountains shall drip sweet wine,
> and all the hills shall flow with it" (Amos 9:13).

Other Old Testament prophetic passages also predict this future time of a wonderful renewal of nature, so that "the desert shall rejoice and blossom like the crocus" (Isa. 35:1), and God will make the "desert" of

Zion "like the garden of the Lord" (Isa. 51:3; cf. 55:13). In New Testament times Peter echoed this in preaching that one day would come "the time for restoring all the things" (Acts 3:21).

I also believe that such restoration of the earth need not completely wait until Christ's return and God's miraculous renewing of the earth, but that the redeeming work of Christ provides the basis for us even now *to work incrementally toward the direction that God shows us is his future good intention for the earth*. Theologian and economist Cal Beisner puts it this way:

> The effects of the atoning death, victorious resurrection, and triumphant ascension of Christ, then, sweep over all of creation, including man, animals, plants, and even the ground itself. They include the restoration of the image of God in the redeemed and through them — and by common grace even through many who are not redeemed — the restoration of knowledge, holiness, and creativity in working out the cultural mandate, including human multiplication, subduing and ruling the earth, transforming the wilderness by cultivation into a garden, and guarding that garden against harm.[1]

3. God now wants human beings to develop the earth's resources and to use them wisely and joyfully

As stated earlier, at the very beginning of human history, immediately after God created Adam and Eve, he told them to

> "Be fruitful and multiply and fill the earth *and subdue it and have dominion* ... over every living thing that moves on the earth" (Gen. 1:28).

He also told them how they were to care specifically for the garden of Eden — primarily "to work it and keep it" (2:15).

This responsibility to "subdue" the earth and "have dominion" over it implies that God expected Adam and Eve and their descendents to explore and develop the earth's resources in such a way that they would bring benefit to themselves and other human beings. (The Hebrew word *kabâsh* means "to subdue, dominate, bring into servitude or bondage" and is used later, for example, of subduing the land of Canaan so that it would serve and provide for the people of Israel; cf. Num. 32:22, 29; Josh. 18:1).

---

1. E. Calvin Beisner, *Where Garden Meets Wilderness* (Grand Rapids: Acton Institute and Eerdmans, 1997), 107.

a. Subduing the earth after the fall

The responsibility to develop the earth and enjoy its resources continued after Adam and Eve's sin, for even then God told them, "You shall eat the plants of the field" (Gen. 3:18).

David also says in Psalm 8,

> What is man that you are mindful of him ...?
> You have given him dominion over the works of your hands;
> you have put all things under his feet,
> all sheep and oxen,
> and also the beasts of the field,
> the birds of the heavens, and the fish of the sea,
> whatever passes along the paths of the seas (Ps. 8:4–8).

Another evidence that our responsibility to "subdue" the earth continues after the fall is the very necessity of cultivating the earth in order to grow food to eat. We have to "subdue" the earth to some extent or we will all starve!

Moreover, the fact that after the flood God explicitly told Noah, "Every moving thing that lives shall be food for you" (Gen. 9:3), confirms the fact that responsibility to exercise dominion over the natural creation, including the animal kingdom, is still given by God to human beings. In the New Testament, Paul implies that eating meat is morally right and no one should pass judgment on another person because of this (see Rom. 14:2–3; 1 Cor. 8:7–13; 1 Tim. 4:4; also Mark 7:19, where it says that Jesus "declared all foods clean").

Jesus also taught that *human beings are much more valuable in God's sight than animals*, and this tends to confirm our continuing responsibility to "have dominion" over the animal kingdom and to seek to make animals useful for us, since they are God's good provision for the human race. Jesus said, "Of how much *more value* is a man than a sheep!" (Matt. 12:12). He also said, "Look at the birds of the air.... Are you not of *more value* than they?" (Matt. 6:26). And again he said, "You are of *more value* than many sparrows" (Matt. 10:31).

However, these commands to subdue the earth and have dominion over it *do not mean that we should use the earth in a wasteful or destructive way* or intentionally treat animals with cruelty. Rather, "whoever is righteous has regard for the life of his beast" (Prov. 12:10), and God told the people of Israel to take care to protect fruit trees during a time of war (see Deut. 20:19–20). In addition, the command, "You shall love your neighbor as yourself" (Matt. 22:39), implies a responsibility to think of the needs of other human beings, even those who will come in future generations. Therefore we should not use the earth in such a way that we destroy its resources or make them unable to be used for future generations. *We should use the resources of the earth wisely, as good stewards*, not wastefully or abusively.

b. Contrasting a biblical view of the earth and a radical environmentalist view

This biblical principle about the moral goodness of developing and enjoying the earth's resources stands in contrast to the views of radical environmentalists, many of whom hold to "untouched nature" as their ideal and therefore object to activities like the use of animals (such as guinea pigs or chimpanzees) in medical research. Environmentalists will attempt to block many new building projects through the use of lawsuits claiming that some species of turtle or other small creature like the pygmy owl will be damaged.[2]

For instance, farmers in California's San Joaquin Valley have had the water they use for growing crops diverted to the Pacific Ocean to save a three-inch fish called the delta smelt.[3] As a result, unemployment rates have hit 40% in the region, which provides much of the produce for the rest of the nation and the world. Thus this environmentalist action has caused food shortages and higher prices, again harming the poor most of all. *The Wall Street Journal* wrote:

> California has a new endangered species on its hands in the San Joaquin Valley — farmers. Thanks to environmental regulations designed to protect the likes of the three-inch long delta smelt, one of America's premier agricultural regions is suffering in a drought made worse by federal regulations.... The state's water emergency is unfolding thanks to the latest mishandling of the Endangered Species Act. Last December, the U.S. Fish and Wildlife Service issued what is known as a "biological opinion" imposing water reductions on the San Joaquin Valley and environs to safeguard the federally protected hypomesus transpacificus, a.k.a., the delta smelt. As a result, tens of billions of gallons of water from mountains east and north of

---

2. "Pygmy owl leaves a conservation legacy." *Arizona Star* (Aug. 5, 2005), www.azstarnet.com/sn/related/87256; and Leslie Carlson and Pete Thomas, "Back off, Bambi," *Los Angeles Times* (June 15, 2004), http://articles.latimes.com/2004/jun/15/news/os-deer15.

3. Peter Fimrite, "U.S. Issues Rules to Protect Delta Smelt," *San Francisco Chronicle* (Dec. 16, 2008). www.sfgate.com/cgi-bin/article.cgi?f=/c/a/2008/12/15/MNDD14OIOF.DTL.

Sacramento have been channeled away from farmers and into the ocean, leaving hundreds of thousands of acres of arable land fallow or scorched.... The result has already been devastating for the state's farm economy. In the inland areas affected by the court-ordered water restrictions, the jobless rate has hit 14.3%, with some farming towns like Mendota seeing unemployment numbers near 40%. Statewide, the rate reached 11.6% in July, higher than it has been in 30 years. In August, 50 mayors from the San Joaquin Valley signed a letter asking President Obama to observe the impact of the draconian water rules firsthand.[4]

Secular environmentalists object to the killing of deer or geese in residential neighborhoods, even when these animals are so numerous they have become a significant public nuisance and even a danger to health (as with the prevalence of ticks that spread Lyme disease).[5] They will object to the killing of mosquitoes with pesticides even when the mosquitoes spread West Nile Virus and (in Africa) spread malaria that kills millions of people.[6] It seems to me a correct application of Matthew 10:31 to think that Jesus would have said, "People are of *more value* than many millions of mosquitoes."

Another tendency of secular culture is to view much use of the earth's resources with *fear* — fear that human beings will damage some part of "untouched nature," which seems to be the environmentalists' ideal. Such fear will lead people to oppose hydroelectric dams (they harm fish),[7] windmills (they harm birds),[8] oil and natural gas development (oil rigs ruin the appearance of nature, and there might be a spill),[9] any burning of coal or oil or gas (they might harm the climate),[10] and any use of nuclear energy (it might lead to an accident).[11]

---

4. "California's Man-Made Drought," *Wall Street Journal* (Sept. 2, 2009), A14. http://online.wsj.com/article/SB10001424052970204731804574384731898375624.html.

5. See www.eradicatelymedisease.org/environment.html.

6. Michael Doyle, "Environmentalists challenge pesticide rule," *McClatchy Newspapers* (Nov. 29, 2006).

7. "How Dams Harm Rivers," www.imhooked.com/for/damsharm.html; and Erik Robinson, "Latest dam plan already under fire from groups," *The Columbian* (May 6, 2008), www.wildsalmon.org/library/lib-detail.cfm?docID=772.

8. John Ritter, "Wind Turbines Take Toll on Birds of Prey," *USA Today* (Jan. 4, 2005).

9. "Congress Lifts Offshore Drilling Moratorium," World Wildlife Fund News. http://wwf.worldwildlife.org/site/PageServer?pagename=can_results_offshore_drilling.

10. See www.energyjustice.net/coal/.

11. "Nuclear Energy = Dangerous Energy." www.greenpeace.org/seasia/en/news/nukes-endanger-indonesia.

They are always emphasizing the dangers (whether real or imagined) and never realistically evaluate an *insignificant risk* of danger in comparison to a *certain promise* of great benefit. Some of them give the impression that they think the major problem with the whole earth is the presence of human beings!

Radical environmentalist Paul Watson of the Sea Shepherd Institute wrote:

> Today, escalating human populations have vastly exceeded global carrying capacity and now produce massive quantities of solid, liquid, and gaseous waste. Biological diversity is being threatened by over-exploitation, toxic pollution, agricultural mono-culture, invasive species, competition, habitat destruction, urban sprawl, oceanic acidification, ozone depletion, global warming, and climate change. It's a runaway train of ecological calamities. It's a train that carries all the earth's species as unwilling passengers with humans as the manically insane engineers unwilling to use the brake pedal.[12]

Watson also called human beings the "AIDS of the Earth" and declared that human beings must reduce the world's population to less than one billion people (from its current 6.8 billion), dwell in communities no larger than "20,000 people and separated from other communities by wilderness areas," and recognize themselves as "earthlings" dwelling in a primitive state with other species. Watson wrote, "Curing a body of cancer requires radical and invasive therapy, and therefore, curing the biosphere of the human virus will also require a radical and invasive approach."[13]

Speaking about the environment in Great Britain, John Guillebaud, co-chairman of Optimum Population Trust and emeritus professor of family planning at University College in London, told the *Sunday Times* that parents ought to consider the environment first when they plan to have a child. He said, "The greatest thing anyone in Britain could do to help the future of the planet would be to have one less child."[14]

A report by that trust entitled *A Population-Based Climate Strategy* said, "Population limitation should therefore be seen as the most

---

12. Paul Watson, "The Beginning of the End for Planet Earth?" Sea Shepherd Conservation Society (May 4, 2007). www.seashepherd.org/news-and-media/editorial–070504–1.html#.

13. Ibid.

14. John Guillebaud, "Having Large Families Is an Eco-Crime," *Sunday Times* (May 6, 2007). http://www.washingtontimes.com/news/2009/jul/14/catastrophic-budget-failure.

cost-effective carbon offsetting strategy available to individuals and nations."[15]

By contrast, God's perspective in the Bible is that the creation of human beings in his image and placing them on the earth to rule over it as his representatives is the crowning achievement of God in his entire work of creation.

A Christian worldview would consider it morally right—and pleasing to God, and no cause for irrational fear—when human beings wisely exercise widespread and effective dominion over the earth and its creatures. This worldview will present no moral objection to eating meat from animals or to wearing leather or fur made from animal skins. (God himself clothed Adam and Eve with animal skins [Gen. 3:21], setting a precedent for the beneficial use of animals for human beings.) Such a Christian worldview would also think it morally right—even morally imperative—to use animals (in a reasonably compassionate way) for medical research that can lead to solutions to human diseases.

Another implication of this component of a Christian worldview is that *we should view the development and production of goods from the earth as something morally good*, not merely an evil kind of "materialism." God placed in the earth resources that would enable man to develop much more than food and clothing. There are resources that enable the construction of beautiful homes, automobiles, airplanes, computers, and millions of other consumer goods. While these things can be misused, and while people's hearts can have wrongful attitudes about them (such as pride, jealousy, and coveting), *the things in themselves* should be viewed as *morally good* because they are part of God's intention in placing us on the earth to subdue it and have dominion over it.

Therefore the creation of large amounts of wealth in some of the world's more economically developed nations should not be seen as something that is morally evil in itself, but rather something that is fundamentally good. It is part of what God intended when he told Adam and Eve to subdue the earth and have dominion over it. This means that wealthy nations and wealthy individuals should not automatically be considered "evil" or even "unspiritual." Rather, we should do what we can to help other nations achieve similar levels of wealth for themselves—as is happening every year in more and more countries around the world. If subduing the earth and making it useful for

---

15. Peter J. Smith and Steve Jalsevac, "Environmentalist Extremists Call Humanity 'Virus' a 'Cancer'; Large Families Guilty of 'Eco-Crime,'" *LifeSiteNews.com* (May 8, 2007). www.lifesitenews.com/ldn/2007/may/07050812.html.

mankind is a good activity, then it is right to encourage many different kinds of development of the earth's resources and many different kinds of production of material goods from the earth.

God's command to subdue the earth and have dominion over it also implies that *it was not his intention for all human beings to live in abject poverty or live as subsistence farmers barely surviving from crop to crop.* Rather, his intention was that all people should enjoy the abundance of the earth's resources with thanksgiving to him. This implies that it is *morally right* for us to seek to overcome poverty wherever it is found. It is also *morally right* for us to help the world's poor to have the ability to develop and enjoy the earth's good resources in abundance.

4. God created an abundant and resourceful earth

Did God create an earth that would run out of essential resources because of human development? That is not the picture given in the Bible. God created an earth that he pronounced to be "very good" (Gen. 1:31). Although he cursed the earth after the sin of Adam and Eve, he also promised a future time when *this same earth* would be renewed and bring forth abundant prosperity (see above, pp. 116–17). That renewed earth will have the same resources (it is not a new creation),[16] but it will have the dangers and harmfulness and painfulness to man removed. It will once more become abundantly productive like the original garden of Eden.

Therefore the Bible's picture of the earth *in general* is that it has abundant resources that God has put there to bring great benefit to us as human beings made in his image. There is no hint that mankind will ever exhaust the earth's resources by developing them and using them wisely.

Does current information about the earth confirm this idea that it has abundant resources? That is the question of the next section.

B. THE CURRENT STATE OF THE EARTH'S RESOURCES

Many questions about applying biblical teachings to environmental questions have to do with *correctly evaluating the facts* about the current situation of the earth. What is the current status of the earth's resources, and what can we learn from long-term trend lines on various resources?

---

16. See Wayne Grudem, *Systematic Theology* (Grand Rapids: Zondervan: 1994), 1160–61.

1. Are we destroying the earth?

People often fear that we are about to run out of land for food or run out of clean water or some other essential resource. That in turn leads them to live with a faint cloud of continual guilt whenever they drive a car or water their lawn or use paper cups and paper plates and to live with a vague fear that in a few decades the earth's resources might be exhausted and unable to sustain human life.

In this section I present data indicating that *there is no good reason to think we will ever run out of any essential natural resource.* God has created for us an earth that has incredible abundance, and whenever it seems that some resource is becoming scarce, he has given us the wisdom to invent useful substitutes. I look at data regarding the following factors:

a. World population
b. Land for growing food
c. Water
d. Clean air
e. Waste disposal
f. Global forests
g. Species loss
h. Herbicides and pesticides
i. Life expectancy

2. The importance of using information from long-term, worldwide trends rather than short-term, local stories of disasters

In many conversations I have found that people's "vague impressions" about what is happening to the earth are almost always wrong. People have developed their opinions, not from actual data showing the true state of the earth as a whole and showing long-term trends, but from a barrage of media reports about specific local incidents where something has gone wrong—a certain oil spill, or a crop failure and famine in some country, or the cutting down of trees and loss of forest area in some country, or a polar bear jumping off a piece of melting ice somewhere in the Arctic, and so forth.

But we should always keep in mind that newspapers need readers and television programs need viewers, and fear is one of the great ways of increasing an audience. Therefore the media have a natural bias toward reporting alarming events—whether an airplane crash or a serial killer or a water or food shortage in some place or another. But such individual events almost always have specific local causes that may not exist elsewhere.

Another factor contributing to people's general impressions of resource scarcity is the existence of a number of special interest organizations that raise more money and keep themselves employed only by putting out press releases declaring that worldwide environmental disaster is just around the corner. Bjorn Lomborg, a Danish environmentalist and economic statistician, cites numerous examples of astoundingly blatant dishonesty in the use of data in publications by environmentalist organizations such as the Worldwatch Institute or the World Wide Fund for Nature or Greenpeace.[17]

For example, Lomborg writes that Lester Brown and the Worldwatch Institute make statements such as "The key environmental indicators are increasingly negative. Forests are shrinking, water tables are falling, soils are eroding, wetlands are disappearing, fisheries are collapsing, range-lands are deteriorating, rivers are running dry, temperatures are rising, coral reefs are dying, and plant and animal species are disappearing." Lomborg adds, "Powerful reading—stated entirely without references."[18]

Lomborg goes on to refute these claims. He says that reports from the Food and Agricultural Organization (FAO) of the United Nations show that global forest cover has increased from 30.04% of the global land area in 1950 to 30.89% in 1994.[19] With regard to water shortages, Lomborg writes:

> One of the most widely used college books on the environment, *Living in the Environment*, claims that "according to a 1995 World Bank study, 30 countries containing 40 percent of the world's population (2.3 billion people) now experience chronic water shortages that threaten their agriculture and industry and the health of their people." This World Bank study is referred to in many different environment texts with slightly differing figures. Unfortunately, none mentions a source.
>
> With a good deal of help from the World Bank, I succeeded in locating the famous document. It turns out that the myth had its origin in a hastily drawn up press release. The headline

17. See Bjorn Lomborg, *The Skeptical Environmentalist: Measuring the real State of the World* (Cambridge: Cambridge University Press, 2001), 8–31.

18. Ibid., 16.

19. Ibid.

on the press release was "The world is facing a water crisis: 40 percent of the world's population suffers from chronic water shortage." If you read on, however, it suddenly becomes clear that the vast majority of the 40 percent are not people who use too much water but those who have no access to water or sanitation facilities — the exact opposite point. If one also reads the memo to which the press release relates, it shows that the global water crisis which Lester Brown and others are worried about affects not 40 percent but about 4 percent of the world's population. And, yes, it wasn't 30, but 80 countries the World Bank was referring to.[20]

Therefore it is important for us to find some reliable data that accurately show the long-term trends in the earth's resources. What is the overall result of human development on the world environment that we live in? Is the presence of mankind actually destroying the earth? Taken as a whole, is human development of the earth's resources a helpful or harmful thing?

These questions are especially important in light of the biblical teachings that I discussed earlier (see pp. 112 — 23), especially the teaching that the earth God created was "very good" (Gen. 1:31) and the teaching that God told Adam and Eve that they were to "be fruitful and multiply and *fill the earth* and *subdue* it and *have dominion* over the fish of the sea and over the birds of the heavens and over every living thing that moves" (v. 28).

If God created an earth for man to subdue and develop, then it is reasonable to think that he created (a) an earth with abundant resources able to be developed, and (b) an earth that would benefit from man's developing it, not one that would be destroyed through such development. In addition, if God wanted human beings to "fill the earth," then it seems reasonable to expect that the spread of human population over the earth could be done without necessarily harming or destroying it.

The "curse" that God put on the earth in Genesis 3:17 – 18 would make development of the earth's resources more difficult and more painful, but it would not change the basic character of such development or turn it into something harmful rather than helpful. Instead, subduing the earth would be even more necessary in a land filled with "thorns and thistles" that had to be removed before the land was a suitable and enjoyable place for human beings.

20. Ibid., 20.

Our overall viewpoint on these matters affects our basic expectations. Do we basically expect that development of the earth's resources will be *helpful* or *harmful* to the earth? Do we expect that obedience to God's commands will bring benefits to ourselves and to the earth or bring harm to both? Do we tend to assume that God made an earth that is about to run out of all sorts of resources necessary for human survival, or do we think that he made an incredibly abundant earth with incredibly rich and diverse resources that would be useful for human life and enjoyment?

If it is God's purpose for us to develop and enjoy the earth's resources with thanksgiving to him, then we would also expect it would be Satan's purpose to oppose and hinder such developmental activity at every point and in every way possible.

In the following section I will refer to *long-term trends* that show remarkable human progress in making the earth useful for mankind and doing so in a sustainable way. As the teachings of Genesis would suggest, modern evidence confirms that *God created an incredibly abundant and resourceful earth*, and he also created human beings with the wisdom and skill to develop and use those resources for God's glory and with thanksgiving to him.

3. Long-term trends show that human beings will be able to live on the earth, enjoying ever-increasing prosperity, and never exhausting its resources

Many of the statistics I cite below come from one of the most influential books of the past decade, *The Skeptical Environmentalist* by Bjorn Lomborg. The advantage of Lomborg's book is that he is an expert in the fair and accurate use of statistics and repeatedly bases his arguments on official, publicly available information from sources such as United Nations agencies and the World Bank.[21] And he quotes long-term trends, not just an isolated bit of data from a two- or three-year period.

Because Lomborg's book mounted a massive challenge to widely accepted environmentalist views, it was severely criticized by a number of writers and organizations. But Lomborg has responded in an articulate and sensible way to the most serious of these criticisms, and anyone can read the exchanges on the Internet. From what I have read of the controversy, it appears clear to me that Lomborg has gotten the best of the arguments and that his critics are careless and emotional in their claims, but not very persuasive. It is not surprising that *Time* magazine

---

named Lomborg one of the world's 100 most influential people in 2004[22] and *Foreign Policy* magazine named him one of the top 100 public intellectuals in 2008.[23] Also in 2008, *Esquire* magazine named him one of the 75 most influential people of the twenty-first century.[24]

a. World population

The world population has grown from 750 million people in 1750 to 6.8 billion people today.[25] As the chart below shows, the rapid increase in growth began around 1950 but is already slowing down and is predicted to end at a world population of about 11 billion around the year 2200.[26] Other, more recent projections show world population stabilizing at even lower levels (such as 8–9 billion) and then declining, as the population already is doing in Western Europe.[27]

WORLD POPULATION 1750-2200

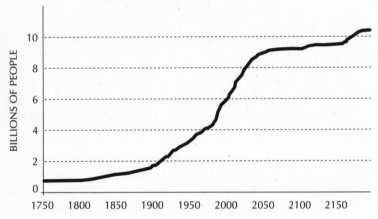

Source: The World at Six Billion, United Nations Population Division (October 1999), 5. www.un.org/esa/population/publications/sixbillion/sixbilpart1.pdf.

---

22. "Bjorn Lomborg," *Time* (April 26, 2004). www.time.com/time/magazine/article/0,9171,994022,00.html?iid=chix-sphere.

23. "The Top 100 Public Intellectuals: Bios," *Foreign Policy* (April 2008). www.foreignpolicy.com/story/cms.php?story_id=4293.

24. "The Heretic's New Book," *Esquire* (Sept. 24, 2007). www.esquire.com/features/esquire–100/globalwarming1007.

25. World Population Clock. www.worldometers.info/population/.

26. "World Population Would Stabilize at Nearly 11 Billion By Year 2200." www.un.org/News/Press/docs/1998/19980202.POP656.html.

27. Chart from Bjorn Lomborg, *The Skeptical Environmentalist*, 46, fig. 11.

The reason world population grew so quickly is that modern development gave people better access to food, water, medical care, and sanitation, so on average they lived much longer. But the reason the world population will stabilize is that as nations increase in wealth, their birth rate declines, as is evident in the smaller birthrates in Europe today, for instance.[28] But will we run out of space on the earth? No, there is much more available space for people to live. Some of the most densely populated countries in the world are in Europe, as shown on the following chart:

Country	Population/sq. mile
Netherlands	1,023
Belgium	880
United Kingdom	693
Germany	598
Italy	500
Switzerland	470

These figures are much higher than the United States, which has a population density of 79.6 persons per square mile.[29] But as anyone who has visited the Netherlands, Belgium, Germany, or the United Kingdom can attest, these countries have vast areas of uncrowded farmland and open spaces.

These can be seen in comparison with the following countries, which are commonly thought to have high population densities:[30]

Country	Population/sq. mile
Japan	873
India	851
China	353

28. Mark Henderson, "Europe Shrinking as Birthrates Decline," *London Times Online* (March 28, 2003). www.timesonline.co.uk/tol/news/world/article1123982.ece.

29. US Census Bureau, Census 2000 Redistricting Data (PL 94–171) Summary File. Cartography: Population Division, US Census Bureau. www.census.gov/population/cen2000/atlas/censr01–103.pdf#page=3.

30. These figures are converted from kilometers to square miles. For population density estimates, see US Census Bureau, International Data Base. www.census.gov/ipc/www/idb/region.php.

To get an idea of what these densities mean, we can compare them with a few states in the United States as well:[31]

State	Population/sq. mile
New Jersey	1,134.4
Massachusetts	809.8
New York	401.9
Florida	296.4
Ohio	277.3
Pennsylvania	274.0
Illinois	223.4
Michigan	175.0
Indiana	169.5
North Carolina	165.2
Wisconsin	98.8

Certainly our more densely populated states have a number of large cities, but they also have vast amounts of land area in forests, parks, and agricultural use.

Nor does increasing population seem to change the total use of land in a nation by very much, mostly because people move into cities and much of the rural area of a country is left untouched. For example, between 1945 and 1992 the US population almost doubled (from about 140 million to about 256 million people; it is now over 307 million).[32] But as the following chart indicates, a doubling of US population resulted in almost no change in the amount of land used for crops, forests, or grasslands.[33]

The urban area of the nation increased from 1% of the land to 3% of the land in 2002 and contains 79% of the population, but there is still an immense amount of land remaining.[34]

---

31. US Census Bureau, Census 2000 Summary File 1. http://factfinder.census.gov/ servlet/GCTTable?_bm=y&-ds_name=DEC_2000_SF1_U&-CONTEXT=gct&-mt_ name=DEC_2000_SF1_U_GCTPH1_US9&-redoLog=false&-_caller=geoselect&-geo_ id=&-format=US–9|US–9S&-_lang=en.

32. Population: 1900 to 2002. www.census.gov/statab/hist/HS–01.pdf and www.census. gov/population/www/popclockus.html.

33. Stephen Moore and Julian Simon, *It's Getting Better All the Time: Greatest Trends of the Last 100 Years* (Washington, DC: CATO Institute, 2000), 203.

34. Major Uses of Land in the United States 2002, Urban and Residential Land Use. www. ers.usda.gov/publications/EIB14/eib14g.pdf

U.S. LAND USE BY TYPE, 1945 AND 1992

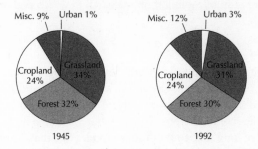

1945

1992

Does an increase in population mean that people are more crowded in their living space? No, because as nations increase in wealth over time, people tend to build larger houses and have more rooms per person rather than fewer rooms. This is seen in the following chart:

ROOMS PER PERSON

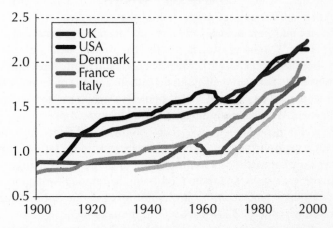

SOURCES: First European Quality of Life Survey: Social Dimensions of Housing, European Foundation for the Improvement of Living and Working Conditions, Table 2: Average number of rooms per person, by age and area, 23. http://www.eurofound.europa.eu/pubdocs/2005/94/en/1/ef0594en.pdf.
University of Liege, International Centre for Research and Information on the Public and Cooperative Economy, Housing Statistics in the European Union (2002), and U.S. Department of Energy, Energy Information Administration, Housing Characteristics 1993 (June 1995), 46-49, Table 3.4: cited in Robert Rector, "How Poor are America's Poor? Examining the 'Plague' of Poverty in America," Heritage Foundation Backgrounder, No. 2064 (August 27, 2007), 7, Table 3. http://s3.amazonaws.com/thf_media/2007/pdf/bg2064.pdf.
Centre for Housing and Welfare, Housing in Denmark (September 2007) http://vbn.aau.dk/ws/fbspretrieve/13695523/Housing_130907.pdf.
Peter Flora, ed. Growth to Limits: The Western European Welfare States Since World War II, Vol. 2 (Berlin: Walter D. Gruyter and Co., 1986), 295, 302, 311, 324.
Stanley Lebergott, The American Economy: Income, Wealth, and Want (Princeton, N.J.: Princeton University Press, 1976), 94-95, 258.

In other words, world population is stabilizing, and there is an immense amount of room left on the earth in which everyone can live comfortably.

b. Land for growing food

But will we run out of land to grow enough food to feed the world's population? No, not at all. Out of the total ice-free land surface of the earth, about 24% of the land is "arable"[35] — that is, it could produce an acceptable level of food crops. That is about 3.2 billion hectares (7.9 billion acres) of land that could produce food. (The remaining land is in areas that are too cold or too dry, are too rocky or hard, or have soil that is too poor for crop use.) But this potential crop land is more than three times the area actually used for growing crops in any given year at the present time.[36] That is, we currently grow crops on *less than one-third of the earth's arable land.* How many people could the available land feed? Roger Revelle, former director of Harvard University's Center for Population Studies, estimated as far back as 1984 that even if this land produced less than half the average production of the "Corn Belt" in the United States, it could feed about 35 billion people "at an average intake of 2,350 kcal per day."[37] Another estimate was that the available land could readily feed about 18 billion people per year.[38] This is still nearly three times the current world population of about 6.8 billion, and it is much more than the best current estimates of world population stabilizing at about 11 billion people. We are not running out of land to grow crops.

In addition, *food production per acre* has increased remarkably in the last sixty years and will likely continue to increase in the future through better farming methods and greater use of modern technology. Our ability to grow more and more food — and better food — on more and more kinds of land should continue to increase, due to the amazing inventiveness that God has placed in the human mind.

As this chart[39] from the Food and Agriculture Organization of the United Nations shows, the amount of cereal grain grown per hectare in

---

35. Roger Revelle, "The World Supply of Agricultural Land," *The Resourceful Earth*, ed. Julian Simon and Herman Kahn (New York: Basil Blackwell, 1984), 184.

36. Ibid., 185.

37. Ibid., 186. A "kcal" is a kilogram calorie — that is, 1,000 grams of calories.

38. "Resources Unlimited," National Center for Policy Analysis" (Feb. 19, 1996). www. ncpa.org/sub/dpd/index.php?Article_ID=12935: citing Thomas Lambert, "Defusing the 'Population Bomb' With Free Markets," Policy Study No. 129, Feb. 1996, Center for the Study of American Business, Washington University, St. Louis, Missouri.

39. Chart taken from *The State of Humanity*, ed. Julian Simon (Oxford and Cambridge, Mass: Blackwell, 1995), 381.

WORLD CEREAL YIELDS 1950–90

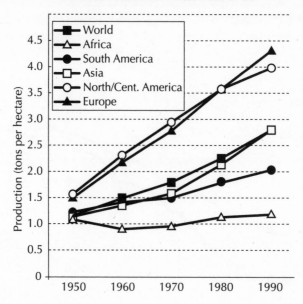

North America, Central America, and Europe more than doubled between 1950 and 1990 (the top two lines), and the amount grown per hectare in the world as a whole was showing a significantly increasing trend. (A "hectare" is a metric unit for measuring area and is equal to 2.47 acres.) These gains have come about through higher-yielding seeds, modern fertilizer, increased pest control, new plants that tolerate colder weather, and giving an earlier start to the growing season. [40]

Because of this increase in production of food crops, the last fifty years have seen a steady increase in the amount of food calories consumed per day per person in the world as a whole and in the developing world in particular, as the following chart indicates:[41]

As this chart indicates, there has been a steady increase in available food and in the food actually consumed. Lomborg says, "Although there are now twice as many of us as there were in 1961, each of us has *more* to eat, in both developed and developing countries. Fewer people are starving. Food is far cheaper." [42] (Of course, the number of calories

---

40. See further discussion in Dennis Avery, "The World's Rising Food Productivity," in ibid., 376–91.

41. Chart from Lomborg, *The Skeptical Environmentalist*, 61, figure 23.

42. Lomborg, op.cit., 60.

DAILY CALORIES PER CAPITA 1964-2030

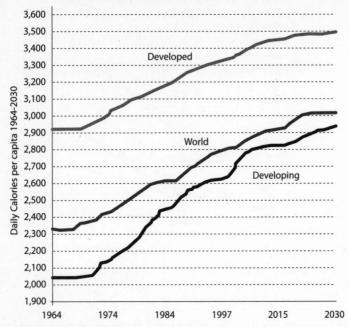

Daily intake of calories per capita in the industrial and developing counties and world. 1964-2030 (projected).
Source: Global and regional food consumption patterns and trends, Food and Agriculture Organization of the United Nations. www.fao.org/docrep/005/ac911e/ac911e05.htm.

consumed has become *too great* for many people in developed countries, but that is another sort of problem!)

This does not mean that there are no remaining problems. Estimates are that the percentage of the population still starving in the world is around 12%. (The United Nations defines "starving" as not getting enough food to perform light physical activity.)[43] But the question is the long-term direction of the trend lines, and these are wonderfully encouraging. From 1970 to 2010 (estimate), a period of forty years, the percentage of the world's people who are starving has fallen from 35% to 12%.[44] However, progress has not been uniform in all parts of the world. While most regions of the world have seen a rapid

43. Ibid., 61.
44. Ibid.

decline since 1970 in the proportion of people living in starving conditions, the progress in sub-Saharan Africa has not kept pace with the progress in the rest of the world, as the following chart indicates:

PROPORTION OF STARVING IN PERCENT – DEVELOPING WORLD BY REGION 1969-2015

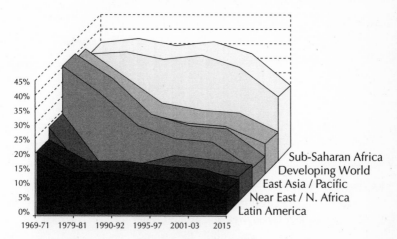

Sub-Saharan Africa
Developing World
East Asia / Pacific
Near East / N. Africa
Latin America

1969-71   1979-81   1990-92   1995-97   2001-03   2015

Sources: The State of Food and Agriculture, United Nations Food and Agriculture Organization (2006), 85, Table 16. www.fao.org/righttofood/kc/downloads/vl/docs/AH523.pdf.
The State of Food Insecurity in the World, United Nations Food and Agriculture Organization (2006), 4. http://ftp.fao.org/docrep/fao/009/a0750e/a0750e00a.pdf.

c. Water

In a remarkable development over a thirty-year period, the percentage of people in developing countries with access to clean drinking water increased from 30% in 1970 to 80% in 2000![45] As mentioned above, Lomborg also documents how a widely used college textbook on the environment quotes erroneous statistics on water shortages that it claims were from a World Bank study.[46]

But are we using up the world's supply of water too quickly? Not at all.

There is a massive amount of water on the earth — 71% of the earth's surface is covered by water. This is how the water is distributed:

---

45. Ibid., 21.
46. Ibid, 20.

PEOPLE WITH ACCESS TO DRINKING WATER AND SANITATION[47]

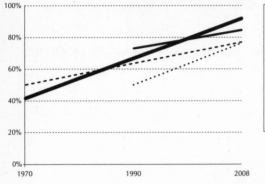

Drinking water (Solid Lines)

World Average

Developing Regions

Sanitation (Broken Lines)

World Average

Developing Regions

TOTAL WATER ON EARTH

Water in the oceans	97.20%
Water in polar ice	2.15%
Remaining water, including all fresh water lakes, river, and ground water (water under the ground)	0.65%
Total	100.00% [48]

Now, of that 0.65% of water that is potentially available for human use, some of it is in areas so remote that it is inaccessible to human beings for all practical purposes. But out of the remaining water that is accessible for human use, *we still use less than 17% of the annually renewable water on the earth.* That is not at all 17% of the fresh water on earth, but just 17% of the "readily accessible and renewable water" that is refreshed each year on the earth.[49] The current high-end predictions of how much will be used in 2025 are just 22% of the readily accessible, annually renewed water.[50] Who uses most of the water? In terms of global usage, here is the breakdown:

Therefore, do we need to be concerned that we will use up the world's water in the future? I do not think so, for at least two reasons:

47. Ibid., 22, figure 5.
48. Ibid., 149–50.
49. Ibid., 150–51.
50. Ibid., 150.

GLOBAL USAGE OF WATER

Agriculture	69.0%
Industry	23.0%
Households	8.0%
Total	100.00%[51]

(1) There is an incredible amount of waste in the current usage of water in many countries, both through leakage and through inefficient agricultural usage.[52] But countries such as Israel have developed highly efficient water use, with both a drip irrigation system and effective water recycling.[53] If water prices were allowed to rise so that users were much more responsible in how they used water, much higher efficiencies could be achieved.[54] (2) Desalination of water is becoming more and more economically feasible. The price today for removing the salt from ocean water is about $.50/cubic meter, or less than one-fifth of a cent per gallon. This is actually less than the $.69/cubic meter that I currently pay at my home in Arizona! The average price of water today in the United States is $.74/cubic meter, while in the United Kingdom it is $2.37 and in Germany, $3.01/cubic meter.[55] Yet many of these costs reflect not only the raw production costs, but also delivery costs and no doubt other governmental fees. Actually, the city of Carlsbad in Southern California was to begin construction of a desalination plant in 2010, which will provide enough water for the daily use of 300,000 people.[56] Some countries today already derive a significant portion of their water supplies from salt water, such as Kuwait (over half of its total use), Saudi Arabia, and Libya. Worldwide, desalted water still makes up just 0.2% of all water use.[57] Therefore, when we take into account the stabilization of world population in the future, the increased efficiencies with which more developed countries use their water supply, the more than 80% of available and renewable fresh water supplies that are not being used today, and the virtually unlimited supply of water found in the oceans for a slightly higher price, we have no reason to expect that the earth will run out of water, *ever*. In providing the earth with water, God truly provided us with a wonderfully abundant resource.

51. Ibid., 154.
52. Ibid., 154–56.
53. Ibid.
54. Ibid.
55. *Wall Street Journal*, Asian edition (July 31–Aug. 2, 2009), 3.
56. Ibid. (July 10–12, 2009), 14–15.
57. Lomborg, *The Skeptical Environmentalist*, 153.

So, are there local and regional areas where water supply is scarce and difficult to obtain? Yes, but those are local problems and deal with *access to water*, not with the total supply of water on the earth. In many cases, local water shortages are due either to lack of economic development of the nation as a whole (and therefore the lack of ability to transport, purify, deliver, and pay for water), or to local or national legal, economic, or political hindrances to water access.

For example, as I mentioned earlier, the state of California sits right next to the inexhaustible water resources of the Pacific Ocean, but local political opposition to constructing desalination plants has hindered Californians from tapping into this inexhaustible source of water to meet all their needs.

In addition, in 2009 there was a terrible and totally unnecessary *man-made drought* in central California. The San Joaquin Valley (including the cities of Fresno and Bakersfield) is one of the most productive agricultural areas of the entire world, but the water needed to flow from upstream rivers into that valley was diverted from it due to enforcement of environmentalist regulations. In December 2008, the US Fish and Wildlife Service issued a "biological opinion" that would protect a tiny three-inch fish called the delta smelt. As a result of this regulation, literally tens of billions of gallons of water have been diverted away and are flowing out into the ocean, leaving much of this agricultural land parched and dry and throwing thousands of farmers and agricultural workers out of work. Both Governor Arnold Schwarzenegger and President Barack Obama had the authority to take action to get the water flowing again, but both refuse to do so, presumably because of their indebtedness to environmentalist forces.[58] The same Jesus who told his disciples, "You are of more value than many sparrows" (Matt. 10:31), would no doubt say to these needlessly drought-stricken Californian farmers, "You are of more value than many delta smelt!" And he would get the water running again, as would anyone who realizes that California's farmers and productive farmlands are much more valuable than an insignificant three-inch fish. (President Obama agreed to order the water restored in exchange for some congressmen's votes for the Obamacare health care plan in March 2010, so the water started flowing again to California farmers shortly thereafter.)[59]

d. Clean air

I remember as a child how unpleasant it was to walk on the sidewalk along any city street when a line of cars was waiting at the stoplight.

---

58. "California's Man-Made Drought," *Wall Street Journal* (Sept. 2, 2009), A14.

59. Lance Williams, "Delta Democrat denies Swapping Health Care Vote for Irrigation Water, *California Watch* (March 19, 2010). http://californiawatch.org/watchblog/delta-democrat-denies-swapping-health-care-vote-irrigation-water.

The air pollution from the exhaust coming from the cars made the very act of breathing unpleasant and on some days would even make your eyes sting. But today if I walk on the same sidewalk beside a line of cars waiting at a stoplight, I can breathe freely and the automobile exhaust is almost undetectable. What happened?

The change came about because the people of the United States (collectively, through their elected representatives) decided that it was worth the extra expense to require pollution controls on automobile engines. They did the same for trucks, factories, home furnaces, and many other sources of air pollution. As a result, the air became much cleaner.

This clean-up of the air is the pattern followed by all countries of the world as their economies grow and they become wealthier overall. They begin to spend the extra money that is required to control air pollution.

To take another example, the chart below shows the concentrations of sulfur dioxide (SO_2) and smoke in London over a 400-year period. Today these major pollutants are present in London's air in lower concentrations than they even have been since before 1585, long before the modern industrial period. Urban pollutants have also decreased 90% since 1930. [60, 61]

AVERAGE CONCENTRATIONS OF SULFUR DIOXIDE
AND SMOKE IN LONDON, 1585–1994/95

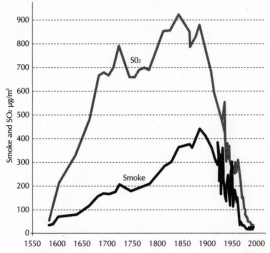

60. Derek M. Elsom, "Atmospheric Pollution Trends in the United Kingdom," in Simon, *The State of Humanity*, 476–90.

61. Chart from Lomborg, *The Skeptical Environmentalist*, 165, figure 86.

Another remarkable graph shows that *economic development is the way that nations can overcome air pollution.* The graph below shows that extremely poor countries (the left side of the graph) have almost no particle pollution in their air. This is because they have almost no cars or trucks or factories to pollute the air. When nations begin to develop economically, they drive older cars and trucks that sputter along but pollute more, and they burn fuels in their homes and factories that increase air pollution until they get to about $3,000/person income per year (the peak of the chart in the center of the graph). But then people decide that the polluted air is so harmful to their quality of life that they begin to impose regulations and fees to decrease pollution. Finally, when nations develop to the point that they have a per capita income of $30,000/year or higher (the right side of the chart), their air has returned to the same quality of purity it had in undeveloped nations with essentially no cars or factories.

What is more encouraging about this chart is to notice the progress that was made between 1972 and 1986. *The entire graph of pollution particles* is lower for every level of economic development. Even the poorer countries were able to develop with less total pollution, because of the use of cheaper and cleaner technology (including less-polluting cars and trucks) that could be imported from more developed countries. (The

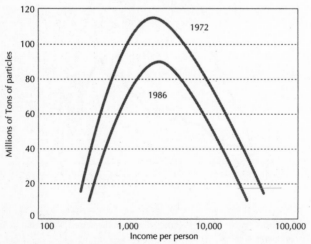

THE CONNECTION BETWEEN GDP PER CAPITA
AND PARTICLE POLLUTION IN 48 CITIES IN 31
COUNTRIES, 1972 AND 1986

Source: See next chart (p. 141)

THE CONNECTION BETWEEN GDP PER CAPITA AND SO$_2$
POLLUTION IN 37 CITIES IN 31 COUNTRIES, 1972 AND 1986

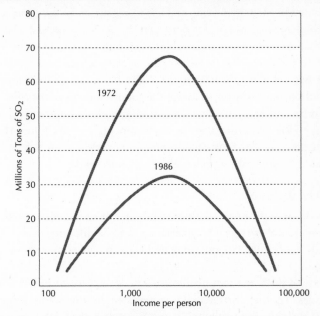

Source: World Development Report (1992), Development and the Environment,
World Bank (Oxford University Press, May 1992), 40-41.
www-wds.worldbank.org/external/default/WDSContentServer/WDSP/IB/2000/
12/13/000178830_9810191106175/Rendered/PDF/multi_page.pdf.

chart also shows that pollution reduction can occur at lower levels of
income over time, as poorer countries come to use technology developed
in wealthier countries.)

As far as future trends in air pollution are concerned, Lomborg points
to the example of the United States:

> In the US, the total number of car miles traveled has more than
> doubled over the past 30 years. The economy has likewise more
> than doubled, and the population has increased by more than
> a third. Nevertheless, over the same period emissions have
> decreased by a third and concentrations by much more. This is
> why it is reasonable to be optimistic about the challenge from
> air pollution.[62]

---

62. Lomborg, *The Skeptical Environmentalist*, 177.

Speaking as a Christian, I am not at all surprised by these findings. It seems to me consistent with the teachings of the Bible, because if God put us on the earth to develop and use its resources *for our benefit*, and *with thanksgiving*, and *for his glory*, and if God is a good and wise creator, then it is completely reasonable to think that he would create in the earth the resources that we need and that there would be ways that we could discover to use these resources wisely. It is reasonable to think that he would make a way for us to use the good resources of the earth in a wonderful and enjoyable way while simultaneously improving human quality of life *and* protecting the environment. We have found that to be true not only with food supplies and water supplies, but also with the increasingly abundant supply of clean air on the earth.

e. Waste disposal

Will nations of the earth continue to produce more and more waste that will eventually overwhelm our cities and make life unpleasant if not actually dangerous? No, not when we look at reliable statistics on waste disposal.

Some of the waste that people generate is recycled or put into compost piles. Another portion of it is incinerated, in some cases in energy-producing incineration plants. Several European countries — especially France, Germany, Denmark, United Kingdom, and Italy — make considerable use of modern incineration plants with extensive measures to minimize any air pollution or waste-disposal pollution from the resulting ashes. France alone has 225 incineration plants for energy production.[63] In addition, energy production from waste incineration seems to be the cheapest of all methods available, when measured per kilowatt-hour.[64]

The rest of the waste that people generate is put into landfills. Modern landfills are highly regulated by the Environmental Protection Agency and are considered very safe for the ground water in the area around them.[65]

---

63. Bernt Johnke, "Emissions from Waste Incineration," *Good Practice Guidance and Uncertainty Management in National Greenhouse Gas Inventories,* 456. www.ipcc-nggip.iges. or.jp/public/gp/bgp/5_3_Waste_Incineration.pdf.

64. The Cornwall Alliance for the Stewardship of Creation, *A Renewed Call to Truth, Prudence, and Protection of the Poor: An Evangelical Examination of the Theology, Science, and Economics of Global Warming* (Burke, VA: Cornwall Alliance, 2009), 66, Table 3, "Index of lifetime generation costs by generating type." Accessed online Feb. 15, 2010, at www.cornwallalliance.org/docs/a-renewed-call-to-truth-prudence-and-protection-of-the-poor.pdf.

65. Lomborg, *Skeptical Environmentalist*, 208.

But landfills are not simply "wasted space." I remember going to watch one of my sons run in a beautiful park with rolling hills when he was part of his high school cross-country team in Illinois. Only later did I find out that the park was built on the site of a landfill that had been carefully covered by soil. In fact, one of the largest landfills in the world, the Freshkills Landfill on Staten Island in New York City, is now closed so it can be turned into landscaped public parkland about three times the size of Central Park. On the New York City Parks website, the New York Department of Parks and Recreation says:

> The transformation of what was formerly the world's largest landfill into a productive and beautiful cultural destination will make the park a symbol of renewal and an expression of how our society can restore balance to its landscape. In addition to providing a wide range of recreational opportunities, including many uncommon in the city, the park's design, ecological restoration and cultural and educational programming will emphasize environmental sustainability and a renewed public concern for our human impact on the earth.[66]

How much space would be required to receive all the garbage being produced in the United States? Even with quite generous assumptions about the amount of waste produced per person and about the size of the growth of the American population, if all the waste generated in the United States for the next hundred years were placed in one landfill, it would fit within a square area less than 18 miles on each side and about 100 feet high (lower than the Freshkills Landfill in New York City). This single landfill would take up less than 0.009% of the land area of the United States.[67] And it could be made into another landscaped public park for people to use in centuries to come. Or if each state had to handle its own waste, it would have to find simply one site for a single square landfill of 2.5 miles on each side.[68] When it was full, of course, it too could be covered with soil and turned into a beautiful state park. (This assumes that it is filled with waste and dirt over each layer and compacted appropriately, according to modern environmental standards.)

In actual fact, thousands of local landfills much, much smaller in size will be used and will be entirely adequate to handle the waste that we generate. Dads like me will also watch their sons run cross-country

---

66. "Freshkills Park: Project Overview," New York City Department of Parks and Recreation. www.nycgovparks.org/sub_your_park/fresh_kills_park/html/fresh_kills_park.html.

67. Lomborg, *Skeptical Environmentalist*, 207.

68. Ibid.

meets on the rolling, wooded hills and never know that a landfill lies under the ground.

Another important factor is that with technological advances we continually discover new uses for waste products and new ways to produce goods with less waste. So the amount of waste generated will probably be much less than these predictions. In any case, we will easily be able to handle that amount of waste. We will never run out of space to store our garbage.

Is recycling worthwhile, then? It does reduce the amount of waste that is put into landfills, but a sensible approach would ask, with respect to each kind of material being recycled, *is it worth the time and effort and expense it takes to do such recycling?* That is simply a *factual* analysis that needs to be carried out. For example, should we put resources into recycling paper, or should we simply burn it at incineration plants and produce energy with it? A quick trip to the local Staples store where I buy copy paper shows me that an ordinary package of twelve of the legal pads that I use costs $5.79, while a twelve-pack of the same size of legal pads on recycled paper costs $8.99! That is 55% higher! So the recycled paper costs *much more* than newly produced paper. Is there any good reason for me to spend 55% more for the paper I use? There is no need to do it to reduce the use of landfills, for which we have abundant space. Well, maybe I should use recycled paper so as not to cut down so many trees? That would only make sense if the world is going to run out of trees to make paper, which is simply not going to happen (see below).

Paper is a *renewable resource*, because trees can be planted and grown, just as oats and wheat and corn are grown. (Trees just take longer, but they are a renewable resource.) If the recycled paper costs more, it means that *the total amount of resources* used to produce recycled paper is *greater* than the resources used to produce new paper—for the price reflects, in general, the cost of production—and it probably reflects less than the cost of production for recycled paper because of government subsidies for recycling plants. Buying the recycled paper is simply wasting my $3.20, which I am not going to do. I buy legal pads made of ordinary paper.

f. Global forests

If we could never grow any more trees in the world, or if we were quickly depleting the amount of trees available for paper and wood production, then of course recycling would make a lot of sense. But is the world running out of trees? Once again, this is simply a question of analysis of *the facts that show worldwide trends.*

About one-third of the earth's land is covered by forests today, and this number has remained relatively stable since World War II, or for the last sixty years.[69] Four countries (Russia, Brazil, the United States, and Canada) together have more than 50% of the world's forests, and in the whole world about two to three times as much land is taken up by forests as by agricultural land used for crops.[70]

As for the United States, from its early history until about 1920 a significant amount of the forest cover was cleared, largely for agricultural use. But since 1920, the amount of forest land has remained quite stable.[71]

When a natural forest area where trees are growing randomly is first cleared for wood or paper use, new trees are planted in neat rows so that much more total wood is grown in each land area. The result of this more efficient use of land has been that the amount of wood that is actually growing in the United States each year *is 3½ times what it was in 1920*.[72] The continuing trend is seen in the bar chart section below where the total number of cubic feet growing in the United States is shown to have increased significantly in the thirty-five years from 1952 to 1987. (Note that the regional trend lines use the left scale and the bar chart for the total nation uses the right scale.) [73]

GROWING COMMERCIAL TIMBER IN THE USA, NET VOLUME

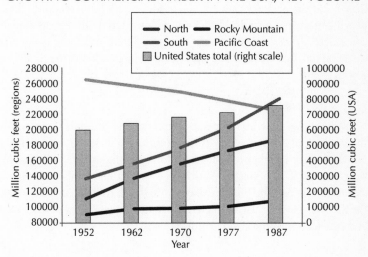

69. Ibid., 117.
70. Ibid., 112.
71. Simon, *The State of Humanity*, 331.
72. Ibid., 331–32.
73. Chart from Simon, *State of Humanity*, 332, figure 33.2.

As far as the entire world is concerned, we have lost about 20% of the original forest cover on the earth since agriculture began,[74] but that percentage has now stabilized (see above). Developing countries tend to clear forests and put more land into agricultural use, but then that trend stabilizes as better agricultural methods are adopted and the food needs of the country are met. Another factor is that less developed societies tend to use wood for fuel in open fires, but with development, other sources of energy are used.

There is still a legitimate concern with loss of tropical rainforests in some countries. But earlier estimates of a loss of 2% or more of tropical rainforests have now been shown to be excessively high.[75] The rate of loss of tropical forests is now about 0.46% per year.[76]

By far the largest proportion of tropical rain forest in the world is in Brazil. The Amazon forest makes up about one-third of the world's tropical forest area. About 14% of the Amazon rain forest has been cut down since earliest human history, with 86% remaining.[77] The Brazilian government has recently imposed new restrictions on deforestation in the Amazon area. Ultimately this is a problem that can only be solved by the governments of each nation that has tropical forests, including Brazil. But the primary cause of loss of forest area is not wood used for paper, but over-use of wood fuel due to low income in less developed countries.[78] In any case, the world consumption of wood and paper can easily be satisfied without any significant deforestation throughout the world.

g. Species loss

Nobody knows how many species of plants and animals there are in the world, and estimates vary from 2 million to 80 million species. By far, the largest number of species is found among insects, followed by fungi, bacteria, and viruses.[79] Although the actual number of species extinctions is certainly higher than those that have been documented, the following table is useful in giving an approximate number of species and extinctions in the last five hundred years: [80]

---

74. Ibid., 112.
75. Ibid., 114: citing William P. Cunningham and Barbara Woodworth Saigo, *Environmental Science: A Global Concern* (Dubuque, IA: Wm. C. Brown Publishers, 1997), 297–98.
76. Ibid.
77. Ibid., 114–15.
78. Ibid., 114.
79. Ibid., 250.
80. Chart from Lomborg, *Skeptical Environmentalist*, 250, table 6.

NUMBER OF SPECIES AND DOCUMENTED
EXTINCTIONS, 1600—PRESENT

Taxa	Approximate number of species	Total extinctions since 1600
Vertibrates	47,000	321
Mammals	4,500	110
Birds	9,500	103
Reptiles	6,300	21
Amphibians	4,200	5
Fish	24,000	82
Mollusks	100,000	235
Crustaceans	4,000	9
Insects	>1,000,000	98
Vascular Plants	250,000	396
Total	Approx. 1,600,000	1,033

Note that the number of insect species is somewhere over 1 million, and this is apparently the group that accounts for the high estimates of 10–80 million species on the earth. Moreover, this chart lists only the species that have been recorded and counted to date.

What is significant is that the total number of documented extinctions is only 1,033 out of 1.6 million species, or 0.06% total over the last five hundred years. The documented rate of species lost among mammals and birds is apparently about one per year.[81] That is far different from the claim of an influential book by Norman Myers, *The Sinking Ark* (1979), where he claimed that we lose about 40,000 every year. But the statement was an entirely unsubstantiated *guess* with no supporting data![82] Unfortunately, environmental advocate and former US Vice President Al Gore has continued to repeat this extraordinarily incorrect claim.[83] Also, Professor Paul Ehrlich, an influential Stanford biologist and environmentalist, claimed in 1981 that we were losing 250,000 species every year and that half the species on earth would be gone by the year 2000 and they would all be gone by 2010–25.[84] These are simply

81. Ibid., 252.
82. Ibid., 249, 252.
83. Ibid., 248.
84. Ibid., 249.

alarmist claims with no legitimate base within statistical reality. Lomborg's best estimate is that the rate of extinction will be about 0.7% per fifty years in the foreseeable future, but even that will probably decline as population growth slows down and the developing world becomes wealthy enough to spend more resources caring for the environment.[85]

Such a low rate of species loss may still be thought to be problematic because of the potential benefits that could come from such biodiversity, but put in the larger perspective of the course of decades or centuries, it is a problem that is certainly capable of a reasonable solution and not one that should be a cause of current panic.

In cases such as the delta smelt in California, mentioned above (p. 138), Jesus' statements about the much greater value of human beings than animals need to be remembered (see Matt. 10:31; 12:12). There is no certainty that the delta smelt will become extinct if the irrigation water is turned back on in the San Joaquin Valley, so even that species might not be lost. But even if the world loses one species of fish that exists only in this one part of California (out of 24,000 species of fish in the world, including 14 other species of smelt), that must be counted as a tiny cost (of no significant measurable economic value) compared with the great benefit of protecting the well-being and actual livelihood of thousands of California farmers and agricultural workers, and also of bringing benefit to the millions of people who eat the food produced in the San Joaquin Valley.

h. Herbicides and pesticides

One of the most significant causes of increased food production around the world has been the invention of modern herbicides (that kill harmful weeds) and pesticides (that kill harmful insects and bacteria). The benefits of herbicides and pesticides are that they improve crop yields and make fruit and vegetables cheaper. If pesticide use were restricted or even prohibited, it would perhaps double the proportion of income that a family in North America or Europe needs to spend on food. With less money to spend, people would eat fewer fruits and vegetables and would buy more primary starch and consume more fat. The effect on the poor would be the greatest, but this might lead to an increase of something like 26,000 additional cancer deaths per year in the United States.[86] Therefore herbicides and pesticides create *great health benefits*, significantly *higher food production*, and *less required use of land*.

---

85. Ibid., 255–56.
86. Ibid., 247–48.

But are pesticides harmful? US government agencies such as the Food and Drug Administration (FDA) and Environmental Protection Agency (EPA) set limits in the use of pesticides based on the measurable amount that gets into the food and water that we consume. The limits are very strictly set. After extensive testing, there is a value established called the NOAEL (No Observed Adverse Effect Level). Then a level below this is a value called the ADI (Accepted Daily Intake). The set ADI limit is usually between 100 and 10,000 times lower than the NOAEL.[87]

One of the most respected studies of various causes of cancer in the United States, for example, concluded that they could find *no significant percentage of cancers caused by pesticides in the United States.* There are many causes of cancer (such as tobacco, diet, sun exposure, and infections), but pesticides do not even make the list. Lomborg concludes that the effect of pesticides on cancer in the United States is so low that "virtually no one dies of cancer caused by pesticides."[88] In another place, Lomborg summarizes a number of studies by saying, "Pesticides contribute astoundingly little to deaths caused by cancer."[89] He says that a "plausible estimate" for the added number of cancer deaths due to pesticide use in the United States is close to 20 deaths per year out of 560,000,[90] or one death out of every 28,000 people who die of cancer. When this is weighed against the immense benefits that come from pesticide use, and the great harm that would come to the world population and world diets if pesticide use were abolished, it appears that there should be no significant objection to their current level of wise and carefully restricted use.

Once again, this conclusion should not be surprising. If God wanted us to subdue the earth and develop its resources in useful ways, then it is reasonable to expect that he would give us the ability to discover means of overcoming the "thorns and thistles" that grow on the earth and also the pests that tend to destroy food crops. In addition, it must be recognized that many of the pesticides used are not synthetic chemical compounds but are derived from natural substances that already occur in one place or another in the plant world—substances that already allow some plants to fight off the pests that would attack them.[91]

---

87. Ibid., 226.
88. Ibid., 228–29.
89. Ibid., 245.
90. Ibid.
91. Ibid., 232–33.

i. Life expectancy

Is the earth becoming a safer or more dangerous place for human beings to live? One very important measure is overall life expectancy. When people have better health, when they can overcome diseases, when they are able to keep themselves safe from natural disasters, and when they have better nutrition, they will live longer. Therefore we would expect that people would have a longer life expectancy as they advance in developing the earth's resources and making them useful for human beings, as God intended them to do.

This is in fact what we find has happened as nations have developed economically and human beings have discovered more ways to make the resources of the earth useful for themselves.

While records from earlier centuries are less detailed, enough information remains to gain a fairly good idea of overall life expectancy in a number of nations. England may be taken as typical of what happens as nations develop economically: [92]

Note that life expectancy in the last 200 years has increased from about 38 years to about 78 years. This is an astounding increase. Other coun-

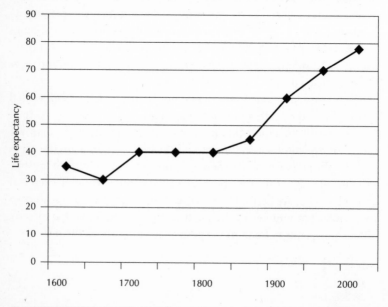

LIFE EXPECTANCY IN ENGLAND AND WALES (1600–2000)

92. Ibid., 51, figure 15.

tries experienced similar growth so that the average life expectancy in developed countries is now 77 years.[93]

In less developed countries, the average life expectancy at the beginning of the twentieth century was under 30 years. By 1950 it had reached 41 years and in 1998 was at 65 years.[94] This is an astounding development, where life expectancy even in less developed countries has more than doubled in the last hundred years.[95] The predictions for future development are continually upward for all parts of the world, as is evident in the following chart:

These statistics are valuable in that they serve as an overall indicator of human progress in the ability to live productive lives on the earth, overcome dangers, and make the resources of the earth beneficial for

LIFE EXPECTANCY FOR INDUSTRIALIZED COUNTRIES, DEVELOPING COUNTRIES, SUB-SAHARAN AFRICA, AND THE ENTIRE WORLD, 1950-2050

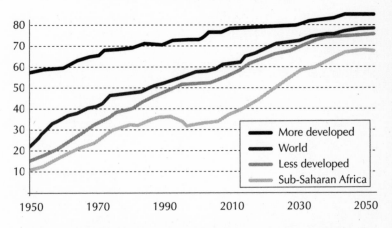

Sources: Monica Ferreira and Paul Kowal, "A Minimum Data Set on Ageing and Older Persons in Sub-Saharan Africa: Process and Outcome," African Population Studies/Etude de la Population Africaine, Vol. 21, No. 1 (2006), 19-36. www.who.int/healthinfo/survey/ageing_mds_pub02.pdf and www.bioline.org.br/request?ep06002.
Social Indicators, United Nations Statistics Division, http://unstats.un.org/unsd/demographic/products/socind/health.htm.
United Nations Population Division, "The World at Six Billion," Table 4 (1999). www.un.org/esa/population/publications/sixbillion/sixbillion.htm.
Life Expectancy at Birth, 1950-2050, Figure 1, Congressional Budget Office, 3. www.cbo.gov/ftpdocs/69xx/doc6952/12-12-Global.pdf.

---

93. Ibid., 50.
94. Ibid.
95. Ibid.

our overall health and well-being. The overall picture that we get is a very encouraging one of continual growth and progress. We are making better use of the environment in which we live, and we are also taking better care of it each year.

God created an abundant and resourceful earth, and we are developing an ever-greater ability to make wise use of the resources that he has placed in it for our benefit, so that we would use these resources with thanksgiving and give glory to him.

Chapter 5

THE ENVIRONMENT: ENERGY, GLOBAL WARMING, AND PUBLIC POLICY

A. ENERGY RESOURCES AND ENERGY USES

Sometimes people naively assume that we are quickly running out of energy sources, but that is simply not true.

To get an overall picture of world energy production, we first need to understand that energy is derived from several different sources. The following diagram shows the distribution of energy sources used in a particular year for the entire world:

1. Wind power

The amount of energy produced by wind power has increased somewhat since that 1998 diagram. In 2008, according to the Global Wind Energy Council, the total amount of world energy capacity from wind-power was 121 gigawatts, growing by 29% from 2007. (A gigawatt is one billion watts of electricity.)[1] However, wind-power "capacity" is not the best

---

1. Global Wind 2008 Report. Global Wind Energy Council. www.gwec.net/fileadmin/documents/Global%20Wind%202008%20Report.pdf.

WORLD ENERGY PRODUCTION BY SOURCE 2006

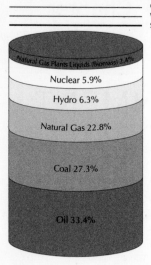

Geothermal 0.5%
Wind 0.6%
Solar 0.9%

Natural Gas Plants Liquids (Biomass) 2.4%

Nuclear 5.9%

Hydro 6.3%

Natural Gas 22.8%

Coal 27.3%

Oil 33.4%

Sources: World Primary Energy Production by Source 1970-2006.
www.eia.doe.gov/aer/txt/ptb1101.html.
Energy Sources: Renewable Energy.
www.green3dhome.com/EnergySources/RenewableSources.aspx.

measure, because wind is unreliable, and actual energy produced may only be around 20% of "capacity." According to the US Department of Energy, wind power presently accounts for about 1.9% of America's electricity.[2] Wind power has some potential, but its contribution to world energy production will probably remain quite small, because it is not dependable in most areas of the world (wind does not blow all the time, and varies in intensity), and the energy is so diffuse that wind farms require huge land areas (or ocean areas) with hundreds of giant windmills that destroy the beauty of the landscape for miles around.

2. Hydroelectric power

While the United States currently gets 5.7% of its energy,[3] or 247,509,974 BTUs,[4] from hydroelectric dams on rivers, it is unlikely that its capac-

---

2. "Wind Powering America Update," U.S. Department of Energy (Aug. 20, 2009). www.windpoweringamerica.gov/filter_detail.asp?itemid=746.

3. BP Statistical Review—Full Report 2009. www.bp.com/liveassets/bp_internet/globalbp/globalbp_uk_english/reports_and_publications/statistical_energy_review_2008/STAGING/local_assets/2009_downloads/hydro_table_of_hydroelectricity_consumption_2009.pdf.

4. Table 1.11, Electricity Net Generation from Renewable Energy by Energy Use Sector and Energy Source, 2003–2007. www.eia.doe.gov/cneaf/solar.renewables/page/trends/table1_11.pdf.

ity is capable of much expansion beyond that amount because most of the good locations where dams can be built already have dams built on them. The situation is similar in most developed countries, so it is unlikely that the 6.6% of the world's energy that is produced by hydroelectric plants will increase very much.

3. Oil

Because of new technology and further exploration, we are constantly discovering new reserves of oil and other energy sources. For example, the following figure shows a comparison of *known oil reserves* with annual production. Note that as oil usage has increased somewhat, the world's *known reserves* of oil have multiplied many times over. This is because people keep discovering new sources of oil.

Moreover, when the price of oil increases, oil in more difficult areas becomes economically more feasible to develop. If we factor in the oil available in tar sands and shale oil fields, the amount of oil remaining is equal to the total energy consumption of the entire world for more than five thousand years![5] But of course, we will also be using other energy

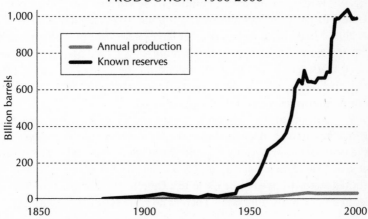

KNOWN WORLD OIL RESERVES AND WORLD OIL PRODUCTION – 1900-2008

Sources: World Oil Production, U.S. Department of Energy.
www.eia.doe.gov/emeu/aer/txt/ptb1105.html.
World Annual Oil Production (1900-2008).
http://people.hofstra.edu/geotrans/eng/ch5en/appl5en/worldoilreservesevol.
html.
CIA Worldfact Book 2009-1002.

---

5. Ibid., 128.

sources as well, and technological developments in the next twenty-five to fifty years will likely shift our usage away from even the amount of world energy that it now produces. In other words, we will never run out of oil.

It seems to me wise for the United States to dramatically reduce its dependence on foreign oil, in two ways: (1) The nation should increase its use of alternative fuels where that is practical to do. But in many cases, oil-based gasoline and diesel fuel are going to remain the preferred fuel for years to come because of their high energy content and easy transportability—you can't burn coal in a car or plane engine, and electric batteries do not deliver enough energy for long enough to power most cars, all larger trucks, or airplanes. Oil is also still relatively cheap and abundant.

(2) The nation should develop more of its own supplies of oil, especially more of the offshore oil deposits off the coast of California and Florida (but far enough from land that they will not be seen, unless they are "disguised"—as some have been in the past—so that they appear as attractive tropical islands). The United States should also develop even more urgently its abundant supplies in the Alaskan National Wildlife Refuge (ANWR), where there are no human inhabitants and where the United States could retrieve as much oil as it now imports from Saudi Arabia each year.[6] The Department of the Interior has estimated that ANWR would provide over 1.3 million barrels of oil a day.[7] (The United States currently imports more than 1 million barrels per day from Saudi Arabia.)[8] In addition, there are other large oil deposits in Western states like Colorado (which could provide more than 46,000 barrels of oil per day)[9] that could be profitably developed, for the good of the nation (by reducing the dependence on foreign oil and by bringing down oil prices due to increased availability of supplies).

In addition to that, we need to expand our oil-refining capacity, which has actually decreased over the last twenty-eight years, keeping the price of gas artificially high. Between 1981, when refineries operated at 69% of their capacity, and 2004, the number of refineries in the United States dropped from 324 to 153. Laurence Goldstein of the Petroleum Research Institute says, "There is no spare refining capacity in the

---

6. "Drill Here. Drill Now. Drill ANWR." www.anwr.org/Latest-News/Drill-here.-Drill-now.-Drill-ANWR.php.

7. See www.doi.gov/news/anwrchart.pdf.

8. "Crude Oil and Total Petroleum Imports Top 15 Countries," Energy Information Administration (Oct. 29, 2009). www.eia.doe.gov/pub/oil_gas/petroleum/data_publications/company_level_imports/current/import.html.

9. Ibid.

US today."[10] We should also take steps to persuade the various states (such as Arizona) to adopt a uniform national standard for the types of gasoline that are sold, rather than paying the extra expense that comes when states pass their own special formulas for boutique mixtures of gas components that are allowed to be sold in each state — a big contributor to higher gas prices and periodic shortages.

4. Coal

Coal is another widely used source of energy, and modern coal-burning power plants are much cleaner and more efficient than in previous years. The total coal resources available in the world will be sufficient for "well beyond the next 1,500 years."[11]

5. Natural gas

Natural gas is an excellent source of energy for home heating and is also widely used to generate electrical power. Some areas have used natural gas to power automobiles and buses, but the special refueling stations are only found in certain places. Its existence in a gas rather than a liquid state under normal temperatures makes it readily transportable by pipelines. But it has to be put under pressure to keep it in a liquid form, so it requires specially pressurized refueling pumps and thick, heavy, reinforced tanks in cars that use it. It burns very cleanly and is now less expensive than gasoline produced from oil.

6. Nuclear power

Nuclear power is also a wonderful source of energy. The energy produced by one gram (that is, 1/28th of an ounce) of uranium–235 is equivalent to the energy produced by almost three tons of coal![12] Nuclear power gives off almost no pollution, but the radioactive waste materials need to be stored safely. This has become a political controversy in the United States, but many nations have already solved this problem for

---

10. "Lack of new refineries also factor in high gas prices," Alexander's Gas and Oil Connections, News and Trends: North America (June 14, 2004). www.gasandoil.com/goc/news/ntn42472.htm

11. Lomborg. *Skeptical Environmentalist*, 127: citing James R. Craig, David J. Vaughn, and Brian J. Skinner, *Resources of the Earth: Origin, Use, and Environmental Impact* (Upper Saddle River, NJ: Prentice Hall, 1996), 159.

12. Ibid., 129: citing Craig et al., *Resources of the Earth*, 164.

themselves, and it should not be a problem in the United States either. Senator Pete Domenici of New Mexico points out that in France, to dispose of nuclear waste, "a single 150-liter class canister contains the waste (fission products and actinides) from 360,000 families of four heating their homes with electricity for one year."[13] To give some comparison, 150 liters is about the size of a common 40-gallon steel drum (or the inner water tank that is inside all the insulation of an ordinary 40-gallon home water heater). This means that the yearly nuclear waste of *over a million people* could be stored in a container of this size. (This would require that the United States adopt a method of reprocessing nuclear fuel that is now used safely in France and other countries.)

According to the US Department of Energy Civilian Nuclear Waste Management, France stores its spent nuclear fuel for one year at its nuclear power plants in specially constructed storage pools. Following storage, spent nuclear fuel is then transported to the La Hague and Marcoule reprocessing plants and stored for two to three years. France has also reprocessed nuclear fuel for Germany, Belgium, Japan, and the Netherlands.[14] The fuel and radioactive waste is buried 400 to 1,000 meters below the ground. In Japan, the waste is buried 300 meters underground.[15] Some 76.8% of the electricity generated in France is from nuclear power.[16] Japan gets 25.6% of its electricity supply from nuclear power.[17]

There are currently 104 operating nuclear power plants in the United States (including the Palo Verde Nuclear Generating Station west of Phoenix, which is probably providing the electricity powering my computer as I type this sentence). They provide over 20% of the electricity generated for the United States.[18]

Several hundred more nuclear power plants had been planned up until about the mid–1970s, but because of endless legal and regulatory barriers, no new nuclear power plants have been built in the United States since 1975.

---

13. Pete Domenici, *A Brighter Tomorrow: Fulfilling the Promise of Nuclear Energy* (Lanham, MD: Rowman & Littlefield, 2004), 157. This book contains an abundance of information on the benefits of more nuclear energy, with detailed responses to objections.

14. "France's Radioactive Waste Program," U.S. Department of Energy Fact Sheet Office of Civilian Nuclear Radioactive Waste Management. www.ocrwm.doe.gov/factsheets/doeymp0411.shtml.

15. The Federation of Electric Power Companies of Japan. www.japannuclear.com/nuclearpower/program/waste.html. See also Nuclear Waste Management Organization of Japan. www.numo.or.jp/en/faq/main1.html.

16. Nuclear Energy Agency. www.nea.fr/html/general/profiles/france.html.

17. Ibid. www.nea.fr/html/general/profiles/japan.html.

18. See www.nea.fr/html/general/profiles/usa.html.

Why is this? Senator Domenici, who has devoted many years to learning about nuclear energy and is a past chairman of the Energy and Natural Resources Committee of the US Senate, attributes the failure of the United States to change these prohibitive barriers to two causes: (1) "many Americans have an irrational fear of anything 'nuclear,'" and (2) "the policy of deliberate misinformation that opponents of nuclear energy employ with shameless disregard of the truth."[19] Contrary to popular impressions, for example, the accident with a cooling system malfunction at the Three Mile Island Nuclear Generating Station in Pennsylvania on March 29, 1979, involved no human deaths and no injuries to plant workers or nearby residents.[20] The generator that had experienced the accident resumed operation in October 1985, after repairs and lengthy litigation.[21]

What about Chernobyl? It is true that in the former Soviet Union, the Chernobyl Nuclear Reactor in Ukraine was destroyed by a terrible accident April 26, 1986, but that was due to flagrantly poor quality construction and maintenance under the communist government, with a blatant disregard for safety that has never been allowed in the United States, France, the United Kingdom, Japan, or other countries with significant nuclear power production. According to the US Nuclear Regulatory Commission, "U.S. reactors have different plant designs, broader shutdown margins, robust containment structures, and operational controls to protect them against the combination of lapses that led to the accident at Chernobyl."[22]

I was pleased to learn that on February 16, 2010, President Obama pledged $8 billion in loan guarantees to build the first new nuclear reactors in the United States in nearly three decades.[23] I hope this initiative will lead to the construction of many new nuclear reactors.

With a special development called a fast-breeder reactor, there is now sufficient uranium for "up to 14,000 years" of energy production.[24] And

---

19. Domenici, *A Brighter Tomorrow*, xii.

20. "Backgrounder on the Three Mile Island Accident," United States Nuclear Regulatory Commission (Aug. 2009). www.nrc.gov/reading-rm/doc-collections/fact-sheets/3mile-isle.html.

21. "Three Mile Island Unit 1 Outage Dates: February 17, 1979 to October 8, 1985." www.ucsusa.org/assets/documents/nuclear_power/three-mile-island–1.pdf.

22. "Background on the Chernobyl Nuclear Power Plant Accident," United States Nuclear Regulatory Commission (April 2009). www.nrc.gov/reading-rm/doc-collections/fact-sheets/chernobyl-bg.html.

23. Jim Tankersley and Michael Muskal, "Obama pledges $8 billion for new nuclear reactors," *Los Angeles Times* (Feb. 16, 2010). http://articles.latimes.com/2010/feb/16/nation/la-na-obama-nuclear17–2010feb17 (accessed Feb. 17, 2010).

24. Lomborg. *Skeptical Environmentalist*, 129: citing Craig et al., *Resources of the Earth*, 181.

then there is another method of producing nuclear energy—not from nuclear *fission*, but from nuclear *fusion*. The fuel for this is not uranium, but is taken from ordinary seawater, and therefore the supply is unlimited. However, this technology has not yet been successful to a level that would be commercially useful, and it is unknown when a technological breakthrough will occur. Even without nuclear fusion, however, plants based on nuclear *fission* could easily provide the energy needs of the entire United States for thousands of years to come, if they were not prevented from being built by opposition "based on irrational fear led by Hollywood-style fiction, the Green lobbies and the media. These fears are unjustified, and nuclear energy from its start in 1952 has proved to be the safest of all energy sources."[25]

7. Solar energy

Prices for both wind energy and solar energy have dropped considerably in recent years, but they are still not widely used, primarily because they are not yet economically competitive with coal, natural gas, oil, hydroelectric power, and nuclear energy. But recent developments with solar cells have made solar energy much more affordable, and its use will likely increase. Solar energy is unreliable in many areas that are frequently overcast, and of course it cannot be generated at night, which requires that the energy generated be stored in large batteries. Solar energy is by far the greatest source of energy available, however. The amount of solar energy falling on the earth *each year* is equal to about 7,000 times our present global energy consumption.[26]

8. Conclusion

In conclusion, there is an incredibly abundant amount of energy available for human use on the earth. Once again, this is not surprising. If God put us on the earth so that we would develop and use his resources wisely, then it is reasonable that he would provide us with multiple sources of energy that we could discover in order to perform the tasks he gives us to do.

Therefore it makes no sense for people to think that there is some virtue in always seeking to "reduce our energy use." Energy is what replaces human physical work (such as walking everywhere and carry-

25. Domenici, *A Brighter Tomorrow*, 211.
26. Lomborg, *Skeptical Environmentalist*, 133.

ing everything by hand rather than driving) and animal work (such as plowing fields or grinding grain with oxen), and energy is what makes economic development possible. When we *increase our use of these energy sources* that God has provided, by using a truck to carry goods hundreds of miles, or flying by airplane to a distant city, or driving quickly to a meeting thirty miles away, or using a tractor to plow a field, or turning on the dishwasher or washing machine, or living comfortably in a climate-controlled house in hot summers and cold winters—when we increase our energy use, we *decrease the time we have to spend* on travel or menial labor, and we *increase the amount of work* we can get done (and thus increase human prosperity), and we *increase human freedom* because we have more time left to devote to more creative and valuable tasks of our own choosing. Using all of these energy sources is a wonderful ability that God has provided the human race, and it sets us far above the animal kingdom as creatures truly made in the image of God. We should be thankful for the ability of the human race to use more and more of the energy resources that God has placed in the world for our benefit and enjoyment.

If people want to reduce their energy use *to save money* (turning off unused lights, for example), that of course is wise. But if reducing energy use means you will get less work done, or you just have to work longer in order to accomplish the same task (washing a large load of dishes by hand when you have a dishwasher), or if it means you will reduce your quality of life (shivering in a cold, dark room on winter nights to "save energy" when you could easily afford to heat and light your home), then I see no virtue in it. You are just wasting your time when God gives you the wonderful gift of abundant energy in the earth.

We should also realize that during the past hundred years the most significant resource of all has been *human ingenuity* in discovering and developing new sources of energy and discovering more efficient ways to carry out various tasks. It is certainly reasonable to expect that human ingenuity will continue to develop new sources of energy and better ways of using energy in the future so that, just as past predictions have vastly underestimated the amount of remaining energy on earth,[27] so it is likely that present predictions of the amount of energy remaining are themselves too pessimistic, and as further technological progress is made, we will realize that the amount of energy remaining in these sources will last even beyond the current predictions.

27. Ibid., 118–36.

B. GLOBAL WARMING AND CARBON FUELS[28]

Before we can decide what to do about the question of "global warming," it is necessary to understand some of the scientific factors related to the earth's temperature and carbon dioxide.

1. The earth's atmosphere has both warming and cooling influences on the earth

a. Warming effects from the atmosphere

We are able to live on the earth only because the earth's atmosphere retains some heat from the sun. If the earth had no atmosphere, its average surface temperature would be about 0°Fahrenheit — too cold to sustain most life. Yet, because there is an atmosphere surrounding the earth, average worldwide temperatures tend to hover around 59°F — but much colder near the poles, much warmer near the equator, and cooler at night and warmer in the daytime, cooler in winter and warmer in summer, and so forth. Over most of the earth, most of the time, the temperature is well-suited to human life and to plant and animal life of various kinds.

The way the atmosphere warms the earth is often called the "greenhouse effect" — that is, some of the atmosphere retains the heat energy that comes from the sun. Not all of the atmosphere does this, however. Nitrogen (which makes up 78% of the atmosphere) and oxygen (which makes up 21%) don't retain the sun's heat. That makes 99% of the atmosphere that does not retain heat or function as "greenhouse gas."

In the remaining 1% of the atmosphere there are fourteen other elements or compounds. Most of these do not have a warming effect either, but the ones that do are called "greenhouse gases," and they constitute about 0.45% of the atmosphere — just under one-half of 1%. Water vapor makes up 89% of these greenhouse gases, or about 0.4% of the entire atmosphere (higher at the earth's surface, but diminishing with altitude). The other greenhouse gases are carbon dioxide (about 0.039% of the total atmosphere), methane (about 0.00018%), nitrous oxide (about 0.00003%), ozone (less than 0.000007%), and miscellaneous trace gases — all of these other greenhouse gases (apart from

28. I wish to thank my friend Dr. E. Calvin Beisner, who (in my opinion) knows more than anyone else about issues related to Christian stewardship of the environment, for writing the initial draft of this entire section on global warming. However, I have rewritten several portions and added others, and the final responsibility for the content of this section is mine.

water) totaling under 0.05% of the atmosphere. The remaining 0.55% of the atmosphere consists of other elements or compounds that do not have a warming effect on the earth.

Water vapor, then, is the most important greenhouse gas. How important is water vapor? It is responsible for about 80% of the total warming effect of the entire atmosphere.

Another 15% of the warming effect of the entire atmosphere comes from clouds. (Clouds are not included in water vapor because they are actually made of water droplets.) But the effect of clouds is complex, because some clouds warm the earth and some cool the earth. The *low-altitude clouds* mostly *cool* the earth by reflecting the sun's heat back into space before it reaches the surface. (We notice this when a cloud passes in front of the sun on a hot day, and the shade from the cloud feels cooler to us than the direct sunlight.) By contrast, the *warming clouds* are mostly high-altitude cirrus clouds, because they retain more heat than they reflect back into space.

For convenience, most scientists just combine water vapor (80% of warming) and warming clouds (15%) to say that water causes about 95% of "greenhouse warming." The remaining approximately 5% of greenhouse warming comes from carbon dioxide (about 3.6%), methane (about 0.36%), nitrous oxide (about 0.95%), and miscellaneous gases including ozone (about 0.072%).[29]

How exactly do these greenhouse gases warm the earth? Despite the metaphor, they don't work at all like a greenhouse, because in a greenhouse the glass walls and roof warm the interior by trapping warm air inside — the glass keeps the air that is warmed by incoming sunlight from rising and blowing away. But greenhouse gases don't keep warm air from rising and blowing away. Instead, they *absorb* heat energy and then *radiate* it outward.

Here is what happens: First, energy comes from the sun mostly in the form of light. When that light hits the surface of the earth, the earth

---

29. Data on composition of the entire atmosphere are readily available in standard sources, but precise amounts vary slightly from source to source, the main variations being in percentage of carbon dioxide, which has risen over recent years, so it is lower in older sources, higher in newer ones. The percentages stated here reflect those in PhysicalGeography.net Fundamentals eBook, Chapter 7, "Introduction to the Atmosphere," Table 7a–1, online at www.physicalgeography.net/fundamentals/7a.html, updated in the case of carbon dioxide from 360 to 385 ppmv. See also John Houghton, *Global Warming: The Complete Briefing*, 3d ed. (Cambridge: Cambridge University Press, 2004), 16. Greenhouse gas composition data are from Geocraft.com, "Global Warming: A closer look at the numbers," online at www.geocraft.com/WVFossils/greenhouse_data.html, Table 4a.

absorbs light energy from the sun and then radiates it back in the form of *infrared energy*—what we call heat. (Imagine holding your hand above a rock that has been sitting out in the sun, and you can feel the heat energy radiating from the warm rock.) Now let's say that after holding your hand above the warm rock, your hand also becomes warm. Your hand has been absorbing heat energy from the warm rock, and now your hand is also radiating heat energy. If you put your hand to your cheek, you will feel the heat energy from your hand.

In a similar way, greenhouse gases *absorb* infrared energy (heat) and then, having absorbed it, radiate it outward. Some of it goes up into space, thus cooling the earth by moving the heat away, but some of it radiates heat back down to the earth's surface and warms the earth.

It is good for us that not all of the sun's energy stays at earth's surface, or we would cook. It is also good that not all of it bounces back into space, or we would freeze. As Christians, we can be thankful that by God's wise design, such infrared absorption by greenhouse gases ensures that the earth retains the right balance of incoming and outgoing energy.

b. Cooling effects from the atmosphere

I mentioned earlier that without the "greenhouse effect," earth's average surface temperature would be about 0ºF and with it, it's about 59ºF. But if the atmosphere didn't have any *balancing factors to modify the greenhouse effect*, there would be another problem: the total warming by the greenhouse gases in earth's atmosphere would keep average surface temperature at about 140ºF—much too hot for most life.[30] So why is the average temperature only 59ºF? Because, in addition to *warming influences*, the atmosphere also has some *cooling influences* that moderate the greenhouse effect. These fall in the general category of climate "feedbacks" (changes in the atmosphere that are caused by other changes in the atmosphere, which then lead to other changes).

These feedbacks, whose net effect is to bring cooling influences to the earth, include such things as evaporation, precipitation (rain, snow, dew, and sleet), convection (upward movement of warm air), and advection (sideways movement of air—that is, wind!). Together we call these "weather," and they include everything from gentle breezes to hurri-

---

30. Earth's temperatures with no greenhouse effect, with greenhouse effect but no feedbacks, and with feedbacks are from S. Manabe and R. F. Strickler, "Thermal equilibrium of the atmosphere with a convective adjustment," *Journal of the Atmospheric Sciences* 21 (1964), 361–65.

canes, from the violent downdrafts of wind shear to the massive, twisting updrafts of tornados, and much more.

There are other feedbacks too, such as changes in cloudiness (which can warm or cool the earth), expansion or contraction of ice (ice reflects solar energy away from earth and so cools it), expansion or contraction of forests and grasslands and deserts, and changes in how rapidly plants take up or give off water through their leaves.

Complete understanding of all these feedbacks is not crucial to the global warming debate. What *is* important is knowing whether, on balance, they *increase* or *decrease* the warming caused by greenhouse gases, and by how much. There is a very simple way to answer that question. With no greenhouse effect, average surface temperature would be about 0°F; with it but without feedbacks, it would be about 140°F; yet, with the greenhouse effect plus feedbacks, it is about 59°F. It seems evident, then, that on balance, these feedbacks decrease the greenhouse effect. By how much? Well, 59 is about 42% of 140, which implies that the feedbacks eliminate about 58% of "greenhouse warming."

c. Then what is the controversy about carbon dioxide?

The global warming controversy has focused mostly on carbon dioxide (CO_2). The people who warn about the dangers of global warming argue that human activities are causing the concentration of greenhouse gases — primarily carbon dioxide, secondarily methane, and to a much lesser extent ozone and chlorofluorocarbons — to increase, and that their increased concentration could warm the earth enough to cause significant, perhaps even catastrophic, harm to people and ecosystems.

The biggest culprit, according to this position, is carbon dioxide, which is responsible for about 3.6% of the total greenhouse effect.

What is carbon dioxide? It is a colorless and nearly odorless gas. It is used to produce the bubbles (carbonation) in carbonated beverages. In a frozen form, it is known as dry ice. When an organic material such as wood burns in a fire, it releases carbon dioxide. Carbon dioxide is also released when coal or gasoline or natural gas (methane) burns. Therefore much energy production releases carbon dioxide into the atmosphere.

In our bodies, carbon dioxide plays an important role in regulating our blood flow and rate of breathing. When we breathe, we inhale oxygen and exhale carbon dioxide in every breath. In fact, all insects, animals, and people emit carbon dioxide when they exhale. In addition, oceans, volcanoes, and other natural sources emit it, too. Carbon dioxide is part of the natural way God has made the world to function.

Carbon dioxide is also crucial for plants, because they need it for photosynthesis, a process that uses light energy to produce various compounds necessary for a plant to live and grow. During photosynthesis, plants absorb carbon dioxide and release oxygen. Thus, in a wonderful cycle of nature that has been designed by God, animals and people continually use up oxygen and release carbon dioxide for plants to use, and then plants use up that carbon dioxide and release oxygen for people and animals to use. *Carbon dioxide is thus essential to all the major life systems on the earth.* We should not think of carbon dioxide as a pollutant, but as an essential part of God's wise arrangement of life on earth.

Many atmospheric scientists believe the concentration of carbon dioxide in the atmosphere has risen from about 270 to about 385 parts per million by volume (ppmv), or from about 0.027% to 0.039%, since preindustrial times (before about 1750).[31] Where did this increase in carbon dioxide come from? Primarily, so goes the theory, from burning carbon-based ("fossil") fuels: coal, oil, and natural gas. (However, there are some reasons to question whether atmospheric carbon dioxide has increased that much, and whether burning fossil fuels caused all or most of the increase.)

What is the effect of increasing carbon dioxide from 270 to 385 parts per million? We can compare that with some estimates of what the temperature effect would be from actually *doubling* carbon dioxide concentration from preindustrial times (from 270 to 540 ppmv). This, according to different estimates, would have a net result of raising earth's average surface temperature, *before feedbacks*, by about 1.8° to 2.16°F.[32] And, frankly, that is a relatively small increase in average temperature that does not scare anybody.

What causes some people to fear much greater warming is the belief that climate feedbacks *magnify* this warming. So that belief is built into the computer models that predict the weather for many decades into the

---

31. Roy W. Spencer et al., "The Science of Global Warming," in *A Renewed Call to Truth, Prudence, and Protection of the Poor: An Evangelical Examination of the Theology, Science, and Economics of Global Warming* (Burke, VA: Cornwall Alliance for the Stewardship of Creation, 2009). www.cornwallalliance.org/docs/a-renewed-call-to-truth-prudence-and-protection-of-the-poor.pdf, 27.

32. The low figure (1.8°F) is from Spencer et al., "Science of Global Warming," 27. The high figure (2.16°F) is from Martin L. Weitzman, "On Modeling and Interpreting the Economics of Catastrophic Climate Change," *Review of Economics and Statistics* 91 (Feb. 2009), 1–19, abstract online at http://ideas.repec.org/a/tpr/restat/v91y2009i1p1–19.html; pre-publication full text online at www.economics.harvard.edu/faculty/weitzman/files/modeling.pdf.

future. All of the computer models used by the United Nation's Intergovernmental Panel on Climate Change (IPCC) assume that climate feedbacks magnify the warming that comes from greenhouse gases.

It is important to understand here that the fears of future global warming rest on *predictions of future weather produced by computer "models"* that give different weights to different factors. The computer programs are not infallible, but will predict whatever is required by the data and formulas fed to them; different data and different formulas, based on different assumptions, will give different predictions.

Therefore the fears of future global warming rest on *hypotheses* represented by computer models, *not on empirical observations* of the real world. These models, *by assuming various feedbacks that add to the greenhouse effect,* predict that warming from *doubled* carbon dioxide since preindustrial time would result in an increase of 3.5°F to a midrange estimate of 5.4°F to a high estimate of about 7°F.

Then some *other* computer formulas (other models) have used the *upper range* of this first set of predictions and have gone on to predict serious harm from such warming. (But remember: model results are not *evidence*; they are merely *hypotheses*. Only empirical observations are evidence.)

Other scientists, however, have raised significant objections to this entire process of making predictions. They point out that climate feedbacks are climate feedbacks, and there is no reason to think the feedbacks will act differently on man-made "greenhouse gases" than on natural ones. Since the feedbacks currently eliminate about 58% of the warming effect of natural greenhouse gases, it stands to reason that they will do the same to the warming effect of man-made ones.

These scientists say that the proponents of global warming *have the feedbacks backward in their computer formulas.* Appealing to what we already know *by observing the real world,* they say that although some feedbacks may be positive and tend to warm the earth, *the combined feedback effect* must be negative—very strongly negative—and therefore the feedbacks will tend to have an overall cooling effect on additional man-made greenhouse gases.

The result? I mentioned above that *if we did not factor in climate feedbacks,* doubling the amount of carbon dioxide from preindustrial times, so that it would increase from 270 to 540 parts per million by volume (ppmv), would have a net result of raising earth's average surface temperature, *before feedbacks,* by about 1.8° to 2.16°F. But if we expect climate feedbacks to *subtract* from warming, we can expect they will lower the warming effects by about 58% to between 0.76°F to 0.9°F—in other words, actually *doubling* the amount of carbon dioxide from preindustrial times would lead to a total "global warming" of less than 1°F.[33]

An increase in average world temperature of less than 1°F is not dangerous. In fact, in general such slight warming would be beneficial, especially to agriculture. This is because most of the warming would occur in higher latitudes (near the poles), in the winter, and at night, not in already hot places at hot times. The result would be *longer growing seasons in cooler climates, less crop damage* from frost, and *fewer deadly cold snaps* (which tend to kill about ten times as many people per day as heat waves). Longer growing seasons would make food more abundant and therefore more affordable, a great benefit to the world's poor.[34]

This way of arguing for low climate sensitivity to increases in greenhouse gases—from the big picture of what we know about the effect of overall feedbacks on "greenhouse warming"—isn't the only way to reach this conclusion. More narrowly focused studies have reached it also. For example, Richard Lindzen and Yong-Sang Choi conclude their analysis from the Earth Radiation Budget Experiment by saying that "ERBE data appear to demonstrate a climate sensitivity of about 0.5°C [0.9°F]."[35] So this study also shows less warming than 1°F.

---

33. Spencer et al., "Science of Global Warming," 26–27, figures recalculated using Weitzman's higher (2.16°F) estimate of warming from doubled carbon dioxide. If Spencer's lower estimate (1.8°F) for warming from doubled carbon dioxide is correct, the IPCC's estimates require much greater added increments—94 percent, 200 percent, or 289 percent—and the net warming after feedbacks is about 0.76°F instead of 0.9°F.

34. William Nordhaus, *A Question of Balance: Weighing the Options on Global Warming Policies* (New Haven: Yale University Press, 2008); Bjørn Lomborg, *Cool It: The Skeptical Environmentalist's Guide to Global Warming* (New York: Alfred A. Knopf, 2007); Robert Mendelsohn, *Climate Change and Agriculture: An Economic Analysis of Global Impacts, Adaptation and Distributional Effects*, New Horizons in Environmental Economics (Northampton, MA: Edward Elgar, 2009).

35. Richard S. Lindzen and Yong-Sang Choi, in "On the determination of climate feedbacks from ERBE [Earth Radiation Budget Experiment] Data," *Geophysical Research Letters* 36 (Aug. 26, 2009), www.drroyspencer.com/Lindzen-and-Choi-GRL-2009.pdf, 5). Stephen E. Schwartz, in "Heat Capacity, Time Constant, and Sensitivity of Earth's Climate System," *Journal of Geophysical Research* 112 (Nov. 2, 2007), (www.ecd.bnl.gov/steve/pubs/HeatCapacity.pdf, 17), concludes that climate sensitivity could range from 1.08° to 2.88°F (1.1 ± 0.5 K). Richard S. Lindzen, Ming-Dah Chou, and Arthur Y. Hou, in "Does the Earth Have an Adaptive Infrared Iris?" *Bulletin of the American Meteorological Society* 82:3 (March 2001), (www-eaps.mit.edu/faculty/lindzen/adinfriris.pdf), provide evidence that clouds respond to surface warming by allowing more heat to escape into space, thus acting as a strong negative feedback. Roy W. Spencer, William D. Braswell, John R. Christy, and Justin Hnilo, in "Cloud and radiation budget changes associated with tropical intraseasonal oscillations," *Geophysical Research Letters* 34 (Aug. 9, 2007), (www.drroyspencer.com/Spencer_07GRL.pdf), reached similar conclusions using different methods.

Therefore, should we believe these predictions of dangerous results that will come from increased temperatures? I don't think so, for three reasons: (1) Actual empirical data about the effects of climate feedbacks show that they do not multiply the warming effect of greenhouse gases as the global warming computer programs would have us believe (as explained above); (2) some principles from the Bible make me doubt these global warming predictions; and (3) some important facts from other scientific evidence make me doubt them as well. The material that follows will explain reasons 2 and 3.

2. The Bible's teaching about the earth

a. Did God design a fragile earth or a resilient one?

The predictions of global warming that have most prominently come from the U.N.'s IPCC require us to believe that the net climate feedback response to "greenhouse warming" is very strongly positive (or warming) and therefore that dangerous global warming is likely.

But should Christians believe that God has actually designed the earth to be this fragile in response to human activity? This would be analogous to believing that an architect designed a building so that if someone leaned against one wall, its structural feedbacks would so magnify the stress of that person's weight that the building would collapse! No one would consider such an architectural design "very good." Yet Genesis 1:31 tells us, "God saw everything that he had made, and behold, it was very good."

If the earth is the product of the infinitely wise and omniscient God and is sustained by his providence, is seems to me more reasonable to think that the fundamental mechanisms of the earth's climate system are robust, self-regulating, and self-correcting—that they are designed to operate somewhat like a thermostat, cooling the planet when it begins to warm, and warming it when it begins to cool.

Evidence that the earth has warmed and cooled cyclically throughout its history is consistent with this view. As Fred Singer and Dennis Avery put it in the prologue to their book *Unstoppable Global Warming—Every 1,500 Years*:

> The history of Earth's climate is a story of constant change. Through at least the last million years, a moderate 1,500-year warm-cold cycle has been superimposed over the longer, stronger Ice Ages and warm interglacials. In the North Atlantic, the

temperature changes about 4°C [7.2°F] from peak to trough during these "Dansgaard-Oeschger cycles."[36]

b. God's promises to maintain stability in seasons and oceans

Some other biblical truths point in this same direction, reflecting details of God's protection of the earth's seasons and oceans. For example, after the great flood of Noah's day, God promised, "While the earth remains, seedtime and harvest, cold and heat, summer and winter, day and night, shall not cease" (Gen. 8:22). This suggests God's commitment to sustain the various cycles on which human, animal, and plant life on earth depend, until the final judgment.

Also following the flood, God promised, "Never again shall there be a flood to destroy the earth" (Gen. 9:11; see also v. 15). While that by itself doesn't rule out the possibility of major sea level increase (probably the most feared effect predicted from global warming), it does indicate that God controls the sea level. Psalm 104:9 likewise says, regarding the waters of the seas, "*You set a boundary that they may not pass, so that they might not again cover the earth.*" And in Jeremiah, God says,

> I placed the sand as the boundary for the sea, a perpetual barrier that it cannot pass; though the waves toss, they cannot prevail; though they roar, they cannot pass over it (Jer. 5:22).

c. People displease God when they fail to acknowledge his control of the weather

In the next verses after Jeremiah 5:22, God rebukes Israel for not acknowledging that he controls their weather:

> But this people has a stubborn and rebellious heart; they have turned aside and gone away. They do not say in their hearts, "Let us fear the LORD our God, who gives the rain in its season, the autumn rain and the spring rain, and keeps for us the weeks appointed for the harvest." Your iniquities have turned these away [that is, the rains and the harvest seasons], and your sins have kept good from you" (Jer. 5:23–25).

This passage sounds remarkably similar to the proponents of dangerous global warming today—they fear a fragile, out-of-control climate pattern that will destroy the earth, but "do not say in their hearts, 'Let us

---

36. S. Fred Singer and Dennis T. Avery, *Unstoppable Global Warming—Every 1,500 Years*, 2d ed. (Lanham, MD: Rowman & Littlefield, 2008).

fear the LORD our God, who gives the rain in its season.'" This suggests that the underlying cause of fears of dangerous global warming might not be science, but rejection of belief in God.

In the New Testament, the apostle Paul speaks similarly of people who "suppress the truth" about God's existence and attributes (Rom. 1:18). These people "did not honor him as God or give thanks to him, but they became futile in their thinking, and their foolish hearts were darkened" (v. 21). Surely that includes people who did not honor God or give thanks to him for the brilliant order and structure of his creation, so, "claiming to be wise, they became fools" (v. 22) and "exchanged the truth about God for a lie and worshiped and served the creature rather than the Creator" (v. 25). Such a description could be applied to much of the environmentalist movement, for whom "Mother Earth" rather than the one true God is their highest object of devotion.

Many other passages of Scripture also affirm God's control over the earth's weather (see Lev. 26:18–20; Deut. 28:12, 23–24; 2 Sam. 21:1; 1 Kings 17–18; Job 37:9–13; Pss. 107:23–38; 148:8; Amos 4:7–8; Jonah 1:4–16; Matt. 8:26–27).

d. God did not design the earth so that we would destroy it by obeying his commands

God originally commanded Adam and Eve (and by implication all mankind):

> "Be fruitful and multiply and *fill the earth and subdue it* and have dominion over the fish of the sea and over the birds of the heavens and over every living thing that moves on the earth" (Gen. 1:28).

This command seems inconsistent with a belief in dangerous, man-made global warming. Do we think God set up the earth so that we would destroy it by obeying these commands to develop the earth's resources and use them for our benefit? Did he set up the earth so that when we burn wood to warm ourselves or cook food, or when we burn gasoline to drive to work or school or church, or when we use diesel fuel to transport food and clothing and household goods from farm or factory to market, or when we burn oil or coal or natural gas to produce electricity to cook with or to heat or cool our homes or to provide light — do we really think God set up the earth to work in such a way that *the more we do these morally right things*, the more we will *destroy the earth*?

I do not think God made the earth to work that way. Rather, I think that God put wood on the earth and coal and oil and natural gas in the earth so that we could have abundant, easily transportable sources of fuel for use in various applications. Of course, all of these things can be used foolishly and dangerously—instead of building a safe fire to cook food, someone can carelessly start a forest fire. And coal-burning plants and factories can spew out soot and chemicals and pollute the air. I am not advocating reckless, dangerous use of these fuels.

But that is not all that global warming alarmists are complaining about. They are also warning against *clean and safe use of all these fuels.* They are saying that there is *no* safe use of these fossil fuels, because even if they are burned with 100% pollution-free flames, *they will still necessarily emit carbon dioxide* because that is an unavoidable by-product of combustion. They object not to the *abuse* of fossil fuels to pollute or destroy the environment but to their very *use.* They want to take away from human beings the best, most convenient, and cheapest energy sources we have.

Do we really think God has created the earth so that it would be destroyed by such morally right human activities, done in obedience to him? Do we really think God created the earth so that its climate system would care off into catastrophe if carbon dioxide rose from 0.027% to 0.054% of the atmosphere (that is, from 27 to 54 *thousandths of one percent* of the atmosphere)? That is what global warming alarmists imply. Or do we think, by contrast, that God has set up an earth that is immensely resilient and will be able to adapt and be useful for human life under a wide variety of conditions?

My own view is that God has placed in the earth and its atmosphere a number of self-regulating, self-correcting mechanisms by which it can manage its own temperature. One example of this is the "global iris" effect of clouds over the oceans.[37] When the surface becomes warmer, high-level clouds diminish, permitting more heat to escape into space. When the surface cools, high-level clouds increase, retaining more heat. This and other studies showing that clouds regulate earth's temperature should, as Christian environmental theologian E. Calvin Beisner puts it, lead

> Christians to praise God for the way in which the Earth, like the human body, is "fearfully and wonderfully made." In some senses this planet, like the eye, may be fragile. But it may also, by God's wise design, be more resilient than many fearful environmentalists may imagine.[38]

---

37. Lindzen et al., "Does the Earth Have an Adaptive Infrared Iris?"
38. E. Calvin Beisner, *What Is the Most Important Environmental Task Facing American Christians Today?* Mt. Nebo Papers, No. 1 (Washington, DC: Institute for Religion and Democracy, 2008), 23, in sidebar "Climate Science and Doxology." www.theird.org/Document.Doc?id=25.

This high-level cloud variation certainly looks like a self-correcting mechanism that God built into the earth's system to keep temperatures relatively stable. Who knows whether there are other systems like this that we have not yet discovered, where a heating factor triggers a balancing cooling factor and vice-versa? It would not be surprising, since the earth's long-term temperature averages tend to go back and forth between warming trends followed by cooling trends followed by warming trends.

e. Global warming alarmists remove our motivation to thank God for his wonderful gifts of cheap, abundant energy resources

The Bible praises God for his creation of the earth:

> And God saw everything that he had made, and behold, *it was very good* (Gen. 1:31).

> The earth is the LORD's and the fullness thereof, the world and those who dwell therein (Ps. 24:1).

> … *everything created by God is good*, and nothing is to be rejected if it is received with thanksgiving (1 Tim. 4:4).

These passages and others tell us that we should give thanks and praise to God for the excellence of the earth that he created. He wants us to develop and use the earth's resources because "he formed it to be inhabited!" (Isa. 45:18). We should use the resources he placed in the earth with thanksgiving to him.

Those who warn that we face dangerous global warming tell us we should feel guilty about using wood, coal, oil, and natural gas to produce energy. Rather than using God's good gifts with thanksgiving, they load us with guilt for using God's good gifts. Therefore they rob people of the motivation to thank God for the wonderful things he has given.

3. What does the scientific evidence say about global warming?

One response to the arguments above is to say that "scientists agree" that human emissions of greenhouse gases are causing global warming that could do great harm. For example, that is the message trumpeted endlessly by Al Gore, whose video documentary *An Inconvenient Truth* has been shown in thousands of schools and even won an Oscar, and who with the IPCC received the Nobel Peace Prize for warning the world of impending climate disaster.

But is the scientific consensus really that clear? No, it certainly is not. Every attempt to prove the existence of such a scientific consensus has failed.

a. Scientific opinion is strongly divided about global warming

First, it is now beginning to seem that more scientists *reject* than embrace the idea of dangerous man-made global warming—possibly many times more. In one list compiled by a US Senate panel, *more than 700 scientists* have published their rejections of the whole or significant parts of the global warming hypothesis.[39]

On another list, *more than 31,000 degreed scientists*, including over 9,000 with PhDs, have signed the "Global Warming Petition" saying:

> There is *no convincing scientific evidence* that human release of carbon dioxide, methane, or other greenhouse gases is causing or will, in the foreseeable future, cause catastrophic heating of the Earth's atmosphere and disruption of the Earth's climate. Moreover, there is substantial scientific evidence that increases in atmospheric carbon dioxide produce many beneficial effects upon the natural plant and animal environments of the Earth.[40]

Another important resource in this regard is Lawrence Solomon's book *The Deniers: The World-Renowned Scientists Who Stood Up against Global Warming Hysteria, Political Persecution, and Fraud*.[41] He shows that those who reject the global warming alarms include many of the world's top experts in their fields.

Second, the published scientific literature is divided about this issue. A 2003 review, by history professor Naomi Oreskes, of scientific abstracts that purported to demonstrate scientific agreement about global warm-

---

39. U.S. Senate Minority Report: Over 700 International Scientists Dissent over Man-Made Global Warming Claims (Dec. 11, 2008). http://epw.senate.gov/public/index.cfm?FuseAction=Minority.Blogs&ContentRecord_id=2674E64F−802A−23AD−490B-BD9FAF4DCDB7.

40. Oregon Institute of Science and Medicine, "Global Warming Petition Project," emphasis added, http://petitionproject.org/. The site includes complete lists of signers and, at http://petitionproject.org/qualifications_of_signers.php, summarizes the numbers from various specialties relevant to the debate.

41. Lawrence Solomon, *The Deniers: The World-Renowned Scientists Who Stood Up against Global Warming Hysteria, Political Persecution, and Fraud* (Minneapolis: Richard Vigilante Books, 2008), 207−8.

ing was shown to have been badly flawed, and a re-examination of the same database found no such consensus.[42] Then a study of the same database covering up to 2007 actually showed a significant shift away from what had earlier (and mistakenly) been claimed as the consensus. As Klaus-Martin Schulte put it in the last of those studies,

> Though Oreskes said that 75% of the papers in her sample endorsed the consensus, fewer than half now endorse it. Only 6% do so explicitly. Only one paper refers to "catastrophic" climate change, but without offering evidence. There appears to be little evidence in the learned journals to justify the climate-change alarm that now harms patients.[43]

Third, as Thomas Kuhn so famously pointed out in *The Structure of Scientific Revolutions*, great advances in science, often involving major paradigm shifts, occur when small minorities patiently—and often in the face of withering opposition—point out anomalies in the data and inadequacies in the reigning explanatory paradigms until their number and weight become so large as to require a wholesale paradigm shift, and what once was a minority view becomes a new majority view. Something like this process seems to be happening now to gradually change the media-driven claims of "consensus" about man-made global warming.

b. The earth's temperature has fallen or remained steady for the past fifteen years, a result not predicted by global warming computer models

The normal process in scientific investigation is to propose a hypothesis and then test it by seeing if the actual empirical data confirm or falsify it. What has happened with respect to global warming? The hypothesis was that recent increases in atmospheric carbon dioxide would lead to

---

42. Naomi Oreskes, "The scientific consensus on climate change," *Science* 306:5702 (Dec. 3, 2004), 1686; www.sciencemag.org/cgi/content/full/306/5702/1686. This was refuted by Benny J. Peiser's Letter to *Science* (Jan. 4, 2005), submission ID: 56001; www.staff.livjm. ac.uk/spsbpeis/Scienceletter.htm. The surveys were reported in Dennis Bray and Hans von Storch, *The Perspectives of Climate Scientists on Global Climate Change* (Geesthacht, Germany: GKSS–Forschungszentrum Geesthacht, 2007); http://dvsun3.gkss.de/BERICHTE/GKSS_Berichte_2007/GKSS_2007_11.pdf.

43. Klaus-Martin Schulte, "Scientific Consensus on Climate Change?" *Energy and Environment* 19, no. 2 (July 2009), 281–86. http://scienceandpublicpolicy.org/images/stories/papers/reprint/schulte_two_colmun_fomat.pdf.

increasing global temperatures. But the actual facts have not shown that hypothesis to be true.

For one thing, there has been no "statistically significant" increase in average global temperatures in the last fifteen years, even according to a BBC News interview on February 13, 2010, with Dr. Phil Jones, long-time director of the Climatic Research Unit at the University of East Anglia (until he stepped down in December under investigation for scientific misconduct). Jones has been the provider of much of the most important data on which the U.N. IPCC and many governments have based fears of global warming. He reported a positive warming trend of 0.12°Centigrade per decade (0.216°F per decade, or an average of 0.02°F per year, too small to be statistically significant) from 1995 to 2009, but also said that there was a negative (cooling) trend of −0.12°C per decade if you calculate from January 2002 to 2009![44] How can this be? Such stability or even cooling in the presence of *increased* carbon dioxide is not the predicted result from the global warming computer models. (In the midst of the fallout from the "Climategate" data-rigging scandal in early 2010 [see below], England was covered in more snow than it has known for many years, and so was Washington, DC, which could lead one to wonder if the frigid temperatures might be an indication of an ironic divine exclamation mark over the scandal!)

In that same interview, when asked about the statement, "the debate on climate change is over," Jones amazingly replied,

> I don't believe the vast majority of climate scientists think this. This is not my view. There is still much that needs to be undertaken to reduce uncertainties, not just for the future, but for the instrumental (and especially the palaeoclimatic) past as well.[45]

In addition, earlier changes in average global temperatures have not coincided with changes in atmospheric concentrations of carbon dioxide. Here is a graph showing changes in global temperatures for the last 150 years:[46]

Note that the increase in temperature from 1910 to 1940 was *prior to* most of the world's increasing production of carbon dioxide (after World War II). Then there was a cooling period from about 1945 to 1975, then a warming period from 1975 to 2000, then a cooling period from

---

44. BBC interview with Professor Phil Jones, at http://news.bbc.co.uk/2/hi/science/nature/8511670.stm (accessed Feb. 25, 2010).

45. Ibid.

46. Chart taken from www.windows.ucar.edu/tour/link=/earth/climate/climate_today_2a.html.

GLOBAL AVERAGE TEMPERATURES 1850–2009

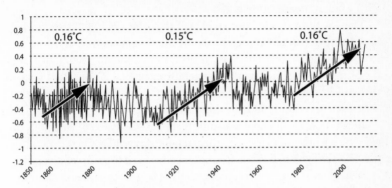

Source: http://joannenova.com.au/2010/03/the-bom-csiro-report-its-what-they-dont-say-that-matters/. Reprinted by permission.

2000 to the present. (And all of these changes are relatively small—the graph is measuring just tenths of a degree Centigrade).

In addition, especially in light of the Climategate scandal, there is some doubt even about the reliability of these temperature measurements, especially whether they adjusted adequately for the "urban heat island" effect—that is, a temperature-monitoring station placed in an uninhabited area that was far from a city thirty years ago might now be surrounded by homes and office buildings and asphalt parking lots, all of which retain heat long after the sun goes down, so the thermometer will have higher average temperatures, but that has nothing to do with carbon dioxide concentrations or trends in overall global temperatures. The weather station might even now be located next to an air-conditioning unit or an exhaust fan![47]

Finally, other factors seem better able to explain the changes that have been observed in global temperatures, especially changes in ocean currents and solar activity.[48]

c. Should the UN's Intergovernmental Panel on Climate Change (IPCC) be trusted to have the last word?

Many people refer to the IPCC as the world's most authoritative body on global warming and describe its pronouncements as those of "thousands of climate scientists." The IPCC certainly warns of dangerous global

---

47. See examples and information at www.surfacestations.org.

48. See 31 of the Cornwall Alliance's statement on scientific analysis of climate: www.cornwallalliance.org/docs/a-renewed-call-to-truth-prudence-and-protection-of-the-poor.pdf.

warming. But we need to understand just what the IPCC has said, and what kind of organization it is.

The "Summary for Policymakers" that the IPCC publishes does not always accurately represent the detailed science in its Assessment Reports (which have been issued in 1992, 1995, 2001, and 2007). Instead, the Summary for Policymakers generally exaggerates the actual scientific conclusions. But because few journalists or politicians ever read the actual science, they tend to be unaware of this problem.[49]

In addition, we should not assume that the IPCC is an *objective* body of *objective* scientists not serving particular political agendas. On the contrary, the IPCC is *highly politicized*. Its charter called for it to study *human* influence on global temperature; consequently, it largely ignores *natural* influences. (And hundreds of staff workers now know that their jobs depend on continuing to find and publish evidence supporting the theory of dangerous man-made global warming, which gives a built-in bias factor in their data.) The crucial chapter 9 of its 2007 Assessment Report, which assesses likely temperature change from human "greenhouse gas" emissions and on which all the rest depends, relies heavily on the work of a small group of scientists prone to "group think" for lack of adequate interaction with others. Structural flaws seriously reduce the IPCC's credibility.[50]

Finally, the IPCC's authority was deeply undermined by a large number of scandals that surfaced in late 2009 and early 2010. These include particularly "Climategate" and discoveries that the IPCC based some of its most frightening predictions on unscientific sources—such as press releases from environmental advocacy groups—while the actual scientific data refuted them.[51]

The term "Climategate" refers to the November 2009 leak, from the Climatic Research Unit at the University of East Anglia in England, of thousands of emails, computer codes, and other documents. These documents

---

49. Mark W. Henderson, "A Closer Look at the IPCC," Center for Vision and Values, Grove City College (May 22, 2009). www.visandvals.org/A_Closer_Look_at_the_IPCC.php.

50. David Henderson, "Governments and Climate Change Issues: A Flawed Consensus" (prior version online at www.heartland.org/custom/semod_policybot/pdf/19306.pdf), and Ross McKitrick, "Response to David Henderson's 'Governments and Climate Change Issues'" (http://ross.mckitrick.googlepages.com/McKitrick.final.pdf), both in *American Education Bulletin* XLVIII:5 (May 2008); John McLean, *Prejudiced Authors, Prejudiced Findings: Did the UN bias its attribution of "global warming" to humankind?* (Washington, DC: Science & Public Policy Institute, 2008), http://scienceandpublicpolicy.org/images/stories/papers/originals/McLean_IPCC_bias.pdf.

51. Mark Landsbaum, "What to say to a global warming alarmist" (Feb. 12, 2010), (www.ocregister.com/articles/-234092-.html), provides a helpful list and summary of such IPCC errors.

revealed that a core group of climate scientists at a wide range of agencies—the CRU, NASA's Goddard Institute for Space Studies, the National Oceanic and Atmospheric Administration, the National Center for Atmospheric Research, the National Climatic Data Center, the UK Meteorological Office, and elsewhere—on which the IPCC and national governments relied for data basic to global warming projections, had committed some serious scientific misconduct. Among the misdeeds were these:

- Fabricating, cherry-picking, suppressing, withholding, and destroying data related to historic and present temperatures;
- Failing to keep proper research archives;
- Using computer programs intentionally designed to exaggerate recent warming and minimize earlier climate variability (both warming and cooling) to create the appearance that recent warming was unprecedented when it was not;
- Refusing to share data and source code with other scholars on request, as required both by standard scientific practice and, in some cases, by the written standards of journals in which their work was published;
- Intimidating dissenting scientists to deter them from publishing research contrary to belief in dangerous man-made global warming;
- Corrupting the peer review process to prevent publication of dissenting research;
- Attempting to have journal editors who published dissenting research removed from their jobs;
- Boycotting journals that published dissenting papers; and
- Violating the law by refusing to turn over information subject to Freedom of Information laws in both the United States and the United Kingdom.

This is simply not the way researchers act when they are confident that the actual facts are overwhelmingly on their side. The misconduct was so serious and systemic that *it simply undercuts the credibility of all historic and contemporary temperature data* published in the IPCC's Scientific Assessment Reports.[52] But these sets of data were the basis for the claims of the

---

52. The three most thorough analyses of "Climategate" at the time of this writing are John P. Costella, *Climategate Analysis*, SPPI Reprint Series (Jan. 20, 2010) from the Washington: Science & Public Policy Institute (2010), (http://scienceandpublicpolicy.org/images/stories/papers/reprint/climategate_analysis.pdf); Steven Mosher and Thomas Fuller, *Climategate: The CRUtape Letters* (Charleston, SC: CreateSpace/Amazon.com, 2010); Brian Sussman, *Climategate: A Meteorologist Exposes the Global Warming Scam* (Torrance, CA: WND Books, 2010); and A. W. Montford, *The Hockey Stick Illusion: Climategate and the Corruption of Science* (London: Stacey International, 2010).

global warming alarmists! In short, the IPCC's authority on global warming is poor. It is doubtful that it will be able to regain the credibility it previously had in the scientific world. It was using distorted, incorrect data.

The top climate-change official at the United Nations, Yvo do Boer, announced his resignation February 19, 2010. The *Washington Times* reported, "The bureaucrat's departure is no surprise because his pseudo-scientific global warming religion was proved to be a hoax on his watch."[53] In the same article, the *Post* also reported the following remarkable disclosure:

> Joseph D'Aleo, the first director of meteorology and co-founder of the Weather Channel, and Anthony Watts, a meteorologist and founder of SurfaceStations.org, are well-known and well-respected scientists. On Jan. 29, they released a startling study showing that starting in 1990, the National Oceanic and Atmospheric Administration (NOAA) began systematically eliminating climate-measuring stations in cooler locations around the world. Eliminating stations that tended to record cooler temperatures drove up the average measured temperature. The stations eliminated were in higher latitudes and altitudes, inland areas away from the sea and more rural locations. The drop in the number of weather stations was dramatic, declining from more than 6,000 stations to fewer than 1,500.[54]

Lawrence Solomon, in *The Deniers*, had already written that the Climategate scandal made the historical temperature data suspect and that carbon dioxide's "contribution to global warming remains approximately nil."[55] The broader implications of Climategate and related data-manipulation scandals were still unfolding at the time of this writing.

d. Are glaciers melting and sea levels rising?

For years now, the public has been bombarded with messages that man-made global warming is causing disastrous consequences, such as melting glaciers, endangered polar bears, and rising sea levels. What should we think of these claims?

53. *Washington Times* (Feb. 18, 2010). www.washingtontimes.com/news/2010/feb/18/more-errors-in-temperature-data/?feat=home_editorials.

54. Ibid.

55. Lawrence Solomon, "The Ozone Hole Did It," *Financial Post* Comment (Jan. 9, 2010). http://network.nationalpost.com/np/blogs/fpcomment/archive/2010/01/09/the-ozone-hole-did-it.aspx.

First, even if we did see glaciers melting and sea levels rising, these might well be due to other factors such as variations in sun activity, variations in ocean currents, and ordinary long-term weather cycles and not due to changes in carbon dioxide levels (as explained above).

Second, none of the claimed disasters is well supported by evidence. Here are some examples:

(1) *Glaciers and ice caps:* Glaciers have been shrinking slowly ever since the end of the last Ice Age (perhaps around 18,000 years ago) — during more than 99% of which time people have not emitted enough greenhouse gas to have any effect on global average temperatures. So the mere fact of their shrinking is nothing new and nothing caused by human beings.

But is there recent shrinkage evidence pointing to accelerated warming and thus, indirectly, evidence that *something* new is going on? No. The data are simply insufficient to establish accelerated shrinkage compared with their long-term rate since the Ice Age.[56]

As for ice caps in the Arctic and Antarctic, short-term observations do not prove much of anything. Ice melts in warmer seasons and freezes in cooler seasons every year, and there are warmer years and colder years, so a photo of melting Arctic ice does not prove a long-term trend. But if people want to use short-term observations, the recent ones show that both Arctic and Antarctic ice has been *expanding*:

> In October 2008, it was reported that Arctic ice was actually increasing at a rapid rate. According to the International Climate and Environmental Change Assessment Project (ICECAP), an organization of respected climatology academics, the Arctic ice had increased at a rate of 31.3% or from 5,663,125 square kilometers in 2007 to 7,436,406 square kilometers just a year later.[57] They also reported in 2008 that Antarctica had set a record for the maximum amount of ice since monitoring began in 1979.[58]

(2) *Sea levels.* Al Gore, in his book *Earth in the Balance*, dramatically claimed, "Many residents of low-lying Pacific Island nations have already had to evacuate their homes because of rising seas" — a claim illustrated

---

56. Idso and Singer, *Climate Change Reconsidered*, 135–52.

57. Joseph D'Aleo, "Arctic Ice Increasing Rapidly" (Oct. 14, 2008). http://icecap.us/index.php/go/joes-blog/arctic_ice_increasing_rapidly/. (It should be noted that 2007 was an especially low year for Arctic ice, so it is not surprising that the following year would show a significant increase.)

58. Joseph D'Aleo, "Latest Antarctic Ice Extent" (Jan. 14, 2008). http://icecap.us/index.php/go/joes-blog/latest_antarctic_sea_ice_extent2/.

by a photo of Tuvalu (an island nation of 12,000 people between Hawaii and Australia).[59]

But as Marlo Lewis pointed out in his 154-page, devastating critique of Gore's book, "Tide gauge records show that sea levels at Tuvalu *fell* during the latter half of the twentieth century. Altimetry data from the Topex-Poseiden satellite show that Tuvalu sea levels fell even during the 1990s...."[60] Indeed, no one has had to evacuate any Pacific island nations because of rising sea level. Gore's claim was just misleading.

In the film *An Inconvenient Truth* Gore claimed that melting ice from West Antarctica and Greenland would cause a twenty-foot increase in sea level worldwide. Although he did not specify *when* this would happen, the context makes it clear that he intends the prediction to prompt action *now* to protect our children or perhaps our grandchildren. Clearly, he had the remainder of this century in mind.

Yet the IPCC, even with its questionable assumption of high warming from rising greenhouse gases, estimated instead that melt from those two locations would add only about *2.5 inches* to sea level over the next hundred years.[61] In fact, sea level, which has been slowly rising ever since the end of the last Ice Age, rose only about 6.3 inches in the entire twentieth century—and the *rate* of increase *declined* in the latter half of the century.[62]

Gore's movie was judged by a British court to have so many and such serious errors that it could no longer be shown in British government schools without an accompanying list and refutation of its errors. Otherwise, said the judge, it would violate an Act of Parliament prohibiting political indoctrination of children.[63]

59. Al Gore, *Earth in the Balance* (Emmaus, PA: Rodale Books, 2006), 186.

60. Marlo Lewis Jr., *Al Gore's Science Fiction: A Skeptic's Guide to An Inconvenient Truth,* Congressional Briefing Paper (Washington, DC: Competitive Enterprise Institute, n.d.), 88, online at http://cei.org/pdf/5820.pdf. See also Cliff Ollier, "Sea Level in the Southwest Pacific is Stable," *New Concepts in Global Tectonics Newsletter* 51 (June 2009), http://nzclimate-science.net/images/PDFs/paperncgtsealevl.pdf.

61. Christopher Monckton, *35 Inconvenient Truths: The Errors of Al Gore's Movie* (Washington, DC: Science and Public Policy Institute, 2007), 4. http://scienceandpublicpolicy.org/images/stories/press_releases/monckton-response-to-gore-errors.pdf.

62. S. J. Holgate, "On the decadal rates of sea level change during the twentieth century," *Geophysical Research Letters* 34 (2007): cited in Craig Idso and S. Fred Singer, *Climate Change Reconsidered: 2009 Report of the Nongovernmental International Panel on Climate Change* (NIPCC) (Chicago: Heartland Institute, 2009), 186–87, www.heartland.org/publications/NIPCC%20report/PDFs/NIPCC%20Final.pdf.

63. Monckton, *35 Inconvenient Truths*, 3. See also William Lee Adams, "British Court: Gore Film 'Political,'" *Time* (Oct. 12, 2007). www.time.com/time/world/article/0,8599,1670882,00.html.

e. What about severe weather and other claims about damage from global warming?

Has there been more frequent or more intense *severe weather* caused by a warming earth? No.[64] The most common claim—that hurricane frequency and strength rose with recent global warming—has been not only refuted empirically but also abandoned by the scientist who most strongly promoted it.[65] An attempt by climatologist Michael Mann (author of the discredited "hockey stick" graph that eliminated the Medieval Warm Period and Little Ice Age to make twentieth-century warming appear extraordinary) to show an increase in hurricanes in recent years brought a devastating rebuttal by Chris Landsea, one of the world's leading hurricane experts.[66]

What about *droughts and floods*? Are they growing more frequent and intense? Even if they were, that alone would not prove that this is caused by increases in carbon dioxide. But in fact, droughts and floods are not increasing in frequency or intensity.[67]

4. The benefits that come from increased carbon dioxide in the atmosphere

We should also not ignore a completely different aspect of the discussion. Carbon dioxide's effect on *global average temperature* is most likely insignificant and benign, as I argued above. But its effect on *plant life*—and therefore on all other life, which depends on plant life—is large and *overwhelmingly beneficial.*

---

64. Idso and Singer, *Climate Change Reconsidered*, 281–360; Randall S. Cerveny, "Severe Weather, Natural Disasters, and Global Change," in *Shattered Consensus: The True State of Global Warming*, ed. Patrick J. Michaels (Lanham, MD: Rowman & Littlefield, 2005), 106–20; Patrick J. Michaels, *Meltdown: The Predictable Distortion of Global Warming By Scientists, Politicians, and the Media* (Washington, DC: Cato Institute, 2004), 111–61.

65. National Oceanic and Atmospheric Adminstration, "NOAA Attributes Recent Increase in Hurricane Activity to Naturally Occurring Multi-Decadal Climate Variability" (Nov. 29, 2005), www.magazine.noaa.gov/stories/mag184.htm; Eric Berger, "Hurricane expert reconsiders global warming's impact," *Houston Chronicle* (April 12, 2008), www.chron.com/disp/story.mpl/tech/news/5693436.html; Kerry Emanuel, Ragoth Sundararajan, and John Williams, "Hurricanes and Global Warming: Results from Downscaling IPCC AR4 Simulations," *Bulletin of the American Meteorological Society* 89:3 (March 2008), 347–67, http://ams.allenpress.com/archive/1520–0477/89/3/pdf/i1520–0477–89–3–347.pdf.

66. Chris Landsea, untitled letter in response to Michael Mann and co-authors. http://icecap.us/images/uploads/LetterMann.pdf.

67. Idso and Singer, *Climate Change Reconsidered*, 281–309.

Hundreds and hundreds of peer-reviewed scientific studies have demonstrated that increased atmospheric carbon dioxide leads to enhanced plant growth. Indeed, on average, doubled carbon dioxide increases plant growth efficiency by about 35%. With enhanced carbon dioxide, plants grow better, whether subjected to higher or lower temperatures and to drier or wetter soil. Consequently, their geographical range expands, and so does that of the various animals that depend on them. The plants also resist diseases and pests better.[68]

Earth's atmospheric carbon dioxide level is now very low compared with many past geologic periods—periods during which its plant and animal life thrived. The IPCC and other global warming alarmists tend to hide this fact by referring to carbon dioxide's increase only since pre-industrial times. As mentioned before, we can see the great variation by comparing earlier periods with our current concentration of 385 parts per million by volume (ppmv). Many scientists believe the concentration was 270 ppmv in preindustrial times.[69]

But what about much earlier periods? One study says that early in the Paleozoic era (540–250 million years ago [mya], according to time scales used in modern geological studies), carbon dioxide climbed from about 5,000 to 7,000 ppmv and then fell back again, then fell in fits and starts to about 3,000 ppmv late in the Silurian period (440–415 mya), rose to about 4,000 in the first half of the Devonian period (415–360 mya), fell to around 400 in the Carboniferous (360–300 mya) and Permian (300–250 mya) periods, rose again to about 2,000 in the Triassic period (251–200 mya), fell stepwise to about 1,300 by the middle of the Jurassic period (240–145 mya), rose for a while in that period to about 2,800, and then began a long decline through the Cretaceous (145–65 mya) and Tertiary (65–3 mya) periods, reaching around 200 to 300 in the Quaternary period (3 mya to present).

Did these changes in carbon dioxide result in massive temperature changes? Contrary to the view that carbon dioxide drives temperature, throughout geologic history there has been no clear correlation between

---

68. The Center for the Study of Carbon Dioxide and Global Change (www.co2science. org) maintains an enormous and growing database of published scientific studies on the subject. A review of the findings is in Idso and Singer, *Climate Change Reconsidered*, 361–578.

69. Roy W. Spencer et al., "The Science of Global Warming," in *A Renewed Call to Truth, Prudence, and Protection of the Poor: An Evangelical Examination of the Theology, Science, and Economics of Global Warming* (Burke, VA: Cornwall Alliance for the Stewardship of Creation, 2009), 27. www.cornwallalliance.org/docs/a-renewed-call-to-truth-prudence-and-protection-of-the-poor.pdf.

the two. Sometimes they rose together, sometimes they fell, and some-times they went in opposite directions.[70]

What is clear is that the periods of higher carbon dioxide have also been periods of *much more prolific plant growth*. As Ian Plimer puts it,

> The CO_2 content of air has hardly ever been as low as today and ecosystems suffer because of this. Early in the Earth's history, the CO_2 content of air was tens to hundreds of times higher than today and, over time, this CO_2 has been stored as carbon compounds in rocks, oil, gas, coal and carbonate rocks.[71]

The release of carbon dioxide now, by our burning of fossil fuels, is restoring some of it to the atmosphere and greatly benefitting life on earth. It appears to be causing deserts to green, and it has contributed significantly to increasing crop yields since 1950, making food more abundant and less expensive and therefore reducing the percentage of the human population experiencing hunger and starvation.

Sherwood Idso, one of the world's foremost researchers on the sub-ject, says, "We appear to be experiencing the initial stages of what could truly be called a *rebirth of the biosphere*, the beginnings of a biological rejuvenation that is without precedent in all of human history."[72]

For this reason, intentionally forcing people to reduce carbon dioxide emissions would actually do enormous harm, not only to human econo-mies but also to the whole biosphere.

5. The unacceptable loss of human freedom that would come with government control of energy use

A neglected factor in this discussion is how much we think that gov-ernments should control our lives. The controversy over global warm-ing is to a very large degree a controversy over human liberty versus

70. Robert A. Berner and Zavareth Kothavala, "Geocarb III: A revised model of atmo-spheric CO_2 over Phanerozoic Time," *American Journal of Science* 301 (Feb. 2001), 182–204: summarized in Ian Wishart, *Air Con: The Seriously Inconvenient Truth About Global Warm-ing* (North Shore, NZ: Howling at the Moon Publishing, 2009), 33–36.

71. Ian Plimer, *Heaven and Earth: Global Warming the Missing Science* (Lanham, MD: Taylor Trade Publishing, 2009), 411.

72. Sherwood B. Idso, *CO_2 and the Biosphere: The Incredible Legacy of the Industrial Revo-lution* (St. Paul: University of Minnesota Department of Soil, Water and Climate, 1995). The Center for the Study of Carbon Dioxide and Global Change offers two excellent video documentaries on the benefits of increased carbon dioxide: *The Greening of Planet Earth* and *The Greening of Planet Earth Continues* (www.co2science.org).

government control. The liberal politicians who continually seek more government control do so because they think that enlightened governing officials can run peoples' lives better than they can run them themselves. Such people will eagerly flock in large groups to the global warming crusade, because it appears to be a wonderful mechanism by which government can control more peoples' lives.

Regulating peoples' use of energy is an incredibly effective way of increasing the control of central governments over our entire lives. If the government can dictate how far you drive your car, how much you heat or cool your home, how much you will use electric lights or computers or a TV, how much energy your factory can use, and how much jet fuel you can have to fly an airplane, then it can control most of the society.

Václav Klaus, president of the Czech Republic, said that in his opinion the alarm about global warming and the campaign to reduce carbon dioxide provide the greatest threat to human liberty that has come to the earth since communism. He wrote in the *Financial Times* that "global warming hysteria has become a prime example of the truth versus propaganda problem." He continued:

> As someone who lived under communism for most of his life, I feel obliged to say that I see the biggest threat to freedom, democracy, the market economy and prosperity now in ambitious environmentalism, not in communism. This ideology wants to replace the free and spontaneous evolution of mankind by a sort of central (now global) planning.
>
> The environmentalists ask for immediate political action because they do not believe in the long-term positive impact of economic growth and ignore both the technological progress that future generations will undoubtedly enjoy, and the proven fact that the higher the wealth of society, the higher is the quality of the environment. They are Malthusian pessimists.[73]

This is significant because Klaus lived through many years of communism in the former Czechoslovakia. He is also a trained economist.

6. The unacceptable costs of reducing our use of carbon fuels

Global warming alarmists want the world to drastically reduce the use of fossil fuels to cut carbon dioxide emissions. But the best economic

---

73. Václav Klaus, "Freedom, Not Climate, At Risk," *Financial Times.com*. (June 13, 2007). www.ft.com/cms/s/2/9deb730a–19ca–11dc–99c5–000b5df10621.html.

analyses show that trying to reduce fossil fuel use would cause far more harm than good.[74] Why? Because abundant, affordable energy is crucial to economic production, especially to societies that seek to climb out of abject poverty. It is important to remember that when we use energy sources, we reduce the need for human work: plowing a field with a tractor rather than walking behind a horse, driving a car rather than walking huge distances, driving a truck rather than pushing a cart, and so forth. Energy use makes possible all human economic progress and frees us to use our time in higher levels of intellectual endeavor or interpersonal human relationships or even various Christian ministries. Energy use gives us freedom that we can use as we choose—for good or for ill.

Where can we obtain energy? Fossil fuels are (along with nuclear energy) the most abundant and affordable sources of energy available. Forcing people to replace carbon fuels would require them to switch to alternative energy sources, and solar, wind, and biofuels—the sources frequently mentioned—tend to cost from two to eight times as much as fossil fuels for generating electricity.[75] Such a switch would mean *drastically increasing the price of energy* and thus slowing economic development, trapping the world's poor in their poverty and perpetuating the high rates of disease and premature death that stem from their poverty.

Human beings already live in climates from the freezing Arctic to the searing Sahara. Temperature is not a significant challenge. The wealthier people are, the better they can cope with heat and cold, droughts and floods, storms, diseases, and other challenges. Forced reductions in fossil fuel use would cause economic harm to every person in the world (as prices for everything would rise), but especially immense harm to the world's poor.

Bjorn Lomborg, a respected Danish environmentalist and professor of statistics, convened a series of meetings under the title Copenhagen Consensus, beginning in 2004. The participants assumed (for the purpose of their discussions) that man-made global warming is occurring and then asked what the best human response to that would be. They concluded that "for some of the world's poorest countries, which will be

---

74. Nordhaus, *A Question of Balance*; Lomborg, *Cool It*; Bjørn Lomborg, ed., *Global Crises, Global Solutions* (Cambridge: Cambridge University Press, 2004); *Solutions for the World's Biggest Problems: Costs and Benefits* (Cambridge: Cambridge University Press, 2007); and *How to Spend $50 Billion to Make the World a Better Place* (Cambridge: Cambridge University Press, 2006).

75. Cornelis van Kooten, "The Economics of Global Warming Policy," in Spencer et al., *A Renewed Call to Truth, Prudence, and Protection of the Poor*. www.cornwallalliance.org/docs/a-renewed-call-to-truth-prudence-and-protection-of-the-poor.pdf, 66.

adversely affected by climate change, problems like HIV/AIDS, hunger, and malaria are more pressing and can be solved with more efficacy."

Consequently, after carefully comparing the severity of many challenges and the cost-benefit ratios of proposed solutions, they agreed that top priority should go to fighting communicable diseases, relieving malnutrition and hunger, and eliminating trade subsidies and barriers—all of which have benefits far outweighing their costs, while proposals to fight climate change were the worst use of funds, with their costs far outweighing their benefits.[76]

Christians who are concerned about alleviating poverty in the world cannot ignore the tremendous economic harm that would come from forcing reductions in carbon-based energy sources. The policies promoted to fight global warming would harm the poor more than the warming itself, even if it were real.

I joined with the twenty-nine evangelical scholars who authored and endorsed the statement *A Renewed Call to Truth, Prudence, and Protection of the Poor: An Evangelical Examination of the Theology, Science, and Economics of Global Warming*[77] in concluding that

> Policies requiring drastic reductions in carbon dioxide emissions are unrealistic and threaten human well-being, especially in developing countries, where, by curtailing use of the most abundant, reliable, and affordable energy sources, they would prolong abject poverty and the miseries of toil, disease, and premature death that accompany it....
>
> The most scientifically, economically, and ethically defensible policy response to alleged dangerous anthropogenic global warming is to promote economic development, especially for the world's poor, through policies that ensure abundant and affordable energy, on the one hand, and reduce specific risks from which the poor suffer regardless of climate change (e.g., under-nutrition and malnutrition; waterborne, pest-borne, and communicable diseases; depressed income because of tariffs, trade restrictions, and corrupt governments; high rates of accidental injury and death because of poor transport and industry infrastructure), on the other hand.

76. Lomborg, *How to Spend $50 Billion to Make the World a Better Place.*

77. See www.cornwallalliance.org/docs/a-renewed-call-to-truth-prudence-and-protection-of-the-poor.pdf, 68. See also the conclusions of Nobel Prize–winning economists of the Copenhagen Consensus Center, http://copenhagenconsensus.com/CCC%20Home%20Page.aspx.

7. Conclusion

In conclusion, the warnings about dangerous man-made global warming are based on poor scientific evidence and poor scientific method, are not proven by previous empirical data, conflict with the Bible's teachings about the nature of the earth and man's purpose on the earth, and propose solutions that would cripple the world's economies and bring immense harm to the poor. These solutions would also bring unacceptable losses of human freedom and immense increases in government power.

While carbon dioxide does not contribute in any significant measure to dangerous levels of global warming, increasing its amount in the atmosphere would bring important agricultural benefits in terms of increased plant growth. Slight increases in global temperature would on the whole bring important agricultural benefits as well, especially in terms of longer growing seasons in cool climates.

In light of these factors, governments should not adopt any policies to regulate the amount of carbon fuel used or to diminish the amount of carbon dioxide in the atmosphere.

C. CAFE STANDARDS FOR AUTOMOBILE MILEAGE

Congress first enacted fuel economy standards for US vehicles in 1975 (after the shock of the Arab oil embargo in 1973).[78] These standards were designed to force Americans to use less oil by manufacturing more fuel-efficient cars. They are called Corporate Average Fuel Economy (CAFE) standards, and they show the average miles-per-gallon performance required for the cars and trucks produced by each manufacturer in each year.

For 1978, passenger cars had to average 18 miles per gallon (MPG). For 1979, it went up to 19 MPG, and light trucks had to average 17.2 MPG. The CAFE standards gradually increased after that and leveled off at 27.5 MPG for passenger cars in 1990. For the category of light trucks (which includes minivans and sport utility vehicles—SUVs), the standard was 20 MPG in 1990 and has increased to 23.1 MPG for 2009.[79]

How did manufacturers reach these averages? Some improvements were made in engine technology to squeeze more miles out of each

---

78. National Highway Traffic Safety Administration. "CAFE Overview, Frequently Asked Questions." www.nhtsa.dot.gov/CARS/rules/CAFE/overview.htm.
    79. Ibid.

gallon, but there is only so much energy in each ounce of gas, so there is a limit to how much improvement can come that way. Moreover, these improvements become increasingly expensive, driving up the price of the vehicle. Therefore the only practical way to meet these standards has been to make a lot of *smaller, lighter cars* that take less energy to power. (You can drive a go-cart a long distance on a gallon of gas!) There are some lightweight composite materials that would increase crash strength in cars, but they are more expensive[80] and would just lead to significantly higher car prices.

This means that most Americans are now driving smaller, lighter cars than they did thirty years ago. This is not because drivers *chose* to ride in smaller, more cramped quarters, or *chose* to drive cars that provide them very little protection in an accident. It is because government standards have driven larger cars (like the family station wagon) off the market; making such cars would drive up the manufacturer's CAFE totals too high, and for that they would face huge government fines.

Therefore manufacturers can only make a very few larger cars to factor into their averages, and they then price them so high that only wealthy customers can afford them. Tom Libby, Senior Director of Industry Analysis for the J.D. Power Information Network said , "Mercedes Benz, for instance, will have to adjust their powertrains and model mix.... It will be difficult for them." Michael Omotoso, also of J.D. Power, added, "Even though they can achieve the standards, they say it may cost $4,000 to $6,000 more per vehicle. So manufacturers can either pass the entire cost onto the consumer, or they will have to eat some of the costs, and thus lower their profits or lose money on every vehicle they sell."[81]

When allowed to choose between cars of similar price, most customers will choose larger cars for safety and comfort. (There are many models with very high fuel efficiency on the market, but they have not been bestsellers.) Yet this choice is being systematically denied to them by government.

What are the costs of the CAFE standards? Smaller cars are demonstrably more dangerous. The death rate in accidents in multivehicle crashes is *twice as high* in minis as in large cars; in single-vehicle crashes involving only a small car, "passengers in minis suffered *three times as*

---

80. Statement by Jeffrey Runge, former head of the National Highway Traffic Safety Administration (NHTSA), in *USA Today* (May 20, 2009), 2B.

81. Don Hammonds, "New Fuel Standards Advancing Lighter Cars, Hybrids," *ScrippsNews.com* (May 27, 2008). www.scrippsnews.com/node/33526.

many deaths as in large cars."[82] Already in 2002, a National Research Council study found that the 27.5 MPG CAFE standards "contributed to about 2,000 deaths per year through their restrictions on car size and weight."[83] That is 2,000 more Americans dead each year (and many thousands more seriously injured) simply because of CAFE requirements imposed by Congress.

It was troubling, therefore, that on May 19, 2009, President Obama announced an agreement with the Detroit automakers (including General Motors and Chrysler, which the federal government now in effect controls) to institute a huge increase of CAFE standards from 27.5 MPG in 2010 to 35.5 MPG by 2016. Passenger cars would have to average 39 MPG.[84] SUVs and minivans will also have to be factored into the overall formula, and this will require even smaller and lighter cars as well as switching to the more-expensive hybrid or all-electric cars. The cost will be paid by the American people in terms of significantly higher prices for cars overall (which makes this a sort of "hidden tax" on everyone who drives). The cost will also be paid through even less safe cars, with even more injuries and more deaths. There is also a significant loss in consumer freedom because, when given a chance, Americans in general prefer to drive larger, safer, more comfortable cars. But those cars will simply be unavailable or unaffordable for most middle-class drivers.

Alan Reynolds of the Cato Institute wrote about how these standards negatively impact auto manufacturers, focusing on General Motors. He said:

> The actual Corporate Average Fuel Economy (CAFE) results will depend on the mixture of fuel-thrifty and fuel-thirsty vehicles consumers choose to buy from each manufacturer — not on what producers hope to sell. That means only those companies most successful in selling the smallest cars with the smallest engines will, in the future, be allowed to sell the more profitable larger pickups and SUVs and more powerful luxury and sports cars....
>
> General Motors is likely to become profitable only if it is allowed to specialize in what it does best — namely, midsize

---

82. "Small Cars Are Dangerous Cars," *Wall Street Journal* (April 17, 2009), A11, citing studies by the Insurance Institute for Highway Safety.

83. Ibid.

84. Steven Mufson, "Vehicle Emission Rules to Tighten," *Washington Post* (May 19, 2009). www.washingtonpost.com/wp-dyn/content/article/2009/05/18/AR2009051801848.html.

and large sedans, sports cars, pickup trucks and SUVs. The company can't possibly afford to scrap billions of dollars of equipment used to produce its best vehicles simply to please politicians who would rather see GM start from scratch, wasting more taxpayer money on "retooling" to produce unwanted and unprofitable subcompacts and electric cars. The average mileage of GM's future cars won't matter if nobody buys them.

Politicians are addicted to CAFE standards because they create an illusion of doing something sometime in the future without voters experiencing the slightest inconvenience in the present. Tighter future CAFE rules will have no effect at all on the type of vehicles we choose to buy. Their only effect will be to compel us to buy larger and more powerful vehicles from foreign manufacturers. Americans will still buy Jaguars, but from an Indian firm, Tata, rather than Ford. They'll buy Hummers, but from a Chinese firm, Tengzhong, rather than GM. The whole game is a charade; symbolism without substance....

The bottom line is that CAFE standards are totally unenforceable and ineffective. Regardless of how much damage the rules do to GM and Chrysler, Americans can and will continue to buy big and fast vehicles from German, Japanese, Korean, Chinese and Indian car companies. CAFE standards might just be another foolhardy regulatory nuisance—were it not for the fact that they could easily prove fatally dangerous for any auto maker overly dependent on the uniquely overregulated U.S. market.[85]

What is the reason for the CAFE standards? The primary reason is a desire to reduce "greenhouse gas emissions" from automobiles, as the Obama administration explained in announcing its plan May 19, 2009.[86] But if (as I argue in the previous section) using carbon fuels has almost no measurable effect on the earth's climate, then these CAFE standards are just forcing Americans to drive smaller, less comfortable, more dangerous cars for no good purpose.

It is also another example of growing government control of more and more of our lives, including the size of cars we are allowed to drive.

85. Alan Reynolds, "Fuel Standards Are Killing GM," *Wall Street Journal* (July 2, 2009). www.cato.org/pub_display.php?pub_id=10326.
86. Statement by Jeffrey Runge, *USA Today*, op. cit.

NATIONAL DEFENSE: JUST WAR THEORY AND INTERNATIONAL TERRORISM

Should governments use military power to defend themselves against other nations? If so, when and how should such forces be used in war? What moral restrictions should nations place on the actions of their military forces in wartime? How should nations respond to the threat of worldwide terrorism?

A. BIBLICAL TEACHING

1. Governments are responsible to defend their nations from attacks by other nations

One of the most basic responsibilities of government is to punish those who do evil. When a government does this, it defends the weak and defenseless and deters further wrongdoing. The apostle Peter says the civil government is intended "to punish those who do evil and to praise those who do good" (1 Peter 2:14). Paul says that the government is authorized by God to "bear the sword" (Rom. 13:4) against evildoers so that it can be "a terror" to bad conduct (v. 3), and it also "carries out God's wrath on the wrongdoer" (v. 4). According to Paul, when the ruler uses superior force—even deadly force—against evil, he is "God's servant for your good" (v. 4).

Now, if a government is commanded by God to protect its citizens from the robber or thief who comes from *within* a country, then certainly it also has an obligation to protect its citizens against thousands of murderers or thieves who come as an army from somewhere *outside of* the nation. Therefore a nation has a *moral obligation to defend itself* against foreign attackers who would come to kill and conquer and subjugate the people in a nation.

Further evidence for this is seen in Old Testament narratives where the nation of Israel repeatedly had to defend itself against attacks by nations such as the Philistines, the Assyrians, and the Babylonians. When God blessed Israel, they defeated their enemies who were attacking them (see Judg. 2:16–18; 1 Sam. 17; 2 Sam. 5:17–25; and numerous other examples in the Old Testament narratives). But when the people disobeyed God and turned from him, he allowed other nations to defeat them as a manifestation of his judgment against them:

> They abandoned the LORD and served the Baals and the Ashtaroth. So the anger of the LORD was kindled against Israel, and he gave them over to plunderers, who plundered them. And he sold them into the hand of their surrounding enemies, so that they could no longer withstand their enemies. Whenever they marched out, the hand of the LORD was against them for harm, as the LORD had warned, and as the LORD had sworn to them. And they were in terrible distress (Judg. 2:13–15).

This was a fulfillment of what God had promised through Moses in Deuteronomy 28. If the people were obedient to God, he promised, "The LORD will cause your enemies who rise against you to be defeated before you. They shall come out against you one way and flee before you seven ways" (v. 7). But if they disobeyed, "The LORD will cause you to be defeated before your enemies. You shall go out one way against them and flee seven ways before them" (v. 25).

These promises were fulfilled multiple times in the history of Israel. They demonstrate that it is a good thing in God's sight—a special blessing—when a government has enough military power to defeat the enemies who would bring armies to attack it (that is, it is a good thing as long as a government has not become so corrupt and evil that God would be pleased to see it conquered).

Sometimes people wonder how it can be consistent for the Ten Commandments to say, "You shall not murder" (Exod. 20:13), and then also command that soldiers and armies go forth to kill the soldiers in an attacking army. Doesn't this mean that soldiers who kill in combat are violating one of the Ten Commandments? No, it does not, because that is not what that verse means.

The Hebrew word translated "murder" in Exodus 20:13 is *ratsakh*, a word used forty-nine times in the Old Testament. It is *never* used to refer to killing in war (other Hebrew words are used for this). Rather, the word refers to what we would call "murder" in English today (the unlawful killing of another human being) and also "causing human death through carelessness or negligence" (as the ESV marginal note says at this verse). The command is not speaking about killing in war, and the original Hebrew readers would not have understood it to apply to soldiers who kill in combat.

In fact, at various times in the Old Testament, God himself commanded the people of Israel to go to war (see Deut. 20:1), and it would be contradictory for him to command something and forbid it at the same time. In the New Testament, soldiers are not condemned for being soldiers in the Roman army, but John the Baptist tells them, "Be content with your wages" (Luke 3:14), and Cornelius, a Roman centurion in charge of one hundred soldiers, came to faith and was baptized as a believer in Jesus with no indication that there was anything morally wrong about the occupation of being a soldier (see Acts 10:1, 44–48; see also Luke 14:31).

B. HOW CAN WE KNOW IF A WAR IS A "JUST WAR"?

Of course, there are wrong wars such as wars merely for conquest and plunder. How can we tell if a war is right or wrong? During centuries of ethical discussions regarding the question of war, one common viewpoint that developed, with much input from Christian scholars, is the "just war" tradition. That viewpoint argues that a war is morally right (or "just") when it meets certain criteria. It also argues that there are certain moral restrictions on the way that war can be conducted.

It seems to me that this "just war" tradition, in general, is consistent with biblical teachings about the need for nations to defend themselves against their enemies. Here is a useful recent summary of the criteria for a just war, together with biblical references that support these criteria. I think that these criteria, in general, are consistent with these biblical teachings:

> Over time, the just war ethic has developed a common set of criteria that can be used to decide if going to war in a specific situation is right. These include the following: (1) *just cause* (is the reason for going to war a morally right cause, such as defense of a nation? cf. Rev. 19:11); (2) *competent authority* (has the war been declared not simply by a renegade band within

a nation but by a recognized, competent authority within the nation? cf. Rom. 13:1); (3) *comparative justice* (it should be clear that the actions of the enemy are morally wrong, and the motives and actions of one's own nation in going to war are, in comparison, morally right; cf. Rom. 13:3); (4) *right intention* (is the purpose of going to war to protect justice and righteousness rather than simply to rob and pillage and destroy another nation? cf. Prov. 21:2); (5) *last resort* (have all other reasonable means of resolving the conflict been exhausted? cf. Matt. 5:9; Rom. 12:18); (6) *probability of success* (is there a reasonable expectation that the war can be won? cf. Luke 14:31); (7) *proportionality of projected results* (will the good results that come from a victory in a war be significantly greater than the harm and loss that will inevitably come with pursuing the war? cf. Rom. 12:21 with 13:4); and (8) *right spirit* (is the war undertaken with great reluctance and sorrow at the harm that will come rather than simply with a "delight in war," as in Ps. 68:30?).

In addition to these criteria for deciding whether a specific war is "just," advocates of just war theory have also developed some moral restrictions on how a just war should be fought. These include the following: (1) *proportionality in the use of force* (no greater destruction should be caused than is needed to win the war; cf. Deut. 20:10–12); (2) *discrimination between combatants and noncombatants* (insofar as it is feasible in the successful pursuit of a war, is adequate care being taken to prevent harm to noncombatants? cf. Deut. 20:13–14, 19–20); (3) *avoidance of evil means* (will captured or defeated enemies be treated with justice and compassion, and are one's own soldiers being treated justly in captivity? cf. Ps. 34:14); and (4) *good faith* (is there a genuine desire for restoration of peace and eventually living in harmony with the attacking nation? cf. Matt. 5:43–44; Rom. 12:18).[1]

C. PACIFISM

Although the just war view has been the one most commonly held throughout the history of the church, a minority view has been that of military pacifism. The pacifist view holds that it is always wrong for *Christians* to use military force against others and thus it is wrong for

---

1. "War," in ESV *Study Bible*, p. 2555.

Christians to participate in military combat, even to defend their own nation. A similar pacifist view holds that it is wrong for *anyone* to participate in military combat and that such "violence" is always morally wrong.

Several of the arguments for pacifism are often related to the "all government is demonic" view advocated by Greg Boyd in *The Myth of a Christian Nation*. Another recent advocate of pacifism is Jim Wallis, in his book *God's Politics*.[2] Similar arguments are also found in Shane Claiborne and Chris Haw's *Jesus for President*, which advocates a pacifist perspective.[3] What follows here is a shorter analysis of the key pacifist arguments as they apply to war.

The arguments commonly used to support pacifism are that (1) Jesus commanded us to turn the other cheek (in Matt. 5:39), (2) Jesus commanded us to love our neighbors as ourselves (Matt. 22:39), (3) engaging in military combat involves failure to trust God, and (4) the use of violence always begets further violence, and pacifism should be adopted to stop that vicious cycle.

In response, I would argue that (1) the pacifist viewpoint wrongly uses Jesus' teaching about individual conduct in turning the other cheek (Matt. 5:39) to apply to civil government, but the explicit teaching on civil governments in Romans is that it should "bear the sword" to oppose evildoers and execute God's wrath on the wrongdoer (Rom. 13:4). In addition, in Luke 22:36 Jesus actually commanded his followers to carry a sword (which was used for self-defense and protection from robbers).

(2) If we truly love our neighbors (as Jesus commanded in Matt. 22:39) then we will be willing even to go to war to protect them from evil aggressors who are attacking the nation. While the pacifist might ask, "How can you love your neighbor or even love your enemy and then kill him in war," the answer has to be that God commanded *both* love for one's neighbor and going to war, for the command "You shall love your neighbor as yourself" is found in Leviticus 19:18 in the Old Testament,

---

2. Jim Wallis, *God's Politics: Why the Right Gets It Wrong and the Left Doesn't Get It* (San Francisco: HarperSanFrancisco, 2005), especially 87–205.

3. Shane Claiborne and Chris Haw, *Jesus for President: Politics for Ordinary Radicals* (Grand Rapids: Zondervan, 2008), especially 199–224 and 338–47 but also at various other places in the book, most of which is structured as a loosely connected set of narratives rather than an organized, sequential, logical argument. Claiborne and Haw also list at least two widely used pacifist books in their recommended bibliography: Greg Boyd, *The Myth of a Christian Nation* (Grand Rapids: Zondervan, 2007), and John Howard Yoder, *The Politics of Jesus* (Grand Rapids: Eerdmans, 1994).

and Jesus quotes it from there. Therefore it must be consistent for God to command *both* things and the one command should not be used to nullify the other. One example of this is found in the tragic story of David sending out his army to defeat Absalom, his son, in 2 Samuel 18:1–33. David had great love for his son Absalom and yet he was responsible to protect the office of king that God had entrusted to him. Therefore, with sorrow, and while still loving Absalom, David sent the army out against him.

(3) Christians have no right to tell others to "trust in God" for things that are different from what the Bible teaches, and Romans 13:1–4 teaches that God authorizes governments to use deadly force if necessary to oppose evil. Therefore, at this point the pacifist argument is telling people to disobey what Romans 13 says about government and then to trust God to protect them anyway. This would be like telling people they should not work to earn a living, but should "trust God" to provide their food anyway! A better approach is to obey what God says in Romans 13:1–4 about the use of government power to restrain evil and then trust God to work through that government power to restrain evil, which is how he intends governments to function.

This is the problem I have with Jim Wallis when he criticizes the American reliance on military power to protect the nation from terrorists as "a foreign policy *based primarily on fear.*"[4] And then he also attributes another wrong motive to Americans when he puts military responses to terrorist attacks in the category of "anger and vengeance" that leads a nation to "indiscriminately retaliate in ways that bring on even more loss of innocent life."[5] Wallis sees military action against terrorism as based on "fear" and "vengeance."

By contrast, Romans 13 teaches that military action used to defend a nation is not a wrongful or sinful activity, *nor is a desire to depend on military action (under God's guidance) a wrongful attitude to have,* because God has *authorized* nations to use such military power. What pacifists like Wallis fail to realize is that it is completely possible — as millions of Christians who have served in military forces have demonstrated — to *trust in God* that he will enable them to use the military power he has put in their hands to successfully defend their country. The solution is not pacifism, but *trust in God* to give success *while obeying him* by using the military defense that he has appointed.

---

4. Wallis, *God's Politics*, 88, emphasis added.
5. Ibid., 92; see also 94.

This is also why pacifists such as Wallis are actually unbiblical when they say that nations like the United States should not act alone and use "unilateral action" to defend themselves, but should rather depend on a "world court to weigh facts and make judgments, with effective multi-national law enforcement."[6] Elsewhere Wallis wants us to depend on a much more powerful "international law" and "global police forces."[7] Wallis says that only such a world court with effective power "will be able to protect us."[8]

There are several objections to Wallis's argument:

(a) It is mere wishful thinking. Such an effective worldwide government over the entire earth has never occurred in the entire history of the human race. (Even the Roman Empire at its largest extent did not reach to China or India or Sub-Saharan Africa or North and South America.) It is foolishness to depend on something that has never existed to save us from a terrorist threat that we are facing at this very minute.

(b) If such a powerful world government ever did exist, it would likely be dominated by the votes of numerous small nations who are largely anti-American because their governments are communist or totalitarian or devoted to expanding the Muslim religion and therefore opposed to the United States. In this way it would be like the present make-up of the United Nations with its frequent anti-American votes.

(c) Depending on such a world government to keep peace in the world would require nations to give up their individual sovereignty and would require the United States to give up a significant measure of its individual sovereignty. This would open the door to reducing the United States to a condition of servitude and domination by nations or leaders that seek its demise.

Far better than the pacifist position of trusting in a world court and world police force is trusting in the Lord to use the means he has designated, which is the use of each nation's own military power, as I have argued above from Romans 13 and other passages.

(4) It is simply untrue to say, as pacifists do, that "violence always begets more violence." The deadly force used by local police in restraining or killing a murderer brings that murderer's violence to an end. It is the same situation when armies are used to defend nations against aggressors. In fact, the use of military power stopped Adolf Hitler from taking over all of Europe and ultimately all the world in World War II. It stopped the North Koreans from taking over South Korea in the Korean War. In the

---

6. Ibid., 106.
7. Ibid., 164.
8. Ibid., 106.

American Civil War, it stopped the Confederate armies from establishing a separate nation in which slavery would be preserved and protected.

The pacifist slogan "violence always begets more violence" is misleading, because it uses the same word, "violence," to refer to two very different things—the morally *good* use of deadly force to stop evildoers and the morally *wrong* use of force to carry out attacks on innocent people. A better slogan is, "Just governments should use superior force to stop criminal violence against innocent people." Or even shorter, "Superior force stops criminal violence."

This is the shortcoming of the pacifist position of Wallis, who says that the solution to international terrorism is "the mobilization of the most extensive international and diplomatic pressure the world has ever seen against the Bin Ladens of the world and their networks of terror."[9] Consistent with that position, Wallis argues that rather than going to war against Iraq,

> The international community could have united in an effective strategy to isolate, contain, disarm and ultimately undermine and remove the brutal and dangerous regime of Saddam Hussein.

Wallis adds, "The Iraqi people themselves could have been supported internationally to create civil resistance within their own country to achieve [regime change]."[10]

But Wallis's pacifist solution here is very much like the wishful thinking of Greg Boyd expressed in his book *The Myth of a Christian Nation*. He is simply saying that we "could have" overthrown Saddam and protected ourselves from international terrorists without military action against them by the United States. The phrase "could have" in pacifist arguments can justify almost any wishful thinking. We "could have" waited for some future day when a supposed international police force would come on the scene. And we "could have" waited for the day when the Iraqi people would rise up and overthrow a brutal dictator who controlled one of the most powerful armies in the world. But in fact, these things did not happen, although alternative solutions had been tried for many years. In actual fact, it was only the superior force of the United States military that overthrew Saddam. It was only the superior power of the United States military that defeated terrorists in Afghanistan. It was only the superior power of the United States military that protected us for many years following 9/11.

This kind of "history could have been different" argument is common in pacifist literature. Instead of acknowledging that military power

---

9. Ibid., 163.
10. Ibid.

is necessary to achieve a triumph over evil forces, it claims, "If the events of history had turned out differently, they would support my case." But that is simply saying, "If the facts were different, they would support my case." That is not a persuasive argument. It is merely wishful thinking.

The logic of pacifism leads ultimately to a total surrender to the most evil of governments, who will stop at nothing to use their power to oppress others. For all of these reasons, the pacifism of Jim Wallis and others is not a persuasive position for Christians to adopt.

D. DEFENSE POLICY IN THE UNITED STATES

If governments have a moral responsibility to defend their nations from attacks, then the first point of application to the United States is that it should have enough military power to be able to defeat any other nation or combination of nations that has the potential to attack it.

Someone might object that having so much military power is dangerous. In fact, someone holding a pacifist position might claim that *military weaponry itself* increases tension and instability in the world and therefore makes war more likely. But this claim comes from an underlying assumption that the ultimate cause of evil is not in the hearts of human beings but is in some influence (such as powerful weapons) *outside of* human beings.

To the contrary, a Christian worldview understands that there is both good and evil in every human heart and also that in some people the tendency toward evil becomes so powerful that those people cannot be reached by reason or negotiation or compromise, but can only be restrained by the superior power of a just government. Therefore God gives civil governments the power of the sword (Rom. 13:4) to restrain such unreasoning commitments to evil. Military weapons for governments are God-ordained and are not themselves the cause of evil.

However, we must be clear that no nation has the right ever to use military power simply to conquer other nations or impose their ideas of social good on another nation.

1. Twentieth-century attacks by nations committed to evil aggression

At various times in history some nations have been ruled by despots who exercised tremendous evil over their own people and also pursued evil acts of aggression against other nations. Hitler was one example in his rule over Germany before and during World War II. Joseph Stalin was another example in his rule over the Soviet Union and his conquering of the nations of Eastern Europe. The leaders of Japan were yet another example before and during World War II, in which they carried out militarized aggression and horrible brutality against Manchuria and much of China. In December 1937, the Japanese Imperial Army marched into China's capital city of Nanking and proceeded to murder 300,000 out of 600,000 civilians and soldiers in the city. The six weeks of carnage would become known as the Rape of Nanking as Japanese soldiers buried Chinese citizens alive or would hack them apart with swords, among other horrible atrocities.[11]

2. Current threats of possible attack against the United States or its allies

At the present time (in early 2010, as I am writing) there are still evil rulers who would use military force to invade and conquer another nation if they thought they could succeed. Countries need to have a strong enough military force to defend against them. Such evil rulers include the leaders of *North Korea* and *Iran*. While these countries are not likely to attack the United States directly, they might launch a missile strike or a terrorist bomb against US territory or US military bases overseas, and it is very possible that they would attack other countries near them (such as Israel or South Korea, both US allies).

What about *Russia*? From 1945 until 1991 — the period of the Cold War — the United States' primary potential enemy was the Soviet Union. The current government of Russia, the successor to the Soviet Union, is not a genuine democracy but essentially a dictatorship run by a small group of Communist Party officials who have continued to tighten their grip on power under Vladimir Putin. Russia sometimes acts as an ally now, but it is unreliable and could again become a threat to the United States as well as to many countries in Eastern Europe.

In Latin America, both *Venezuela* (under Hugo Chavez) and *Cuba* (under Fidel Castro) are military dictatorships that have destabilized several countries in Central and South America. Chavez has engaged in ongoing military threats against Colombia through the placement of troops on their border,[12] and he has convinced Ecuador to go along

---

11. "1937 Nanking Massacre." www.nanking-massacre.com/RAPE_OF_NANKING_OR_NANJING_MASSACRE_1937.html.

12. "Hugo Chavez Warns of War in South America," *London Telegraph* (Aug. 11, 2009). www.telegraph.co.uk/news/worldnews/southamerica/colombia/6007459/Hugo-Chavez-warns-of-war-in-South-America.html.

and place troops there as well.[13] In addition, Cuba has a long history of supporting anti-democratic thugs within Nicaragua, the Dominican Republic, Bolivia, and El Salvador, attempting to weaken their governments.[14] The more this Castro-Chavez influence grows and overthrows governments in Latin America, the more the United States will have to deal with hostile neighboring countries on its doorstep.

China now has good relationships with the United States, especially because of trade. We should hope that those relationships continue, but China's government is totalitarian and autocratic, not democratic. The government in China is controlled by nine members of the Politburo Standing Committee. This means that the future direction of China is unknown. China has been establishing bases of influence in Asia,[15] Latin America,[16] and Africa[17] that could become centers to project its military power. With regard to Asia, the late Congressman Henry Hyde said, "I fear that a future American generation may awaken from its Pacific slumber to find our influence removed entirely from the Asian mainland."[18] Regarding Africa, Peter Brookes of the Heritage Foundation wrote, "The most pernicious effect of the renewed Chinese interest in Africa is that China is legitimizing and encouraging Africa's most repressive regimes, thereby increasing the likelihood of weak and failed states."[19]

China has an increasingly powerful navy with 255,000 men, 58 active submarines, 77 principal surface combatants, 387 coastal warfare vessels, and approximately 500 amphibious warfare vessels,[20] along with

13. "Ecuador Follows Chavez in Deploying Troops to Columbian Border," Associated Press (March 3, 2008). www.foxnews.com/story/0,2933,334409,00.html.

14. Eileen Scully, "The Castro Doctrine Makes Gains," *Heritage Foundation Backgrounder #289* (Sept. 12, 1983), (www.heritage.org/Research/LatinAmerica/bg289.cfm), and Clifford Krauss, "The Last Stalinist," *New York Times* (Feb. 10, 1991), (www.nytimes.com/1991/02/10/books/the-last-stalinist.html).

15. Testimony of Lisa Curtis before the U.S.-China Economic and Security Review Commission" (March 18, 2008). www.heritage.org/Research/AsiaandthePacific/tst032008.cfm.

16. Peter Brookes, "China's Influence in the Western Hemisphere," *Heritage Foundation Lecture #873* (April 19, 2005). Remarks were delivered at a hearing of the Subcommittee on the Western Hemisphere of the House Committee on International Relations.

17. Peter Brookes and Ji Hye Shin, "China's Influence in Africa: Implications for the United States," *Heritage Foundation Backgrounder #1916* (Feb. 22, 2006). www.heritage.org/Research/AsiaandthePacific/bg1916.cfm.

18. Tyler Marshall, "China Poised to Dominate Influence in Asia," *Boston Globe* (Aug. 13, 2006). www.boston.com/news/world/asia/articles/2006/08/13/china_poised_to_dominate_influence_in_asia/.

19. Brookes and Shin, "China's Influence in Africa."

20. "Chinese Naval Forces." www.sinodefence.com/navy/default.asp.

a total amount of armed forces of 2.3 million personnel[21] and a space system that demonstrated its ability in January 2007 to shoot US communications satellites out of the sky.[22] Chinese hackers with remarkable skills continue to launch periodic attacks against the highest levels of US military information networks. In a 2008 report to Congress, it was stated that "China even now is planting viruses in US computer systems that they will activate" in the event of a military conflict with the United States.[23] In 2008, China announced a 14.9% rise in military spending, to 480.68 billion yuan ($70.36 billion).[24] In January 2007, John D. Negroponte, the Director of National Intelligence, reported, "The Chinese are developing more capable long-range conventional strike systems and short- and medium-range ballistic missiles with terminally guided maneuverable warheads able to attack US carriers and airbases."[25] Although we hope it would never happen, it is possible that China could become an extremely powerful aggressor nation in the future.

Islamic terrorist threats stemming from groups within various Muslim countries continue to pose the most prominent military challenge today and constitute the most imminent current threat to the security of the United States.

3. Defense alliances and responsibilities to help protect other countries

Another factor makes the responsibility of the United States more complicated. In 2009, the United States was the most powerful military force in the world, far surpassing every other nation in its military power, with 1,454,515 people on active duty,[26] and an additional 848,000 in reserve.[27]

---

21. "China's Navy 2007," Office of Naval Intelligence. www.fas.org/irp/agency/oni/chinanavy2007.pdf.

22. "China Confirms Satellite Downed," *BBCNews.com* (Jan. 23, 2007). http://news.bbc.co.uk/2/hi/asia-pacific/6289519.stm.

23. Eric McVadon: as quoted in Dave Ahearn, "U.S. Can't Use Trade Imbalance to Avert China Invasion of Taiwan," *Defense Today* (Aug. 2, 2005), 1–2: cited in "China Naval Modernization: Implications for U.S. Navy Capabilities — Background and Issues for Congress," CRS Report for Congress (Feb. 4, 2008). http://assets.opencrs.com/rpts/RL33153_20080204.pdf.

24. Henry Sanderson, "China's Navy to Build New Ships, Planes," Associated Press (April 16, 2009). www.boston.com/news/world/asia/articles/2009/04/16/chinas_navy_to_build_new_ships_planes/?rss_id=Boston.com+ — +World+news.

25. John D. Negroponte, Annual Threat Assessment of the Director of National Intelligence (Jan. 11, 2007), 10.

26. Department of Defense Active Military Personnel by Rank/Grade (Feb. 28, 2009). http://siadapp.dmdc.osd.mil/personnel/MILITARY/rg0902.pdf.

The US defense budget was $515.4 billion, the largest in the world.[28] As of November 2009, the US Navy had 328,798 active personnel, 109,158 reservists, 286 deployable battleships, and 3,700 aircraft.[29] As of September 2008, the US Air Force had 327,452 personnel on active duty, 115,299 in the Selected and Individual Ready Reserves, 106,700 in the Air National Guard, and 5,603 active aircraft.[30] The Army had 549,015 active and 563,688 reserve personnel.

Because of the great military power of the United States, we also carry a great deal of responsibility for maintaining world peace in several ways. Many other nations look to us and depend on us to help defend their freedom. For example, membership in the NATO Alliance (North Atlantic Treaty Organization, formed in 1949), of which the United States is a member, involves a pledge that other members will come to the aid of any NATO member that is attacked by another country.

But such a sense of responsibility to join in the defense of allies is not new to US history. The Monroe Doctrine was a policy first stated by President James Monroe on December 22, 1823. It affirmed that if any European nation attacked or attempted to colonize any nation in North or South America, the United States would intervene to oppose such action. Although there is dispute today over how extensively the Monroe Doctrine should be applied, it has been invoked on numerous occasions by US presidents.

In addition, the United States has entered into mutual defense treaties or agreements with other friendly nations, such as Taiwan and Israel.

Are such defense agreements appropriate? As long as nations voluntarily enter into such agreements and believe that both countries benefit from them, I see no reason in principle to say that they are wrong. The United States has decided in the past that it is in the best interest of the nation and that it contributes to the protection of world peace for it to enter into such agreements, because they provide a significant deterrence against other countries beginning to take over various parts of the world. The countries with which we have such agreements are valuable

---

27. Bryan Bender, "Gates calls for buildup in troops," *Boston Globe* (Jan. 12, 2007). www.boston.com/news/nation/washington/articles/2007/01/12/gates_calls_for_buildup_in_troops/.

28. Department of Defense Budget 2009. www.gpoaccess.gov/usbudget/fy09/pdf/budget/defense.pdf.

29. See www.navy.mil/navydata/navy_legacy_hr.asp?id=146.

30. "2009 Air Force Almanac," *Air Force Magazine* (May 2009), 48–49. www.airforce-magazine.com/MagazineArchive/Magazine%20Documents/2009/May%202009/0509facts_fig.pdf.

to the United States in many ways, through mutual trade, tourism, cultural and educational exchange, and the preservation of stability in different regions of the world.

Another reason why the United States is right to commit itself to defending the independence and freedom of democratic nations is that its foundational document, the Declaration of Independence, asserts that *we as a nation* hold certain truths to be "self evident" and that among those truths are the following:

> That all men are created equal, that they are endowed by their Creator with certain unalienable rights, that among these are life, liberty, and the pursuit of happiness—that to secure these rights, governments are instituted among men, deriving their just powers from the consent of the governed.[31]

This means that *as a nation* the United States has formally declared from the beginning that God (the "Creator") has granted to every individual on earth certain basic rights, including both "life" and "liberty." This implies that it is in our best interest and also *consistent with our foundational convictions as a nation* to promote the protection of life and human freedom in various nations around the world. Therefore such alliances for the purpose of defending other countries are based on convictions that are at the basis of our very existence as a nation.

For these reasons, I disagree with the "noninterventionist" viewpoint of Congressman Ron Paul. In his book *The Revolution: A Manifesto,* Ron Paul quotes from some of America's Founding Fathers, including Thomas Jefferson and George Washington, to argue that we should not use military force to intervene in other nations. Therefore, for example, Ron Paul opposed the Iraq War.[32] Paul says, "In time it will become apparent to all of us that foreign interventionism is of no benefit to American citizens, but instead is a threat to our liberties."[33]

Paul also says, "I oppose all foreign aid on principle," and that means that he is opposed even to any foreign aid to Israel.[34] He also opposes the stationing of US troops in places such as Korea, Japan, and Europe, saying, with regard to them, "How many years is enough?"[35] Paul's non-

---

31. Transcript of the Declaration of Independence. www.archives.gov/exhibits/charters/declaration_transcript.html.

32. See Ron Paul, *The Revolution: A Manifesto* (New York: Grand Central Publishing, 2008), 10–17, 19, 21–24.

33. Ibid., 17.

34. Ibid.

35. Ibid, 37.

interventionism even led him to blame the United States for the attacks on 9/11, saying, "Have you ever read about the reasons they attacked us? They attack us because we've been over there. We've been bombing Iraq for 10 years."[36] I think that such blaming of the United States for the attacks of 9/11 shows how deeply flawed Ron Paul's understanding of foreign policy actually is.

I disagree with Ron Paul for three primary reasons. (a) It is significant that while he quotes some of the American Founding Fathers to defend noninterventionism, he cannot quote the US Constitution in support of this view, because it cannot be found there. While some of the Founding Fathers, including George Washington and Thomas Jefferson, may have *thought* that it would be wise for the United States to stay out of foreign disputes at a time when we were a new and tiny nation, they and the others who drafted the Constitution were wise enough not to set that opinion about the current situation in concrete as they wrote the Constitution. They no doubt realized that situations might change and that what was not appropriate for a young, relatively weak nation might be very different for a more mature, more powerful nation. Today we have grown more powerful and more influential in the world than Washington and Jefferson could ever have imagined.

(b) I see no reasons from the teachings of the Bible that would lead me to support Ron Paul's noninterventionism. In fact, at one point God, through the prophet Obadiah, rebuked the nation of Edom for its "noninterventionist" policy with regard to Israel:

> On the day that you stood aloof,
> on the day that strangers carried off his wealth
> and foreigners entered his gates
> and cast lots for Jerusalem,
> you were like one of them (Obad. 11).

When the foreign invaders (the Babylonians) attacked Jerusalem, the neighboring country of Edom "stood aloof" and failed to give military support to help Jerusalem defend itself. God says that Edom was guilty of failing to intervene in that conflict and help their neighbor: "You were like one of them."

(c) It seems to me that the great power of the United States gives us an obligation to help weak nations who are attacked when we have made alliances with them and are able to help them. The NATO alliance was

---

36. "Ron Paul Gets Turn in Spotlight in South Carolina Debate," Reuters.com (May 16, 2007).

a major factor in preventing Soviet expansion of its power into Western Europe after 1949. The US alliance with Taiwan has been the major reason that China has not attacked it. Our alliance with and military presence in South Korea has been the primary deterrent that has kept the fanatical and militaristic regime in North Korea from overrunning its neighbor. And the US agreements to defend Israel, together with massive amounts of military aid, have been a significant factor in preventing Arab nations from destroying that country. If we had not driven Saddam Hussein out of Kuwait in the First Gulf War (1990–91), he would have controlled the Kuwaiti oil fields and very likely would have invaded and captured Saudi Arabia as well.

All of these relationships and others have extended the protections of democracy and the benefits of "certain unalienable rights" to millions of people in the world, and they have made the world more peaceful and more secure for the last two centuries. It is consistent with our foundational convictions as a nation, as embodied in the Declaration of Independence, that the United States should promote the protection of life and human freedoms in various nations around the world. For this reason also, I strongly disagree with the noninterventionist views of Congressman Paul.

Does Ron Paul really think that the world would be better off with the horrible communist government of North Korea controlling South Korea, with Communist China controlling Taiwan, and with Saddam Hussein controlling Saudi Arabia and Kuwait and exporting terrorism around the world? Does he think the world would be better off if the Soviets under Stalin had been allowed to overrun Western Europe, including Germany and France and other countries, after World War II? Does he think the world would be a better place if the US Navy did not protect the international shipping lanes of all the oceans of the world? I am convinced that these actions by the United States have made the world a much better and more peaceful place.

For all of these reasons, I cannot believe that Paul's noninterventionist policies would do anything but bring about a much less free, much less peaceful, and much more antagonistic and dangerous world.

4. The value to the world of a strong US military

If we do not accept a pacifist position that weapons are in themselves evil, then it is wise to realize that *superior military weaponry* in the hands of a nation that protects freedom for itself and other countries *is a good thing for the world*, not a harmful thing. The existence of superior military power in the hands of a peace-loving, freedom-supporting nation brings great benefits to the world.

Genuine peace in the world comes through the strength of the United States and other democratic, peace-loving nations. By contrast, US military weakness would simply invite war and provoke multiple attempts at conquest by aggressive nations led by evil rulers.

Unfortunately, the facts show that President Obama in 2009 began reducing the strength of US military forces, just as Democratic President Jimmy Carter did in the 1970s. Practically the only area of government spending that was cut in 2009 by President Obama was defense spending. The *Wall Street Journal* wrote:

> More ominously, Mr. Obama's budget has overall defense spending falling sharply starting in future years—to $614 billion in 2011, and staying more or less flat for a half decade. This means that relative both to the economy and especially to domestic priorities, defense spending is earmarked to decline. Some of this assumes less spending on Iraq, which is realistic, but it also has to take account of Mr. Obama's surge in Afghanistan. That war won't be cheap either.
>
> The danger is that Mr. Obama may be signaling a return to the defense mistakes of the 1990s. Bill Clinton slashed defense spending to 3% of GDP in 2000, from 4.8% in 1992. We learned on 9/11 that 3% isn't nearly enough to maintain our commitments and fight a war on terror—and President Bush spent his two terms getting back to more realistic outlays for a global superpower.[37]

One example among many such cuts is the most advanced jet fighter in the world, the F–22 "Raptor." In early 2009, in the midst of massive increases in federal government spending—far in excess of any increases promoted by any administration in American history—President Obama insisted on cutting funds for the F–22.[38] No aircraft in the world comes close to the fighting capabilities of this plane. It is so advanced that it can fight battles against multiple attacking aircraft and defeat them all simultaneously. Its advanced electronics allow it to "see" an approaching enemy aircraft over the horizon and destroy it before the

---

37. "Declining Defense," *Wall Street Journal* (March 2, 2009). http://online.wsj.com/article/SB123595811964905929.html.

38. "Senate Sides with Obama, Removes F–22 Money," *Associated Press* (July 21, 2009). www.sfgate.com/cgi-bin/article.cgi?f=/n/a/2009/07/21/national/w000457D19.DTL&tsp=1

enemy is even able to see the F–22 approaching.[39] W. Thomas Smith, a former US Marine rifle-squad leader and counterterrorism instructor, wrote in *Human Events,* "The F–22 was built for speed: Though her numbers are classified, she can outrun, outclimb, and outmaneuver any fighter aircraft a potential adversary might be able to put up against us."[40]

But following President Obama's insistence, the US Senate voted on July 21, 2009, to end production of the F–22 at 187 fighters, far less than the 250–380 that were originally planned and needed.[41] The President signed the defense authorization bill killing the production of more F–22s, as he wished, on October 28, 2009.[42] In making such cuts, the President "rejected the notion that 'we have to waste billions of taxpayer dollars to keep this nation secure.' "[43] I think this was a tragic mistake.

E. ISLAMIC JIHADISM (INTERNATIONAL TERRORISM)

The greatest threat of attack against the United States today comes not from any specific nation, but from an international terrorist movement that is sometimes called Islamic Jihadism. This term actually refers to a number of loosely related Islamic terrorist groups such as al-Qaeda, Hamas (a Palestinian group), Hezbollah (based in Lebanon), the Muslim Brotherhood (in several countries, but with strong roots in Egypt), and various other smaller movements with similar convictions and goals.

In my judgment and in the judgment of many other analysts, such radical Islamic Jihadism constitutes the single greatest threat to American peace and security in the world today. Its cause is ultimately not poverty in certain Muslim nations (for many terrorist leaders come from wealthy backgrounds, such as Osama bin Laden). Nor is its cause any

---

39. "F–22: Unseen and Lethal," *Aviation Week* (Jan. 8, 2007). www.f22-raptor.com/media/documents/aviation_week_010807.pdf.

40. W. Thomas Smith, "We Need Both," *Human Events* (Oct. 29, 2009). www.humanevents.com/article.php?id=34173.

41. "Senate Sides with Obama, Removes F–22 Money," Associated Press.

42. "Obama Inks Defense Bill With Hate Crimes Provision," Associated Press (Oct. 28, 2009). www.washingtonpost.com/wp-dyn/content/article/2009/10/28/AR2009102803147.html?hpid=moreheadlines.

43. Roxana Tiron, "Obama Signs Defense Bill, Attacks Waste," *The Hill* (Oct. 28, 2009). http://thehill.com/homenews/administration/65183-obama-signs-defense-bill-attacks-waste.

recent action by the United States (for there were numerous terrorist attacks on American interests even prior to the First Gulf War, and certainly prior to the Iraq War—see historical details below). Its cause is a profoundly evil religious belief that the use of any violent means, even the intentional murder of civilians, is justified in order to advance the goal of forcible Muslim domination of other nations and eventually of the entire world.

1. Origins and beliefs of al-Qaeda and similar organizations

The most extensive and authoritative history of Islamic terrorism in recent times is *The Looming Tower: Al-Qaeda and the Road to 9/11* by Lawrence Wright.[44] The great majority of Muslims around the world would not hold to the beliefs of Islamic Jihadism, and Wright points out that views common to today's terrorists have been a *minority* voice within Islam for centuries, beginning with Abdul Wahhab (1703–1792), a Muslim teacher and revivalist who in 1744 came under the protection of Mohammed bin Saud, the founder of the first Saudi state.[45] Wahhab taught that his followers could kill and rape and steal from people who would not obey his teachings. He also taught that men should not trim their beards and that there was "no difference between religion and government."[46] People sometimes refer to modern followers of Wahhab's teachings as Wahhabi Muslims and to the viewpoint itself as Wahhabism (though Wahhab's followers do not prefer that name for themselves).

In recent years the most influential writer persuading Muslims to use violence to purify and advance Islam was the Egyptian author Sayyid Qutb (1906–1966), in his book *Milestones* (published in 1964). Before he left Egypt, Qutb (pronounced *kuh*-tub) was already one of that country's most popular writers, and when he came to America as a foreign student in 1948, he sailed in a first-class stateroom on a cruise ship.[47] Qutb studied in New York City, in Washington, DC, and especially at Colorado State College for education in Greeley, Colorado (in 1949). During his time in America, he became hardened in his opposition to what he saw as the evils of American society, with its commitment to modern ways of life and what he saw as frequent immorality.[48]

---

44. Lawrence Wright, *The Looming Tower: Al-Qaeda and the Road to 9/11* (New York: Alfred Knopf, 2006).

45. Ibid., 63.

46. Ibid.

47. Ibid., 7.

48. Ibid., 16–23.

When he returned to Egypt, Qutb became increasingly troubled that the Egyptian government, under Gamal Nasser, was not sufficiently strict in enforcing Islamic law. He became vocal in his opposition to Nasser through editing a Muslim Brotherhood (or Muslim Brothers) magazine. After some members of the Muslim Brothers tried to assassinate Nasser in 1954, Qutb was put in prison, where he stayed until 1965.[49] He experienced much physical suffering in prison, but also wrote extensively. His book *Milestones* was smuggled out of the prison in Cairo and published in 1964.[50] Although Qutb was released for a few months at the end of 1964, he was soon arrested again, charged with conspiracy to overthrow the government, and sentenced to death. He was hanged August 29, 1966,[51] but his influence continues today.

Another influential leader in Islamic terrorism has been Ayman al-Zawahiri (1951 –), also an Egyptian. Zawahiri was a brilliant student from a prominent Egyptian family who finished medical school and became a recognized surgeon.[52] He was influenced by Qutb's writings and became the leader of a group of Egyptians who were determined to overthrow the leadership of Egypt, including President Anwar Sadat.[53]

Zawahiri was closely involved with the group that successfully planned the assassination against Sadat that occurred on October 6, 1981. Zawahiri was arrested and imprisoned and was tortured severely in an Egyptian prison.[54] He then became the public spokesman for all three hundred defendants at the trial that began December 4, 1982,[55] and during his time in prison he became a hardened radical and recognized leader for Islamic militant beliefs. But he had not directly participated in the assassination, and he was released from prison in 1984, after which he traveled to Saudi Arabia and then to Afghanistan, where he would meet Osama bin Laden.[56]

Osama bin Laden (1957 – 2011) was born to an extremely wealthy family in Saudi Arabia. His father was Muhammad bin Laden, who owned a huge construction company that was responsible for building many of the highways as well as the largest mosques in the country,[57]

49. Ibid., 27–30.
50. Ibid., 29.
51. Ibid., 30–31.
52. Ibid., 32–34.
53. Ibid., 40–42, 48–49.
54. Ibid., 50–54.
55. Ibid., 54.
56. Ibid., 57–58, 60–61.
57. Ibid., 64–68.

including the Grand Mosque in Medina.[58] Bin Laden joined the Muslim Brothers while he was in high school. He studied economics in the university in Jeddah, but spent more of his time involved in campus religious activities.[59]

Bin Laden eventually traveled to Afghanistan, where he became a leader of the forces that fought to drive out the Soviets. He then returned to Saudi Arabia and worked in the family business overseeing construction projects. His share of the company at that time was about equal to $7 million (US), plus he had a substantial annual income. But his deepest commitment was to advancing Islam through radical means, and he eventually returned to Afghanistan, where he connected with other leaders and radicals who shared his convictions, including Zawahiri.

Although the United States had helped him and his followers drive the Soviets out of Afghanistan, bin Laden eventually turned against the United States because of his commitment to radical Islam. Lawrence Wright explains it this way:

> Why did these men turn against America, a highly religious country that had so recently been their ally in Afghanistan? In large part, it was because they saw America as the locus of Christian power.... Viewed through the eyes of men who were spiritually anchored in the seventh century, Christianity was not just a rival, it was the archenemy. To them, the Crusades were a continual historical process that would never be resolved until the final victory of Islam.... Yet bin Laden and his Arab Afghans believed that, in Afghanistan, they had turned the tide and that Islam was again on the march.[60]

Wright goes on to explain how radically opposed to western values this brand of Islam is:

> By returning the rule of Sharia [Islamic law governing all of life], radical Islam could draw the line against the encroaching West. Even the values that America advertised as being universally desirable—democracy, transparency, the rule of law, human rights, the separation of religion from governments—were discredited in the eyes of the jihadis because they were Western and therefore modern.

---

58. Ibid., 66–71.
59. Ibid., 78.
60. Ibid., 171.

Wright also reports that Zawahiri, who partnered with bin Laden in Afghanistan, had become convinced of an extreme interpretation of Islam known as *takfir* ("excommunication"), which was applied to those who are thought to have abandoned true Islamic beliefs. Wright explains that this is an extreme view, but so influential that it led to the assassination of President Sadat in Egypt:

> *Takfir* is the mirror image of Islam, reversing its fundamental principles.... The Quran explicitly states that Muslims shall not kill anyone, except as punishment for murder.... How, then, could groups ... justify using violence against fellow Muslims in order to come to power? Sayyid Qutb had pointed the way by declaring that a leader that does not impose Sharia on the country must be an apostate. There is a well-known saying of the Prophet that the blood of Muslims cannot be shed except in three instances: as punishment for murder, or for marital infidelity, or for turning away from Islam. The pious Anwar Sadat was the first modern victim of the reverse logic of *takfir*.[61]

Wright then explains how this doctrine was taken farther and farther by the new Islamic militants, because they

> extended the death warrant to encompass, for instance, anyone who registered to vote. Democracy, in their view, was against Islam because it placed in the hands of people authority that properly belonged to God. Therefore, anyone who voted was an apostate, and his life was forfeit. So was anyone who disagreed with their joyless understanding of Islam.... [They] believed that they were entitled to kill practically anyone and everyone who stood in their way; indeed, they saw it as a divine duty.[62]

On August 11, 1988, a few months before the final withdrawal of Soviet forces from Afghanistan in 1989, bin Laden and other leaders of the Arab resistance had a decisive meeting in Peshawar and decided to form an organization called al-Qaeda (meaning "the base") that would be "the solid base ... for the hoped-for society" that would implement a strict Islamic rule in many nations.[63]

Wright goes on to describe how al-Qaeda's philosophy developed. It increasingly focused on carrying out terrorist attacks against civilians

---

61. Ibid., 124.
62. Ibid., 125.
63. Ibid., 130–34.

in strategic locations around the world: "al-Qaeda would concentrate not on fighting armies but on killing civilians."[64] Yet the main focus of al-Qaeda's attacks would be the United States because it stood in the way of establishing Islamic rule over more and more nations:

> America was the only power capable of blocking the restoration of the ancient Islamic *caliphate* [government], and it would have to be confronted and defeated.[65]

To get a picture of what kind of life Islamic terrorists would impose upon a nation if they obtained power, we can look at the Taliban regime that was imposed in Afghanistan before the American military attack drove them out of power in November 2001. Here is a picture of life under the Taliban:

> Work and schooling for women were halted at once, which destroyed the health-care system, the civil service, and effectively eliminated elementary education.... The Taliban ... forbade kite-flying and dog racing.... "Unclean things" were banned, an all-purpose category that included ... satellite dishes, cinematography, any equipment that produces the joy of music, pool tables, chess ... alcohol ... computer, VCR's, television ... nail polish ... sewing catalogues, pictures, Christmas cards.... The fashion dictators demanded that a man's beard be longer than the grip of his hand. Violators went to jail.... Should a woman leave her home without her veil, "Her home will be marked and her husband punished."[66]

From the perspective of the Bible, my response to such a view is as follows: Although militant Muslims frequently refer to the United States as "the great Satan," it seems evident that the movement truly motivated by Satan himself is such a movement that would justify killing anyone who disagrees with it. Jesus said that Satan "was a murderer from the beginning" (John 8:44), and such a movement that believes it right to violently suppress and murder all disagreement shows marks of having its deepest spiritual motivation, not in God, but in demonic forces that are opposed to God and his truth. The results of such a reign of strict Sharia law are an intolerable loss of human freedom, essentially reducing human beings to dehumanizing slavery ruled by the Islamic religious

---

64. Ibid., 175.
65. Ibid.
66. Ibid., 230–31.

leaders. This is a work of Satan, not a work of God. Jesus said, "The thief comes only to steal and kill and destroy. I came that they may have life and have it abundantly" (John 10:10). He also proclaimed not slavery, but liberty: "The Spirit of the Lord is upon me, because he has anointed me to proclaim good news to the poor. He has sent me *to proclaim liberty to the captives* and the recovering of sight to the blind, to set at *liberty* those who are oppressed" (Luke 4:18).

I have devoted so much space to explaining the background of al-Qaeda because it is crucial to understand that the terrorist attacks directed against the United States and other countries *are not caused by people experiencing poverty or oppression in poor nations.* Qutb, Zawahiri, and bin Laden were all well-educated and well-to-do (bin Laden was a multi-millionaire). Wright points out that most young men who joined up with al-Qaeda in Afghanistan were "middle or upper class" and "were largely college-educated, with a strong bias toward the natural sciences and engineering."[67]

Even al-Qaeda's opposition to the presence of American troops in Saudi Arabia and to the US attack against Iraq in the First Gulf War[68] were essentially *religious* objections as well, since these were non-Muslim troops in Muslim countries, even if they were there to protect Saudi Arabia from Saddam Hussein's Iraq.

Therefore the explanation for al-Qaeda and similar Islamic terrorist movements can only be rightly understood as a deeply and profoundly *religious motivation*—a conviction that they must use murder and terrorism to advance the rule of Islamic law by force throughout the nations of the world. The movement has its modern origins in a campaign to institute more strict Islamic law in Egypt (Qutb, Zawahiri), in Saudi Arabia (bin Laden[69]), and then in other countries.

Radical Islamic opposition to Israel must also be understood in this light. Whereas Islam is the dominant religion in all the countries of the Middle East that surround Israel, the presence of Judaism as the dominant religion in Israel stands out as an intolerable exception, and therefore many Muslim leaders declare that Israel has no right to exist and that they will not rest until all the Jews are driven out of the land of Palestine or driven into the sea. Then pure Islamic rule can be established in Palestine as well. Islamic scholar Nihal Sahin Utku has written, "History has shown, as the Torah states, that the Palestinian land, the

---

67. Ibid., 301.
68. Ibid., 234, 247, and 259–60.
69. Ibid., 246.

promised land of God, really belongs to the descendents of Abraham. However, not those who descended from Isaac, but those who descended from Ismail, one of whom was Prophet Muhammad."[70]

Elsewhere in his analysis Wright returns again and again to the religious domination goals as the true explanation of the convictions of al-Qaeda and related groups:

> On August 23, 1996, Osama bin Laden issued a "declaration of war" against America.[71] His first reason given was American support for Israel and the second was the presence of American troops in Muslim lands, particularly in Saudi Arabia (following the First Gulf War).[72]

In 1998 Zawahiri and bin Laden wrote a formal declaration with three reasons for terrorist attacks against the United States: (1) the continuing presence of American troops in Saudi Arabia even though the First Gulf War had ended (and even though they were there with the blessing of the Saudi government because of the continuing protection they provided against Saddam Hussein), (2) America's action against Iraq (in the First Gulf War), and (3) America's support of Israel. Therefore they issued a *fatwa* (authoritative religious opinion) signed by bin Laden, Zawahiri, and others with this chilling statement:

> The ruling to kill the Americans and their allies—civilian and military—is an individual duty for every Muslim who can do it in any country in which it is possible to do it.[73]

2. Explanations that primarily blame America for terrorism are mistaken and harmful

This historical analysis of the origins of Islamic terrorism shows why the primary explanations for terrorism that are given again and again in Jim Wallis's book *God's Politics* simply misunderstand the causes of terrorism. I realize that at one point Wallis rightly says that "the root of the terror attacks is not a yearning for economic justice for the poor and oppressed of the world," and "it is motivated rather by the ambition

70. Nihal Sahin Utku, "Palestine: The Eternal Domain of the Prophet's Descendents," *LostProphet.info.* www.lastprophet.info/en/nihal-sahin-utku-phd/palestine-the-eternal-domain-of-the-prophet-s-descendents.html.

71. Wright, *The Looming Tower*, 234.

72. Ibid., 247.

73. Ibid., 259–60.

of a perverted religious fundamentalism for regional and global power; one that rejects the values of liberty, equality, democracy, and human rights."[74] But those brief comments are not at all central to his argument, nor are they emphasized at all. In his overall discussion of terrorism Wallis minimizes the underlying religious causes and points instead to what he sees as *American shortcomings* that provided great help for the terrorist cause.

For example, Wallis says, regarding his recommendation for Americans,

> An even more courageous national commitment would be to face honestly the grievances and injustices that breed rage and vengeance and are continually exploited by terrorists to recruit the angry and the desperate.... It is indeed impossible to comprehend adequately the terrorist acts of September 11 without a deeper understanding of the grievances and injustices felt by millions of people around the world.[75]

Wallis returns again and again in his book to what he thinks are shortcomings of the United States that have led to these "grievances and injustices" that have given support to the terrorist cause. He mentions US support for military dictators, the United States' failure to be "an honest broker for Middle East peace," "American and Western appetites for oil," and the fact that "the United States sits atop and is the leader of a global economy in which half of God's children still live on less than two dollars a day." Wallis says that "the United States will be blamed around the world for the structures of injustice that such a global economy daily enforces."[76] He says that "we have contributed to the grievances and injustices that breed terrorism."[77] Again and again Wallis returns to this "blame America" theme, saying that a serious agenda of "global poverty reduction" would be a good strategy for opposing terrorism.[78]

Then Wallis also says that our military attacks on terrorists lead to "recruiting even more terrorists, and fueling an unending cycle of violence."[79] This particular argument has the situation exactly backward, because it says that our successful military attacks actually help

74. Wallis, *God's Politics*, 99.
75. Ibid., 96.
76. Ibid., 97.
77. Ibid., 101. Similar statements are found on pages 104, 105, and 106.
78. Ibid., 99.
79. Ibid., 101.

the terrorists. In other words, when we defeat the terrorists militarily, it helps them. Another way of putting this argument is to say that winning is actually losing! Wallis fails to recognize that the supply of terrorist recruits dries up as soon as it becomes evident that they will be defeated by superior military power at every point and that their cause is futile.

Wallis's argument here is just the opposite of the apostle Paul, who gives this explanation for the military power of civil government: "*But if you do wrong, be afraid*, for he does not *bear the sword* in vain. For he is the servant of God, an avenger who carries out God's wrath on the wrongdoer" (Rom. 13:4). The sword in the hand of good government is God's designated weapon to defeat evildoers.

It is important to recognize that Wallis's arguments when he heaps blame on America for terrorism are not carefully reasoned and well-documented proofs that supposed American wrongdoing has led to terrorist attacks. They are simply broad accusations thrown out as if they needed no proof or argument. But they lack any convincing substantiation.

What is the function of this kind of "blame America" argument for a pacifist position? *It allows a pacifist always to change the subject* from how to defend against evil terrorists to accusations against the United States for contributing to the terrorism that attacked it! Although the United States was attacked on 9/11, the entire force of Wallis's discussion is to turn the victim (the United States) into the culprit! He is saying that the victim was mostly responsible for the attacks against it.

By this kind of argument, the continuing existence of *any poverty anywhere in the world* provides Wallis with a basis for accusing the United States of wrongdoing. He can always bring up world poverty to argue how "evil" the United States is, using vague and unsubstantiated accusations. (He makes these accusations even though world poverty is not the fault of the US government or US citizens or American corporations and even though the people of the United States do more than any other nation to alleviate poverty throughout the world [see discussion in chap. 2].)

The harmful result of these repeated accusations from Jim Wallis is *to undermine any sense of moral right and wrong in the battle against terrorism*. In actual fact, the terrorists who attack innocent civilians in the United States are committing profound evil, and the military forces of the United States who defend against such terrorists are doing good, according to Romans 13 and 1 Peter 2. So there is a clear distinction between "good" and "evil" *with respect to the specific question of terrorist attacks and defense against them*. I am not saying that the United States is a perfect nation, or that it has no shortcomings, which it certainly does. I am saying that in the matter of the attacks by Islamic terrorists such as 9/11 and elsewhere (see the list in the next section), there was clearly a moral right and wrong. Terrorists who attack innocent civilians are wrong. Innocent civilians whom they attack and military actions that attempt to stop such attacks are morally good with respect to this particular issue. Wallis just muddies the waters and confuses this clear moral difference.

Wallis erodes the sense of moral rightness we should have as we defend our nation, saying over and over that we too are "evil." This is a profoundly mistaken argument and will cripple the ability of any nation to defend itself against evil.

3. Terrorist attacks carried out by al-Qaeda and its allies

Here is a brief list of terrorist attacks by al-Qaeda and related forces:[80]

February 26, 1993	First World Trade Center bomb
June 25, 1996	Bombing of Khobar Towers, a US military barrack in Saudi Arabia
August 7, 1998	Bombing of US embassy in Nairobi, Kenya
August 7, 1998	Bombing of US embassy in Dar es Salaam, Tanzania
October 12, 2000	Bombing of USS Cole in port in Yemen
September 11, 2001	Attack on the World Trade Center and the Pentagon

Therefore the attacks of 9/11 did not suddenly appear out of the blue, but were the culmination of a series of militant actions undertaken *with the goal of imposing radical Islam on the nations of the world*—attacks that had begun (long before the formation of al-Qaeda) in an assassination attempt against President Gamal Abdel Nasser in Alexandria, Egypt, on October 26, 1954, carried out by members of the Muslim Brothers, with whom Sayyid Qutb was already associated.[81] These attacks continued in the 1981 assassination of Anwar Sadat. They continue to be perpetuated in terrorist attacks in various countries of the world to this day.

---

80. Wright, *The Looming Tower*, 177.
81. Ibid., 27–28.

4. Solutions to Islamic Jihadism

Defeating Islamic Jihadism will require several solutions.

a. Superior force

The hardened supporters of al-Qaeda have a deeply religious commitment to violent evil deeds. There should be no reasonable expectation that they can be turned from their commitment to violence *by any reasoning or bargaining or concessions or negotiation*, nor is there any persuasive historical evidence that negotiation will ever deter them from their single goal of imposing radical Islamic law on the nations of the earth.

The only method that has shown any success, or that shows any promise of success in stopping them, is *the use of superior force by military and police forces* within each nation, so that these hardened supporters can be captured or killed before they are able to carry out an attack. Lawrence Wright's book recounts in various places how Nasser and Sadat in Egypt and the Royal Family in Saudi Arabia attempted to appease the terrorist elements in their own countries with various concessions at various times, but without any success.[82]

The use of superior military and police power to defeat such evildoers is the proper role of government, because, as said earlier, God has appointed it to "bear the sword" (Rom. 13:4), to be a "terror" to those who would do evil (v. 3), and to act as "an avenger who carries out God's wrath on the wrongdoer" (v. 4). Therefore it is right for the United States and other countries who would oppose Islamic terrorism to use all their military and police might to capture and imprison or, if necessary, to kill hardened supporters of al-Qaeda and those with similar commitments. The United States in particular should use all of its military, electronic, economic, and diplomatic power to defeat followers of al-Qaeda wherever they are in the world.

But defeat of such terrorists poses a particular law-enforcement problem, because many of them are committed to giving their lives in what they think of as "martyrdom in the cause of God" in carrying out terrorist attacks.[83] This means that the older forms of criminal investigation that are aimed at capturing and punishing the wrongdoer *after the attack* will simply not work, because with a suicide bomber, the wrongdoer is already dead. Therefore they must be defeated before they can launch an attack.

---

82. Ibid., 26, 31, 39, 48, 209–10.
83. Ibid., 302.

b. What about wiretapping?

The technological expertise of American counter-terrorism specialists gave them two particularly effective weapons that were being used secretly and very successfully against terrorism. But they were both compromised by a combination of media leaks and the opposition of anti-war members of Congress.

One method was the secret tracing of inter-bank transfers of terrorist funds, many of which were going through large banks in Europe to which American and European anti-terrorist specialists had been given access. Therefore they were able to trace the destination of funds that were to be used to prepare for terrorist attacks. But such tracking of funds was recklessly exposed in an article in the *New York Times* on June 23, 2006.[84] Edward Turzanski of LaSalle University said, "I do know that the government official who told *The Times* reporter about this broke the law, ought to be prosecuted, and *The New York Times* ought to wake up and get it. They are harming our ability to prevent terror attacks. This isn't some sort of academic game. This is going to cost lives, and they are harming our abilities to connect the dots. And that's what the 9/11 commission was all upset about is our inability to connect dots."[85]

This reckless publication of a highly classified secret anti-terror program meant that terrorists largely stopped using these banks for transfers of funds and that this effective anti-terrorism tool was taken away from the US government. I consider this action by *The New York Times* so damaging to our national security interests that I think it was treasonous and should be prosecuted as such. But the liberal opposition to President Bush and to the War on Terror was so strong that the government did nothing in response to this publication of defense secrets.

The second effective technological tool was the ability of the US government to listen in on telephone conversations between terrorists even when they were *both* outside the United States. Because of some particular aspects of international telecommunications, many calls made around the world, even from one cell phone to another when both are outside the United States, still are transferred electronically through switching equipment in the United States. According to Wired.com,

---

84. James Risen and Eric Lichtblau, "Bank Data Sifted in Secret by U.S. to Block Terror," *New York Times* (June 23, 2006). www.nytimes.com/2006/06/23/washington/23intel.html.

85. "New York Times Outs Another Anti-Terror Program," *The Big Story with Jon Gibson, Fox News* (June 26, 2006). www.foxnews.com/story/0,2933,201011,00.html.

"International phone and internet traffic flows through the United States largely because of pricing models established more than 100 years ago in the International Telecommunication Union to handle international phone calls. Under those ITU tariffs, smaller and developing countries charge higher fees to accept calls than the US-based carriers do, which can make it cheaper to route phone calls through the United States than directly to a neighboring country."[86] Therefore US anti-terrorism forces were able to eavesdrop on many terrorist phone calls around the world and discover plots for terrorist attacks before the attacks were to occur. They were also able to locate and capture many terrorist leaders.

In addition to monitoring these calls entirely between foreign callers, the National Security Agency, which collects such telephone calls as well as email traffic, was monitoring communications from places such as the area of Afghanistan where Osama bin Laden was thought to have been hiding to various locations in the United States (which were then suspected to be indications of a possible al-Qaeda cell within the United States).

But when liberal opponents of the War on Terror discovered that this was happening, once again they betrayed the urgent defense interests of the United States and opposed what they called "warrantless wiretapping." Of course, if you are listening to a call between terrorists that lasts two minutes, there is no time to go to a local court and get the nearest judge to issue a warrant for that call because you will miss it. And with terrorists using disposable cell phones for a short time and then discarding them, the requirement for specific warrants in each case would make such listening to terrorist conversations impossible.

Opponents of this electronic anti-terror procedure have claimed that it violates the civil rights of Americans and also violates a law passed in 1978 called the Foreign Intelligence Surveillance Act (FISA) because it intercepts telephone communications without a warrant. So it was called "warrantless wiretapping." But the Bush administration steadfastly maintained that it was not violating any American law. Law professor John Yoo of the University of California, Berkeley, who was a Justice Department official in the Bush administration, notes the following:

> Every Federal Appeals Court to address the question has agreed that the President may gather electronic intelligence to protect against foreign threats. This includes the special FISA appeals

---

86. Ryan Singel, "NSA's Lucky Break: How the U.S. Became Switchboard to the World," *Wired.com* (Oct. 10, 2007). www.wired.com/politics/security/news/2007/10/domestic_taps.

court, which in a 2002 sealed case upholding the constitution-
ality of the Patriot Act held that "the President did have inherent authority to conduct warrantless searches to obtain foreign
intelligence information." The court said … that "FISA could
not encroach on the President's constitutional power."[87]

Because of his support for former President Bush's attempt to keep
the country safe, Yoo was labeled a "war criminal" by the "far left."[88]

The very existence of this top-secret program to monitor terrorist
phone calls was also first revealed to the public by an article in *The New
York Times* on December 16, 2005. Even the liberal *Times* had to admit
that the program was successful:

> Several officials said the eavesdropping program had helped
> uncover a plot by Iyman Faris, an Ohio trucker and naturalized
> citizen who pleaded guilty in 2003 to supporting Al Qaeda by
> planning to bring down the Brooklyn Bridge with blowtorches.
> What appeared to be another Qaeda plot, involving fertilizer
> bomb attacks on British pubs and train stations, was exposed
> last year in part through the program, the officials said.[89]

The primary opposition to this program has been from the American
Civil Liberties Union (ACLU), which has filed numerous lawsuits to stop
it,[90] and many Democratic members of Congress. After an incredibly
long battle with Congress, President Bush was finally able to persuade
enough members of Congress to pass a bill granting immunity to telecommunications companies that would help in this process; he signed
the bill July 10, 2008. Without this law, the companies that owned the
telecommunications equipment could have been driven out of business
by having to defend themselves against lawsuits regarding this program.
The ACLU immediately promised to challenge the law in court.[91]

---

87. John Yoo, "Why We Endorsed Warrantless Wire-Taps," *Wall Street Journal* (July 16,
2009), A13.

88. Glenn Greenwald, "John Yoo's War Crimes," *Salon.com* (April 2, 2008), (www.salon.
com/opinion/greenwald/2008/04/02/yoo/index.html); and Maria L. La Ganga, "Scholar
Calmly Takes Heat for His Memos on Torture," *Los Angeles Times* (May 16, 2005), http://
articles.latimes.com/2005/may/16/local/me-yoo16.

89. James Risen and Eric Lichtblau, "Bush Lets U.S. Spy on Callers Without Courts," *New
York Times* (Dec. 16, 2005). www.nytimes.com/2005/12/16/politics/16program.html?ex=12
92389200&en=e32072d786623ac1&ei=5090&partner=rssuserland&emc=rss.

90. For examples of how the ACLU has tried to stop the surveillance program, go to www.
aclu.org/national-security/surveillance.

91. "Bush Signs Terror Surveillance Bill Granting Legal Immunity to Companies That Aided
Eavesdropping," *Fox News* (July 10, 2008). www.foxnews.com/story/0,2933,379843,00.html.

My own viewpoint is that such a program is essential to national security and essential in the battle against the threat of terrorist attacks. Because it is limited to protecting against terrorist attacks, the small threat of invasion of the privacy of ordinary citizens is insignificant in comparison to the huge benefit of protection against deadly attacks. The program should be continued.

c. Holding nations accountable that harbor terrorists

Another step in defeating Islamic Jihadism was begun by President Bush when he declared on September 20, 2001 — just after the attacks of 9/11 — that the United States would hold accountable any nation that harbored terrorists or gave support to terrorists. The President said:

> We will starve terrorists of funding, turn them one against another, drive them from place to place, until there is no refuge or no rest. And we will pursue nations that provide aid or safe haven to terrorism. Every nation, in every region, now has a decision to make. Either you are with us, or you are with the terrorists. From this day forward, any nation that continues to harbor or support terrorism will be regarded by the United States as a hostile regime.[92]

This is an important step, because without at least passive tolerance by a national government, it is hard for terrorist training camps and cells to remain for long within any nation.

The US government under the leadership of President Bush began to pursue aggressive policies to intercept and attack terrorists before they could attack us, and the result was an amazing success that no one would have believed possible shortly after 9/11. For the entire remaining seven years of the Bush administration, and so far in President Obama's administration (as I am writing in early 2010), no successful terrorist attack has been carried out inside the United States.

Journalist Ronald Kessler, an expert on anti-terrorism, writes, "Terrorists haven't attacked during the past seven years because of the work of the FBI, the CIA (Central Intelligence Agency), and our military, as well as the sweeping changes President Bush instigated in the intelligence community."[93] Kessler goes on to say, "When Bush proclaimed that any

---

92. George W. Bush, Address to a Joint Session of Congress Following 9/11 Attacks. www.americanrhetoric.com/speeches/gwbush911jointsessionspeech.htm.

93. Ronald Kessler, "The secret to why we have not been attacked," *Newsmax.com* (accessed Sept. 11, 2008).

country harboring a terrorist would be considered terrorist, Arab countries began cooperating in the War on Terror, turning over thousands of terrorists and leads."[94] He adds, "Since 9/11, the FBI, the CIA, and the military have rolled up about 5,000 terrorists world-wide."[95]

d. Persuading people in Muslim nations to turn against terrorist groups

We can be thankful that the vast majority of Muslims throughout the world have not advocated or supported such terrorist activities. In fact, it was the resistance of the Muslim governments in Egypt to the imposition of strict Islamic law that made them the first targets of Islamic Jihadism. As journalist and former Army Green Beret Michael Yon explains again and again in his book *Moment of Truth in Iraq*,[96] the local populations in one region after another have turned decisively against al-Qaeda and told American and Iraqi forces where terrorists were hiding and where they had planted bombs. But this turn of events happened only after Americans did two things: They used military power to provide security and safety, and they used local contacts and charitable acts to build confidence and trust with the Iraqis who had been terrorized by violent al-Qaeda members.

To the extent that this happens in areas where al-Qaeda pockets are found in the world, the local forces opposing these terrorists will find and imprison or destroy them, and terrorism will be marginalized and given no place to thrive. But as Yon points out, it will require a strong, committed US military presence in Iraq and Afghanistan to provide the neighborhood security within which such other peace-making efforts can be successful.

Moreover, Christians must realize that as we hope to persuade Muslims to turn against terrorism and renounce the idea that Islam can be imposed by force on non-Muslim peoples, we are asking them to reject a conservative, more literal reading of the Quran (as promoted by terrorist factions), in which "peace" means not coexistence with other religions, but total surrender to Muslim rule over society. Therefore, when Muslims claim they hold to a "religion of peace," we should ask for clarification about what is meant by "peace."

e. Moral reformation in American culture

One factor that gives Islamic radicals "intellectual ammunition" to vilify America is the very evident moral breakdown in American society,

---

94. Ibid.
95. Ibid.
96. Michael Yon, *Moment of Truth in Iraq* (Minneapolis: Richard Vigilante Books, 2008).

which they can criticize in order to argue that every nation badly needs the imposition of strict Islamic law. The radicals point to widespread moral decline in America characterized by alcoholism, addiction to drugs or gambling, pornography, widespread break-up of marriages, sexual immorality before and after marriage, undisciplined and disrespectful children in schools, the breakdown of parental authority, widespread shoplifting and employee theft, dishonesty in all areas of life, and more.

At this point Christians should realize that historically it has been *the proclamation by Christian pastors of the moral law of God* and of universal accountability before God that has brought positive moral transformation in many societies. Christians would do well to consider again at this point in history how they might persuasively teach the society at large about God's moral standards in the Bible.

f. Spiritual revival

The type of moral proclamation and transformation that I mentioned in the previous section can bring beneficial changes to the accepted moral standards in a society. But genuine transformation will not come about unless a substantial number of people in a society or nation also have their hearts transformed by the message of the Christian gospel that proclaims forgiveness of sins and the opportunity for new life through faith in Jesus Christ. This has application in two ways.

First, if there is a spiritual revival that brings many people to personal faith in Christ in the United States or other nations, it will bring about a more effective kind of moral transformation in society and thereby will begin to provide a better answer to the attempts by Islamic terrorists to claim the moral high ground in terms of personal morality and Islamic law.

Second, such a revival would also have the potential for reaching even the hardened hearts of al-Qaeda terrorists, if they would give consideration to it. If such a spiritual revival were to occur not only in the United States but also in nations with large Muslim populations, it would provide evidence that genuine Christianity is not represented by the kind of decadence that many Muslims see in popular American culture and especially in movies, but that genuine Christianity results in a transformation of the heart and shows itself in moral conduct and love for one's neighbor as manifested in the life and teachings of Jesus Christ.

Chapter 7

NATIONAL DEFENSE: CURRENT WARS AND RELATED ISSUES

In addition to the broader issues of just-war theory and international terrorism, many specific political issues related to national defense must be addressed:

What should be done about the wars in Iraq and Afghanistan?

Should the United States have nuclear weapons, and if so, how many?

Should the United States develop a more extensive missile defense system?

What should be the role of the CIA, and what limits should be placed on its activity?

What should the nation's policy be regarding torture of enemy forces in its custody?

Should homosexuals be allowed to serve in the military?

Should women serve in combat situations?

A. WARS IN IRAQ AND AFGHANISTAN

According to the criteria for a just war mentioned in the previous chapter, I believe that the wars in Iraq and Afghanistan were just wars.

(1) These wars were undertaken for a *just cause*, first, because the United States had already been attacked by Islamic terrorists on 9/11 and previously, and second, because these wars were launched against hotbeds of Islamic terrorism. Therefore their primary justification was to defend the United States against another similar terrorist attack that could come, not from one specific nation, but from a worldwide network of terrorists that was receiving support or at least safe harbor from various nations. The Taliban and the al-Qaeda forces were controlling Afghanistan and carrying out terrorist attacks from there. In the Middle East, Saddam Hussein was giving repeated support to terrorist activities, providing training grounds, paying $25,000 to the family of every terrorist who committed a suicide attack in Israel,[1] and developing or perhaps possessing weapons of mass destruction. With respect to Iraq, another *just cause* was that Saddam had never complied with the terms of surrender in the First Gulf War in 1993, because he was continuing to prevent site visits to verify that he had no nuclear weapons.

Although no weapons of mass destruction were found after the invasion of Iraq, the intelligence services of the United States and many other Western countries were convinced that he had chemical and biological weapons (he had used them previously against Kurds in the northern part of Iraq), and there was substantial evidence that he was attempting to acquire nuclear weapons as well. (Israel had destroyed Saddam's Osirak nuclear reactor as far back as June 7, 1981, in a surprise air attack, because Israel was convinced that Saddam was soon going to be able to develop nuclear weapons from it.) According to the British Broadcasting Corporation (BBC), "The Israeli Government explained its reasons for the attack in a statement saying, "The atomic bombs which that reactor was capable of producing, whether from enriched uranium or from plutonium, would be of the Hiroshima size. Thus a mortal danger to the people of Israel progressively arose.'"[2]

In addition, there is still reason to believe that these intelligence reports were accurate, because some apparently reliable sources have reported that Saddam transported large quantities of weapons of mass destruction to Syria just prior to the American invasion. In January 2004, *Agence France Presse* (the French news service) reported:

---

1. Hohn Esterbrook, "Salaries for Suicide Bombers," *CBSNews.com* (April 3, 2002). www.cbsnews.com/stories/2002/04/03/world/main505316.shtml.

2. "1981: Israel Bombs Iraq Nuclear Reactor," *BBCNews.com* (June 7, 1981). http://news.bbc.co.uk/onthisday/hi/dates/stories/june/7/newsid_3014000/3014623.stm.

An exiled Syrian dissident has reiterated claims that Iraqi biological and chemical weapons were smuggled into Syria just
before the start of the United States–led attack on Iraq in
March last year. "The Iraqi chemical and biological weapons
were at first put in (Syrian) Presidential Guard depots, at its
headquarters in Damascus," Nizzar Nayyouf told the French-
based Internet news site Proche-Orient.info, which specialises
in news from the Middle East. He said the operation took place
"between February and March 2003, when Saddam Hussein
realised that the Americans had decided to act" against Iraq.
The operation took place under supervision of General Zoul-
Himla Shalich, the head of the guard in Syria and considered
close to Syrian President Bashar al-Assad, Nayyouf said, citing
as his sources "superior officers who themselves took part in
the operation."[3]

Then-Israeli Prime Minister Ariel Sharon also made this claim in
December 2002, saying, "We have some information to that effect. We
are now working to confirm the information."[4]

But an even broader justification for the war was the conviction
of President Bush and others in the leadership of both parties that if
a genuinely functioning free and democratic government could begin
to succeed in Iraq, *it would provide a more effective long-term antidote
to Islamic terrorism*, a movement that had attacked us several times,
because *countries that are governed by open democratic processes do not
launch wars of conquest against other nations*. This position was argued, I
think persuasively, by Natan Sharansky in *The Case for Democracy*.[5] But
Sharansky contends that in order to be a *genuine* democracy, a country
must pass this "town square test": Can a citizen stand in the middle
of the town square and openly criticize the government without fear
of arrest, imprisonment, or physical harm?[6] Therefore, Sharansky says,
the present government of Hamas in Gaza does not constitute a genuine
democracy, for example, because it cannot pass that town square test.
I would add, nor does the current government of Russia pass the town

3. "Iraq Hid Weapons in Syria, Dissident Claims," *Agence France Presse* (Jan. 19, 2004).
www.iol.co.za/index.php?click_id=3&art_id=qw1074472561910B262&set_id=1.

4. "Syria Denies It Received Iraqi Weapons," Associated Press (Dec. 25, 2002). www.usa-
today.com/news/world/2002–12–25-syria-iraq_x.htm

5. Natan Sharansky, *The Case for Democracy: the Power of Freedom to Overcome Tyranny
and Terror* (New York: Public Affairs, 2004).

6. Ibid., 40.

square test, nor does the government of China. These are not now genuine democracies.

But Iraq is a genuine, functioning democracy. It has held successful elections, first to elect delegates to a constitutional convention, then later to approve the constitution (Oct. 15, 2005), in an election in which 63% of eligible Iraqis voted, passing it with 78% of the vote.[7] Still later, another successful election was held to elect members of Parliament (Dec. 15, 2005),[8] and another successful parliamentary election was held on March 7, 2010. Afghanistan is also a functioning democracy.[9] These countries still have internal struggles and conflicts (as all countries do, and especially new democracies as they begin to function), but they are living proof that functioning democracies are able to work within predominantly Muslim nations.

Some people object that predominantly Muslim countries will never be able to function as democracies. But Turkey is 99.8% Muslim and has a democratically elected government,[10] and Pakistan is 95% Muslim and has a democratically elected government as well.[11] Indonesia is 86% Muslim (and 6% Protestant and 3% Roman Catholic) and is a functioning democracy.[12]

The hope of President Bush was that a successful, peaceful, economically growing Iraq would be a persuasive, visible model that would challenge the people of other Islamic nations, because it would demonstrate that even the nation with the Middle East's worst Islamic dictatorship (under Saddam Hussein), once the oppressive government is overthrown, can begin to function with a non-oppressive, democratic government. This would provide impetus for the same process happening in other Muslim nations (such as Iran). In this way this model has the potential to change the course of history in the Middle East.

My own expectation is that this process holds the most hope of long-term defeat of Islamic terrorism. Functioning democracies in Muslim

---

7. Kenneth Katzman, "Iraq: Elections, Government, and Constitution," *CRS Report for Congress* (Feb. 27, 2007). http://fpc.state.gov/documents/organization/81355.pdf.

8. Ibid.

9. Griff Witte, "A Sign of Democracy in Afghanistan," *Washington Post* (Dec. 20, 2005). www.boston.com/news/world/middleeast/articles/2005/12/20/a_sign_of_democracy_in_afghanistan/.

10. "Turkey," *The World Factbook*, Central Intelligence Agency (Oct. 28, 2009). www.cia.gov/library/publications/the-world-factbook/geos/tu.html.

11. "Pakistan," *The World Factbook*, Central Intelligence Agency (Oct. 28, 2009). https://www.cia.gov/library/publications/the-world-factbook/geos/pk.html.

12. "Indonesia," *The World Factbook*, Central Intelligence Agency (Feb. 7, 2010). https://www.cia.gov/library/publications/the-world-factbook/geos/id.html.

nations will eventually give Islamic terrorists no place to train and no place to hide.

Therefore the war in Iraq was a necessary, strategic, and highly significant step in defending the United States against radical Islamic terrorism. It was undertaken for a *just cause.*

(2) The Iraqi and Afghan wars were declared by a *competent authority* (the President, with Congress authorizing the expenditures).

(3) There was truly *comparative justice* on our side, because of the great evil propagated by the Taliban in Afghanistan and Saddam Hussein in Iraq.

(4) We had the *right intention,* to free both countries from oppressive dictatorships and simultaneously to remove the threat of terrorism against us that was coming from those countries.

(5) Both were wars of *last resort,* because other negotiations had gone on for years without any significant change in those countries.

(6) The United States had a great *probability of success.*

(7) The *proportionality of projected results* was massively in favor of these two wars because of the world-threatening nature of terrorism emanating from those countries and because of the great good that would come about if their governments were changed. As a matter of fact, the *actual* results have been that these two nations are now functioning democracies, and a total of nearly 60 million more people (nearly 29 million in Iraq[13] and more than 28 million[14] in Afghanistan) who were formerly under extremely oppressive regimes are now living in comparative freedom. This is an excellent result.

(8) The wars were carried out in a *right spirit,* with regret that war had to be undertaken, but with determination to bring it to a successful conclusion.

Therefore I strongly disagree with Jim Wallis when he writes in *God's Politics* that the Iraq War did not meet the criteria of a just war.[15] And it is seriously misleading when he says repeatedly that most churches from various denominations were opposed to the Iraq War (see pp. 109, 113, 134, and 155). Wallis gives almost no documentation for this claim, except at one point (p. 155) he does list some signers to a vague anti-

---

13. "Iraq," *The World Factbook,* Central Intelligence Agency (Oct. 28, 2009). https://www.cia.gov/library/publications/the-world-factbook/geos/iz.html.

14. "Afghanistan," *The World Factbook,* Central Intelligence Agency (Oct. 28, 2009). https://www.cia.gov/library/publications/the-world-factbook/geos/af.html.

15. Jim Wallis, *God's Politics: Why the Right Gets It Wrong and the Left Doesn't Get It* (San Francisco: HarperSanFrancisco, 2005), 111, 113.

war statement. What he does not mention is that the signers are mostly people who are already committed to his pacifist position or are from much more liberal rather than evangelical colleges and seminaries. In actual fact, very few evangelical churches ever considered or voted on any resolutions in support of the war or against it (and Wallis himself notes that Southern Baptists supported it).[16] Certainly Wallis is mistaken if he is implying that opposition to the Iraq War was a dominant "evangelical Protestant" viewpoint, which it certainly was not.

My present concern, however, is that President Obama might actually lose both Iraq and Afghanistan to terrorists once again through weakness and indecision. He is decreasing our military presence in Iraq and seems to be weakening our resolve to establish a strong and successful government there that can successfully oppose terrorist forces. He has insisted on an arbitrary timetable for withdrawal of American troops from Iraq,[17] and there were early indications that this may be destabilizing some regions and giving terrorists new hope that they might yet be able to defeat the forces of freedom that have brought such stability to the nation. Regarding Afghanistan, he delayed for thirteen weeks[18] a response to General Stanley McChrystal's request for 60,000 more troops in Afghanistan,[19] and he eventually agreed to send approximately half that number or 34,000.[20] But that might not be enough strength to defeat the terrorists and preserve the hard-won peace in Afghanistan.[21]

If the United States loses both the war in Iraq and the war in Afghanistan, so that these countries once again fall under terrorist domination, the destructive consequences for America and for the rest of the world would be far beyond anything that has happened up to this point. If that happens, the responsibility for such losses and such a renewed cam-

---

16. Ibid., 113.

17. Karen DeYoung, "Obama Sets Timetable for Iraq," *Washington Post* (Feb. 28, 2009). www.washingtonpost.com/wp-dyn/content/article/2009/02/27/AR2009022700566.html.

18. President Obama took from September 2 to November 24, 2009, to respond to the request. See Toby Harnden, "Barack Obama to Send 34,000 More Troops to Afghanistan," *Telegraph.co.uk* (Nov. 24, 2009). www.telegraph.co.uk/news/worldnews/northamerica/usa/6646411/Barack-Obama-to-send-34000-more-troops-to-Afghanistan.html?utm_source=Left+Foot+Forward+List&utm_campaign=f3bbdd60a7-Left_Foot_Forward8_18_2009&utm_medium=email.

19. Peter Spiegel and Yochi Dreazen, "Top Troop Request Exceeds 60,000," *Wall Street Journal* (Oct. 9, 2009). http://online.wsj.com/article/SB125504448324674693.html?mod=WSJ_hpp_sections_news.

20. Harnden, "Barack Obama to Send 34,000 More Troops to Afghanistan."

21. Yochi Dreazan, "Afghan Troop Request Simmers," *Wall Street Journal* (Sept. 26, 2009). http://online.wsj.com/article/SB125391851405042437.html?mod=rss_Politics_And_Policy.

paign of terror throughout many nations will belong solely to President Obama. I deeply hope that this does not happen.

B. NUCLEAR WEAPONS

1. History of nuclear weapons

The only two nuclear weapons ever used in war were exploded by the United States over Hiroshima and Nagasaki, Japan—on August 6 and 9, 1945, respectively. Both of these large cities had industrial and military significance for the Japanese war effort. Estimates ranging from 90,000 to 150,000 people were killed in Hiroshima (out of 340,000), and about 80,000 people were killed in Nagasaki (out of 212,000).[22] (About half of those numbers were killed immediately, and half died afterward from burns, radiation, and other injuries.) In both cases, the bomb destroyed everything within a one-mile radius in all directions and caused fires as far as two miles from the bomb.

President Harry S. Truman's goal in authorizing the use of these bombs was to bring an end to World War II, and that was in fact the result. Six days after the second bomb, Japan announced its surrender to the Allied Powers. While dropping these bombs caused the loss of approximately 200,000 Japanese lives, a commonly repeated estimate (from analysts who understand the US and Japanese force strength at that time) is that if the war had gone on without these bombs, the result would have been the loss of at least 500,000 American lives and possibly hundreds of thousands of Japanese lives.[23]

In his 1955 autobiography, President Truman affirmed that the atomic bomb probably saved half a million US lives, not to mention many Japanese casualties. The Japanese had already shown in previous battles in the Pacific campaigns that they would not surrender. Still, leftist critics claim that the number of 500,000 possible casualties was a "myth." In an article in the *New England Journal of History* in 2007, Michael Kort, professor of General Studies at Boston University, answered those critics:

> Writing in *The Journal of Military History*, [military historian] D. M. Giangreco explained that in military hands these pro-

---

22. C. Peter Chen, "Atomic Bombing of Hiroshima and Nagasaki," World War II Database. http://ww2db.com/battle_spec.php?battle_id=49.

23. Jing Oh, "Hiroshima and Nagasaki: The Decision to Drop the Bomb," University of Michigan. www.umich.edu/~historyj/pages_folder/articles/Hiroshima_and_Nagasaki.pdf.

jections took three forms: Medical estimates, manpower estimates, and strategic estimates. He then demonstrated that there
was substantial documentation for high-end casualty projections—which, to be sure, varied widely—from both military
and civilian sources that reached upward of 500,000. Equally
important, one estimate that reached Truman—from former
president Herbert Hoover, who had high-level government
contacts—led the president to convene an important meeting
with the Joint Chiefs of Staff and top civilian advisors on June
18, 1945, to discuss the projected invasion of Japan. In short,
as Giangreco stressed in a later article in the *Pacific Historical
Review*, Truman both saw and was concerned about high-end
casualty estimates prior to the scheduled invasion.[24]

Whatever the precise number would have been is impossible to know,
but it is clear that the use of the atomic bombs saved countless numbers
of lives.

Since 1945, several other nations have acquired nuclear weapons, but
no other nuclear weapon has ever been used in war. What prevented
their use, for example, during the entire period of the Cold War between
the Soviet Union and the United States and its allies? What prevented
the Soviets from launching nuclear attacks against the United States or
Western Europe? It was primarily the fear of overwhelming retaliation
by the United States, the United Kingdom, and France that would result
in horrifying destruction of the Soviet Union itself. In other words, it
was *the possession of overwhelming numbers of nuclear weapons* by peace-
loving nations that prevented their use by any aggressor nation. That
system of deterrence has worked perfectly now for more than six decades
(since 1945).

2. Which nations have nuclear weapons today?

According to the Pentagon, the United States now has a total of 5,113
operational nuclear weapons,[25] and current estimates are that Russia has 5,200.[26] The US total is what remains after the nation "has

24. Michael Kort, "The Histography of Hiroshima: The Rise and Fall of Revisionism,"
New England Journal of History 64:1 (Fall 2007), 31–48. http://theamericanpresident.us/
images/truman_bomb.pdf.
25. "U.S. Releases Details of Nuclear Weapons Inventory," Associated Press (May 3, 2010).
Accessed at www.foxnews.com/politics/2010/05/03/release-details-nuclear-weapons-inventory/.
26. "To Russia with Love," editorial in *Wall Street Journal* (April 4–5, 2009), A10.

dismantled more than 13,000 nuclear weapons since 1988."[27] The reason for retaining such a large number is that in the event of a nuclear war, many weapons might be destroyed before they could be launched, others would fail, and others would not reach their targets. (The weapons depend on a three-part delivery system: bombers, missiles, and submarines.)

In addition to the United States and Russia (which now controls the nuclear arsenal of the former Soviet Union), the following nations also possess nuclear weapons: (3) United Kingdom, (4) France, (5) China, (6) India, (7) Pakistan, and (8) North Korea. In addition, (9) Israel is widely thought to possess nuclear weapons but has never publicly confirmed this.

Besides these nations, Iran is aggressively pursuing nuclear power, and al-Qaeda has tried to obtain nuclear weapons. Moreover, when Israel destroyed Saddam's Osirak nuclear reactor on June 7, 1981, it temporarily destroyed Iraq's ability to develop nuclear weapons.[28]

3. Can the world successfully abolish nuclear weapons?

Many people today believe that the danger from nuclear weapons comes from the *mere presence* of so many of them in the world. If people believe this, then it seems evident to them that reducing the number of nuclear weapons in the world would reduce the threat that any nation would ever launch a nuclear attack. Their goal, then, is complete nuclear disarmament around the world. Their hope is that the world will be able to get rid of all nuclear weapons once and for all. Democratic Senator Diane Feinstein of California has said that nuclear weapons are "not a deterrent, but a grave and gathering threat to humanity."[29]

Will worldwide nuclear disarmament ever be possible? The short answer is no.

The history of the world shows that once new weapons are developed, they never disappear from the earth. Crossbows were declared illegal by the Second Lateran Council in 1139, but people kept using them anyway. After airplanes were invented, The Hague Convention banned aerial bombardment in 1899, but people continued to use planes

---

27. Jack David, "There's No Reason for a Nuclear Test Ban," *Wall Street Journal* (Feb. 21–22, 2009), A9.

28. "1981: Israel Bombs Iraq Nuclear Reactor," *BBCNews.com* (June 7, 1981).

29. Dianne Feinstein, "Let's Commit to a Nuclear-Free World," *Wall Street Journal* (Jan. 3–4, 2009), A9.

to drop bombs.[30] The reason is that the earth will always have people whose hearts are evil and who will pursue the most destructive weapons they can obtain in order to carry out their evil purposes. "The heart is deceitful above all things, and desperately sick; who can understand it?" (Jer. 17:9).

Therefore, to hope that nuclear weapons can be abolished from the nations of the earth is merely wishful thinking, with no basis in reality. To say it is possible would be to say that it is possible to reverse the entire course of all of human history from the beginning of time with regard to the development of new weapons. Such an expectation should not qualify as a rational defense policy for a nation.

Just after President Obama proclaimed to the United Nations his goal of a world without nuclear weapons, the editorial board of the *Wall Street Journal* rightly observed:

> In the bitter decades of the Cold War, we learned the hard way that the only countries that abide by disarmament treaties are those that want to be disarmed.[31]

4. How can we effectively reduce the risk of using nuclear weapons?

If it is not possible to rid the world of nuclear weapons, then the most important question is, how can we prevent nations from using nuclear weapons? There are two answers to this question: (1) deterrence by the credible threat of a superior nuclear force, and (2) an anti-missile defense system that will prevent nuclear weapons from reaching their targets.

Since it is the responsibility of governments to protect the people over whom God has placed them in authority, it is now necessary, in a world with nuclear weapons, for nations to be able to defend themselves in these two ways or else be able to depend on more powerful peaceful nations to defend them against such attacks. That is why the United States, in particular, has a weighty responsibility to maintain a clearly superior nuclear force that can defeat any potential attacker, and it must speak and act in such a way that the potential attacker is convinced the United States will overwhelmingly retaliate if a nuclear weapon is launched against it. To fail to do this would be to fail to protect the citizens of this nation effectively.

---

30. "To Russia with Love," *Wall Street Journal*.
31. "The Disarmament Illusion," *Wall Street Journal* (Sept. 26, 2009), A14.

In addition, there are more than thirty other allied nations who depend on the United States for their protection from nuclear attack.[32] If the United States were to fail to maintain a sufficiently strong nuclear response capability, it would also be failing these allies who depend on our protection — and would prompt them to decide they have to develop their own nuclear arsenal.

In addition, because of the persistent threat of the use of nuclear weapons by an aggressor nation (whether Russia or North Korea or Iran or perhaps even China), the United States has a clear responsibility to continue to develop and deploy an effective anti-missile defense system that would shoot down an attacking missile before it could reach its target.

In fact, the anti-missile defense system that the United States has now partially deployed in Alaska and California is a wonderful alternative to the horrible possibility of having to launch a nuclear attack in response to an attack against us. Instead of two nations blowing up each others' cities, anti-missile defense systems will shoot down the incoming missile from an attacker before it reaches its target, so that no nuclear weapons are exploded in the first place. (The nuclear payload would ordinarily not detonate in such cases.) All Christians who love peace and believe in the protection of human life should rejoice greatly that military technology has advanced to the place where such systems are actually quite effective, as they have shown in many tests. On January 26, 2002, it was reported that a ground-based interceptor missile fired from a Navy ship hit a dummy armed missile in space that had been fired over the Pacific.[33] In another test, conducted on September 1, 2006, a missile was fired from a silo at Vandenberg Air Force Base and shot down a missile launched from Kodiak Island in Alaska.[34] In a test of an airborne anti-missile system, on February 11, 2010,

> A flying Boeing 747 jumbo jet equipped with a massive laser gun shot down a Scud-like missile over the Pacific late Thursday night, marking what analysts said was a major milestone in the development of the nation's missile-defense system.... The laser shot a heated, basketball-size beam that traveled 670

32. "Atomic Bombshells," Wall Street Journal (Jan. 24–25, 2009), A10; Jack David, "No Reason," Wall Street Journal (Feb. 21–22, 2009), A9.

33. "Missile Shield Test Dubbed A Hit." Associated Press (Jan. 26, 2002). www.cbsnews.com/stories/2002/01/26/national/main325718.shtml.

34. Robert Jablon, "Anti-Missile Test Succeeds," Chicago Tribune (Sept. 2, 2006). http://archives.chicagotribune.com/2006/sep/02/news/chi–0609020154sep02.

million mph to incinerate a missile moving 4,000 mph, the Pentagon said.[35]

When President Reagan first proposed such anti-missile defense systems, he was ridiculed by the political left and the media in the United States, who called it a "Star Wars" system and predicted that "it will never work." But now such a system actually has been shown to work in tests time and again. Christians should eagerly and enthusiastically support such a defensive system.

These two means of defense against nuclear attacks (maintaining strong nuclear weapon capabilities and building a strong anti-missile defense system) have another advantage as well: When the United States has such great superiority to other nations in both areas, it discourages any potential enemies from trying to match our power or engage in an arms race with us.

By contrast, if the United States proceeds in a unilateral way to disarm itself further and further, it will simply encourage hostile nations into an immediate rush to begin to develop more nuclear weapons and delivery systems that they think might possibly be able to attain a victory over the United States if they were able to attack. Thus America's *disarmament* would lead to an *arms race* on the part of other nations. It would also lead many of the allies who depend on US protection to think that they themselves must acquire nuclear weapons for their own defense, which would lead to further proliferation of the weapons.

During 2009, however, it became increasingly clear that President Obama would pursue exactly the opposite strategy from what I have advocated here, for he took several steps to weaken the US nuclear weapons arsenal and opposed further anti-missile defenses. He sought a new treaty with Russia that would set a maximum of 1,000 nuclear warheads each for the United States and Russia[36] (down from our current total of 5,113 warheads). He sought to kill the Reliable Replacement Warhead program, which would modernize and update the nuclear arsenal for a long time to come and which is supported by both Defense Secretary Robert Gates and Chairman of the Joint Chiefs of Staff, Admiral Mike Mullen. Killing this program would leave our nuclear arsenal in its current state of "gradual physical deterioration."[37] He also asked the

35. W. J. Hennigan, "Pentagon: Laser shoots down missile in test," *Arizona Republic* (Feb. 13, 2010), A8.
36. "To Russia with Love," *Wall Street Journal*.
37. Ibid.

Senate to ratify the Comprehensive Test Ban Treaty (CTBT), which the Senate had rejected in 1999.[38] Such an action would unwisely commit the United States to never being able to test its nuclear weapons systems, which would leave them vulnerable to gradually becoming outmoded.

Even more harmful to world peace than these decisions was President Obama's decision on September 17, 2009, to abandon a missile defense agreement that President George W. Bush had negotiated with Poland and the Czech Republic to station anti-missile defense systems in these two important countries in Eastern Europe.[39] Abandoning this program betrayed the trust that the Poland and Czech governments had placed in us. This missile system would have protected Europe from Iranian or Russian attacks, and it would have provided significant protection for us against missiles launched from Russia or Iran toward the east coast of the United States, since it would have intercepted them early in their flight paths.

Russia was delighted with President Obama's decision—a decision that left Eastern Europe more vulnerable to future Soviet attempts to attack and regain control over it. One Polish newspaper proclaimed, "Betrayal! The U.S. sold us to Russia and stabbed us in the back." A respected newspaper in the Czech Republic said, "An ally we rely on has betrayed us, and exchanged us for its own, better relations with Russia, of which we are rightly afraid."[40] *The Wall Street Journal* on the next day wrote this:

> The reality is that the U.S. is working hard to create antagonists where it previously had friends.... Officials in Warsaw surely noticed that President Obama cancelled the missile system 70 years to the day that the Soviet Union invaded Poland.[41]

The Obama administration also canceled the Kinetic Energy Interceptor project for basing anti-missile defenses in Germany and Turkey. It canceled this as part of the $1.4 billion in cuts to the Pentagon's missile defense budget in early 2009, while it was in the midst of increasing government spending in almost every other area, far in excess of spending

38. Jack David, "No Reason," *Wall Street Journal* (Feb. 21–22, 2009), A9.

39. "Obama's Remarks on Strengthening Missile Defense in Europe," *Council on Foreign Relations* (Sept. 17, 2009). www.cfr.org/publication/20226/obamas_remarks_on_strengthening_missile_defense_in_europe_september_2009.html.

40. Vanessa Gera, "Poles, Czechs: U.S. Missile Defense Shift a Betrayal," Associated Press (Sept. 18, 2009). www.washingtontimes.com/news/2009/sep/18/poles-czechs-us-missile-defense-shift-betrayal/print/.

41. "Obama's Missile Offense," *Wall Street Journal* (Sept. 18, 2009), A22.

done by any previous administration in history.[42] The administration was so opposed to such military spending that this was the only budget area subject to significant cuts. These were tragic decisions, immensely harmful to future national security.

C. THE CIA

The Central Intelligence Agency (CIA) is the primary organization that gathers and analyzes information about other countries, especially about potential enemies of the United States. In other words, the CIA coordinates America's spy network abroad.

Is this a good thing? It seems to me that a necessary part of defending a nation is seeking to know about potential enemies and possible attacks before they happen, so that the nation can be defended against them. Because of this function, the CIA has no doubt prevented immense harm to the United States and to its interests both at home and elsewhere.

In the Bible, spies were not unknown. Joshua sent spies into the Promised Land before the conquest of Canaan (Josh. 2:1), David sent out spies to learn the whereabouts of King Saul (1 Sam. 26:4), and David later sent Hushai the Archite to serve as an undercover agent when Absalom was about to capture Jerusalem (2 Sam. 15:32–37; 16:15–19; 17:5–22).

Americans should, in general, be thankful for the CIA and the valuable intelligence it provides for our government. But instead of appreciation, the CIA constantly faces hostility and criticism from much of the American media and Hollywood. Because of unrelenting criticism over the years, much of which cannot be effectively answered without revealing national secrets, a sort of anti-CIA attitude has grown up in the United States. One example is the recent series of three movies called "The Bourne Trilogy," starring Matt Damon as Jason Bourne. Although I have enjoyed several of Robert Ludlum's novels (from which the lead character was taken), and although these movies were great fun to watch and very well made, their plots were completely different from Ludlum's novels, and the main villain turns out to be not any evil terrorist but the CIA itself!

Such an anti-CIA mindset is both unfortunate for the country and highly inappropriate to the crucial work that is carried out by the agency. Although there are no doubt occasional breeches of good conduct and unwise decisions, for the most part the tens of thousands of people who

---

42. "Our Missile-Defense Race Against Iran," *Wall Street Journal* (Sept. 21, 2009), A19.

work for the CIA do so at the cost of significant personal sacrifice and often in the face of great danger. Criticism of the CIA or its activities in general has a destructive effect on the nation because it undermines the morale of CIA employees who often perform extremely dangerous tasks at great personal sacrifice, largely out of devotion to protecting the nation. It also creates an atmosphere in which it is more difficult for the agency to recruit employees and carry on its work.

Opposition to the CIA *as a general attitude of mind* or a general policy position runs contrary to the very ability of the nation to defend itself; it is therefore opposition to the United States itself.

Of course, it is necessary that Congress have some oversight of the activities of the CIA and related intelligence agencies, all of which are part of the executive branch and ultimately report to the President. But too often congressional oversight has led to damaging leaks of information (from anti-CIA congressmen or their staff members), leaks that have been destructive to the CIA's ability to protect national security and have actually hampered the CIA in fulfilling its tasks.

Christians who believe it is right, according to Romans 13 and 1 Peter 2, for nations to defend their citizens should be supportive of the CIA in general rather than being instinctively critical of activities about which they actually know very little.

D. COERCIVE INTERROGATION OF PRISONERS

What should the policy of a government be regarding what the press commonly calls the "torture" of captured prisoners? This question has been the focus of significant debate in the United States as a result of the terrorist attacks of 9/11 and the subsequent capture of al-Qaeda operatives who were thought to have information about plans for future attacks in the US and elsewhere.

The discussion has been made more difficult by lack of clarity in definition of terms, especially the word "torture." Some people think "torture" means extreme measures like cutting off a person's fingers or toes or gouging out an eye. Others think that merely shouting at a prisoner is torture, or waking him up from a sound sleep for more questioning under a bright light. In ordinary English today, "torture" can be used very broadly, as in, "Listening to that boring sermon for thirty minutes this morning was sheer *torture!*"

When a word has this many different meanings, it becomes difficult to use the word in a way that does not confuse at least some hearers. Ethicist Daniel Heimbach rightly criticized a statement on torture issued by the National Association of Evangelicals on March 11, 2007, by noting, "While it loudly renounces 'torture,' it nowhere—in 18 pages of posturing—defines what signers of the document claim so vehemently to reject."[43]

Therefore, in this section I will attempt to define explicitly what I am talking about, but I will try to avoid the word "torture" unless I specify clearly what is meant or when I am directly quoting others. The word's wide variety of meanings only confuses the discussion.

Former presidential candidate Senator John McCain, who had himself endured severe torture that caused permanent physical harm as a prisoner in North Vietnam, insisted that the US policy should be "no torture, ever."[44] He said, "One of the things that kept us going when I was in prison in North Vietnam was that we knew that if the situation were reversed, we would not be doing to our captors what they were doing to us."[45] His amendment prohibiting any "cruel, inhuman, or degrading" treatment of prisoners passed the US Senate by a vote of 90–9 in 2005.[46]

But under questioning, McCain admitted he did not intend this prohibition to be absolute! When asked what to do if we captured a terrorist who had planted an atomic bomb that was set to go off in New York City, he responded, "You have to do what you have to do. But you take responsibility for it."[47] So the language of the amendment allowed *no exceptions,* but McCain himself admitted *there had to be exceptions.* This is inconsistent. Worse than that, even if a president authorizes extreme coercive measures and extracts the location of the bomb, and a bomb squad then diffuses it and saves thousands of lives, that same president and everyone who participated in the questioning of the terrorist would later be subject to prosecution and imprisonment for violating McCain's amendment. Given the power of pacifist and anti-violence lobbying groups in the United States, it is nearly certain that some prosecuting

43. "Ethicist: NAE torture declaration 'irrational,'" *Baptist Press* online edition (March 15, 2007). www.sbcbaptistpress.org/BPnews.asp?ID=25190 (accessed Oct. 29, 2009).

44. John McCain: quoted in Charles Krauthammer, "The Truth about Torture," *Weekly Standard* (Dec. 5, 2005). http://weeklystandard.com/Content/Public/Articles/000/000/006/400rhqav.asp.

45. Marc Santora, "McCain Finds Sympathy on Torture Issue," *New York Times* (Nov. 16, 2007). www.nytimes.com/2007/11/16/us/politics/15cnd-.mccain.html?ex=1352869200&en=73fdf47bcf1916b9&ei=5088&partner=rssnyt&emc=rss

46. Charles Babington and Shailagh Murray, "Senate Supports Interrogation Limits," *Washington Post* (Oct. 6, 2005). www.washingtonpost.com/wp-dyn/content/article/2005/10/05/AR2005100502062.html.

47. Evan Thomas and Michael Hirsh, "The Debate Over Torture," *Newsweek* (Nov. 21, 2005). www.newsweek.com/id/51198.

attorney could be persuaded that such prosecutions should go forward "so that it will be clear to the world that we will always take the high moral ground and never torture anyone, and those who do will be held accountable." Therefore Senator McCain's position is contradictory and would ultimately prove to be vindictive against those who are most responsible for protecting the nation from attack.

What, then, should the US policy be? My own conclusion is that we should have a standard policy, but with some carefully defined exceptions.

1. Standard policy

The standard policy of the United States regarding the treatment of prisoners of war should be one of humane treatment that exhibits compassion and care in accordance with the Geneva Conventions of 1949. These policies for the proper treatment of prisoners captured in wartime say in part:

> Protected persons are entitled, in all circumstances, to respect for their persons, their honour, their family rights, their religious convictions and practices, and their manners and customs. They shall at all times be humanely treated, and shall be protected especially against all acts of violence or threats thereof and against insults and public curiosity. Women shall be especially protected against any attack on their honour, in particular against rape, enforced prostitution, or any form of indecent assault. Without prejudice to the provisions relating to their state of health, age and sex, all protected persons shall be treated with the same consideration by the Party to the conflict in whose power they are, without any adverse distinction based, in particular, on race, religion or political opinion. However, the Parties to the conflict may take such measures of control and security in regard to protected persons as may be necessary as a result of the war.[48]

Such humane treatment of prisoners of war is entirely consistent with the purpose of keeping such prisoners in confinement, for the purpose should not be *to punish them* (for they were breaking no law by merely serving in the army of their country) but simply *to prevent them from re-engaging in war against the United States* as long as that war is going on. Therefore their confinement should not include any measures whose primary purpose would be to cause them suffering or pain.

---

48. Convention (IV) relative to the Protection of Civilian Persons in Time of War, Part III: Status and Treatment of Protected Persons, Geneva (12 Aug. 1949). www.icrc.org/ihl. nsf/FULL/380?OpenDocument.

Abraham Lincoln concluded his Second Inaugural Address with this kind of spirit, which exemplifies well what the United States has so long stood for:

> With malice toward none; with charity for all; with firmness in the right, as God gives us to see the right, let us strive on to finish the work we are in; to bind up the nation's wounds; to care for him who shall have borne the battle, and for his widow, and his orphan — to do all which may achieve and cherish a just and lasting peace, among ourselves, and with all nations.[49]

Such a policy is consistent with Jesus' command, "Love your enemies" (Matt. 5:44). Such treatment of enemy soldiers also holds up for any foe and for all the world a standard of moral conduct that takes the "high road" and exemplifies what is so good about our nation. We will defend ourselves when attacked, as governments have an obligation before God to do, but we will not be vindictive against those who are defeated. (In a similar spirit, the United States helped to rebuild both Germany and Japan, its defeated enemies, after World War II.)

2. Exceptions

Should there be any exceptions to this policy?

When someone enters the United States to carry out a terrorist attack, that person forfeits the status of prisoner-of-war for two reasons: (1) he is deliberately attacking civilians, and (2) he is fighting out of uniform (since he is trying to disguise himself as an innocent civilian). Therefore, according to international law, *he is not entitled to the protections of the Geneva Conventions.*

How should the United States treat a captured terrorist, especially when it has strong reason to believe the terrorist has planned a future terrorist attack against it or has detailed knowledge about a future attack? Newspaper columnist Charles Krauthammer has called this the "ticking time bomb" problem.[50]

The moral and legal status of this terrorist is different because he is still *currently* engaged in the immoral and illegal process of concealing information that could save thousands of lives from terrible destruction — that is, he is *currently* complicit in mass murder on an

---

49. Abraham Lincoln Second Inaugural Address (March 4, 1865). www.bartleby.com/124/pres32.html.

50. Krauthammer, "The Truth about Torture," op. cit.

unimaginable scale. The moral question in this case is whether the US government has a moral right to use less-than-humane treatment, including treatment that causes discomfort and even significant pain, *in order to attempt to compel the terrorist to do what is morally right*, namely, to disclose the location of the ticking bomb or the identities and locations of those planning to carry out the future evil attack.

In such cases I think the US government has a right—even a moral obligation—*within specified limits*, to use such compulsion. Not to do this would be to completely fail in the government's God-given responsibility to "rescue the weak and the needy" and to "deliver them from the hand of the wicked" (Ps. 82:4). It would also utterly fail in its responsibility to "bear the sword" as a "servant of God" to be a "terror" to evildoers and thus protect its citizens from attack (Rom. 13:3–4).

Someone might object that the *terrorist* thinks it is *morally wrong* to reveal his plans to murder thousands of civilians. He thinks he is morally right to carry out his terrorist attack! Who am I to say that his plans are morally wrong? Pastor-author Greg Boyd argues along these lines when he says to Americans:

> You probably passionately believe that our cause is just, and theirs is evil, but the terrorists passionately believe that their cause is just and ours is evil. Your passion for American justice is mirrored by their passion for Islamic justice.[51]

My response is that there is a clear moral difference. The Islamic terrorists' actions are clearly morally wrong, because (1) their war is contrary to the historic standards for a just war in that its purpose is to conquer other nations and impose Islamic law (see pp. 195–96 above), and (2) they are intentionally targeting innocent civilians, which is contrary to the Bible's standards for the conduct of war (see pp. 193–95) and contrary to international law. In 2004 the Security Council of the United Nations said, "The Security Council reaffirms its strong condemnation of all acts of violence targeting civilians or other protected persons under international law."[52] Boyd has lost all sense of moral compass when he sees Islamic terrorist attacks and American defense against those attacks as morally equivalent. He is simply wrong.

---

51. Greg Boyd, *The Myth of a Christian Nation* (Grand Rapids: Zondervan, 2007), 25.

52. "In Presidential Statement, Security Council Reaffirms Strong Condemnation of Violence Targeting Civilians in Armed Combat," United Nations Press Release SC/8267 (Dec. 14, 2004). www.un.org/News/Press/docs/2004/sc8267.doc.htm.

But what about taking the "high moral ground"? Critics of enhanced interrogation techniques argue that if we inflict pain to extract information, it will cause us harm in terms of world opinion — other nations will cease to respect us. But they fail to recognize that what our terrorist enemies respect is not timidity and weakness, but courage and superior strength. It is not pampering captured terrorists but rather the use of superior military force and intelligence that will defeat hardened al-Qaeda terrorists. The "high moral ground" must certainly exclude doing things that are always morally wrong (see the next section), but it also must surely include doing everything we can to defend our nation from attack. What our allies also respect *and depend on us for* is to use our strength to protect ourselves *and them* from terrorist attacks when we are able to do so.

3. Inherently evil actions should be prohibited in all circumstances, without exceptions

However, there still must clearly be limits to what a government should be allowed to do in *any* situation, no matter what ticking time bomb scenario arises. Even if *some* infliction of pain would be morally right (under circumstances and limits that I describe below), no agency of government should *ever* be allowed:

(1) To commit actions that are in themselves always immoral, such as raping a prisoner;

(2) To deny medical treatment;

(3) To carry out the sadistic humiliation of prisoners such as what occurred at Abu Ghraib prison in Iraq (which had nothing to do with intelligence gathering, and for which the military persons responsible were punished);[53]

(4) To attempt to force a prisoner to violate the religious convictions that he has *that pose no threat to the United States or its defense* (for example, it would be wrong to give a Muslim prisoner only pork to eat or only alcoholic beverages to drink, so as to force him to sin against his religion or starve to death);

(5) To carry out any actions that would "shock the conscience" of a US court, such as doing anything that would cause lasting physical damage to the prisoner. This would include cutting off fingers

---

53. Regarding the Abu Ghraib controversy, see, for example, www.globalsecurity.org/intell/world/iraq/abu-ghurayb-prison.htm (Jan. 5, 2006).

or toes, gouging out eyes, branding someone's face, or twisting and binding limbs so severely as to cause permanent disability of the type that Senator McCain has from his imprisonment in North Vietnam (he cannot raise his arms above his shoulders).

None of these actions serve any valid purpose in obtaining the needed information when it could be more readily obtained by inflicting bodily pain (within the moral limits described below) in a way that does no long-term damage.

4. What kind of means of coercion?

What kind of infliction of pain do I mean in these exceptional cases? I can give two personal examples, both of which are quite minor but may clarify what I mean. When our children were young and would engage in actions of willful disobedience, my wife or I would sometimes use a quick "shoulder squeeze." This was squeezing the trapezius muscle that runs between the shoulder and the neck. It hurts! And it was an effective means of discipline with no physical damage.

When my sons were in high school, I paid the fees for them to take martial arts classes for self-defense (in this case, Tae Kwan Do). After a few weeks they wanted to demonstrate what they had learned about certain "pressure points" in the human body. So I volunteered, and I soon learned that by merely pressing their thumb firmly against a certain point in my back, for example, they could cause immense pain. I ended the demonstration!

These are minor examples, but skilled military interrogators would no doubt be able to inflict even more acute pain in various ways (and I suppose they would find my examples humorous and trivial—but I am just making the point that real pain can be inflicted without causing lasting physical damage).

I cannot see any biblical basis for prohibiting governments from using these and similar means of inflicting pain—even much more significant pain—on a terrorist in order to coerce him into revealing the location of a hidden time bomb that will soon go off. (Some of the stress positions and confinement used in the CIA's enhanced interrogation procedures would achieve this.) In Proverbs, the disciplining of children with "the rod" (which caused pain but not lasting damage) was required: "Whoever spares the rod hates his son, but he who loves him is diligent to discipline him" (Prov. 13:24; see also 22:15; 23:13–14; 29:15). So how can there be moral objection to *all* infliction of pain to attempt to compel a right action?

A related issue is the injection of Sodium Pentathol, commonly called "truth serum." It tends to reduce a person's inhibitions and make him more willing to talk with interrogators. It has also been widely used in previous years as an anesthetic for surgery. I see no moral objection to the use of this or similar drugs in exceptional cases to obtain valuable information about terrorist attacks.

What about "waterboarding"? This involves holding a prisoner down so that his head is lower than the rest of his body while he faces up. Then a cloth is put over his nose and mouth, and water is poured over the cloth, giving the prisoner a sensation of drowning. For a number of years this same process has been used on thousands of US troops in giving them Survival Evasion Resistance Escape (SERE) training to resist an enemy if captured, and this has been done "with the full knowledge of Congress."[54]

Waterboarding was the most controversial of the "enhanced inter-rogation methods" used in questioning of al-Qaeda terrorists under the Bush administration. According to Victoria Toensing, former chief counsel for the Senate Intelligence Committee, the US Senate in September 2006 rejected, by a vote of 53–46, an amendment that would have made waterboarding illegal.[55] So the US Senate refused to prohibit it. However, President Obama completely prohibited it in an executive order on his second full day in office in January 2009.[56]

This procedure does not seem to me to be inherently morally wrong. It inflicts pain and a feeling of panic, and apparently it is very persuasive in getting a terrorist to reveal hidden information. When used within appropriate guidelines, it causes no permanent damage. (US interrogators were given specific limitations to prevent water from getting into the person's lungs and prevent any lasting physical damage.)

Daniel Heimbach, former deputy undersecretary of the Navy and now an ethics professor, formulates some "just war" criteria that would prescribe limits on the use of coercion in interrogation:

> [Charles] Krauthammer's appeal to the principles of proportion-ality (no more force than necessary), right intent (only to obtain

---

54. David B. Rivkin Jr. and Lee A. Casey, "The Memos Prove We Didn't Torture," *Wall Street Journal* (April 20, 2009), A15.

55. Victoria Toensing, "Critics Still Haven't Read the 'Torture' Memos," *Wall Street Journal* (May 19, 2009); Martin Kady II, "Mukasey, GOP Waffle on Waterboarding," *Politico.com* (Oct. 31, 2007), www.politico.com/news/stories/1007/6660.html.

56. Executive Order, Ensuring Lawful Interrogations (Jan. 22, 2009). www.whitehouse. gov/the_press_office/Ensuring_Lawful_Interrogations.

necessary information and nothing more), last resort (only when no other means will work), competent authority (only with authorization from cabinet-level political authority), and no evil means (no sick sadomasochism) are certainly apropos.

In fact, we should go beyond Krauthammer to also consider other just-war principles such as just cause (only to correct injustice), comparative justice (only if stakes on our side are more worthy than stakes on theirs), probability of success (only if good reason to believe the one interrogated actually knows important information), proportionality of projected results (only if information needed is worth more than what it costs to obtain), right spirit (only with regret), and good faith (never breaking promises).... after setting proper boundaries for moral use, we should without apology defend [the] obligation to exercise justified coercion within proper restraints.[57]

5. But does it work?

Critics of waterboarding and similar enhanced interrogation methods sometimes point to "expert" academic opinions arguing that "torture never works" and that the prisoner will make up all sorts of lies just to bring the pain to an end. But the facts of recent history show that argument to be incorrect.

Former CIA director Michael Hayden and former US Attorney General Michael Mukasey disclosed publicly on April 17, 2009, that the coercive interrogation techniques used on al-Qaeda operatives brought very significant results:

As a result of such coercive methods, terrorist Abu Zubaydah disclosed information that led to the capture of Ramzi bin al Shibh, another of the planners of Sept. 11, who in turn disclosed information which ... helped to lead to the capture of KSM [Khalid Sheikh Mohammed, mastermind of 9/11 attacks] and other senior terrorists, and the disruption of follow-on plots aimed at both Europe and the U.S.[58]

57. Daniel R. Heimbach, "Untitled Essay on Torture," n.p. http://evangelicaloutpost.com/archives/2005/12/daniel-r-heimbach.html. For Krauthammer's column, see www.weeklystandard.com/Content/Public/Articles/000/000/006/400rhqav.asp.

58. Michael Hayden and Michael B. Mukasey, "The President Ties His Own Hands on Terror," *Wall Street Journal* (April 17, 2009), A13.

Far from being secret, details of these methods and their results were widely known in Congress, and there was no congressional action to prohibit them:

> Details of these successes, and the methods used to obtain them, were disclosed repeatedly in more than 30 congressional briefings and hearings beginning in 2002.... Any protestation of ignorance of those details, particularly by members of those committees, is pretense. The techniques themselves were used selectively against only a small number of hard-core prisoners who successfully resisted other forms of interrogation, and then only with the explicit authorization of the director of the CIA.... as late as 2006 ... *fully half of the government's knowledge about the structure and activities of al Qaeda came from these interrogations.*[59]

William McSwain, a lawyer and former Marine who was deeply involved in Defense Department reviews of these techniques, wrote:

> It is doubtful that any high-level al Qaeda operative would ever provide useful intelligence in response to traditional methods [of interrogation]. Yet KSM and Zubaydah provided critical information after being waterboarded — information that ... helped to prevent a "Second Wave" attack in Los Angeles.[60]

In other words, these enhanced interrogation techniques *worked remarkably well.* The claim that they "don't work" is disproven by recent US history. Hayden and Mukasey say that the idea that these measures never work is an "ignorant view."[61] These techniques prevented several attacks and saved thousands of American and European lives. Any residents of Los Angeles, for example, who are still alive today because there was no second wave of attacks should be thankful that the government used them. *Not to have used them would have been morally wrong,* because it would have meant *having the ability to stop the murder of thousands and thousands of people* and not doing it. What could be a greater moral wrong for any government than this?

But in 2009 Attorney General Eric Holder began to threaten prosecutions against some Justice Department lawyers in the recent Bush administration who wrote internal memos arguing that such methods, within

---

59. Ibid., emphasis added.

60. William M. McSwain, "Misconceptions About the Interrogation Memos," *Wall Street Journal* (April 27, 2009), A15.

61. Ibid.

clear limits, were legal. He said, "We are going to follow the evidence, follow the law, and take that where it leads. No one is above the law."[62] *Prosecutions* for writing a legal memo? For carrying out what the Justice Department's Office of Legal Counsel told the CIA was legal? This is a vindictive attempt by the highest legal officer in the nation to use the courts to bring retribution against people for holding a different opinion on a widely debated political question. It is an attempt to criminalize political differences after you have won an election — something done by Third World despots but deeply unworthy of the United States of America. It can only poison the political atmosphere in the country still further.

Such threats will also breed institutional timidity in the CIA and the Department of Justice, and eventually we will suffer more horrible attacks. Even if a future president reauthorizes such enhanced interrogation techniques in exceptional cases, how will the CIA and the Justice Department know that some future administration won't release all the details of what was done and then attempt to send those involved to prison? The "safe" route now will be for government officials to pamper terrorists, opening the country both to their contempt and to their future attacks.

E. HOMOSEXUALS IN THE MILITARY

The US military policy had always been that known homosexuals should not serve in the armed forces. The enforcement of the previous policy, officially repealed in late 2011, was called by the press "Don't ask, don't tell" because military officials were not allowed to launch an investigation of someone in the absence of some evidence indicating homosexual conduct or intent.

The actual wording of the policy was this:

> Sexual orientation will not be a bar to service unless manifested by homosexual conduct. The military will discharge members who engage in homosexual conduct, which is defined as a homosexual act, a statement that the member is homosexual or bisexual, or a marriage or attempted marriage to someone of the same gender.[63]

---

62. Terry Frieden, "'No One Is Above the Law,' Holder Says of Torture Inquiry," *CNN* (April 22, 2009). www.cnn.com/2009/POLITICS/04/22/torture.prosecution/index.html.

63. "Gay Rights in the Military; The Pentagon's New Policy Guidelines on Homosexuals in the Military," *New York Times* (July 20, 1993). www.nytimes.com/1993/07/20/us/gay-rights-military-pentagon-s-new-policy-guidelines-homosexuals-military.html?sec=&spon=&pagewanted=all.

The policy said that anyone who "demonstrate(d) a propensity or intent to engage in homosexual acts" would be prohibited from serving in the military. The reason was that "it would create an unacceptable risk to the high standards of morale, good order and discipline, and unit cohesion that are the essence of military capability."[64]

I am convinced that homosexual conduct is contrary to the moral standards of the Bible. Therefore I believe that Christians who follow the moral authority of the Bible should uphold the reintroduction of our previous policy.

Military personnel have repeatedly stated that inclusion of homosexuals in the armed forces harms combat preparedness and effectiveness. In her testimony before Congress, Elaine Donnelly of the Center for Military Readiness said:

> Repealing the 1993 law would be tantamount to forcing female soldiers to cohabit with men in intimate quarters, on all military bases and ships at sea, on a 24/7 basis. Stated in gender-neutral terms, forced cohabitation in military conditions that offer little or no privacy would force *persons* to live with *persons* who might be sexually attracted to them.
>
> Inappropriate passive/aggressive actions common in the homosexual community, short of physical touching and assault, will be permitted in all military communities, to include Army and Marine infantry battalions, Special Operations Forces, Navy SEALS, and cramped submarines that patrol the seas for months at a time.
>
> The ensuing sexual tension will hurt discipline and morale, but commanders will not have the power to improve the situation. Individuals whose beliefs and feelings about sexuality are violated by the new policy will have no recourse. The only option will be to avoid or leave the service. Forced cohabitation with homosexuals in the military, 24/7, would be unfair, demoralizing, and harmful to the culture of the volunteer force, on which our national security depends.[65]

One thousand military officers sent a letter to President Obama asking him to maintain the Don't Ask, Don't Tell policy, stating that

---

64. Ibid.

65. Testimony of Elaine Donnelly before the House Armed Services Personnel Subcommittee (July 23, 2008). http://armedservices.house.gov/pdfs/MilPers072308/Donnelly_Testimony072308.pdf.

abolishing it "would undermine recruiting and retention, impact leadership at all levels, have adverse effects on the willingness of parents who lend their sons and daughters to military service, and eventually break the All-Volunteer Force."[66]

Among the signatories were General Carl E. Mundy Jr., a former commandant of the Marine Corps; Admiral Leighton W. Smith, a former commander of US Naval Forces Europe; General Charles A. Horner, who commanded US aerial forces during the 1990–91 Gulf War; and Admiral Jerome L. Johnson, a former vice chief of Naval Operations.

Unfortunately, President Obama, in his State of the Union Address on January 27, 2010, called for an end to the former policy so as to allow homosexuals to serve openly in the US military. On September 20, the policy was officially repealed. This despite the fact that when the troops were surveyed by the Military Officers Association of America, they said, by a 2–1 margin, that the armed forces should have an even stronger policy against homosexuals in military service.[67] The MOAA survey also found that 68% of respondents believe that repeal of the law would have a very negative effect (48%) or moderately negative effect (20%) on troop morale and military readiness.[68] I believe the recent change in policy was exactly wrong.

F. WOMEN IN COMBAT

Historically the position of the United States has been that women should never be sent into combat. Women could serve in other capacities in the armed forces, but not in responsibilities where they were likely to engage in combat. In the last thirty years there has been pressure to change that policy, and we already have some women serving as fighter pilots in Afghanistan. The first female fighter pilots were employed in Kosovo in 1993, and the first woman who joined the Navy specifically to be a pilot did so in 1981.[69]

---

66. David Crary, "Retired Military Officers: Keep Ban on Gays," Associated Press (March 31, 2009). www.guardian.co.uk/world/feedarticle/8431955.

67. Grace Vuoto, "Is Obama Administration Listening to the Troops?" *Washington Times* (July 30, 2009). www.cmrlink.org/CMRDocuments/WT070309.pdf.

68. Ibid.

69. "Women Fighter Pilots Flying Combat Missions over Afghanistan with Little or No Fanfare," Associated Press (Oct. 23, 2001). www.military.com/Content/MoreContent?file=FL_womenpilots_102301.

I believe that the historic position of the United States is correct and that it is wrong to send women into combat. The biblical argument for this position is expressed well in the ESV *Study Bible* article on "War":

> Most nations throughout history, and most Christians in every age, have held that fighting in combat is a responsibility that should fall only to men, and that it is contrary to the very idea of womanhood, and shameful for a nation, to have women risk their lives as combatants in a war. The assumption that only men and not women will fight in battle is also a frequent pattern in the historical narratives and is affirmed by leaders and prophets in the OT (see Num. 1:2–3; Deut. 3:18–19; 20:7–8; 24:5; Josh. 1:14; 23:10; Judg. 4:8–10; 9:54; 1 Sam. 4:9; Neh. 4:13–14; Jer. 50:37; Nah. 3:13).[70]

70. ESV *Study Bible*, "War," p. 2555.

Chapter 8

FOREIGN POLICY: FUNDAMENTAL PRINCIPLES

How should the government of a nation relate to the other nations of the world?

What should be the goals of the foreign policy of a nation?

Is it right for the United States to try to promote freedom and democracy in other nations?

A. BIBLICAL TEACHING

The biblical basis for foreign policy in a nation flows from our understanding of the purpose of government in general, and the responsibility of government in particular to defend itself and its citizens against other nations, as discussed in chapter 6 (see pp. 193–95). The civil government is established by God to do "good" for its people, as God's "servant" (Rom. 13:4), and it should "praise those who do good" (1 Peter 2:14). It must also "punish those who do evil" (1 Peter 2:14), both to prevent wrongdoing and protect its citizens and also to act as God's "servant" who "carries out God's wrath on the wrongdoer" (Rom. 13:4).

Therefore the foreign policy of a nation must first of all work toward the goal of defending itself against attack or harm from other nations. As I argued in chapter 6 (pp. 204–8), it is appropriate for governments to form mutually beneficial alliances with other nations in order to further this purpose of defending themselves.

These considerations lead to several principles regarding foreign policy.

1. The foreign policy of a nation should serve to protect the sovereignty and independence of that nation and to protect and defend the interests of its citizens in their relationships with other countries

Protecting the sovereignty and independence of a nation serves the purpose of protecting it from conquest and oppressive domination by some other aggressive foreign country. As governments function to protect their own sovereignty, they also serve, in the wise providence of God, to protect the nations of the world from the horrible tyranny that would result from the dissolution of the sovereignty of individual nations and the establishment of one worldwide government. Such a government would have far too much power, which would lead to immense corruption in the government. (Since power nearly always corrupts, such corruption would then lead to a horrible kind of oppression from which there would be no place to flee.)

2. Governments should seek to do good for other nations as they are able to do so

The command of Jesus, "You shall love your neighbor as yourself" (Matt. 22:39), gives warrant for thinking that nations should seek to do good for other nations insofar as they have opportunity to do so. A government's first obligation should be to defend and seek the good of its own citizens, but it can often bring positive influences to other nations without significantly hindering that primary goal.

Such positive influence can come through diplomatic negotiation. It can also come through cultural exchanges, educational exchanges, commercial relationships, and fair and honest media reporting about events in other nations. Another means is military alliances, as I discussed in chapter 6 (see pp. 204–8). In addition, nations can sometimes help other countries through foreign aid of various sorts, as discussed in the section below.

The United States carries out, I suppose, hundreds of unheralded activities that bring benefit to the world as a whole. One example is protecting the sea lanes of the world from piracy or from one nation's ships attacking the merchant or passenger ships of another nation. It is primarily the US Navy that keeps the sea lanes of the world free in this way, a fact that is seldom known. Thomas Keaney, acting director of the Strategic Studies at the Paul H. Nitzke School of Advanced International Studies at Johns Hopkins University, writes:

> Oceans and other waterways have long figured prominently in commercial activity, transportation routes and, ultimately, warfare. Even in an age of air, space and cyberspace, the sea remains the prime mode of transportation of goods worldwide, and thus vital to the world's economies—access to oil supplies serves as the key example of this dependence.
>
> For the United States, concerns for the security of international trade, energy supplies and even fishing rights have played a prominent part in its history and have led to two parallel interests advocated by U.S. policymakers through the years. The first is the promotion of freedom of the seas for commerce and international trade. The second is the impulse to build a powerful navy to protect those activities. Those interests continue today in a world of globalized trade networks, as the United States has extended itself to assure freedom of the seas for international trade on a worldwide basis. It is a mission of enormous responsibilities and consequences.
>
> While the United States has committed itself to the defense of freedom of the seas worldwide, it is not alone in its desire for free transit—all countries engaged in intercontinental trade or who import oil share that goal. Few countries other than the United States have any capability to defend the freedom of the seas for that trade.[1]

The continuation of piracy off the coast of Somalia is an aberration due to the absence of any legitimate governmental authority in Somalia and the ambiguities of international law in the ocean next to Somalia because of that situation. According to France 24/7, the country's national news service, "Somalia's transitional government has very little real authority.... Experts and military personnel have been saying that policing the seas to stop pirates simply won't work as long as Somalia remains a lawless country. It's been without an effective government since the fall of Siad Barre [the former president of Somalia] 17 years ago."[2]

1. Thomas Keaney, "Ruling the Waves: American Sea Power," Paul H. Nitzke School of Advanced International Studies at Johns Hopkins University, Washington DC (2008). www.sais-jhu.edu/pressroom/publications/saisphere/2008/keaney.htm.

2. "Somalia: A Failed State?" France 24/7 (Nov. 20, 2008). www.france24.com/en/20081120-pirates-thrive-lawlessness-ethiopia-somalia.

Another benefit the United States provides has been the maintenance of the Internet system for the benefit of the entire world. Until a few years ago, 70% of all Internet traffic sent between two locations passed through the United States. Recently, other governments have taken steps to maintain their own Internet systems.[3] In November 2005, scholars with the Heritage Foundation outlined the role the United States has played in maintaining the Internet and the reasons why other countries want to seize control or turn control over to the United Nations. They wrote:

> For decades, the Internet has developed with a minimum of government interference. The core governance of the medium has been performed by non-governmental entities and overseen by the U.S. government, which has exercised a light regulatory touch. It is no coincidence that the medium has prospered from this benign neglect, growing from a research curiosity into a major force in the world economy and an invaluable venue for the exchange of information.
>
> Most people appreciate this success as a convenience that makes their lives easier and their work more productive. However, the Internet represents something quite different to many foreign governments. Some, including members of the European Union, are frustrated by their inability to regulate or tax it as they desire. Others, such as China and Iran, see the Internet as a threat and are desperate to prevent their citizens from encountering ideas that might undermine their authority or communicating with foreigners. As a result, the United States is coming under increasing criticism that because the Internet is an international resource, no one country should control it.
>
> The result of a UN-controlled and regulated Internet would be that non-democratic countries that oppose the right to free speech such as China and grasping, anti-market impulses like those of the European Union would have a greater voice in guiding the Internet in a direction away from "freedom, education, and innovation."[4]

---

3. John Markoff, "Internet Traffic Begins to Bypass the U.S.," *New York Times* (Aug. 30, 2008). www.nytimes.com/2008/08/30/business/30pipes.html?_r=3&oref=slogin&pagewanted=print.

4. Brett D. Schaefer, John J. Tkacik Jr., and James L. Gattuso, "Keep the Internet Free of the United Nations," *Heritage Foundation WebMemo #904* (Nov. 2, 2005). www.heritage.org/Research/InternationalOrganizations/wm904.cfm.

A third benefit is that NASA's Earth Science Enterprise operates more than thirty Earth-observation satellites, many in cooperation with other agencies and countries. These satellites provide images and data on many aspects of the Earth's atmosphere, ocean, and land, including atmospheric temperature, moisture content, clouds, and precipitation.[5]

Still another benefit is the substantial role that the United States plays in the linking of telecommunication lines from various nations of the world. However, in 1992, President George H. W. Bush split the oversight and licensing jurisdiction of commercial satellites, allowing commercial communication satellites that do not incorporate advanced technologies to be exported as civil or commercial goods under the supervision of the Commerce Department.[6]

An additional benefit is allowing the United Nations headquarters to be in New York City and providing all the police and security protection required in the area surrounding the presence of representatives of so many nations. According to the US Mission to the United Nations,

> In accordance with its obligations under the United Nations Headquarters Agreement, the United States, as host country to the United Nations, is committed to assuring the safety and security of the United Nations Headquarters, the Permanent and Observer Missions accredited to the United Nations, and the members of the United Nations diplomatic community. This responsibility is one of the most important of our obligations, and is codified in United States law under the Act for the Protection of Foreign Officials and Official Guests of the United States.[7]

(I realize that the United Nations does many things that are now contrary to the best interests of the United States and that hinder democracy and human rights around the world, so housing the UN is a mixed benefit!)

In addition, the United States gives massive amounts of both private and public aid to other nations and groups within other nations. According to a 2003 report by Lino J. Piedra, a member of the US Delegation to the United Nations Commission on Human Rights,

---

5. George Abbey and Neal Lane, "United States Space Policy: Challenges and Opportunities," American Academy of Arts and Sciences (2005), 4. www.amacad.org/publications/spacePolicy.pdf.

6. Ibid., 8.

7. Security and Protective Services, United States Mission to the United Nations. http://usun.state.gov/about/host_aff/c32154.htm.

In 2003, the United States was the origin of over seventy percent of all financial flows reaching developing countries from
the G–7 developed world, through private investment, private
philanthropy, public aid and private remittances. When net
purchases of goods and services, private investment, private
philanthropy, public aid and private remittances are all added
together, the United States accounted for over $340 billion in
financial flows to developing countries in 2003. Private remittances from the United States totaled almost $28 billion, while
US aid accounted for almost one-third of all overseas development assistance from developed countries.[8]

3. The United States should seek to promote freedom and respect for human rights in other nations

Is it right for the United States to use noncoercive means such as diplomatic negotiations, cultural and educational exchanges, public relations strategies, media reporting, and foreign aid to attempt to promote
greater human freedoms and human rights in other nations? To that
question, it seems to me that the answer is certainly yes.

One objection should be addressed, however. Sometimes people
object to trying to influence other countries, saying something like,
"We should not impose our view of human rights and freedom on other
nations." But this way of phrasing the matter is highly misleading. The
word "impose" implies using military conquest to forcibly change the
government of another nation. That is a "just war" question (see chap. 6,
pp. 193–95), which is not the issue I am discussing here. I am talking
about *influencing* another nation, not *imposing* anything.

The first reason I think we should try to *influence* nations positively
for human freedom and human rights is that according to the moral
standards found in the Bible, the promotion of human liberty within
nations is a morally good thing. Slavery and oppression are always
viewed negatively in Scripture, while freedom is viewed positively (see
Exod. 20:2; Lev. 25:10; Deut. 28:28–29, 33; Judg. 2:16–23; Isa. 61:1).
Moreover, the Bible gives indirect but significant support to the idea
that governments should be chosen by the people over whom they govern, and this implies the desirability of some kind of democracy. Some
kind of democracy gives greater accountability to rulers, helps prevent

---

8. Statement by Lino J. Piedra, "Item 7: The Right to Development" (March 22, 2005).
http://geneva.usmission.gov/humanrights/2005/0322Item7.htm.

a misuse of power, and helps to guarantee that government will serve for the benefit of the people rather than for the benefit of the rulers, as Scripture says it should (Rom. 13:4; 1 Peter 2:13–14).

The Declaration of Independence, the document on which the existence of the United States is based, declares that we as a nation are committed to the idea that all human beings "are endowed by their Creator with certain unalienable rights," and that those rights include "life, liberty, and the pursuit of happiness." This means that the nation has declared as a founding belief the idea that human rights come ultimately from God ("their Creator"), that these rights can never be legitimately taken away (they are "unalienable rights"), and that one of those rights is the right to "liberty" or human freedom. Then the Declaration of Independence in the very next sentence says that governments are established among people "to secure these rights," and that governments that are set up are "deriving their just powers from the consent of the governed," that is, by some kind of democratic process that elects or affirms governments in power.

In brief, the beginning of the Declaration of Independence declares that the United States as a nation is committed to the idea that God has given people the right to liberty and that governments are only valid if they have the consent of the people over whom they govern. This means that promotion of human freedom, human rights, and democratic government is consistent with the most foundational convictions of our nation.

A further reason why the United States should seek to increase human freedom and democracy in other nations is that this promotes the nation's self-interest. This is because *genuine democracies* are less likely than any other form of government to launch aggressive attacks against other countries, as was persuasively argued by Natan Sharansky in *The Case for Democracy*.[9] Thus, promoting human liberty and the rule of genuine democratic governments is a very effective way to promote world peace.

My conclusion, therefore, is that biblical moral standards, our Declaration of Independence, our own self-interest as a nation, and the promotion of world peace all argue that the United States should promote freedom and democracy wherever it is able to do so around the world. We should help our friends who similarly promote freedom and democracy. We should help to support forces within oppressive nations that are

---

9. Natan Sharansky, *The Case for Democracy: The Power of Freedom to Overcome Tyranny and Terror* (New York: Public Affairs, 2004).

working for increased freedom and democracy. We should also oppose the enemies of freedom and democracy wherever we are able to do so.

For many years, one of the most effective means of doing this was through Voice of America, a radio network that transmitted radio broadcasts in dozens of languages that were heard by oppressed peoples in various nations of the world. But in the last two decades or so, its budgets have been cut and the Voice of America has significantly curtailed its broadcasts. When we are increasing spending on everything else, why should we reduce our promotion of democracy and our explanations of what is good about America to counter its many critics? Have our government officials become hesitant about angering oppressive governments around the world?[10] According to Helle C. Dale of the Heritage Foundation, "Due to budget cuts and emphasis on the use of surrogate radio outlets, Voice of America does not send a single broadcast under its own name to the Middle East. And yet, an integral part of VOA's mission is to inform others about American society and US policy. In a world where anti-Americanism is rampant, that mission surely has not become obsolete."[11]

This is a tragic turn of events that gives one sign that the leadership of the United States has become confused about the fundamental values that are essential to the founding documents on which the very existence of our nation is based, and beliefs that are essential to our deepest values as a nation. Rather than being embarrassed about advocating freedom and democracy for all peoples of the earth, we should be vastly expanding the scope of the broadcasts both by radio and by Internet and through the use of any other media (such as documentary films, pamphlets, and books). We should be clearly and unashamedly promoting the values of freedom and genuine democracy to all nations of the world, especially to people living in countries hostile to these values, such as communist nations or nations with oppressive governments. We should be unashamedly proclaiming that a system of democracy that includes freedom of religion is far superior to any oppressive government that seeks to impose the Muslim faith and practices on entire populations.

10. Kasie Hunt, "Voice of America Shifts Priorities," Associated Press (Feb. 23, 2007), www.foxnews.com/printer_friendly_wires/2007Feb23/0,4675,USVOACuts,00.html; "Former VOA Directors Appeal for Reversal of Plan to Reduce Network's Presence on the World's Radio Airwaves" (March 5, 2007), www.publicdiplomacy.org/78.htm; Helle C. Dale, "Voices of America," *Heritage Foundation Commentary* (May 3, 2007), www.heritage.org/Press/Commentary/ed050307a.cfm.
11. Dale, "Voices of America."

In addition, if it is morally right and in our best interest to promote freedom and democracy, then we should do this through our use of all diplomatic channels (including the United Nations) and all of our foreign aid as well.

4. A mistaken policy of encouraging enemies and hindering friends

Unfortunately, President Obama's administration, rather than *helping* our friends who promote freedom and democracy and *opposing* our enemies who fight against freedom, began in various ways throughout 2009 to do exactly the opposite. They followed policies that seemed quite evidently to be *abandoning* our friends and *helping* our enemies. This can be seen with respect to several countries in different regions of the world.

In Iran, when President Ahmadinejad shamelessly stole the election on June 12, 2009, and courageous protestors took to the streets by the tens of thousands—no doubt hoping for support from the United States in the court of world opinion—President Obama remained indecisive and noncommittal. He merely said that he was "deeply troubled" but would "pursue a tough, direct dialogue between our two countries."[12] Yet he did nothing to voice immediate support of the protestors, some of whom were killed. Jamie M. Fly, a former member of the National Security Council, wrote:

> By sanctioning the fraudulent re-election of [President] Ahmadinejad and overseeing the brutal crackdown underway in its aftermath, [Supreme Leader of Iran] Khamenei has revealed the true despotic nature of the regime he oversees. Additionally, Khamenei oversees Iran's support for Hezbollah, Shiite militias in Iraq, and the Taliban in Afghanistan, which has resulted in thousands of deaths, including those of many Americans. This man, now with the blood of his own people on his hands, is the person the Obama administration is attempting to curry favor with during this time of uncertainty in Iran."[13]

Thus President Obama abandoned the pro-democracy forces and allowed Ahmadinejad to retain power with no effective pressure from the United States. But Ahmadinejad is so deluded that he denies the

12. Jamie M. Fly, "Obama's Iran Election Ineptitude Worsens Nuclear Threat," *U.S. News and World Report* (June 19, 2009). www.usnews.com/articles/opinion/2009/06/19/obamas-iran-election-ineptitude-worsens-nuclear-threat.html.
13. Ibid.

Holocaust ever existed, saying, "They have created a myth today that they call the massacre of Jews and they consider it a principle above God, religions and the prophets,"[14] and he insists he is going to wipe Israel off the map.[15] So this opportunity to call for international sanctions against Iran's sham elections and its despotic regime was lost.

In Latin America, Fidel Castro's government in Cuba and Hugo Chavez's government in Venezuela are the two greatest threats to freedom and democracy in North and South America. Both Castro and Chavez are military dictators who send money and soldiers to other Latin American countries to attempt to destabilize their governments and bring them into the Cuba-Venezuela orbit of totalitarian states that incline toward socialism or communism (see chap. 6, pp. 202–3).

As one expert on Latin America writes, "A Chavez-style takeover of institutions in Bolivia, Ecuador and Nicaragua has quashed political pluralism, free speech, and minority rights in those countries. There is now a heavy presence of Cuban state intelligence throughout the Venezuelan empire.... Argentina is also in his [Chavez's] sights."[16]

But President Obama simply took steps to endorse the continued legitimacy of these governments and gave no help for any democratic opposition within those countries. After he took office, he promised a "new beginning" with Cuba, lifting restrictions on travel, commerce, and mail to that nation.[17]

President Obama has failed again and again to give public support to democratic movements within oppressive countries. Daniel Henninger, deputy director of the *Wall Street Journal* editorial page, wrote:

> If the Obama team wanted to make a really significant break from past Bush policy, it would say it was not going to just talk with the world's worst strongmen but would give equal, public status to their democratic opposition groups. Instead, the baddest actors in the world get face time with Barack Obama, but their struggling opposition gets invisibility.
>
> Iran's extraordinary and brave popular opposition, which broke out again this week at two universities, seems to have

14. "Iranian Leader Denies Holocaust," *BBCNews.com* (Dec. 14, 2005). http://news.bbc.co.uk/2/hi/middle_east/4527142.stm.

15. Ibid.

16. Mary Anastasia O' Grady, "Anti-American Amigos," *Wall Street Journal* (Aug. 27, 2009), A9.

17. Jake Tapper and Emily Friedman, "Obama Deals with Cuba, Venezuela—as Chavez Gives Him Book Assailing U.S.," *ABCNews.com* (April 18, 2009). http://abcnews.go.com/Politics/story?id=7370989&page=1.

earned these pro-democracy Iranians nothing in the calculations of U.S. policy....

In July, Mr. Obama made a historic journey to Africa, giving a widely praised speech in Ghana in support of self-help and self-determination. In August, Secretary of State Hillary Clinton grandly visited seven African nations with a similar message. Three days ago in Guinea, government troops fired on a pro-democracy rally estimated at 50,000 in the capital of Conakry, killing more than 150 people. The State Department got out a written statement of condemnation. Why is it not possible for President Obama or Secretary of State Clinton, having encouraged these aspirations, to speak publicly in their defense, rather than let democratic movements rise, fall and die?

In trying to plumb why the U.S. won't promote or protect its own best idea, one starts with Mr. Obama's remarks at the "reset" visit in Moscow: "America cannot and should not seek to impose any system of government on any other country, nor would we presume to choose which party or individual should run a country."

Setting aside that no one is talking about the U.S. literally "imposing" a government in this day and age, what is one to make of a left-of-center American political leader taking such a diffident stance toward democratic movements? The people who live under the sway of the top dog in all the nations that have earned high-level Obama envoys are the world's poor, and one would expect the social-justice left to support them. That may no longer be true on the American or European left....

Our dictator chat partners are getting brazen about staging and then rigging elections. Iran's mullahs proved there will be no sustained push-back from the U.S. or Western Europe to a fraudulent election. Instead the great powers' energies go into pounding tiny Honduras, which tried to save itself from the Chávez- and Castro-admiring Manuel Zelaya.

What if the world's real democrats, after enough bullets and dungeon time, lose belief in the American democracy's support for them on this central idea? They may come to regard their betters in the U.S. and Europe as inhabiting a world less animated by democratic belief than democratic decadence.[18]

18. Daniel Henninger, "Obama, Dictators, and Democrats," *Wall Street Journal* (Oct. 1, 2009), A21. http://online.wsj.com/article/SB20001424052748704471504574444890430083018.html.

With regard to China, President Obama has raised not even a whisper of protest against increasing harassment and imprisonment of leaders of the house church movement, a loose network of evangelical, Bible-believing churches that have remained independent of government registration and control, despite pleas from human rights groups to do so.[19] In fact, he refused to meet with the Dalai Lama when he visited Washington, DC, breaking a precedent set by former presidents.[20] Before a visit to China in February 2009, Secretary of State Hillary Rodham Clinton said advocacy for human rights could not "interfere with the global economic crisis, the global climate-change crisis and the security crisis."[21]

By contrast, President George W. Bush visibly and publicly expressed his support for the house-church movement when he was in China, thus giving significant support and encouragement to the Christians who were leading these meetings and seeking to gain greater freedom and protection from the Chinese government. In an interview with NBC's Bob Costas, President Bush said, "I went to church here, and I'm sure the cynics say, 'Well, you know, it was just a state-sponsored church,' ... and that's true. On the other hand, it gave me a chance to say to the Chinese people, 'Religion won't hurt you; you ought to welcome religious people.' And it gave me a chance to say to the government, 'Why don't you register the underground churches and give them a chance to flourish?' "[22]

What about other nations that are actually encouraging democracy? President Obama and the Democrats in Congress have made life hard for these friends. Congress has repeatedly refused — even before Obama took office — to ratify an excellent free-trade agreement that would help the nation of Colombia, which has courageously overcome much of its drug-trafficking problem under the leadership of strongly pro-American president Alvaro Uribe.[23] And so the United States has abandoned the poor farmers of Colombia, one of our closest allies, making it impossible for them to export agricultural products to us at a competitive price and essentially refusing to open our huge market to them. This refusal to

---

19. Penny Starr, "Obama Should Address Human Rights Abuses during Trip to China, Group Says," *CNSNews.com* (Nov. 11, 2009). www.cnsnews.com/news/article/56958.

20. James Pomfret, "Obama's Meeting with Dalai Lama Delayed," *Washington Post* (Oct. 5, 2009). www.washingtonpost.com/wp-dyn/content/article/2009/10/04/AR2009100403262_pf.html.

21. Ibid.

22. "Bush Attends Church in China," *Baptist News Service* (Aug. 11, 2008). www.bpnews.net/bpnews.asp?id=28660&ref=BPNews-RSSFeed0811.

23. Henninger, "Obama, Dictators, and Democrats."

ratify the agreement was due to the opposition of the US labor unions, strong supporters of Democratic candidates, who did not want more trade with Colombia even though there would be considerable economic benefit to both nations. The *Wall Street Journal* editorial board writes, "The U.S. failure to get this deal done is a long-running travesty," and points to the primary culprit as then House Speaker Nancy Pelosi, who was giving in to pressure from labor union leaders.[24]

In Honduras, the term of President Manuel Zelaya was going to expire in January 2010. The constitution of Honduras limits presidents to one term. But Zelaya, with the encouragement and financial support of Hugo Chavez in Venezuela, decided to call for a referendum to rewrite the constitution so that he could seek a second term. The Honduran courts then determined that to be an illegal activity, and when he persisted in attempting to hold this referendum — even flying in ballots that had been printed in Venezuela — the Supreme Court in Honduras ordered him removed from office.[25]

The Honduras military forces then forcibly removed President Zelaya. Governmental power, including the office of president, was lawfully taken over by Roberto Micheletti, a man from Zelaya's own political party, who was selected by the Congress in a process that followed Honduran law.

Therefore it seemed as though Honduras had successfully resisted the attempts of Chavez to subvert its freedom and establish a Chavez-controlled president for years to come. This should have been wonderful news for freedom-loving people everywhere. This was also the conclusion of respected Roman Catholic Oscar Rodriguez Maradiaga, who was joined by all the Roman Catholic bishops in Honduras in stating that the removal of Zelaya was lawful according to Honduran law and that democratic processes were continuing to function. Miguel Estrada, a Honduran native who had been nominated to the US Court of Appeals by President Bush but was denied confirmation by Senate liberals because of his conservative views, reported that all of this was legal, writing:

> Something clearly has gone awry with the rule of law in Honduras — but it is not necessarily what you think. Begin with Zelaya's arrest. The Supreme Court of Honduras, as it turns out, had ordered the military to arrest Zelaya two days earlier. A second order (issued on the same day) authorized

---

24. "Southern Discomfort," *Wall Street Journal* (June 27, 2009), A12.
25. "The Wages Chavismo," *Wall Street Journal* (July 1, 2009), A12.

the military to enter Zelaya's home to execute the arrest. These orders were issued at the urgent request of the country's attorney general. They make for interesting reading.

What you'll learn is that the Honduran Constitution may be amended in any way except three. No amendment can ever change (1) the country's borders, (2) the rules that limit a president to a single four-year term and (3) the requirement that presidential administrations must "succeed one another" in a "republican form of government."

In addition, Article 239 specifically states that any president who so much as proposes the permissibility of re-election "shall cease forthwith" in his duties, and Article 4 provides that any "infraction" of the succession rules constitutes treason. The rules are so tight because these are terribly serious issues for Honduras, which lived under decades of military rule.

Zelaya is the type of leader who could cause a country to wish for a Richard Nixon. Earlier this year, with only a few months left in his term, he ordered a referendum on whether a new constitutional convention should convene to write a wholly new constitution. Because the only conceivable motive for such a convention would be to amend the unamendable parts of the existing constitution, it was easy to conclude—as virtually everyone in Honduras did—that this was nothing but a backdoor effort to change the rules governing presidential succession.[26]

But the Obama administration immediately responded exactly the wrong way, calling Zelaya's removal a "coup" and demanding that Honduras return him to the presidency. The President said:

> It would be a terrible precedent if we start moving backwards into the era in which we are seeing military coups as a means of political transition rather than democratic elections. The region has made enormous progress over the last 20 years in establishing democratic traditions in Central America and Latin America. We don't want to go back to a dark past.[27]

---

26. Miguel A. Estrada, "In Honduras, 'Coup' Was Legal Reaction to Zelaya," *Atlanta Journal Constitution* (July 20, 2009). www.ajc.com/opinion/in-honduras-coup-was-95580.html.

27. Jake Tapper, "In Russia, President Obama Expresses His Support for Ousted President of Honduras," *ABCNews.com* (July 7, 2009). http://blogs.abcnews.com/politicalpunch/2009/07/in-russia-president-obama-explains-his-support-for-ousted-president-of-honduras.html.

Obama said this even though Zelaya was trying to subvert his country's constitution. The United States cut off $30 million in foreign aid to Honduras[28] and brought other forms of diplomatic pressure against the country. Hilary Clinton, as Secretary of State, continued to bring pressure against Honduras, issuing a statement that read, "The action taken against Honduran President Mel Zelaya violates the precepts of the Inter-American Democratic Charter, and thus should be condemned by all."[29] Latin American expert Mary Anastasia O' Grady wrote, "In its actions toward Honduras, the Obama administration is demonstrating contempt for the fundamentals of democracy."[30] Adding to the international insult, the US State Department revoked the US visas of all fifteen justices of the Honduras Supreme Court because of their interpretation of their own constitution![31]

In other words, while President Obama refused to "meddle" in the affairs of Iran and give any kind of support to the *pro-democracy* demonstrators, he did decide to meddle in the affairs of tiny Honduras and give support to the *anti-democratic* forces attempting to bring the nation under essentially increasing dictatorial control. Thus, former president Zelaya was supported by Fidel Castro, Hugo Chavez, and Barack Obama. Obama sided with our enemies and opposed our friends.

Why has President Obama followed such policies? One possible explanation is that the most liberal elements of the Democratic party, from which he originates, are sympathetic toward socialism (government ownership of factories, companies, and other means of production) and therefore would like to see several socialist-leaning (Venezuela) or even communist (Cuba) governments succeed, but would not like to see free market-oriented countries like Colombia succeed.

In spite of US opposition, Honduras appears to have resolved its own internal conflict. On October 29, 2009, the various sides to the conflict in Honduras signed an agreement that President Zelaya would be temporarily returned to office, but the November 29 elections would go forward, and a vote in Congress would decide the outcome of the leadership

28. Arhsad Mohammed and David Alexander, "U.S. Cuts More Than $30 Million in Aid to Honduras," *Reuters.com* (Sept. 3, 2009). www.reuters.com/article/honduras/idUS-TRE58251N20090903.

29. Statement by Secretary of State Hillary Rodham Clinton, "Situation in Honduras," U.S. Department of State (June 28, 2009). www.state.gov/secretary/rm/2009a/06/125452.htm.

30. Mary Anastasia O'Grady, "Hilary's Honduras Obsession," *Wall Street Journal* (Sept. 29, 2009), A17.

31. Ibid.

of the country if necessary. The Honduran Embassy reported that the result was a landslide victory for the National Party and its candidate, Porfirio Lobo. They took more than 55% of the vote, while the Liberal Party only took 40%. The National Party won 70 of the 128 seats in the Congress and also carried 200 out of 298 mayorships.[32]

A similar refusal to help a friend happened in 1999–2000, when Democratic President Bill Clinton—I think shamefully—refused to grant asylum to Elian Gonzalez, a young Cuban boy who was living with relatives in Florida. Elian's mother had drowned while trying to help him escape the Castro dictatorship, but Elian survived and did reach the United States. Attorney General Janet Reno sent in US agents to forcibly remove the young boy from his relatives and have him sent back to Cuba.[33] Why support dictators who are our enemies and refuse to help a child who nearly lost his life trying to escape to freedom?

B. THE UNITED NATIONS

Because the United Nations is now the only effective forum where representatives of all nations can meet and negotiate and debate, I think the United States has no choice but to stay actively involved with it. If the United States were to pull out, the United Nations' decisions and policies would become even more forcefully anti-democratic and anti-American.

But the fact remains that with a large block of Muslim nations, supported by a number of other dictatorial or autocratic nations such as North Korea, Cuba, Venezuela, and sometimes Russia and China as well as several anti-democratic African nations, the United Nations has become dominated by a significant majority of countries who are anti-American and even more strongly anti-Israel. So the United States must recognize that the United Nations, by majority vote of a number of smaller nations, has come to the point where it is hostile to freedom and to actions that are consistent with biblical standards of moral conduct in many areas of the world. Former State Department official Stefan Halper wrote back in 1996:

> The vastly expanded General Assembly was soon dominated
> by non-Western states whose elites seldom shared the political
> culture of the democratic West, much less any belief in market

---

32. Honduras Election Analysis, The Embassy of Honduras (Dec. 9, 2009). http://hondurasemb.org/2009/12/09/honduras-election-analysis/.

33. "Federal Agents Seize Elian in Pre-Dawn Raid," *CNN.com* (April 22, 2000). http://archives.cnn.com/2000/US/04/22/cuba.boy.05/index.html.

economics. The new majority felt free to exercise its power by passing resolutions favorable to the Third World and its member-states' various pet projects. Although the Third World was hardly homogeneous, operating on an identical agenda, a mutually convenient system of logrolling soon came into being. For example, Arab states would vote for black African resolutions against South African apartheid, provided that the black African countries in turn voted against Israel when called upon to do so. All factions frequently voted against the United States, although they were seldom as harsh with the Soviet Union— as President John F. Kennedy discovered when the nonaligned states refused to condemn the USSR for resuming aboveground nuclear tests in September 1961.[34]

The United Nations has also become incredibly corrupt in its use of funds. Halper reported:

> The salary and benefits packages of UN employees based in New York City are incredibly lucrative. Statistics compiled in 1995 revealed that the average annual salary for a midlevel accountant at the United Nations was $84,500. The salary for a comparable position in non-UN businesses and agencies was $41,964. A UN computer analyst could expect to receive $111,500 compared to $56,836 paid counterparts outside the UN bureaucracy. An assistant secretary general received $190,250; the mayor of New York City was paid $130,000. The raw figures do not convey the extent of the disparity, however, since the salaries of UN employees are free of all taxes. In addition to their bloated salaries, UN bureaucrats enjoy an array of costly perks, including monthly rent subsidies of up to $3,800 and annual education grants (also tax-free) of $12,675 per child. The UN pension program is so generous that entry-level staffers whose pay rises only as fast as inflation can retire in 30 years with $1.8 million.[35]

Halper added that the UN Children's Fund lost approximately $10 million because of mismanagement in Kenya. Nearly $4 million in cash was stolen outright at UN headquarters in Mogadishu, Somalia.[36]

---

34. Stefan Halper, "A Miasma of Corruption: The United Nations at 50," *Cato Institute Policy Analysis 253* (April 30, 1996). www.cato.org/pubs/pas/pa–253.html.
35. Ibid.
36. Ibid.

When asked about the United Nations' waste of funds, *Fox News* correspondent Eric Shawn, author of the book *The UN Exposed: How the United Nations Sabotages America's Security and Fails the World*, replied:

> I titled one chapter of the book "$400,000 in a Desk Drawer" because a review of 58 audits released by the [Paul] Volcker investigation revealed billions frittered away, from the 400 grand stashed in a U.N. office in Iraq with "unrestricted access" that the staff would dip into for "loans," to overpaying Gulf War reparations to Kuwait by $2 billion. A recent internal U.N. investigation found what it called "a culture of impunity" when it comes to U.N. spending. It said peacekeepers spent $10.4 million leasing a helicopter that should have cost $1.6 million. $65 million was spent for fuel in the Sudan and Haiti that wasn't needed, $2.4 million for hangers in the Congo that were never used, and on and on. In January, one U.N. study found overpayments in the Peacekeeping department amounted to more than $300 million.[37]

Therefore the United States should seek to minimize the influence of the United Nations wherever it is bringing harmful and destructive results throughout the world.

On the other hand, the United Nations does some good in educational and scientific areas and in matters of cultural exchange. In addition, it has sent peacekeeping forces to a number of hotspots in the world, and they have probably done some good. Former US diplomat James Dobbins cited the Sinai in the 1950s–1960s and again in the 1970s and Cyprus since 1964 as U.N. peacekeeping missions that were successful.[38]

There does not appear to be much hope for reforming the corruption in the United Nations or for bringing about fundamental change in its anti-American stance or its refusal to protest human rights abuses by some of the worst governments in the world. Former US Ambassador to the United Nations John Bolton said:

> ... the quality of membership of the Human Rights Council is going to go a long way to determining its success. The Commission on Human Rights was widely discredited on many fronts, but the most visible sign of the Commission's decay was the inclusion,

---

37. Cited in Paul Weyrich, "United Nations: A Human Rights Farce," *RenewAmerica.com* (May 16, 2006). www.renewamerica.com/columns/weyrich/060516.

38. George Gedda, "Lebanon Peacekeeping Force Hard to Create," Associated Press (Aug. 23, 2006). www.foxnews.com/printer_friendly_wires/2006Aug23/0,4675,USUNPeacekeepers,00.html.

and in some cases the leadership, of such countries as Cuba, Zimbabwe, and Sudan. We cannot allow that to happen again.

Additionally, the membership of the inaugural Council will be of particular procedural importance. Many of the processes that will permanently characterize the meeting and the actions of the Council will be decided by the first collection of nations to hold those seats.

Members elected this week include Algeria, China, Cuba, Pakistan, Russia and Saudi Arabia. Heritage Foundation analyst Brett D. Schaefer [has concluded] ..., "These countries were key players in undermining the effectiveness of the now-defunct Commission on Human Rights, and so it is very likely that they will play the same role on the Council, steering it away from confronting human rights abuses within their borders and in general."[39]

Therefore it would seem wise for the United States also to become more aggressive in building alternative associations of freedom-loving nations in the world—associations (or perhaps one association) that could provide a counterbalance to the negative influence of the United Nations in future years.

C. FOREIGN AID

Foreign aid is a specific area that the United States can use to promote its own interests and also do good for other nations.

1. Military aid

Military aid, whether through gifts or sales of weapons and airplanes and military training, should be used to help other nations defend themselves against attack and to maintain their freedom, in accordance with just war principles (see discussion in chap. 6, pp. 193–208).

2. Humanitarian aid

Humanitarian aid in the form of food, clothing, medical supplies, and funds should be sent to areas where there are *natural disasters* such as floods, hurricanes, or droughts. The United States gives large amounts of such aid—more than any nation in the world—both directly from

39. Cited in Weyrich, "United Nations: A Human Rights Farce."

the government (which is from tax dollars) and also through private organizations (see above, pp. 260–61).

3. Economic development aid

Should the United States give financial aid also for *economic development* in poor nations? For years we have assumed that we should, and we and other nations have given *over $1 trillion* in foreign aid, especially to African countries.[40]

But more recently a number of studies have sharply criticized the policy of giving foreign aid to poor nations for economic development or related purposes (as distinct from emergency relief in cases of disaster and as distinct from medical relief). Several books have argued that such aid has been harmful rather than helpful to poor nations because the aid has always been channeled through corrupt governments and *has simply tended to entrench these corrupt governments more firmly in power*, since government officials are the ones who dispense the aid! In addition, this aid *creates a culture of dependency* in poor nations, and this in effect prevents them from becoming self-sustaining, economically healthy countries.[41] I think these critiques are largely correct.

4. Debt forgiveness

Some Christians propose that the United States and other wealthy countries should forgive the debts of extremely poor nations, arguing that

---

40. See especially Dambisa Moyo, *Dead Aid: Why Aid Is Not Working and How There Is a Better Way for Africa* (New York: Farrar, Straus and Giroux, 2009).

41. Ibid. (Moyo is a native of Zambia who holds a PhD in economics from Oxford and a masters degree from Harvard and who has worked both at Goldman Sachs and at the World Bank. She explains how *more than $1 trillion in aid* has been transferred from rich countries to Africa in the last fifty years, with harmful results). See also the earlier work by British economist and foreign aid expert P. T. Bauer, *Equality, the Third World and Economic Delusion* (Cambridge, Mass.: Harvard University Press, 1981); also, William Easterly, *The White Man's Burden: Why the White Man's Efforts to Aid the Rest Have Done So Much Ill and So Little Good* (New York: Penguin, 2006). (Easterly has worked for most of his life as an economist in Africa, Latin America, and Russia). See also Easterly's earlier book, *The Elusive Quest for Growth: Economists' Adventures and Misadventures in the Tropics* (Cambridge, Mass.: MIT Press, 2001). These books from experts on Third World economic development provide strong refutations of the widely publicized book by Jeffrey Sachs, *The End of Poverty: Economic Possibilities for Our Time* (New York: Penguin, 2005). Sachs, who helps the United Nations allocate much aid to poor nations, recognizes that previous decades of aid have done little good. But he argues that if we would just give more aid, it would solve the problem—as if constant repetition of a failed solution makes for a wise plan!

they will never be able to repay them anyway. For example, Jim Wallis spends several pages in *God's Politics* extolling the virtues of a grassroots campaign among churches in the United States and the United Kingdom to cancel such debts. "Jubilee 2000 is now the Jubilee Network, and its supporters still call on the World Bank and IMF to cancel 100 percent of the debt owed to them."[42] Wallis makes reference to the Jubilee Year in Leviticus 25:8–55, when debts were canceled after forty-nine years.

What Wallis does not discuss, however, is a crucial difference between today's debts and those in ancient Israel: *People made loans knowing the Jubilee rules in advance.* In ancient Israel, everyone was aware that debts would be canceled after forty-nine years, and financial arrangements were made taking that into account. For instance, in transactions concerning land, the law said, "If the years are many, you shall increase the price, and if the years are few, you shall reduce the price, for it is the number of the crops that he is selling to you" (Lev. 25:16).

But modern loans to poor nations were not made with the expectation that they would be canceled after forty-nine years or any other period of time. So it is not fair to the lenders when Christians suddenly demand that they live up to a "Jubilee" law that they were not aware of when they made the loan. It is changing the rules after the agreements have been made.

Therefore these campaigns for debt forgiveness must be understood for what they are: *A plea to lenders that they should make voluntary charitable contributions toward the poor countries that have borrowed from them.*

In addition, the frequent moral flavor of these pleas places an implicit accusation of guilt against the lenders. The banks and governments that made loans to poor nations in good faith—probably thinking they were helping the poor nations by making these loans—*are suddenly viewed as wrongdoers* because they actually expect that the loans will be repaid!

Of course, if a country simply cannot repay a debt, then the lender (the World Bank or the International Monetary Fund) is forced to simply write it off as a bad debt. That is a business loss, and there should be accountability for those who make such loans that cannot be repaid. No public campaign is needed for declaring the loan a bad debt. But the borrowing nations do not want this, because this would make them unable to borrow in the future, a condition these nations are not willing to accept.

---

42. Jim Wallis, *God's Politics: Why the Right Gets It Wrong and the Left Doesn't Get It* (San Francisco: HarperSanFrancisco, 2005), 276.

The campaign for "debt forgiveness" was something other than a campaign to decide that these loans were just bad debts. It was a plea for wealthy nations to somehow provide the equivalent funds to pay off these loans so they would not be classified as bad debts. It was really a campaign for more welfare payments to poor countries.

For instance, in 2005 the G8 Summit voted to cancel $40 billion in debt owed to the International Monetary Fund, the World Bank, and the African Development Fund. According to the United Nations Environment Programme, the US was expected to pitch in up to $1.75 billion over ten years. The UN Programme reported, "This amount is its share of a pledge by rich nations to cover $16.7 billion in debt repayments the 18 countries would have made. The International Monetary Fund (IMF) will pay one of the larger bills (some $6 billion). Under the deal, the IMF is supposed to cover those debts from its own 'existing resources.' "[43] But those resources come from member nations; they are not created out of thin air. (The largest share comes from the United States.)

The Jubilee 2000 movement was an international coalition of people from over forty countries that called for the cancellation of Third World debt by the year 2000. The University of Iowa Center for International Finance and Development reported on its efforts:

> Jubilee 2000 staged demonstrations at the 1998 G–8 meeting in Birmingham, England.... The protestors caught the attention of Prime Minister Tony Blair, who met with the directors of Jubilee 2000 to discuss the issue of heavy debt in poor countries. Subsequently, the Prime Minister publicly expressed his personal support for, and dedication to, debt forgiveness. Other notable successes that resulted, at least in part, from Jubilee 2000 pressure included a promise from the United States during the G–7 (G–8 financial ministers, excluding Russia) meeting in Cologne, Germany, in 1999 to cancel 100% of the debt that qualifying countries owed the U.S. Jubilee also lobbied the U.S. Congress to make good on this promise. Congress responded to the growing pressure to address debt relief issues in 2000 by committing $769 million to bilateral and multilateral debt relief.[44]

---

43. United Nations Environment Programme, African Ministerial Conference on the Environment (A.M.CEN). Debt Cancellation, Nairobi (Oct. 26, 2005). www.unep.org/roa/docs/amcen/Brief_Debt_Cancellation.doc.

44. Enrique Carrasco, Charles McClellan, and Jane Ro, "Forgiveness and Repudiation," *The University of Iowa Center for International Finance and Development* (April 2007). www.uiowa.edu/ifdebook/ebook2/contents/part4-I.shtml.

But then the center went on to discuss some of the potential pitfalls of such debt relief:

> ... debt relief has been the subject of much criticism. Some crit-
> ics view debt relief as counter-productive. For example, many
> object to the criteria used to determine which governments
> qualify for debt relief. Some fear that debt forgiveness perpetu-
> ates corrupt regimes in the same manner as illegitimate debt
> because it frees up government funds without any guarantee
> that the government will apply them to legitimate social or
> development programs. Another fear, referred to as the "moral
> hazard," is that countries relieved of their debts will engage in
> reckless over-borrowing with the expectation that, once their
> debts reach unsustainable levels, international creditors will
> forgive them again.[45]

The central difficulty with focusing so much attention on such debt forgiveness is this: *Will debt forgiveness really solve the problems that kept these poor nations in poverty in the first place?* What these poor nations need most of all is to develop productive, self-sustaining, grow-ing economies. Forgiving debt or giving aid may meet some short-term need, but it does not change the governmental corruption, oppression, and destructive economic policies that have caused the poverty in the first place and continue to perpetuate it. Debt forgiveness and foreign aid to corrupt nations will often have the same effect: entrenching in power a corrupt government in that nation. Therefore debt forgive-ness, though well-intended, has the potential of doing more harm than good.

Who exactly are the nations that are receiving the benefits of such debt reduction programs? The International Monetary Fund lists thirty-five countries that have qualified for debt reduction. Twenty-six have reached what the IMF calls a "completion point," where they are eligible for the full measure of debt forgiveness that is being offered. Nine other countries are between the "decision point" and the "completion point" in the IMF reform program, and they have received partial debt forgive-ness. Here is the list of countries:

---

45. Ibid.

LIST OF COUNTRIES THAT HAVE QUALIFIED FOR ... HIPC [HEAVILY INDEBTED POOR COUNTRIES] INITIATIVE ASSISTANCE (AS OF JULY 1, 2009)

Post-Completion-Point Countries (26)		
Benin	Guyana	Niger
Bolivia	Haiti	Rwanda
Burkina Faso	Honduras	São Tomé
Burundi	Madagascar	Senegal
Cameroon	Malawi	Sierra Leone
Central African Republic	Mali	Tanzania
Ethiopia	Mauritania	Uganda
The Gambia	Mozambique	Zambia
Ghana	Nicaragua	

Interim Countries (Between Decision and Completion Point) (9)		
Afghanistan	Democratic Republic of Congo	Guinea Bissau
Chad	Côte d'Ivoire	Liberia
Republic of Congo	Guinea	Togo [46]

What is distinctive about these countries? Even after completing the "reforms" required by the International Monetary Fund, they still are among the most unfree and oppressive countries in the world.

Here is the same list again, but with a number beside each country that shows where it ranks in economic freedom among the 179 nations of the world that are rated each year by the Heritage Foundation and the *Wall Street Journal*. In the scale, *1* indicates the most free country and *179* indicates the least free (North Korea).[47]

46. International Monetary Fund information, from www.imf.org/external/np/exr/facts/hipc.htm (accessed Feb. 4, 2010).

47. These rankings are taken from Terry Miller and Kim R. Holmes, eds., *2010 Index of Economic Freedom* (Washington, DC: Heritage Foundation, and New York: *Wall Street Journal*, 2010). The information here is taken from the summary chart inside the front cover.

Post-Completion-Point Countries (26)		
Benin 115	Guyana 153	Niger 129
Bolivia 146	Haiti 141	Rwanda 93
Burkina Faso 90	Honduras 99	São Tomé & Principe 149
Burundi 160	Madagascar 69	Senegal 119
Cameroon 132	Malawi 122	Sierra Leone 157
Central African Republic 152	Mali 112	Tanzania 97
Ethiopia 136	Mauritania 133	Uganda 76
The Gambia 118	Mozambique 111	Zambia 100
Ghana 87	Nicaragua 98	

Interim Countries (Between Decision and Completion Point) (9)		
Afghanistan N/A	Democratic Republic of Congo 172	Guinea Bissau 167
Chad 159	Côte d'Ivoire 123	Liberia 163
Republic of Congo 169	Guinea 134	Togo 161

The *2010 Index of Economic Freedom* is the current edition of a report that is published annually. It ranks countries in ten categories of economic freedom, including property rights, freedom from corruption, business freedom, investment freedom, and trade freedom, among others. All but one of the thirty-five countries receiving debt forgiveness were rated for this 2010 report. (Afghanistan was not ranked because of a lack of reliable data due to political and military instability.)

What is significant about this chart of countries receiving debt forgiveness is that they all rank quite low in terms of economic freedom. In fact, thirty-one of the thirty-four countries that were ranked fell in the "unfree" or "repressed" categories. (Any number higher than 89 indicates a country that is "mostly unfree," and any number higher than 144 indicates a country that is "repressed," the worst category.) This means that 91% of the countries receiving debt forgiveness are still governed by oppressive, corrupt governments.

On this list of countries, only Ghana, Madagascar, and Uganda *even rank in the top half* of all the nations of the world with respect to these ten factors of economic freedom. Yet they all qualify for debt relief because they have carried out at least some of the "reforms" required by the IMF!

When I look at these statistics, it seems to me that a lot of the moral fervor that Christians have aimed against nations and banks that have made loans to poor countries should be redirected toward the corrupt governments of these repressive countries, where honest, skilled workers and business owners are not free to enjoy the fruits of their labors, and where bribery and routine violations of the law are accepted as a way of life. Debt relief given to these countries is not going to change these underlying problems or provide any long-term solutions.

In addition, debt forgiveness is likely to increase the dependence of the poor nation on funds from other nations. Where is the evidence that debt forgiveness has ever reduced a country's dependence on other nations for economic aid?

In 2005, I received a copy of an email with evangelical megachurch pastor Rick Warren's plea for "The ONE Campaign: To Make Poverty History." This June 3, 2005, email urged people to write to President Bush, urging him to support a campaign to "cancel 100% of the debts owed by the poorest countries." A few days later, Gordon Brown, then the British Chancellor of the Exchequer (similar to America's Secretary of the Treasury), announced that the G8 finance ministers had "agreed to 100 percent debt cancellation for Heavily Indebted Poor Countries."[48]

But did this 2005 campaign really "make poverty history"? No. The poor countries are still poor, more than four years after the world supposedly "made poverty history."

Therefore I have significant reservations about debt forgiveness for poor countries. At first it sounds like a good-hearted idea, and I'm sure that proponents can point to some specific development projects that seem like successful results in the short term. But where is the clear evidence that it will bring a country long-term economic good?

Finally, there is the question of fairness in forcing "contributions" from unwilling donors. Who actually pays for this debt forgiveness? Sometimes people imagine that it is just some rich banker somewhere who loses some money. But if the debt was from a bank, then *the stockholders of that bank*, including many retired people who have their pension plans or retirement savings in stock, have paid for that debt

---

48. *Fox News,* "G–8 Ministers OK $40B Debt Relief" (June 11, 2005). www.foxnews.com/story/0,2933, 159260,00.html.

forgiveness. Do they really want to do this? On the other hand, if the forgiven loan was made by the United States government (or by the World Bank, which gets the largest amount of its funds from the US government), then debt forgiveness means that it is actually *the taxpayers of the United States* who have made a multimillion dollar "contribution" to this debt forgiveness. And if many of the benefits actually brought further power to corrupt governments in these poor countries (and much of the money will go to the wealthy rulers and their friends in such countries), do Americans and citizens of other nations really want to pay more taxes for such a program?

5. Restrictions on foreign aid

It is important that the United States not give aid that will advance agendas in other nations that are morally wrong. For example, the Bush administration was correct when it refused to give foreign aid to any population control measures in China that would involve promoting abortions or forced abortions.

Nor should we give aid that will simply help oppressive totalitarian regimes stay in power (such as the horribly evil rule of Robert Mugabe in Zimbabwe).

6. The United States gives far more aid to other countries than any other nation

Earlier in this chapter I mentioned the statement of Lino J. Piedra, a member of the US Delegation to the United Nations Commission on Human Rights, that the United States was the origin of more than 70% of all financial flows reaching developing countries from the G–7 developed world, through private investment, private philanthropy, public aid, and private remittances.

Chapter 9

FOREIGN POLICY: ISRAEL AND IMMIGRATION

Building on the fundamental principles discussed in the first part of the previous chapter, this chapter tackles specific questions related to Israel and immigration:

> Should Israel be treated just the way we treat any other nation, or does Israel have some special status in the eyes of God?

> What should be the policy of the United States regarding the immigration of people from other countries?

> What should we do about illegal immigrants who are now in the United States?

A. ISRAEL

1. History of Israel: how did we get to this place?

The earliest recorded history of the people of the region of Palestine is that it was occupied by various Canaanite nations (see Gen. 10:15–19). But God promised that he would give this land to Abraham's descendents.

> On that day the LORD made a covenant with Abram, saying, *"To your offspring I give this land*, from the river of Egypt to the great river, the river Euphrates, the land of the Kenites, the Kenizzites, the Kadmonites, the Hittites, the Perizzites, the

284   The Economic and Foreign Policy Issues

Rephaim, the Amorites, the Canaanites, the Girgashites and the Jebusites" (Gen. 15:18–21).

God also told Abraham something similar in Genesis 17:

"And I will give to you and to your offspring after you the land of your sojournings, all the land of Canaan, for an everlasting possession, and I will be their God" (v. 8).

This promise found its initial fulfillment when the Jewish people, under the leadership of Joshua, entered the Promise Land and drove out the Canaanite people who had been living there but who came under God's judgment. God said to Joshua:

"Moses my servant is dead. Now therefore arise, go over this Jordan, you and all this people, into the land that I am giving to them, to the people of Israel. Every place that the sole of your foot will tread upon I have given to you, just as I promised to Moses. From the wilderness and this Lebanon as far as the great river, the river Euphrates, all the land of the Hittites to the Great Sea toward the going down of the sun shall be your territory. No man shall be able to stand before you all the days of your life. Just as I was with Moses, so I will be with you. I will not leave you or forsake you. Be strong and courageous, for you shall cause this people to inherit the land that I swore to their fathers to give them" (Josh. 1:2–6).

The succeeding chapters in Joshua show how the people of Israel began to conquer the Canaanites and take possession of the land, but that process was not completed in Joshua's lifetime (see Josh. 13:1–7). Nevertheless, the nation of Israel was established in the land.

The remaining history of Israel in the Old Testament shows that its largest expansion of territory occurred under the kingships of David and Solomon (1 Sam. 16—2 Sam. 24 for David, and 1 Kings 1–11 for Solomon). Then the kingdom was divided and gradually diminished until the Babylonians finally conquered the last of the kingdom of Judah and carried the people off to Babylon in exile in 586 BC.

The history of the land of Israel from earliest times to the present may be summarized in the following chart:[1]

---

1. The dates in this chart prior to the first century are taken from *ESV Study Bible*, pp. 385, 1788–89.

Before 1406 BC	Canaanite nation
1406 (or 1220) BC	Conquest by Israel
1010-971 BC	King David
971-931 BC	Solomon (followed by various Israelite kings)
586 BC	Babylonian Empire (beginning with Nebuchadnezzar)
539 BC	Persian Empire (beginning with Cyrus)
333 BC	Greece (beginning with Alexander the Great)
142 BC	Independent Israel (Maccabean revolt began in 167 BC)
63 BC	Roman Empire (beginning with Pompey)
330 BC	Byzantine Empire
636 AD	Muslim rule, then various Muslim or Christian (Crusader) rulers
1517 AD	Ottoman Empire (Turkish)
1917 AD	British rule
1948 AD	Israel as independent nation

One implication of this overview is that *there has never been a time in its entire history when an independent "Palestinian" nation existed in this land.*

On November 29, 1947, the United Nations passed General Assembly Resolution 181, which recommended the establishment of two separate nations in the land, the nation of Israel and an Arab nation, with specific boundary lines defined for each nation, a special power-sharing arrangement for the government of Jerusalem, and special arrangements for cooperation in economic, transportation, and agricultural matters. But the Arab residents of the land refused to accept this solution and refused to constitute themselves as a separate nation.

Israel, however, declared its independence on May 14, 1948, in accordance with the policy of the British government that had been declared November 2, 1917, in the Balfour Declaration, a formal statement of policy by the British government. The Balfour Declaration read as follows:

His Majesty's Government view with favour the establishment in Palestine of a national home for the Jewish people, and will use their best endeavors to facilitate the achievement of this object, it being clearly understood that nothing shall be done which may prejudice the civil and religious rights of existing non-Jewish communities in Palestine, or the rights and political status enjoyed by Jews in any other country.[2]

The situation in Palestine in 1947–1948 leading up to the declaration of independence was marked by considerable fighting between Arabs and Jews. Then the very day after that declaration — May 15, 1948 — the armies of five Arab countries (Egypt, Syria, Jordan, Lebanon, and Iraq) attacked Israel. These were all four of the nations that bordered Israel to the north, northeast, west, and south, plus Iraq, which was farther east. To the surprise of much of the world, during the next year Israel increasingly took the offensive and became victorious in the war. Finally a cease-fire was declared and temporary new borders were established. Israel was admitted as a member of the United Nations on May 11, 1949.

Retired Princeton professor Bernard Lewis, who is one of the world's most widely recognized authorities on the history of Islam, notes that "during the fighting in 1947–1948" there was "an exchange of populations." He writes, "About three-fourths of a million Arabs fled or were driven (both are true in different places) from Israel and found refuge in the neighboring Arab countries.... A slightly greater number of Jews fled or were driven from Arab countries.... Most Jewish refugees found their way to Israel."[3]

But Lewis points out that what happened to these refugees was very different. The Jewish refugees from other countries — whether European or Middle Eastern — were accepted as citizens in Israel, but the Palestinian Arab refugees were refused acceptance in most of the surrounding Arab countries:

The government of Jordan granted Palestinian Arabs a form of citizenship, but kept them in refugee camps. In the other Arab countries, they were and remained stateless aliens without rights or opportunities, maintained by U.N. funding. Paradoxically, if a Palestinian fled to Britain or America, he was eligible for naturalization after five years, and his locally-born

2. The Balfour Declaration, November 2, 1917. www.mfa.gov.il/MFA/Peace%20Process/Guide%20to%20the%20Peace%20Process/The%20Balfour%20Declaration.
3. Bernard Lewis, "On the Jewish Question," *Wall Street Journal* (Nov. 26, 2007), A21.

children were citizens by birth. If he went to Syria, Lebanon or Iraq, he and his descendents remained stateless, now entering the fourth or fifth generation.

The reason for this has been stated by various Arab spokesmen. It is the need to preserve the Palestinians as a separate entity until the time when they will return to reclaim the whole of Palestine; that is to say, all of the West Bank, the Gaza Strip and Israel. The demand for the "return" of the refugees, in other words, means the destruction of Israel.[4]

2. Present-day negotiations

What about current "negotiations" between Israel and the Palestinians? Lewis writes frankly:

> The first question (one might think it is obvious but apparently not) is, "What is the conflict about?" There are basically two possibilities: that it is about the size of Israel, or about its existence.... If the issue is not the size of Israel, but its existence, negotiations are foredoomed. And in light of the past record, it is clear that is and will remain the issue, until the Arab leadership either achieves or renounces its purpose — to destroy Israel. Both seem equally unlikely for the time being.[5]

3. Arabs living in Israel

A number of Arabs chose to remain in the land that was governed by the new nation of Israel. These Arabs have citizenship rights and can vote in Israeli elections. In fact, Arab citizens of Israel in late 2009 held 12 of the 120 seats in the Israeli parliament (called the Knesset). There is a Christian Arab of Lebanese descent who is a permanent member of the Israeli Supreme Court. And there are Arab generals in the Israeli army.

By contrast, all Jews have been driven out of Arab lands since 1948, even though many of them and their families had lived peacefully in various Arab nations such as Israel, Syria, and Jordan for many centuries. The Arab nations of the Middle East (Egypt, Saudi Arabia, Yemen, Oman, United Arab Emirates, Qatar, Kuwait, Iraq, Jordon, Syria, Iran) include a total population of 266,807,498 and have a total land area

4. Ibid.
5. Ibid.

of 6,336,746 sq. kilometers,[6] compared with the total population of 7,233,201 in Israel with a land area of 21,642 sq. kilometers (8,522 sq. miles).[7] Most of these Arab nations continue to insist that Israel has no right to exist. They have nearly forty times the population and nearly three hundred times the land area, but still claim the right to destroy the nation of Israel. In fact, Jordan[8] and Egypt[9] are the only Arab countries in the Middle East that have signed a peace treaty with Israel and recognize its existence. In addition, Iraq, since it recently established a democratic government, has not declared itself in favor of the destruction of Israel.

I do not mean to say that Israel is without blame in its treatment of minorities within its borders. In particular, I have been concerned about reports of a lack of adequate protection of religious freedom within Israel. Sometimes Christians—particularly Palestinian Christians— have experienced hostile persecution from both Arabs and Israeli Jews.

Dr. Justus Weiner, a scholar in residence at the Jerusalem Centre for Public Affairs and a leading authority on Christian persecution in Palestine, says that the Christian population in Bethlehem has dropped from a high of 75–80% in the 1940s to approximately 12% today. He notes that the entire Christian population on the West Bank declined to 1.5 to 1.7% of the total population and is "practically close to disappearing."[10]

A 2006 report from the House International Relations Committee of the US Congress led to a letter from Congressman Henry J. Hyde, chairman of the committee, to President Bush on May 19, 2006, that contained the following statement:

> It is becoming increasingly difficult for Christians and Muslims living in the occupied territories to practice their faith. The security barrier, checkpoints, permit system, and segregated highway system render getting to religious services extremely

---

6. *The CIA World Factbook.* www.cia.gov/library/publications/the-world-factbook/region/region_mde.html.

7. Ibid.

8. Israel Ministry of Foreign Affairs, Israel-Jordan Peace Treaty, October 26, 1994. www.mfa.gov.il/MFA/Peace%20Process/Guide%20to%20the%20Peace%20Process/Israel-Jordan%20Peace%20Treaty.

9. Israel Ministry of Foreign Affairs, Israel-Egypt Peace Treaty, March 26, 1979. www.mfa.gov.il/MFA/Peace%20Process/Guide%20to%20the%20Peace%20Process/Israel-Egypt%20Peace%20Treaty.

10. Michelle Vu, "Persecution Fuelling Drastic Decline of Christians in Palestine," *ChristianToday,Com* (July 23, 2007). www.christiantoday.com/article/persecution.fuelling.drastic.decline.of.christians.in.palestine/11791-2.htm.

difficult. In addition, the security barrier cuts through religious properties and impedes access to important holy sites. Consequently the fabric of religious life is being destroyed. The Christians in the area view the security barrier as something that is seriously damaging religious freedom in the Holy Land, impeding their access to important holy sites, and tearing at the social fabric of Christian life by destroying the important linkages between Bethlehem and Jerusalem, resulting in a decreasing Christian presence in both cities.[11]

Congressman Hyde also stated:

> There has been a decline of Christians in the Holy Land.... There are recent and very troubling indications that this decline will be exacerbated and accelerated by actions of the Israeli government and the ascendancy of Islamic fundamentalism.[12]

4. Suicide bombing and the Israeli security fence

For many years Israel sought to defend itself against Arabs who had the right to live in their cities but who would enter crowded buses or marketplaces and blow themselves up in suicide terrorist attacks, killing and wounding hundreds of Israeli Jews. The strategy was to intentionally target innocent civilians for death and thereby spread terror among the population.

Finally Israel decided that its only solution was to build a tall security fence that would separate areas that were dominantly Arab from those that were dominantly Jewish. The security fence was started in 2003[13] and is not yet complete. It is actually a series of concrete walls up to eight meters (twenty-four feet) high in some places. It is also called the "West Bank Barrier" in one area and the "Gaza Strip Barrier" in another.

There has been controversy over whether the placement of the fence is correct, but it has been without question a major factor in a significant reduction in the number of suicide bombings in Israel. The Israeli government therefore defends the fence as a necessary part of its essential self-defense. Palestinian Arabs, including Palestinian Christians, have objected

11. "Staff Report on the Holy Land," in *Palestine — Israel Journal of Politics, Economics and Culture* 13:2 (2006), 114.

12. Ibid., 113.

13. Israel Ministry of Foreign Affairs, "Saving Lives: Israel's Security Fence." www.mfa.gov.il/mfa/mfaarchive/2000_2009/2003/11/.

that it has caused significant disruption in many of their lives because of its requiring much longer travel distances and delays at security checkpoints.

5. Controversy over Gaza

The Gaza Strip is a portion of land on the coast of the Mediterranean Sea located in the southwest corner of Israel. It is about 25 miles (41 kilometers) long and it varies in width from 4 to 7.5 miles (6–12 kilometers) wide. It has a total area of 139 sq. miles (360 sq. kilometers) and a population of 1.5 million people.

The Gaza Strip was intended to become part of the new Arab state, according to the 1947 partition plan passed by the United Nations General Assembly. But during the 1948 Arab-Israeli war, Egypt occupied the Gaza Strip, and it remained in effect under Egyptian control, yet never became an official part of Egypt. Then Israel took over the Gaza Strip after the Six-Day War in June 1967. Israel then created twenty-one new Jewish settlements, Jewish people built homes in the Gaza Strip, and Israel retained control of the area.

In 2005, pursuing the goal of "land for peace," Israel decided to withdraw from the Gaza Strip and remove all Israeli homes that were there. In an address to the UN General Assembly on September 25, 2009, Israeli Prime Minister Benjamin Netanyahu explained what happened:

> In 2005, hoping to advance peace, Israel unilaterally withdrew from every inch of Gaza. It was very painful. We dismantled 21 settlements, really, bedroom communities, and farms. We uprooted over 8,000 Israelis. We just yanked them out from their homes. We did this because many in Israel believed that this would get peace.
>
> Well, we didn't get peace. Instead we got an Iranian-backed terror base 50 miles from Tel-Aviv. But life in the Israeli towns and cities immediately next to Gaza became nothing less than a nightmare. You see, the Hamas rocket launches and rocket attacks not only continued after we left, they actually increased dramatically. They increased tenfold. And, again, the UN was silent — absolutely silent.[14]

The rockets fired from Gaza by Hamas forces had attacked Israeli civilian population centers in southern Israel, particularly the city of

---

14. Benjamin Netanyahu, transcript of remarks to the UN General Assembly, September 25, 2009 (accessed at washingtontimes.com Sept. 25, 2009).

Sderot. Netanyahu said that Israel was faced with "an enemy committing a double war crime, of firing on civilians while hiding behind civilians."[15] The attacks had begun as early as 2000 from sections of the Gaza
Strip, but when Israel completely pulled out of the Strip—hoping that
giving up some land would lead to further concessions toward peace on
the part of the Palestinians—they found that the attacks simply intensi-
fied. Israel's defense minister explained:

> After enduring eight years of ongoing rocket fire—in which
> 12,000 missiles were launched against our cities, and after all
> diplomatic efforts to stop this barrage failed—it was my duty
> as Defense Minister to do something about it. It's as simple and
> self-evident as the right to self-defense.[16]

What did Israel do to avoid killing civilians? The situation Israel
faced was difficult because Hamas was "an enemy that intentionally
deploys its forces in densely populated areas, stores its explosives in
private homes, and launches rockets from crowded school yards and
mosques."[17] Nevertheless, Israel attempted to target only military sites
and warned civilians to move from the path of the attacks. General and
former prime minister Ehud Barak says, "In Gaza, we reached out to the
civilians via millions of leaflets, telephone calls and text messages, urging them to leave areas before we acted."[18]

On December 27, 2008, Israel sent fighter jets in a series of air strikes
against specific targets in Gaza. This was followed by a ground invasion
on January 3, 2009.

The United Nations Human Rights Council subsequently issued a
report (the Goldstone Report) accusing Israel of carrying out war crimes
in Gaza while mentioning nothing that condemned the 12,000 missiles that were launched indiscriminately against civilian targets over a
period of eight years. In response, Prime Minister Netanyahu said to the
UN General Assembly, "What a perversion of truth. What a perversion
of justice."[19]

My own evaluation of these events is that I find it hard to see how
Israel could have acted any differently and still have fulfilled its responsibility to defend its citizens from attack. In fact, when Barack Obama

---

15. Ibid.
16. Ehud Barak, "At the U.N., Terrorism Pays," *Wall Street Journal* (Sept. 25, 2009), A15.
17. Ibid.
18. Ibid.
19. Netanyahu, address to UN General Assembly, September 25, 2009.

visited the city of Sderot while he was a presidential candidate, he said, "If somebody was sending rockets into my house where my two daughters sleep at night, I would do everything to stop them, and would expect Israel to do the same thing."[20] But now as President, he has given signs of increasing opposition to Israel, such as publicly demanding that they stop all settlement construction.[21]

6. What is the solution to the Arab-Israeli conflict?

What is the solution to the current conflict? As long as the Palestinian Arab leaders and the surrounding Arab nations insist that their goal is the total destruction of Israel, and as long as they continue to insist that Israel has no right to exist as a nation, I see no point in negotiation between Israel and the Palestinians. There is no intermediate bargaining point between existing and not existing as a nation. Israel is not going to give up its right to exist or its right to defend itself, nor do I think it should ever give up those things. Therefore, until the most basic Palestinian position changes from this fundamental commitment, the only way to maintain a reasonable amount of peace in that region is for Israel to maintain a strong military force and use that force to defend itself when necessary. This seems to me to fit into the classic description of a just war, because of the fundamental right of a nation to defend itself against an evil enemy who continues to attack and seek to destroy it.

Another way to explain the differences between the two sides is to say this: If the Palestinians would agree to lay down their arms and acknowledge the legitimate existence of Israel, they could have a separate Palestinian nation tomorrow and live in peace and increasing economic prosperity with their Jewish neighbors. But if Israel were to lay down its arms, it would be annihilated; it would cease to exist as a nation. That distinction shows the fundamental difference between the two sides in this conflict.

Therefore, if Western nations, including the United States, are serious about ending the Arab-Israeli conflict, *the first step* should be publicly demanding that Arab nations give up claiming that Israel has no right to exist and that they are going to destroy it. That is the root cause of the entire ongoing conflict and has been since 1948. The Arab states should

---

20. "Israel's Gaza Defense," *Wall Street Journal* (Dec. 29, 2008), A12.
21. Chris McGreal and Rory McCarthy, "Obama: Halt to New Israeli settlements is in America's security interests," *guardian.co.uk* (May 29, 2009). www.guardian.co.uk/world/2009/may/28/barack-obama-jewish-settlements-israel-palestine-relations.

immediately join the other 160 nations of the world that have recognized Israel as a nation.

7. Does God still give special favor and protection to the nation of Israel?

Evangelical Christians differ over the question of whether God gives special protection today to the nation of Israel. Those evangelicals who hold to a dispensational system of biblical interpretation say that God's promise of the land of Israel to the descendents of Abraham was an eternal promise and it will yet be fulfilled in even greater measure in a time yet to come.

On the other hand, non-dispensationalists (including me) argue that the Jewish people at the time of the New Testament rejected Jesus as their Messiah and thereby forfeited the promises to blessings from God that were to come as part of the new covenant in Christ. Non-dispensationalists place much more emphasis on the fact that *many of the promises made to Israel* in the Old Testament were seen by the New Testament authors to be *fulfilled in the church.*

For example, in Hebrews 8:8–13 the author takes a long quotation from Jeremiah 31:31–34, where God makes promises to "the house of Israel" and "the house of Judah" (Heb. 8:8), and he argues that *these are fulfilled in the new covenant,* which is now being experienced by the church of Jesus Christ, to whom the author was writing. Similarly, 1 Peter 2:1–10 sees many Old Testament promises to Israel *fulfilled in the church.* Therefore non-dispensationalists place much less expectation on the Jewish people receiving the fulfillment of God's *promise of the land* that was given in the Old Testament. While dispensationalists would argue that these promises of the land will be *literally fulfilled in a future time of great tribulation* after Christ returns to remove the church from the earth, non-dispensationalists like me do not think there will be such a time of tribulation when the church is removed from the earth. (They think that any future time of tribulation will happen before Christ returns and that Christians will still be on earth during that time.)

But even without resolving the differences between dispensationalists and non-dispensationalists, *is there anything that both sides in this discussion should be able to affirm about the future of Israel?*

First, both sides should clearly affirm that the Jewish people do not have a separate path to salvation apart from trusting in Jesus as their Messiah. Jesus said, "I am the way, and the truth, and the life. No one comes to the Father except through me" (John 14:6). Paul wrote, "There is one God, and there is one mediator between God and men, the man Christ Jesus" (1 Tim. 2:5). The New Testament teaches again and again that apart from trusting in Christ, no one can find forgiveness of sins and eternal salvation. There is no special "second path" of salvation for people just because they come from Jewish ancestry.

But it also seems clear that in the very section of Romans in which Paul expresses such sorrow that the Jewish people have rejected Jesus Christ as their Messiah (see Rom. 9:2–3, 6–8), he speaks about *a distinctive future for the very people of Israel who have rejected Christ*. Paul looks forward to a future time when the Jewish people will be fully included into the people of God, for he says:

> Now if *their trespass* means riches for the world, and if *their failure* means riches for the Gentiles, how much more will *their full inclusion* mean! (Rom. 11:12).

The phrases "their trespass" and "their failure" are speaking about the Jewish peoples' refusal to accept Jesus as their Messiah. During this present age (while Paul was preaching the Gospel) God had opened salvation to the Gentiles and there was great blessing for Gentiles; but this same verse looks forward to a still-future time that Paul calls "full inclusion," a time when apparently a great majority of the Jewish people will become part of God's true people by trusting in Jesus as their Messiah.

Paul speaks of the same idea a few verses later:

> For if *their rejection* means the reconciliation of the world, what will *their acceptance* mean but life from the dead? (Rom. 11:15).

In speaking of a future time that Paul calls "their acceptance," he looks forward to a time of turning to Christ by large numbers of Jewish people.

Next, Paul uses the image of an olive tree to say that because the Jewish people had rejected Jesus as the Messiah, they were like branches that were "broken off" from the olive tree (representing God's true people, Rom. 11:17). Paul says they "were broken off because of their unbelief" (Rom. 11:20). Then he looks forward to a future time when he says, "How much more will these, the natural branches, be grafted back into their own olive tree" (Rom. 11:24).

Paul speaks again of the Jewish peoples' rejection of Christ as temporary, for he says, "A *partial hardening* has come upon Israel, *until* the fullness of the Gentiles has come in. And in this way all Israel will be saved" (Rom. 11:25–26). Paul goes on to speak of ethnic Israel, the Jewish people, and says that "As regards the Gospel, *they* are enemies of God for your sake. But as regards election, *they* are beloved for the sake of *their* forefathers" (v. 28). The *same* Jewish people who are "enemies of God" — that is, who have rejected Jesus as the Messiah — are still the objects of some future purpose that God has in mind, for of these same people he says in the next sentence, "As regards election, *they* are beloved for the sake of their forefathers" (v. 28). Therefore, although they have rejected Christ and do not now have salvation, God still has a plan in mind for the Jewish people and in some sense (other than possessing salvation through Christ) he still counts them "beloved" and has a future purpose in mind for them, "for the gifts and the calling of God are irrevocable" (v. 29).

All of this shows that Paul still believes that *God views the Jewish people who have rejected Christ as a special ethnic group out of all the people of the earth*, a group that God still considers to be "beloved for the sake of their forefathers." And because of this, at some future time "all Israel will be saved" (v. 26), most likely referring to a future turning to trust in Jesus Christ on the part of a significant majority of the Jewish people on earth at that time.

Does God still give special favor and protection to the Jewish people today? Even if evangelical Christians do not agree on how many of the Old Testament promises to Israel will still be fulfilled among the ethnically Jewish people, all Christians should be able to agree that Romans 11 speaks of the Jewish people in the new covenant age, which is the age in which we presently live. Romans 11 still sees a special purpose and special love of God for the Jewish people, whom he will bring to salvation through Christ in great numbers in a future day. Therefore Paul can say that even today, "They are beloved for the sake of their forefathers" (v. 28).

I find it hard to read this as saying anything other than that God still has a kind of special favor and care for the people of Israel who are today "enemies" of God regarding the Gospel, but who will someday experience a "full inclusion" among the people of God and will "be grafted back into their own olive tree" (vv. 12, 24).

8. Should the United States give special protection and favor to Israel?

Regarding the United States' policy toward Israel today, I want to make it very clear, first, that we should never say about any nation that we will always support whatever it does, whether or not we agree with it. And clearly we should not say that about Israel. The vast majority of Jewish people in Israel today have made exactly the wrong decision on the most important question of all of life, namely, whether to trust in Jesus as their true Messiah and Savior and Lord. We cannot say they have made the right decision on that question!

Moreover, if Israel's military forces were to commit immoral acts, such as the intentional murder of innocent civilians rather than strictly attacking military forces and targets, then we should certainly criticize them for any such wrongdoing.

In September 2009, Israel's Defense Minister (and former Prime Minister) Ehud Barak agreed with this stance when he said:

> Israel is not perfect. As much as we as a society try to uphold the IDF's [Israeli Defense Force's] ethical code, mistakes sometimes happen.... And when we are told that things may not be right, we check it out and, when necessary, prosecute those involved. We are now pursuing two dozen criminal investigations regarding events that occurred in Gaza.[22]

Therefore our policy as a nation should never be "Israel is always right," any more than it should be "England is always right" or "Canada is always right" or "The United States is always right." We must be willing to hold even our closest allies and even our own nation up to criticism when we believe it has done something that is inconsistent with the moral standards of the Bible.

Having said that, I still believe that we should treat Israel as a very special and close ally. We should cooperate with and support it in many ways. We should be willing to defend it if attacked and also to defend and support it in diplomatic circles, especially in the United Nations. We should defend its right to exist and its right to defend itself. We should be seeking to find many ways in which we can help Israel grow and prosper as a nation, through free trade, cultural exchanges, educational and technological exchanges, access to military technology, the promotion of tourism, and so forth.

Therefore I disagree with Ron Paul's "noninterventionist" policy, which opposes any defense alliance with Israel and all foreign or military aid to Israel.[23]

I believe the United States should treat Israel as a favored ally for several reasons:

a. Israel is our most reliable ally out of the entire group of nations in the Middle East. From a military and strategic standpoint in terms of

22. Barak, "At the U.N., Terrorism Pays."
23. See Ron Paul, *Revolution: A Manifesto* (New York: Grand Central Publishing, 2008), 10–17, 34–35.

maintaining world peace and world commerce, Israel is crucial to our national interests.

b. Israel is now one of the most advanced nations in the world in terms of scientific and technological inventions, information processing, and financial management. When it finally decided to reject the socialistic economic system it had in place for several decades, it became one of the most successful entrepreneurial, free market economies in the world.[24]

These remarkable advances in the last ten years are described in fascinating detail in George Gilder's recent book *The Israel Test*.[25] Gilder's thesis is that the Jewish people as a whole have demonstrated throughout history amazing achievements far beyond their small numbers, especially in mathematics, science, military strategy, invention, and entrepreneurial and business success.

What Gilder calls "the Israel test" is the question of how the people of the world respond to the nation of Israel. He argues that nations and cultures that hate Israel fail this "Israel test" because they react out of envy and hatred for a nation that has achieved so much success in so many areas. But nations and cultures that appreciate Israel because of the contributions it makes to the entire world pass Gilder's "Israel test" and respond to the success of others in a morally right way.

Although I do not think that Gilder has fully explained the reasons for the hatred of Israel by some people and nations (he fails to consider sufficiently the high moral standards of historic Judaism and the spiritual component of opposition to God's plans for Israel), I think he is correct that envy of Israel's success is certainly a significant factor. The great value of Gilder's book is that he points out the immense benefits that have come to the entire world through Jewish intellectual achievements. (Gilder himself is not Jewish.)

c. We should support Israel because its establishment as a nation in 1948 was morally legitimate and was affirmed by a significant majority of countries in the United Nations at that time. The legitimacy of Israel's existence was again affirmed by its acceptance as a member of the United Nations in 1949, and so far 160 nations of the world have granted Israel diplomatic recognition.[26] The United States was the first nation to grant

---

24. Ron Paul incorrectly implies that Israel's economy lacks sufficient economic freedom to develop rapidly: see his *Revolution*, 35.

25. George Gilder, *The Israel Test* (Minneapolis: Richard Vigilante Books, 2009).

26. Israel Ministry of Foreign Affairs, "Israel's Diplomatic Missions Abroad: Status of Relations," February 8, 2009. www.mfa.gov.il/mfa/about%20the%20ministry/diplomatic%20missions/Israel-s%20Diplomatic%20Missions%20Abroad.

recognition, by an act of President Harry Truman eleven minutes after the Israeli Declaration of Independence was signed on May 14, 1948.[27]

It is important to remember that this establishment of Israel as a nation came in the aftermath of World War II and the attempt by Adolf Hitler and the Nazis to destroy the Jewish people. Jewish refugees had fled from persecution in many nations and were actively seeking a homeland that they could make their own — a place where they would be free from persecution in the future. The nations of the world largely agreed with this solution to the problem of where Jewish refugees could settle and be safe.

d. There are biblical reasons why Christians should support the continued existence and health of the nation of Israel. First, in a world filled with much moral relativism and confusion and also influenced by the harsh, totalitarian governments in strict Islamic nations, Israel provides a refreshing ally in terms of the similarity of its convictions to the moral standards held by Christian believers and taught in the Bible. Both Christians and Jews have moral values that trace their origin to the moral standards that God gave in the Ten Commandments in the Old Testament (Exod. 20:1–17). Therefore the nation of Israel can become a useful ally for Christians in seeking positive moral influence on the world.

Second, because the Bible clearly teaches God's sovereignty over the affairs of nations and also teaches that God has a future plan for the salvation of large numbers of Jewish people, it seems right to see the establishment of the nation of Israel in 1948 and the present gathering of 5.5 million Jews there as a significant preparation that God has made so that the future salvation of many Jewish people through trust in Jesus as Messiah will be evident to the entire world as a fulfillment of what Paul predicted in Romans 11. Throughout history God has worked through human means and human influences to implement his plans for history, and therefore it seems very likely that supporting Israel's continued existence and well-being as a nation is also a way of contributing to the preparation for the "full inclusion" of the Jewish people among the people of God at some time in the future.

Third, although I do not accept the dispensationalist system of interpretation of Scripture, and although I believe that many of the Old Testament promises to Israel have been fulfilled by God in the blessings given to the church in the new covenant, I think there is still legitimate

---

27. "Press Release Announcing U.S. Recognition of Israel," May 14, 1948.

room for *uncertainty about whether the promise of God to Abraham in Genesis 17 has been completely fulfilled in the church.* There God promised Abraham the following:

> "And I will give to you and to your offspring after you the land of your sojournings, all the land of Canaan, for an *everlasting* possession, and I will be their God" (Gen. 17:8).

What does God mean when he says he will give to Abraham's offspring (that is, the Jewish people) "all the land of Canaan, for an *everlasting* possession"? Only the Mosaic covenant (beginning at Exod. 20) is ever called "the old covenant" in the New Testament, and that earlier covenant with Abraham is never called the "old covenant." Although I am somewhat uncertain about this, it seems to me quite possible that the establishment of the Jewish people as a nation in 1948 *in that same land that God had promised to Abraham before 2000 BC*(!) was one step that God made toward his eventual plan to fulfill this promise of the nation of Israel having that land "for an *everlasting* possession," and so, when they turn to Jesus as their Messiah, the last phrase of the verse will also come true: "and I will be their God" (Gen. 17:8).

Therefore it seems that even non-dispensational interpreters like me should at least retain a considerable measure of *uncertainty* about the question of God's present providential favor on Israel. I think we should consider it at least possible that God was even in recent times working to bring about steps leading to a fulfillment of Genesis 17:8 through the establishment of Israel in 1948. As Paul says about God's future plans for the very Israel that had rejected Jesus as Messiah, "For the gifts and the calling of God are irrevocable" (Rom. 11:29).

This line of thought also helps us understand a spiritual component behind the current Israel-Arab conflict. Because Romans 11 teaches that God has a future plan for the salvation of large numbers of the Jewish people, Christians might well suspect that there is a deeper spiritual source behind the intense anti-Semitism, the often-violent and irrational hatred of the Jews, that has occurred in various areas throughout history. It seems reasonable to think, for example, that the spiritual source behind the horrendous evil in the attempt of Hitler and the Nazis to destroy the Jews was none other than Satan himself, who, according to Jesus, was "a murderer from the beginning" (John 8:44). It is not surprising that Satan would try to exterminate the Jewish people and prevent the fulfillment of God's plan to save large numbers of them in the future.

This same demonic hatred, then, seems to me to be the most likely source behind the inhuman evil of the suicide bombers who for years have blown themselves up in the midst of groups of Jewish civilians in Israel. This demonic opposition to God's plan for the Jews also helps to explain the irrational commitment of many Muslim nations today to destroy Israel at all costs.

As for how this affects the United States, it is, of course, our nation's support for Israel that is one of the primary reasons behind the terrorist attacks against us (see above, pp. 217–20). Our nation's steadfast resolve to be Israel's greatest defender in the world today leads naturally to the desire of radical jihadists to destroy the United States as well. In this way the opposition of Satan to the fulfillment of God's plans for the Jewish people can be seen as one of the deep spiritual causes behind the terrorist attacks on the United States.

For several reasons, therefore, it seems to me that the United States should count Israel as a close ally and, while not supporting Israel when it does wrong, should still give special favor and protection to that nation.

B. IMMIGRATION

What should be the policy of the United States (or any other nation) regarding the immigration of people from other countries?

1. Biblical teaching

The Old Testament has many verses that command the people of Israel to treat the "sojourner" (other versions say "alien") fairly and with kindness and love. For example,

> "You shall not wrong a *sojourner* or oppress him, for you were sojourners in the land of Egypt" (Exod. 22:21).

Is the "sojourner" in verses like this the same as a foreign immigrant in a nation today?

In his very perceptive book *The Immigration Crisis*, Old Testament scholar James Hoffmeier says that the verse translated "alien" (NIV) or "sojourner" or "stranger" (ESV; sometimes NASB, KJV) in these Old Testament verses was "a person who entered Israel and followed legal procedures to obtain recognized standing as a resident alien."[28] Hoffmeier points out that there was a specific Hebrew word (*gçr*) used to refer to such an "alien" or "sojourner." In other words, Hoffmeier

---

28. James Hoffmeier, *The Immigration Crisis: Immigrants, Aliens, and the Bible* (Wheaton, IL: Crossway Books, 2009), 52.

shows that these verses about the "sojourner" (Hebrew *gçr*) refer to "legal immigrants" into a country.[29] But other people who did not have this recognized standing were simply termed "foreigners"—using other Hebrew terms—and they did not have the same benefits or privileges that sojourners did.[30]

Therefore Hoffmeier concludes that while "the legal alien ought to have most of the rights of citizenship," on the other hand,

> illegal immigrants should not expect these same privileges from the state whose laws they disregard by virtue of their undocumented status. The Bible clearly distinguishes between the status of a legal alien (*ger*) and a foreigner (*nekhar* and *zar*), and one consequence is that there really is a difference between the legal standing of a present-day documented alien and an illegal immigrant. Therefore it is legally and morally acceptable for government to deal with those in the country illegally according to the nation's legal provisions. The Christian insists, however, that they be dealt with in a humane manner.[31]

With this distinction in mind, we can notice other verses that command God's people to treat sojourners fairly and justly:

> "You shall not oppress a *sojourner*. You know the heart of a sojourner, for you were sojourners in the land of Egypt" (Exod. 23:9).

> "When a *stranger* sojourns with you in your land, you shall not do him wrong" (Lev. 19:33).

> "Love the *sojourner*, therefore, for you were sojourners in the land of Egypt" (Deut. 10:19).

Hoffmeier also emphasizes that nations in the world of the Old Testament clearly placed a high priority on protecting their borders and having the right to decide who would enter their nation and who would not: "Were ancient territorial borders taken seriously and was national sovereignty recognized? The answer is emphatically yes."[32] Hoffmeier also adds, after a survey of the biblical data, that

---

29. Ibid.
30. See Hoffmeier, 52, 89, 156, and elsewhere throughout the book.
31. Ibid., 156–57.
32. Ibid., 32.

> Nowhere in the Old Testament is there any sense that a nation had to accept immigrants, nor was being received as an alien a right.[33]

Another important consideration from the Bible concerns the general responsibilities of governments to seek the good of the nations that they rule (Rom. 13:1–7; 1 Peter 2:13–14) and thereby truly serve as "God's servant for your good" (Rom. 13:4). This means that the immigration policies of a nation *should be designed to bring benefit to that specific nation.*

This purpose of seeking the good of the nation is reflected in the opening paragraph of the Constitution of the United States, where the purposes of the new government included "ensure domestic tranquility" and "provide for the common defense" and "promote the general welfare." The government of the United States was established so that it would *do good for the nation* in these and other ways.

Therefore, in the United States in particular but in nations generally, immigration policies should be designed to bring *benefit to the well-being of the nation as a whole.*

This would imply, for example, that *the United States should control all immigration processes* so that the country gives priority to accepting those people who will most likely make a positive contribution to US society. It is appropriate that *priority* in immigration be given, for example, to those who have sufficient education and training to support themselves and contribute well to American society, those who have demonstrated significant achievement in some area or another, and all those who otherwise give evidence that they will make a positive contribution. It is appropriate, also, to *exclude* those with a criminal record, those who have communicable diseases, or those who otherwise give indication that their overall contribution would likely be negative rather than positive in terms of advancing the well-being of the nation.

2. We have a historically different situation today

It is undoubtedly true that nearly everyone in the United States has some kind of immigrant background, so that we are a "nation of immigrants" (except for Native Americans). But there are two problems that have become acute within the last decade or so and make the present situation different from our entire history of past immigration.

---

33. Ibid., 156.

(1) *Illegal immigrants*: There are many immigrants who have come here *illegally*, outside of the normal system for entering the United States. Estimates are that this number runs as high as 13 million or more[34] (or 4% of a nation of 307 million people).

(2) *Permanent lack of assimilation*: Too many immigrants who have come here *legally* within the last forty years do not seem to be assimilating well into American culture, but have formed their own ethnic communities in which their primary loyalty is not to the United States but to their nation of origin, and many remain as unskilled laborers, unable to rise above the lowest level of annual income. Many of these people (by some estimates) drain more resources from the nation than they provide to the nation.[35] That certainly is true if we include many illegal immigrants in that total.

According to the Center for Immigration Studies, households headed by illegal aliens imposed more than $26.3 billion in costs on the federal government in 2002 and paid only $16 billion in taxes, creating a net fiscal deficit of almost $10.4 billion, or $2,700 per illegal household. They found that the largest costs are Medicaid ($2.5 billion); treatment for the uninsured ($2.2 billion); food assistance programs such as food stamps, WIC (the Special Supplemental Nutrition Program for Women, Infants and Children), and free school lunches ($1.9 billion); the federal prison and court systems ($1.6 billion); and federal aid to schools ($1.4 billion).[36]

Some influential immigrant leaders promote the lack of assimilation into the United States. For example Raul Yzaguirre, former president of the Hispanic immigration advocacy group called La Raza, apparently wants to perpetuate the situation of people living in the United States for generations without being able to speak English, because he was quoted as saying, "U.S. English is to Hispanics as the Ku Klux Klan is to blacks."[37] Another advocate for Mexican immigrations into the United States, Juan Hernandez, said, "I want the third generation, the seventh generation, I want them all to think 'Mexico first.'"[38] Allowing such

---

34. "How Many Illegal Immigrants?" Federation for American Immigration Reform, www.fairus.org/site/News2?page=NewsArticle&id=16859&security=1601&news_iv_ctrl=1007. Also see Center for Immigration Studies, Illegal Immigration, www.cis.org/Illegal.

35. See Mark Levin, *Liberty and Tyranny: A Conservative Manifesto* (New York: Threshold Editions, 2009), especially 154–70.

36. Steven A. Camarota, "The High Cost of Cheap Labor: Illegal Immigration and the Federal Budget," Center for Immigration Studies (July 2004). www.cis.org/node/54.

37. Quoted by Mark Levin, *Liberty and Tyranny*, 162.

38. Ibid., 164.

viewpoints to prosper is completely contrary to the best interests of the United States as a whole.

What is the solution to these two problems?

3. Step 1: Close the borders

Before any other solutions to the current immigration problems can be discussed, it is crucial to come to an agreement that the United States must take immediate action to immediately and effectively close its borders, especially the border with Mexico, from which most of the illegal immigrants originate.

It seems to me inexcusable that Congress has delayed so long in simply authorizing and clearing the way to build a secure fence that would effectively stop something like 99% of illegal immigration from Mexico. The United States as a nation must get control of its borders, as all strong nations throughout history have done. As long as the borders are ineffective, we have no control and no ability to keep criminals, terrorists, and others who would harm our nation from entering. Even those who enter with no intent of breaking any further laws but only of finding employment do this in a way that is unfair to thousands of others who decide to abide by the law and wait many years to be admitted as immigrants by legal means.

Then these illegal immigrants become part of a growing underground economy and a permanent "underclass" that is not really protected by the law because the legal system does not have a record that they exist! It means that they can be easily exploited because they won't seek legal help when wrong has been done against them, for fear they will be discovered and deported. On the other hand, it means that American citizens are not protected from the harm that illegal immigrants might do to others, because the legal system has no easy way to track them if they commit wrong.

These illegal immigrants have very little incentive to try to integrate into the society (as other immigrants from other nations have historically done when they came by legal means). Therefore illegal immigrants are much more likely to form isolated communities who think of their first national loyalty as to Mexico (or some other nation) rather than to the United States. They do not feel themselves responsible to contribute to the well-being of society, as through military service or paying taxes or obedience to laws. Because their status here is already "illegal," their very presence generates disrespect for the rule of law in the nation as a whole.

In addition, these illegal immigrants are living in constant disobedience of Paul's command, "Let every person be subject to the governing authorities" (Rom. 13:1). It is not just that they have broken the laws of the United States by entering the country illegally, but they also continue living in the country in an undocumented status without the legal permission of the United States. They can hardly be subject to the governing authorities when those authorities do not even have a record that they exist. In this way, the continuing presence of a growing illegal minority *that is invisible to the entire legal recordkeeping system of the society* is a destructive force in the society itself—one that will increasingly bring negative consequences to the respect for law and the legal fabric of the nation.

It therefore astounds me that anyone in either party, whether Democrat or Republican, would oppose having Congress and the President take the necessary steps to *complete* a secure and impenetrable border fence immediately. This is not a high-tech problem, such as building a jet fighter or sending a rocket to the moon. A secure fence—that is, a double one with high-tech monitoring devices and a patrol road in between the two parts—that covers the entire 1,951-mile length of the border between the United States and Mexico could be built on an emergency basis within a few months, if the nation had the will to do this. But instead it has dragged on for years, with only partial individual sections being complete. Congress could pass special legislation, if it had the will, that would override environmental challenges to the building of the fence and override legal challenges to the use of eminent domain to obtain the right to build on the property all along the border. A secure fence could and should be built at once.

Closing the border is simply a matter of establishing the rule of law more effectively in a nation. I can see no valid reason to oppose it. I can see no valid argument to delay it. I can see no excuse for making it a bargaining chip for negotiations about other aspects of the immigration question. The United States should have the right to *determine* who enters the country and to *know* who enters the country.

4. Step 2: We should enact comprehensive reform of the immigration system

a. Stopping chain migration and exercising rational control over immigration

Prior to 1965, the United States had much more effective control over who would be allowed to enter the nation as an immigrant. Priority was rightfully given to those people *who would most clearly bring benefit to American society* as well as to their spouses and their immediate minor children.

But under pressure from President Lyndon Johnson, Congress passed the Hart-Celler Act of 1965. It established a new system by which citizens of the United States could sponsor not only a spouse and immediate children for immigration, but also *all of their brothers and sisters as well as their parents who are living in other countries.*

For example, let's say that a couple has eight children in Mexico and then enters the United States and has a baby daughter. Even if they were just here for a few days to give birth to her, she will automatically become an American citizen by virtue of being born here, and once she reaches the age of twenty-one, she becomes immediately able to sponsor her father, her mother, and all seven of her brothers and sisters to migrate to the United States (nine more persons). By that time the brothers and sisters, ranging in age from the early twenties to late thirties, are probably also married, so they can sponsor *their* spouses and also all of *their* children. (So now one person has been able to bring in maybe fifty more people, none of whom gained entry by demonstrating a willingness or ability to contribute to American society.)

Or if an adult aged forty, with six unmarried sons and daughters aged fifteen to twenty-five, comes to the United States legally and obtains permanent resident alien status (also legally, because of work, for example), he is able to sponsor all his unmarried sons and daughters as well as his spouse and parents to immigrate legally into the country. While this chain migration system is sometimes called the "family reunification" process, this pleasant-sounding name masks the reality of what is actually happening.

The differences in immigration patterns after this 1965 act became immense. There was *no limitation on the number of people who could become legal immigrants by this chain migration process,* so the number of *legal* immigrants into the United States, largely as a result of this law, soared from 2.1 million in the 1950s to 4.2 million in the 1970s to 6.2 million in the 1980s to about 9.7 million in the 1990s.[39] Some people may think this is a good thing (see discussion below on the benefits that immigrants bring), but the important point here is that the nation no longer even has control over the number.

Another problem traces back to 1986, when the Immigration Reform and Control Act (enacted under President Reagan) granted a one-time amnesty to about 3 million illegal immigrants who had

---

39. "Persons Obtaining Legal Permanent Resident Status: Fiscal Years 1820 to 2008," *Yearbook of Immigration Statistics,* U.S. Department of Homeland Security. www.dhs.gov/xlibrary/assets/statistics/yearbook/2008/table01.xls.

entered the United States before January 1, 1982.[40] This act was supposed to be a one-time fix that would solve the problem of illegal
immigrants in the United States, but it failed to do this, and in fact
set a precedent that probably made future illegal immigrants hope
that one day it would happen again, thereby giving added incentive to
illegal immigration.

The problem with these immigration laws, and especially with chain
migration prompted by the Hart-Celler Act, is that *the United States no
longer has effective control over either the number of immigrants that come
into the country or the qualifications that it can expect from immigrants.*
With succeeding generations of immigrants who enter under this chain
migration system, the problem will only multiply year after year into the
future.

Therefore the United States no longer has the ability to decide on who
can enter the nation *based on giving priority to those who show that they
will contribute in the most positive way to the well-being of the nation as
a whole.* Thousands upon thousands of immigrants come who do not
speak English well and who do not have sufficient training for specialized jobs. They will continue to be an increasing burden to the US welfare system, will make it harder and harder for teachers to teach using
the English language, will provide an increasing burden to the medical
care system of the nation, and will contribute to the growing size and
increasing feelings of resentment of various isolated segments of society
that do not really feel part of the nation and do not feel loyalty to the
nation but feel primary loyalty to another country instead.

An even more dangerous result would occur if a single man from a
Muslim country came to the United States, lived as an upstanding citizen, applied for citizenship, and obtained it. He could then sponsor for
immigration five or six unmarried brothers and sisters, all of whom had
trained as terrorists in a foreign nation and were coming to the United
States for the purpose of bringing destruction to it.

Thus any immigration reform should repeal the chain migration
system of the Hart-Celler Act and provide that a US citizen could *only*
sponsor the immigration of a spouse or a minor child. Mark Levin
wisely says, "No society can withstand the unconditional mass migration of aliens from every corner of the earth."[41]

---

40. U.S. Citizenship and Immigration Services. www.uscis.gov/portal/site/uscis/menuite-
m.5af9bb95919f35e66f614176543f6d1a/?vgnextoid=04a295c4f635f010VgnVCM1000000ec
d190aRCRD&vgnextchannel=b328194d3e88d010VgnVCM10000048f3d6a1RCRD.

41. Levin, *Liberty and Tryanny*, 149.

b. The benefits of controlled immigration

On the other hand, we must recognize that *if it can be controlled with respect to who is allowed to enter, immigration is a great benefit to a nation.* Immigrants who want to come to the United States are, by and large, *producers* who bring benefit to the economy and *helpers* who bring other benefits to the society as a whole. The United States has immense land and resources, has the world's largest and most productive economy, and is able to accept and assimilate many thousands of people each year, all with beneficial results to the nation.

One of the great benefits of receiving immigrants was illustrated in October 2009, when the Nobel Prizes were announced. Nine people won Nobel Prizes in chemistry, physics, and medicine. Eight of them were American citizens, but of those eight, *four* were born outside the United States and came here only as graduate students or postdoctoral students or scientific researchers. In other words, nearly half of the Nobel Prizes in the scientific fields that year were won by American immigrants![42] Similar stories could be told hundreds of times in small businesses, medical research laboratories, and other ventures, where year after year recent immigrants have brought great benefits to the nation.

c. Needed patriotic and educational reforms in the schools and the immigration processes

The immigration process should also be accompanied by reform in the educational systems in the United States, so that the cultural ideals and values that have made America great are taught and passed down to each succeeding generation. In that way, children growing up in American schools can be taught the moral standards and ideals that have historically been true of the nation.

In addition, the need to protect the well-being and security of the nation means that we should certainly continue to require that any new citizens must renounce allegiance to any other nation and swear allegiance to the United States. However, some have called for this requirement to be dropped! In an op-ed column for the *Wall Street Journal*, law professors Peter Shuck of Hofstra University and Peter J. Spiro of Yale called for dropping the "renunciation clause" from the Oath of Renunciation and Allegiance. They said immigrants should consider them-

---

42. See Susan Hockfield, "Immigrant Scientists Create Jobs and Win Nobels," *Wall Street Journal* (Oct. 20, 2009), A19.

selves to be "Mexican and American," for example, and basically have dual citizenship.[43]

Another reform is that we should place much greater emphasis on the need for all immigrants from every nation *to learn English well*. Out of a current US population of 307 million, current estimates are that 55 million (19.6%) now speak a language other than English at home.[44] More than 34 million of these (12.2% of the population) speak Spanish at home.[45]

If for no other reason than *care for the future well-being of Spanish-speaking people*, we should require that they speak English. I travel and teach in many countries of the world, and I can say from personal experience that *English is the one language that enables people to communicate in whatever nation they travel.* The leaders who are influencing the society in every nation largely speak English as a second language. I travel to China and find that little Chinese children are learning to speak English. I travel to a conference in Hungary attended by representatives of forty nations and find that they are all speaking English to each other. And that makes sense, because when the Swedes want to communicate with the Italians or the Czechs want to communicate with the Spaniards or the Bulgarians want to talk to the Dutch, the only language that they can all understand is English. Business conferences and scientific conferences around the world are conducted in English. English has now attained a status in the world similar to the status that Greek had in the first century, when the apostle Paul could travel to any country and speak Greek and find that he was understood. English is the second language of the whole world.

Therefore it is simply foolish and cruel to children to allow them to grow up without gaining an excellent knowledge of the English language. Lack of knowledge of English will seriously hinder their ability to achieve excellence and advancement in nearly any career field they choose.

There is another reason for requiring more English skill. The United States needs a population that speaks the same language so that people can communicate well with each other in all parts of the nation and

43. Peter H. Schuck and Peter J. Spiro, "Dual Citizens, Good Americans," *Wall Street Journal* (March 18, 1998).

44. U.S. Census Bureau, "Language Spoken at Home." http://factfinder.census.gov/servlet/STTable?_bm=y&-geo_id=01000US&-qr_name=ACS_2008_3YR_G00_S1601&-ds_name=ACS_2008_3YR_G00_.

45. Ibid.

gain a sense of being one nation and one society. If people from different national backgrounds stay in their own language group—that is, Somalis only speak to each other, Muslims only speak (in Arabic) to each other, and Mexicans only speak Spanish to each other—then we will forever remain a nation of small groups isolated from each other, and we will find it almost impossible to attain any kind of reconciliation or unity across ethnic lines.

d. Expanding the number of skilled workers who are admitted to the United States

Immigration reform should also expand the number of highly skilled people allowed into the country each year in various categories and from various countries. While we have vastly expanded the number of *unskilled* immigrants we admit through chain migration, we maintain restrictions that are far too severe on the visas granted to highly trained scientists, inventors, medical professionals, university researchers, and others with similar qualifications.

After September 11, 2001, the United States placed severe restrictions on individuals seeking visas. Officials with the National Academy of Science have said:

> Recent efforts by our government to constrain the flow of international visitors in the name of national security are having serious, unintended consequences for American science, engineering, and medicine. Ongoing research collaborations have been hampered.... Outstanding young scientists, engineers, and health researchers have been prevented from or delayed in entering this country, (and) important international conferences have been canceled or negatively impacted; and ... such conferences will be moved out of the United States in the future if the situation is not corrected.[46]

5. Step 3: Enforce tighter regulations on employers regarding illegal immigrants

There are two kinds of harm that come when employers hire illegal immigrants. First, they can exploit them, treat them unfairly, and pay them inadequately because they are quite confident that illegal immi-

---

46. Randolph Schmid, "U.S. Scientists Criticize Post–9/11 Visa Restrictions," Associated Press (Dec. 13, 2002). www.space.com/scienceastronomy/science_visas_021213.html.

grants will not appeal to any legal authority to correct any injustice done to them. Employers should not do this, because it is morally unjust, but to prevent it, there should be further enforcement of provisions that require employers to verify the immigration status of employees.

The second harm is that when illegal immigrants find jobs in the United States, this provides an incentive for other illegal immigrants to try to enter, thinking that they too will find jobs. This too would stop if more effective enforcement were carried out preventing employers from hiring illegal immigrants.

In Arizona (where I live), I have been told in private conversation that on January 1, 2008, the state began strict enforcement of the E-Verify program that requires employers to electronically verify the legal status of all their employees with the databases of the Social Security Administration and the Department of Homeland Security. But nationally this is still a voluntary program for most employers.[47]

6. Step 4: What should be done about illegal immigrants who are already here?

The most difficult problem with regard to immigration is what to do with illegal immigrants who are already in the United States.

I honestly do not think that any national consensus can develop on this question until the general public is persuaded not simply that politicians are *promising* to close the border, but that an effective border fence *has already been built and is effectively stopping the flow of illegal immigration into the United States* (see discussion above, pp. 304–5). At that point, the frustration, fear (sometimes well-grounded), and anger that people have, feeling that their country is being overrun by people who do not truly belong to this country, may cool down enough for a more rational discussion to occur. Once that happens, the following provisions would probably gain increasing assent:

a. Deport all known criminals

Political analyst and author Michael Medved rightly says:

> First, all parties to this debate agree that the 450,000 criminals and violators for whom outstanding deportation orders

---

47. "E-Verify," U.S. Citizenship and Immigration Services. www.uscis.gov/portal/site/uscis/menuitem.eb1d4c2a3e5b9ac89243c6a7543f6d1a/?vgnextoid=75bce2e261405110VgnVCM1000004718190aRCRD&vgnextchannel=75bce2e261405110VgnVCM1000004718190aRCRD.

currently exist (but who the government finds it next to impossible to apprehend) must become the focus of an aggressive new effort to remove them from the country. These would include known gang members and others who have committed crimes. They constitute a real danger to the well-being of society, and I do not think that there is any reason why they should be allowed to stay within the country.[48]

b. Require immediate temporary registration of some kind for immigrants to receive any service from any facility in the United States

The first step in dealing with the remaining large number (perhaps 13 million or more) of illegal aliens should be that they must let the United States government know who they are and where they are. This would allow them to come out from the shadows and have some kind of temporary status that at least begins to put them within the legal system as long as they remain in this country. If that could be accomplished, it would take away their fear of participating in the legal system.

But how could they be persuaded to do this? It would require a national law saying that if they signed up to have temporary registration, they would not be immediately deported and proof of such temporary registration would be required before they could receive *any* kind of benefits such as medical care or welfare or having their children attend schools or certainly working at any job.

This temporary registration would have to be coupled with a system by which they would have to seek full US citizenship or else permanent resident (green card) status or have their permission to stay in the country revoked after a certain number of years. (This required decision process could be a long time, such as five or ten years, and the temporary registration that they obtain could be subject to renewal if conditions and circumstances warrant it.)

c. A difficult but possible path to full citizenship

The United States discovered in 1986 that immediate amnesty given to about 3 million people was a mistake. It made the path to citizenship far too easy. However, for those who truly want to stay in the United States and also abide by the law, and *for those illegal immigrants who are*

---

48. Michael Medved, "Immigration surprise: broad agreement, not polarization," *Townhall.com* (July 19, 2006). http://townhall.com/columnists/MichaelMedved/2006/07/19/immigration_surprise_broad_agreement,_not_polarization.

contributing most positively to American society, the biblical requirements of mercy and compassion, as well as the well-being of the nation, should make us want those immigrants to stay and continue to contribute positively to our society.

The requirements for citizenship should include a fine (which is an acknowledgment that the person has broken the law), some arrangement regarding back-taxes that need to be paid, the need to learn a good working knowledge of English, the need to swear allegiance to the United States above any other country, the need to learn the values of American society and culture, the need to show a record of employment that is continuing over time, and the need for a background check to show that they do not have a prior criminal record.

How much time should be required before they are allowed to obtain citizenship? This raises the question of fairness with respect to those who have been unable to enter the United States but have been waiting for many years for the right to enter it legally. Yet that consideration has to be balanced with the recognition that these people who want to stay and become citizens and meet these requirements have already been contributing in a very positive way to American society, and their contribution to society should be welcomed and encouraged. While it would be a question to be decided by the political process, it seems to me that a waiting period of something like five-to-ten years would be appropriate for obtaining full citizenship.

If this kind of immigration reform and this kind of path to citizenship were enacted, along with the immediate deportation of all known criminals who are illegal immigrants, then our difficult immigration problem would finally be solved, and the country would be stronger as a result. The United States would once again be opening its doors to a continual influx of citizens of many other nations who come here for the purpose of seeking a new and better life, but who also come because they admire and want to be a part of the kind of nation that we are. It seems to me that welcoming such people into our country would be all gain and no loss for the nation.

One objection that might be raised is that "foreign workers will take jobs away from Americans." However, this perspective is based on a misunderstanding of economics. The number of jobs in a society is never fixed, but is always changing. When talented new people come into a society, they may take some jobs, but they also create other jobs, because they produce goods and services that make the entire society wealthier, and their work also produces some demand for many products. In other words, they contribute to overall growth in the economy, which benefits the nation as a whole and leads to more jobs being created in the entire society. The number of jobs in the United States has never been static—and is not now static—and the benefits that come from productive immigrants far outweigh the disadvantages.

7. What should American churches do about immigrants?

With this background, we can now ask, what should American churches do with regard to immigrants who are part of their congregations?

For immigrants who are here *legally*, churches should be a wonderful home away from home, a welcoming community that will work in many ways to help families from other nations adjust and adapt to life in this new country. (My wife, Margaret, and I remember with fondness and gratefulness the Baptist church that welcomed us, as foreign immigrants, to England from 1973 to 1976, and we also remember the Christians who have warmly welcomed us as temporary "sojourners" to many other countries.) Churches must remind employers to treat legal immigrants justly and fairly, never taking advantage of them because of their lack of language skills or lack of knowledge of American culture. All of the biblical verses regarding the "sojourner" ("alien" in the NIV) would apply to this situation.

But what about immigrants who are here *illegally?* Churches must kindly but honestly counsel such illegal immigrants that the Bible teaches that we are all to be "subject to the governing authorities" (Rom. 13:1). Therefore God requires us to be obedient to the laws of the nation in which we live. The current immigration laws of the United States require that people come here through an established legal process, and obeying that process does not require anyone to sin against God, so it does not fall under the category of the laws that we may in good conscience disobey. Illegal immigrants are obligated before God to obey the immigration laws of the United States.

In many cases it may be possible for churches to help illegal immigrants find an immigration lawyer who can help them work out a process to be able to stay in the United States legally. James Hoffmeier tells in his book about a church he was part of that did exactly this,[49] and he also speaks about a case where, with sadness, he counseled a good friend whose visitor's visa to Canada had expired, and he was fearing deportation. Hoffmeier rightly says, "My instincts told me he should do what was right and legal and trust that things would work out for

49. See Hoffmeier, *The Immigration Crisis*, 159.

him. So I helped him think through his options and encouraged him to leave Canada and apply for landed status [that is, a status that would enable him to stay in Canada permanently]." More than ten years later, Hoffmeier found out that this friend did exactly that and did eventually get his permanent resident status and was once again living in Canada. Hoffmeier says, "It was good to hear he did the right thing, followed the law, and things had worked out for him."[50]

But we must be honest and admit that there are times when this will not be possible and, in order to obey the law, illegal immigrants will have to leave and apply for entry into the United States on the same basis as everyone else, through proper legal channels. In such cases, we must encourage them to trust God that obedience to him in the long run will be the path of greatest blessing in their lives, though they might not be able to see at the moment how that can be true.

Margaret and I had a similar situation that we encountered a few years ago. A wonderful, hard-working Hispanic woman had been coming to our home to clean it on a regular basis, and we liked her very much. But when our payments to her reached a total of $600 for the year, I asked her if she had a Social Security number. (A lawyer friend had told me that the law required me to begin making Social Security payments for her at the $600 point.) The woman said in broken English that she did not have an SSN, so with sadness we explained to her that we could not have her continue with us because we did not want to violate the laws of our country. We gave her a very generous severance check and told her, with tears, that we could not have her work for us again.

8. What about a guest worker program?

It does not seem to me that a temporary "guest worker" program would be a wise idea. Some people argue that seasonal agricultural workers should be allowed to come into the country (to California, for example) for temporary work and then exit afterward.

The difficulty—and I think the decisive objection—to such a program is that it seems almost impossible to get all such workers to abide by their agreements and return to their country of origin. Many of them simply fall beneath the radar and stay as a new group of illegal immigrants. So in this way a guest worker program becomes a pipeline for illegal immigration into a nation.

50. Ibid., 15.

Peter Salins, political science professor at Stony Brook University, writes the following about the guest worker programs in Europe, where they have many years of experience in such a system:

> True enough, the guest workers in Germany, France, the Netherlands, Scandinavia did not assimilate; *but the majority have stayed, legally and illegally,* residing in alienated economic and cultural enclaves, resentful of and resented by their unwelcoming host citizenry. If we are determined to replicate Western Europe's full decade-old guest-worker experiment, we may soon reap the same civil discord it is experiencing today.[51]

In addition, I do not think that such a guest worker program is needed for American businesses. The economic system of supply and demand should provide enough labor even for agricultural work and should do so at a fair wage for people in the United States. There are certainly millions of *fully legal* recent immigrants who will stay in agricultural jobs.

In the future, if the market-determined wage level for agricultural workers in the United States is so low that it does not attract enough workers, employers will simply have to raise wages to get enough workers to meet their needs, and the prices of the food products will have to go up accordingly. But then *the free market will be determining what the United States can produce,* and at what price, by employing people within its own borders to work at its own farms and factories.

Some people will object at this point, "But what if this means that some American farmers are driven out of business because they cannot compete with the cheaper food that is grown in other nations?" I do not think that that will happen in any significant measure, because American farmers are so resourceful and skillful that they are often able to find more productive ways to raise various crops with lower labor costs and more labor-saving machines used per worker. American farmers are the most productive farmers in the world. But if this happens to some degree, then this is simply a result of natural economic forces bringing about some shift in world markets.

Perhaps one day more strawberries will be grown in Mexico than in California. That will help Mexico and will also help ease pressure on our borders, and we should not think that American workers will then have nothing to do, because they did not want the jobs anyway at the pay that was offered. Historically, at one point about 60% of the American

---

51. Peter Salins, "The 'Guest-Worker' Folly," *Wall Street Journal* (June 6, 2007), A19.

population was working in agriculture, but today only about 2% of the population works in agriculture. *What happened to the 58% that had to find jobs elsewhere, and their descendants (such as me—the first generation not connected at all to farming)?* They found more productive, generally higher-paying jobs in other fields, and the transition ultimately brought benefit to the economy as a whole.

Chapter 10

APPLICATION TO DEMOCRATIC AND REPUBLICAN POLICIES TODAY

It is now time to look back on our study and draw some conclusions about the way in which biblical teachings compare to the current policies favored by the Democratic and Republican parties in the United States. (Readers in countries other than the United States can take this list of policy questions and consider how the various political parties in their own nation measure up to these conclusions as well.)

When I was writing this book, some people told me that they hoped it would be "nonpartisan." They hoped I would simply look at the issues and not at the individual parties. They hoped that the book would even-handedly support Democrats where their policies were more consistent with biblical teaching and support Republicans where their policies were more consistent with biblical teaching.

But the policies favored by Democrats and Republicans today are so different that it is unlikely that anyone with a consistent worldview and a consistent view of the purpose of government will support Democratic policies about 50% of the time and Republican policies about 50% of the time. This is because the parties' basic views of the role of government are so different, and their fundamental principles are so different.

That is why, for example, Jim Wallis's book *God's Politics: Why the Right Gets It Wrong and the Left Doesn't Get It*[1] is not at all nonpartisan. The title makes people think that Wallis is going to criticize both Republicans and Democrats equally, but the book actually turns out to be an extended argument for supporting Democratic candidates and positions and opposing Republican ones.

Wallis ends up supporting Democratic policies regarding war, the economy, and capital punishment and (for the most part) even giving mild support to a more liberal view of same-sex marriage. With regard to abortion, Wallis refuses to support the Republican position that we should have *laws* prohibiting abortion (except to save the life of a mother). Rather, he tells Democrats that they should be more tolerant of pro-life Democrats within the party[2] and also tells them they should do more to reduce teen pregnancy and to support low-income women who are at greater risk for unwanted pregnancies.[3] Then he tells readers that the differences between Democrats and Republicans on abortion are not enough reason to support Republicans, because Republicans do not support "a consistent ethic of life" regarding other issues, since they support capital punishment and nuclear weapons and do not do enough to eradicate poverty and racism, all of which are "critical components of a consistent ethic of life."[4]

In other words, Wallis gives readers no reason that they should support Republican policies and makes the entire book an argument to support Democrats and policies favored by the Democratic Party. The entirety of *God's Politics* ends up saying, in essence, that God supports the Democratic Party.

Why does Wallis reach these conclusions? They are strongly informed by (1) his pacifist convictions regarding war and military power and international relations, (2) his view that the primary solution to poverty is more government redistribution of income from the rich to the poor, and (3) his decision that biblical standards regarding abortion and homosexual conduct should not be the determining factor regarding the kinds of laws that governments should make.

Although Wallis says that "God is not a Republican or a Democrat," and he and his organization Sojourners supported a campaign with that slogan,[5] his book in actuality ends up arguing "God's politics" are the

---

1. Jim Wallis, *God's Politics: Why the Right Gets It Wrong and the Left Doesn't Get It* (San Francisco: HarperSanFrancisco, 2005).
2. Ibid., 298–99.
3. Ibid, 300.
4. Ibid, 301.
5. Ibid, 9.

politics of the Democratic Party. I encourage readers to read Wallis's book if they want to hear an argument that God supports the Democrats and their positions.

I have come to quite different conclusions in this book, for the reasons discussed in the preceding chapters. Although I disagree with Republican policies at some points, I have concluded that the policies endorsed by the leadership of the Republican Party have been much more consistent with biblical teachings.

Where does that leave us? Wallis and others say that God supports the positions of the Democrats. I think that the teachings of the Bible, as I understand them, mostly support the current policies of the Republicans. How can people decide between these two views? They can decide in the way people have always decided: by reading the arguments, reading their Bibles (where biblical arguments are used), and then deciding which arguments are the most persuasive. They can discuss their thinking about these matters with others, and when they disagree, they can do so while maintaining a respectful attitude toward the other person. This is a healthy process, and it is essential to a well-functioning democracy.

Sometimes people say they "vote for the candidate, not the party." I think this view is naïve. It simply fails to recognize how decisions are actually made in our current political system. Because only parties — not individuals — can get bills passed in Congress and confirm or reject judicial appointments, *every vote for every candidate is a vote for the candidate's party as much as it is for the candidate.* It is impossible today to vote for a candidate and not also vote for and give support to that candidate's party. And the party in power will determine the course of the nation.

The Democratic and Republican parties have come to represent very different basic positions today, and the elected officials of those parties support those positions, both by their individual votes (usually along party lines) and by the votes they bring to electing the leaders in the House and Senate — leaders who determine the course of all legislation. In the current situation in the United States, the policies favored by the Democratic and Republic parties have moved far apart on dozens of very important issues.

The Republican Party has been dominated by people favoring smaller government, lower taxes, strong defense, traditional moral standards regarding abortion and marriage, the promotion of democracy, and the promotion of free market economies. These stances seem to me to be consistent with biblical teachings on government and a biblical worldview.

By contrast, the Democratic Party has come to be dominated by people favoring larger government, higher taxes, more reliance on negotiations rather than superior military force in dealing with enemies, opposition to biblical moral standards on abortion and homosexual "marriage," and promotion of a more Socialist-leaning economy that is highly controlled by the government. These policies seem to me to be at odds with a biblical worldview and with biblical teachings regarding government.

In this chapter I summarize the earlier discussions in the book and compare my policy conclusions with the policies favored by the majority of Republicans and the majority of Democrats, or by those who have determined the policy decisions in their respective parties.

A. ECONOMIC POLICIES

In chapters 2 and 3 I argued that the teachings of the Bible support a system of private ownership of property and an emphasis on a free market as opposed to extensive government regulation of the economic decisions in any nation.

With regard to these questions, Democrats have commonly tended to favor much more government regulation of people's use of private property and government regulation to direct how the economy works and how income is distributed. Democrats have generally favored higher taxes, in part because this is one way they can redistribute income from the rich to the poor. Republicans, by contrast, have tended to favor more protection of property rights and more emphasis on allowing the free market and free competition between businesses to solve the problems of allocating goods and services in the economy.

I argued also that businesses, in general, are the primary means by which wealth is created and increased in the economy, and therefore businesses should be viewed as basically "good" in what they are trying to carry out (although businesses can do evil things, for which they should be punished by the law).

In recent US history it is primarily Democrats who have been in favor of placing higher taxes and increasing government regulation on businesses, while Republicans have generally (but not uniformly) favored lower taxes and fewer regulations on businesses.

Concerning the rich and the poor, Democrats have often tended to use rhetoric that portrays "the rich" as evil and to support policies that tend to take money from the rich and give it to the poor—in other words, income redistribution policies. Democrats have favored tax laws that strongly trend in this direction. On the other hand, Republicans have tended to favor allowing individual freedom and allowing everyone in the economy, whether rich or middle-class or poor, to keep the fruits of their labors. And Republicans have tended to think of wealthy people, in general, as those who have created much economic good for a society and who have rightfully gained personal benefit from those actions.

I also argued that lower taxes are, in general, beneficial for an economy and, in addition, lower taxes have the great benefit of giving individuals much more freedom to decide how to use their own money. On this issue, the consistent goal of Democrats in state and national government has been to increase taxes more and more (as seen particularly in the Democratic-controlled states of California and New York, for example). But Republican positions (not uniformly, but generally) have tended to *decrease* tax rates, not temporarily but permanently and not for just certain favored groups, but for the entire nation, thus promoting greater economic growth and prosperity throughout the economy.

Regarding health care, I argued that a competitive free market is a much better provider of health care than any government-run and government-managed system. I also argued that steps that would encourage the free market, such as eliminating state mandates for expensive "all-inclusive" policies, allowing consumers to buy insurance across state lines, limiting medical malpractice awards, and giving private individuals the same tax breaks that are given to individuals working for large companies when buying insurance. All of these actions would bring down health care costs, improve health care coverage, and avoid having the government take over and ruin the system that now provides Americans with the best health care in the world.

Republicans generally are in support of policies such as the ones I favored, while Democrats generally favor much more government control of the entire health care segment of the economy (as shown in President Obama's 2009 health care proposal).

B. THE ENVIRONMENT

In chapters 4 and 5 I argued that God has created a wonderfully resourceful earth in which there are abundant resources of every kind, a viewpoint in contrast to the fear-generating rhetoric of much modern media coverage of the environment.

I also argued that we should develop and use energy resources from many types of sources (wind, hydroelectric, oil, coal, natural gas, nuclear power, and solar energy). God has placed in the earth abundant energy sources for us to use for our benefit. In particular, there are huge energy resources remaining in oil, coal, natural gas, and nuclear power, and we should wisely make use of these abundant energy resources while we continue to work on developing alternative forms of energy as well. The great value of energy for human use is that it saves us work, saves us time, and makes our lives more enjoyable and more comfortable. Therefore we should see the earth's abundant energy resources as a blessing from God that he put there for our benefit.

Again and again, it has been Democrats who have blocked the development of these energy resources, preventing further drilling of abundant oil on America's own land (whether they are offshore sources of oil or the abundant sources found in the Alaskan National Wildlife Refuge). Democrats have also stood in the way of enabling new nuclear power stations to be built and sensible nuclear storage facilities to be opened. Therefore, Democrats (in general) have hindered the development of energy resources again and again in the United States. By contrast, many Republicans (but not all) have favored the development of such energy resources, all of which would make products less expensive for everyone and would make the cost of living less for everyone, thus promoting more individual freedom. All these things can be done without any significant danger of doing harm to the earth in the long term.

I also argued that it is highly doubtful that human production of carbon dioxide is having any significant effect on the earth's temperature, and that the alarmist predictions of massive global warming heard so commonly in the media are without substantial basis in fact. It does not seem to me to be likely that God would set up the earth to work in such a way that we would destroy it by doing morally good things that he wants us to do, such as building a fire to keep warm or to cook food, or driving a car or a truck (with appropriate pollution controls, but carbon dioxide is not a pollutant), or flying in an airplane, or running a factory to produce goods for people.

Democrats have by and large supported the "man-made global warming" hypothesis and have therefore strongly favored proposals that would actually *reduce* our carbon output each year until it is far below the current level. This would require either substantial reductions in our standard of living (we would no longer have enough energy to do many things) or else the largest increases in the cost of living that we have ever seen (because of huge increases in costs due to using much more expensive alternative energy sources). Republicans have claimed that these government plans to force us to reduce our carbon energy usage are prohibitively expensive, are harmful to the poor more than anybody else, create a massive increase in government control of our lives, and are an entire waste of money and effort because carbon dioxide is not to be considered a pollutant, but something that occurs naturally in the earth that God made for us. Carbon dioxide has no demonstrated danger of causing people or the earth any harm, and it actually does much good (enabling plants and crops to grow larger).

Finally, I argued that the fuel efficiency (CAFE) standards for auto-mobile mileage, strongly supported by Democrats (with some excep-tions in car-producing states like Michigan) but generally opposed by most Republicans (but not all), have done much more harm than good to the nation, forcing people to drive smaller and more dangerous cars than they would otherwise choose to drive, and resulting in far more injuries and fatalities in auto accidents than otherwise would have hap-pened.

C. NATIONAL DEFENSE

In chapters 6 and 7 I argued that a strong military defense is a moral obligation that God places on nations so that they will be able to protect their national sovereignty and protect their citizens from attacks coming from the outside. Therefore a strong US military force should be seen as a *good* thing and not as something evil in the world. US military power increases peace because it deters any potential enemy from thinking it can benefit from attacking our nation. This promotes peace in the world.

All Republicans of national prominence and some (but not all) Dem-ocrats agree with this perspective. But the Obama administration and its more liberal supporters in the Democratic Party have, like President Jimmy Carter before them, pressed for massive reductions in defense spending, even canceling further production of the greatest fighter plane ever produced, the F–22 ("Raptor") fighter. President Obama insisted on killing authorization for any further production of this remarkable aircraft, something I argued was a significant mistake. But it comes from a mentality that believes that military conflicts are caused by weapons rather than by evil in the hearts of people.

I argued that Islamic Jihadism (international Islamic terrorism) is fundamentally a religious movement and is based on a strong religious belief, namely, a small minority view within worldwide Islam that argues that the rule of Islamic law should be promoted by military conquest and terrorist attacks in various nations of the world, and then, once nations are conquered, Islam should be imposed on nations by the application of superior military power. The cause of such terrorism, therefore, is not poverty, or any perception of oppression of certain nations by the United States, or any failure to negotiate adequately with terrorists, but is rather a profoundly evil and deeply held religious view. I argued that Islamic Jihadism will only be overcome, from a human perspective, by the use of superior military force to find and imprison or otherwise defeat those who would promote it.

Republicans in general have agreed with this position, while Democrats generally have minimized the religious component behind Islamic Jihadism, have tended to downplay the need for the use of superior military force, and have emphasized instead the hope that more negotiation in good faith, more money, and more apologies for supposed US misconduct could lead us to come to terms with those who are opposed to the United States and its policies.

I argued that the war in Iraq and the war in Afghanistan were necessary and morally right in terms of traditional just war theory, because they were founded on the need to defend ourselves against international terrorist attacks. However, we need to have sufficient resolve and sufficient commitment of military forces to pursue those conflicts until the national governments within those countries are well established and secure in their democratic processes, and until they voluntarily decide, on their own accord, that they can take care of themselves and would like American forces to leave.

Republicans have in general agreed with this policy and supported the approach of President George W. Bush to these wars. Most Democrats, by contrast, have continued to push for immediate withdrawal from these countries, an approach that, it seems to me, recklessly risks losing everything we have gained in those countries and risks allowing them to be overrun once again by the terrorist forces of al-Qaeda and the Taliban. It is good that President Obama, in late 2009, committed to sending an additional 30,000 troops to Afghanistan. However, this was only half of what our military commanders said they needed, and President Obama's weak resolve might still result in Afghanistan reverting to Taliban control. In addition, President Obama's commitment to bring back all US troops from Iraq by December 2011 risks losing what we have fought to establish in Iraq, which is presently a functioning democracy.

I argued that it is hopeless and wishful thinking to imagine that the world will ever be free of nuclear weapons, because world history shows that once new weapons are developed, they are never subsequently abandoned. Therefore the United States and other major peace-loving nations that now have nuclear weapons must maintain a strong nuclear arsenal in order to guarantee their ability to defend against attack by any other nations.

While it is true that President Reagan, a Republican, supported some reduction of the US nuclear arsenal, Republicans generally have tended to support a strong nuclear force, while Democrats have in general sought to impose greater and greater reductions in the nuclear arsenal and greater restrictions on the development and testing of these weapons. (This has been the recent policy of President Obama, for example.)

With regard to missile defense systems that would destroy enemy missiles before they could reach the United States, it seems to me that this is a wonderful idea that no impartial, thinking person should oppose. That is because they provide an excellent, life-saving alternative to defending ourselves by sending massive numbers of nuclear weapons against an attacking country. They allow us, instead, to destroy an incoming missile before it can reach our country or do any harm to anyone.

Republicans have favored further development and deployment of such systems, which were first begun by President Reagan. Democrats, by contrast, have opposed and even mocked such systems from the beginning (calling President Reagan's plans a hopeless "Star Wars" scheme based in fiction, not reality). But these systems have proven increasingly accurate in test after test. Unfortunately, President Obama canceled the planned deployment of such anti-missile systems in Poland and the Czech Republic in 2009.

I also argued that a spy network such as the CIA is necessary to gain intelligence against enemies who would attack us, and that Americans should, in general, support the CIA and not automatically assume (from the influence of a biased media and entertainment industry) that it is constantly doing evil things. The CIA performs a necessary function in defending the nation. Republicans in general have supported the activities of the CIA, but many Democrats have attempted to investigate and restrict it with the goal of limiting its ability to carry out its task.

I argued that the use of the word "torture" is not helpful in the discussion of the treatment of enemy prisoners, because it has so many different meanings for people. It seems to me that the best policy for the United States would be to treat prisoners humanely and with significant care, never to attempt to punish them. But in exceptional cases where an enemy was captured who had knowledge of a "ticking bomb" or other likely terrorist attack, I argued that coercive measures, stopping short of anything that would actually be immoral, should be applied to extract information from such prisoners, and that abundant evidence indicates that this kind of treatment actually worked with regard to some high-ranking captured terrorists after 9/11.

Republicans have generally tended to support such coercive interrogation methods (within strict guidelines), but not entirely. For instance, Senator John McCain, among others, expressed opposition to any such use of "coercive interrogation"—but he later backtracked on this somewhat. On the other hand, Democrats have been much more insistent that no such means should ever be used, and Obama issued an executive order banning the use of such means of interrogation within a day after becoming President.

D. RELATIONSHIPS WITH OTHER NATIONS

In chapters 8 and 9, with respect to other nations, I argued that our foreign policy should be to seek the good of the United States and the protection of its citizens in relationships with other nations, but also that we should attempt to give help to other nations and do good for them where we are able to do so. For example, it is right to give various kinds of foreign aid to other nations, both through government sources and through private channels and private charitable organizations.

With regard to Israel, I argued that the United States should continue to support that nation as a close ally, both because it is the most dependable ally for the United States in the Middle East, and because it is a functioning democracy and a growing economy with which we have multiple, mutually beneficial relationships.

Another reason to support Israel is an argument from the Bible that God still has a future purpose for the Jewish people, in which he will bring many of them back to a personal relationship with himself through trust in Jesus as the Messiah (Rom. 11). It seems likely to me that the establishment of the nation of Israel in 1948 and the gathering of millions of Jewish people in that land are one providential step toward the realization of that future plan of God. This is a further reason why, it seems to me, the United States should support Israel. It also seems to me that this plan of God in Romans 11 probably explains the deep spiritual reason why many Muslim nations surrounding Israel are so adamantly opposed to the very existence of Israel as a nation.

What is the origin of the Arab-Israeli conflict in the Middle East? It goes back to the establishment of Israel as a nation by the United Nations in 1948. The same United Nations resolution that established the nation of Israel also authorized the establishment of a separate Arab nation alongside Israel, and specified boundaries for each nation, so that two nations would have been created in 1948. But the Arab nations surrounding Israel and the Palestinian-Arab people themselves rejected this two-state solution and refused to acknowledge the legitimacy of Israel as a nation or to establish the separate Arab nation in Palestine that had been authorized by the United Nations. In addition, the surrounding Arab nations also refused to accept any Palestinian refugees as permanent citizens in their own countries, such as Egypt and Jordan. Therefore, it is ultimately the refusal of Arab nations to accept even the legitimacy of the existence of Israel as a nation that is the unsolvable barrier to peace in the Middle East.

Up to this point in history, both Democrats and Republicans have largely been supportive of Israel as a nation and supportive of Israel's right to defend itself and our obligation to act as an ally toward Israel. Some recent statements of President Obama have begun to call into question his commitment to this policy, but no major change in policy has yet come about.

With regard to immigration, I argued that the Bible requires us to treat immigrants from other nations with love and respect and equality before the law, so long as they fall in the category of the "sojourner" or "alien" that is talked about quite often in the Old Testament. But we must understand that these were people who came into another nation with the full knowledge and permission of the host nation. They were not the same as illegal immigrants who enter a nation today.

With respect to illegal immigration, I argued the following:

(1) A complete and secure border fence must first be built before the nation is ready to work toward any other kind of solution to this problem.

(2) The system must be reformed to stop the pattern of "chain migration" that allows huge extended families to multiply their presence many times over in the United States. In addition, the teaching of English and American traditions and values should be required for people who want to become American citizens.

(3) With regard to illegal aliens who are already in the country, those who are criminals or who have outstanding warrants for their arrest should immediately be deported (about 450,000 people). For the rest, there should be a program of registration plus a difficult but clearly attainable path to citizenship for those who desire it, with appropriate fines, learning of English, and a waiting period that would not unfairly preempt people who have already been in the citizenship process for a long time.

(4) Finally, it does not seem to me that a "guest worker" program would be appropriate, because too many would fall beneath the radar again and create another large illegal-immigrant problem.

Many Republicans have been supportive of plans such as the general policies that I have explained here, but unfortunately, among Republican ranks there have been some hyper-conservative people who have opposed any elements of a plan that would allow any path to citizenship whatsoever for the illegal aliens who are now here in the United States. Democrats, on the other hand, have tended to favor much more liberal policies that would lead to much quicker citizenship (and therefore, they hope, more Democratic votes) for those who are here illegally. Moreover, Democrats have tended to block efforts to carry out a quick completion of a totally secure fence along the border with Mexico. This seems largely to be because of the thought that the larger the immigrant population that comes into the United States, the more political power Democrats and their candidates will have. This is putting concerns for their own political power ahead of the good of the nation.

E. WHAT ABOUT THE SOCIAL AND MORAL ISSUES OFTEN DEBATED IN POLITICS?

Some readers at this point might feel persuaded that conservative or Republican policies are closer to the Bible's values on economic and foreign policy issues. But they may want to know more about how the political parties align with biblical stances on social issues like abortion, homosexual marriage, pornography, freedom of religion, and the like.

I encourage such readers to consider the companion volume to this book, *Voting as a Christian: The Social Issues*. In that volume I argue that biblical teachings also lead to conservative positions on these issues, because conservative positions more consistently uphold the moral guidelines and protections that are healthier for any society.

F. WHY DO THE TWO PARTIES ADOPT THESE DIFFERENT POLICIES?

Is there a reason why Republicans have far more often ended up supporting policies that are consistent with biblical teachings, whereas Democrats have far more frequently ended up opposing these policies? I suggest that there are several factors that account for this difference. I have listed them here in an order that moves from the obvious political differences that anyone can see to the deeper factors that involve a person's entire worldview and deeper spiritual commitments.

(1) *Liberal versus conservative views of government:* The Democratic Party has attracted and has come to represent people who favor much more government control of individual lives and much more government-enforced equality of income among people. The Republican Party, on the other hand, has tended to attract people who believe in much smaller and more limited government and believe in allowing people to keep the fruits of their labors as long as they have been earned legally. This is a classic difference between a "liberal" and a "conservative" view of government. Thus there is a basic policy difference between those who believe in *big government* and *making everybody equal* and those who believe in *small government* and *allowing greater individual differences among people and greater individual freedom.*

Because of the Bible's emphasis on individual freedom and a limited role for government, this means that Republicans have tended to favor policies that seem to be more consistent with biblical teachings.

(2) *Individual human responsibility for good and evil:* With regard to the existence of good and evil in the heart of every individual, and therefore the rightness of holding people accountable for the choices they make, it seems to me that Republicans have, in general, come down on the biblical side of this fundamental question as well. Therefore they have tended to favor stronger military forces (to defend against evil from other nations), stronger police forces, and stronger enforcement of criminal laws (to defend against evil deeds done by people within the nation). Democrats, on the other hand, have been more likely to blame the evil things that people do on forces outside the individual, such as family or society or guns or corporations or national governments. This tends to minimize an emphasis on individual accountability for one's own actions, and this, in turn, makes people think that those who do wrong can simply be persuaded to change their minds with more conversation and more negotiation, whether it be with a criminal within the nation or with leaders who attempt evil things from outside the nation.

(3) *Beliefs about the relationship between the human race and the natural world:* Belief that mere chance has brought about the origin of all living things through evolution leads a person to believe that human beings are just a higher form of animal that has evolved from the material universe. Then it is an easy step to reason that we should not think of human beings as deserving any kind of special role with regard to the earth or the animal kingdom. Because of this belief, people who hold to materialistic evolution as the explanation of all life tend to assume that all development of the earth's resources will cause damage to the environment, and such people will likely support the stricter environmen-

talist policies of the Democratic Party. They will also be more likely to fear that, since random processes *created* human life on earth, random or careless events in the future might cause the *destruction* of the earth and the human race.

Yet there is still something in human nature that makes people seek to serve a cause greater than themselves. If people do not think it is possible to know God as a person, then that longing to serve a cause greater than themselves can easily propel people toward a "save the earth" campaign. (What could be a greater cause than saving the whole earth, especially if you do not think anyone can know about God?) In this way, people who tend toward having environmentalism as their substitute religion would also gravitate toward the Democratic Party.

But people who take the Bible as their reliable guide for life tend to believe that God has created a good earth, a resourceful earth, and one that he wants us to develop and use wisely for our own benefit (according to Genesis 1:28). These people will tend to think that development of the earth's resources is a good thing, something that God wants us to do. Even apart from such a religious basis for this view of the earth, mere observation and common sense have led many people to think that human beings are obviously far superior to any other living creature, and this has led these people to think that the earth's resources and the plant and animal kingdoms should rightfully be developed and used (but in a wise and nondestructive way) for the benefit of mankind. Such people have gravitated toward the Republican Party, whose policies have more strongly favored "wise use" of the environment for the benefit of mankind.

(4) *Beliefs about whether we can know right and wrong:* If a person does not believe that absolute truth and absolute right and wrong can be known, then it follows that one person's views are just as good as another's. There is no way to know whether someone is right or wrong. Once a person reaches that conviction, he or she no longer feels accountable to any moral standard, or any standard of truth that is higher than any other, and certainly not to any God (who probably can't be known anyway, even if he does exist).

It follows that if there is no right and wrong that can be known, the people who are *most dangerous* are those who have strongly held religious convictions (such as fundamentalist Muslims and fundamentalist Christians!). These people must not be allowed to have their viewpoints influence the society.

Taking this reasoning one step further, if there is no absolute right and wrong, then the people who can have the most beneficial influence on society (according to what they personally think is "good" for society) are simply those who have the most power. It follows, then, that if you think there is no absolute right and wrong, it is right to seek more and more power, and that power comes, in most nations, through the attaining of political office and the power of the government. Therefore the Democratic Party tends to attract to itself people for whom gaining power through the government, and then increasing that power, is the best way they know to do something "good" with their lives (as they understand what is "good"). That is why Democrats seek to continually increase government power over individual lives.

Republicans, by contrast, have many more people who believe that there are absolute moral standards (as found in the Bible, or for some conservatives in traditional Jewish teaching, or the Bible plus Roman Catholic Church tradition, or the Book of Mormon, and so forth). These people also tend to think that they will be held accountable for their actions to a personal God who will one day judge them. This means that they believe there are absolute moral standards, and the *attainment of power* is not the ultimate goal, but rather *being obedient to the moral code that God has given to us.* They will tend to resist increases in government power, thinking that God has given to government a limited role.

In addition, these people tend to think that the religious system on which they base their beliefs places a high value on individual responsibility and individual freedom of choice. This is another reason why they tend to want smaller government—government that allows more individual freedom. But this individual freedom should be limited to prevent evil people from harming others through murder or rape or theft or breaking contracts and so forth. Therefore Republicans tend to emphasize individual freedom (within certain boundaries of the law).

(5) *Conclusion:* The differences between Democrats and Republicans today have great significance. These differences are not accidental, but stem from differing convictions about several moral and theological issues.